Conor

CONOR

A Biography of Conor Cruise O'Brien

Volume II
Anthology

Donald Harman Akenson

McGill-Queen's University Press
Montreal & Kingston

© Donald Harman Akenson 1994
ISBN 0-7735-1256-X

Legal deposit third quarter 1994
Bibliothèque nationale de Québec

Published simultaneously by Cornell University Press in the United
States.

Printed in Canada on acid-free paper

McGill-Queen's University Press is grateful to the Canada Council for
support of its publishing program.

Canadian Cataloguing in Publication Data

Akenson, Donald Harman
    Conor: a biography of Conor Cruise O'Brien
    Contents: v. 1. Narrative. – v. 2. Anthology.
    Includes bibliographical references and index.
    ISBN 0-7735-1255-1 (v. 1: McGill-Queen's University Press) – ISBN
    0-8014-3086-0 (v. 1: Cornell University Press) – ISBN 0-7735-1256-X (v. 2:
    McGill-Queen's University Press) – ISBN 0-8014-3087-9 (v. 2: Cornell
    University Press).
    1. O'Brien, Conor Cruise, 1917–
    2. Intellectuals – Ireland – Biography. I. Title.
    PR6065.B67Z54 1994   828.914   C94-900377-8

Contents

Introduction

The selections from the writings of Conor Cruise O'Brien which follow are arranged chronologically. They are intended to be read in tandem with the narrative of Conor's life: references to these selections are provided at appropriate points in the narrative. They can, however, be read on their own, sequentially, to provide an idiographic chart of Conor's style of writing and of the matters on which he focused his attention.

Where Conor will eventually be seen to fit into the literary history of the twentieth century inevitably will be determined not only by the character of his writings, but by all the ever-changing industrial sociology of the business of critical assessment. And it is a business, both in the sense that people are paid to assay the product and that, as in any industry, certain products are in demand in one era, others in the next.

Conor's work fits most easily into a literary field that is not much studied or honored in our own time, namely, serious nonfiction. A glance at any university catalogue indicates that the standard industrial categories of fiction and poetry are receiving the overwhelming bulk of attention, with scant notice being taken of nonfiction in most departments of literature. (Under the pressure of recent developments in critical theory, this may be changing; but the shift, if such it is, is as yet in kernel.)

Nonfiction is frequently taken to be a genre dominated by pedants (who are said to write impenetrable monographs) and of their antipole, journalists (who are said to write schlock). There are indeed bales of head-splitting scholarly monographs, enough to create an academic Maginot Line, and, also, there seems to be no level of taste beneath which a truly awful journalist cannot limbo. Yet, much of the best writing of our own time is done by academicians and by journalists. Too often it is easy to denounce scholarly writing as muddy, when in fact our own technical incompetence in the field is at fault; and in adjudging journalism in general to be shabby and subliterate, we may be either masking our fear of the demos, or veiling in the guise of taste our contempt of the mass.

The tradition of writing to which Conor's work belongs is the nineteenth-century line of nonfiction masters: Thomas Babington Macaulay, Matthew Arnold, and, especially, the great Irish intellect W.E.H. Lecky. Each of these men ranged across a wide area, from literary criticism to social history, and each could write brilliantly in short forms (in periodicals and, occasionally, newspapers) and long (full-length books). Of these three, it is Lecky who comes closest to being Conor's intellectual godfather: in his Enlightenment skepticism; in his optimistic belief that ideas actually can make a country, even Ireland, better; and in his confident and individualistic style which, like a good bespoke suit of clothes, fits him alone, but perfectly. The tie is also historical: Conor's father had edited for republication one of Lecky's less well-known essays.

I suspect that when the dust of our own century settles, Conor will be seen as the most important Irish nonfiction writer of the twentieth century. Suggesting that is not to denigrate other Irish nonfiction writers, for their company is a goodly one. In addition to Irish academic writers (whose works are rather thinner on the ground than one would wish, because of the heavy teaching and administrative load at most Irish universities) and to Irish newspaper columnists (who, blessedly, are very much in evidence, Irish newspapers being one of the last places in Western culture where a report's having wit does not preclude its publication), there is a central line of great talents. Robert Lynd of Belfast served as literary editor of the *Daily News* (London) and wrote essays for the *New Statesman* for decades. He is sometimes dismissed as light and charming, but when he wrote about Irish matters (as in his discussions of Irish politics in the era of the First World War, and in his appreciation of Tom Kettle), he was no lightweight. (Lynd, it will be recalled, was for a time a relative of Conor's, through Conor's first wife, who was Lynd's niece.) Sean O'Faolain, although remembered chiefly as a short story writer and novelist, was genuinely at home with nonfiction. In his biographies of Daniel O'Connell, and of Hugh O'Neill, he managed the difficult trick of being a lyrical historian, which is a high-wire act performed without a net: if one misses a step, the lyrical becomes instantly lugubrious. O'Faolain succeeds, brilliantly. Hubert

Butler's work is known for its consistent high quality, although his output is limited. The most underrated of Irish nonfiction writers of this century in my view has been Brian O'Nolan. Although well recognized in his various garbs—as Flann O'Brien and Myles na gCopaleen chiefly—for his satire and his pioneering postmodern fiction, his nonfiction has been largely overlooked. In the two and a half decades that he did his "Cruiskeen Lawn" column in the *Irish Times*, he was not solely skywriting, he was also presenting a good deal of shrewd commentary on everyday Irish life, and this at a time when commentary other than fiction was generally flabby. (O'Nolan, incidentally, was private secretary for many years to Sean MacEntee, Conor's second father-in-law, and that was a rather tense relationship.)

These Irish nonfiction writers serve as an appropriate cultural peer group for Conor, for he always has been an Irish writer. His range of subjects is vast—Biafra, Israel, the Congo, Southern Africa, Northern Ireland, French literature, nationalism, religion, and, of course, Dublin and its politics—but always he has written as an Irishman. This is usually explicit in his books, periodical articles, and pieces in newspapers, but it is structural as well. It is inherent, like an endoskeleton. What he has been most concerned with all over the world is the international version of the Irish problem: namely, what happens when religion and nationalism intersect within the context of postmedieval social structure. One can argue that he has rarely written about anything except Ireland.

Part of the problem of evaluating Conor's stature in the nonfiction field is that his writings are so widely scattered. As the bibliography which follows the selections indicates, he has published all over the world, with the result that many of his individual pieces are admired by critics, but that the tonality and density of his entire *oeuvre* is lost. Further, Conor has frequently published in unfashionable places, particularly newspapers. For some reason, an essay in the *Irish Independent* is seen to be mere journalism, but when the same piece is printed in the *New Republic* (as was the case with some of his essays on South Africa), then it becomes serious nonfiction. No: it is serious wherever it appears. And like all truly serious writing, it is not only luminous, but often very funny.

In his book-length writings, Conor has frequently confused the critics by playing with forms and vaulting from one mode to another. Ideally, if one wants to be recognized as a serious nonfiction essayist, one plays the game as international figure skaters play theirs: one does the same thing just a little bit better each year and slowly moves up the ladder until, finally, the judges give the performance a "5.9." One receives a nice medal and can then retire. In contrast, Conor's most important books are neither predictable nor simple. *To Katanga and Back* is a brilliant picaresque novel, one composed of facts and thus a nonfiction novel, but a novel nonetheless. Conor's monumental biography of Edmund Burke was an amalgam of immensely erudite scholarship concerning Burke, and of both conscious and unconscious autobiography. *States of Ireland*, arguably the most influential work of Irish historical writing since Ireland became independent, was both history and autobiography, a mixture unprecedented in Irish writing and beyond imitation.

Another characteristic of Conor's writing that stands in the way of full appreciation is that he is very much a writer-with-an-attitude, and this runs strongly against the Irish grain. Anthony Claire, the Irish host of the BBC's "In the Psychiatrist's Chair," recently summarized his own experience when he asserted his personality in his homeland. "The Irish view is, or was, that the world is *not* your oyster. You're fortunate to be here at all. And now shut up!" (*Observer*, 16 August 1992). Well, Conor will not shut up, and he will not stop reminding his readers that there is a live human being behind what they are reading. He refuses to draw a distinction between his public voice and his private voice. What he writes is what he is. Yet, his assertion of self is disciplined. His anecdotes and personal reflections work because the stories are not simply exercises in self-assertion. They are a means to an end, the end being to convince his reader of the rightness of an argument that he is presenting. (See, for example, Selection 44, "Death in the Afternoon.")

And that raises the greatest obstacle to appreciating his stature. If, in Conor's writing, the distinction between private and public voice disappears, it is because he understands that literature and action are not separate entities. He believes that what he writes affects the real world; and conversely, his writing, therefore, is largely reality-driven. Because Conor wants to change people's minds, and thus to make them act better, more humanely, sensibly, and morally, he forswears metalanguage. There is no missing what he means, and for the critic this leads to a conundrum: how does one judge an essay, say, on Northern Ireland, with whose conclusion one disagrees, but whose style and structure one finds admirable? This is the problem that Conor presents to Irish literary criticism in particular. It is a heavy demand indeed to ask someone to read and appreciate work of whose substantive conclusion one disapproves—the more so because the greater the writer's art, the more damage he inevitably will do to one's own side.

If current trends continue into the twenty-first century, Conor Cruise O'Brien's stock is apt to rise high. This is because (as Geoffrey

Harpham argues in the *Times Literary Supplement*, 28 August 1992), issues of power and identity are increasingly replacing theories of literature within the field of literary studies. A critical profession with less of
a linguistic bent, and more of a pragmatic orientation, will find Conor's
writings at once congenial and challenging.

That said, one must never approach Conor's *oeuvre* without a sense
of irony and thence with a recognition that every critical exercise has its
limits. Conor himself well understands the limits not only of his own
work, but of the entire O'Brien enterprise. In a review of Desmond
Ryan's quirky biography of James Stephens' *The Fenian Chief* (in the
Listener, 7 March 1968), he noted an item in the book's eccentric index:

O'Brien, An:
    never turn his back on an enemy, p. 32
    would never retreat from fields of which ancestors were kings, p. 33
    does, p. 34

As Conor mildly protested, "this kind of thing can be pushed too far."
And so can any critical viewpoint.

It is a pleasure to acknowledge the help and kindness of the several publishers who have aided in my bringing together the following selection
of Conor's shorter essays (and two early poems). In almost every instance, Conor himself owns the copyright and items are here reprinted
with his permission. However, in each case the original publishers (and
where traceable in the instance of defunct firms, the legal receivers)
have also given their approval and, indeed, encouragement. The place
of first publication is indicated in a note for each selection.

D.H.A.
Kingston, Ontario

Selections

1

"POISSON D'AVRIL" / "POISON D'AUTRUI"

POISSON D'AVRIL

Les haut-parleurs
Des travailleurs
Ne sont menteurs
Que quand la peur
Des noirs pasteurs,
Leurs inspecteurs
    Ecclésiastiques,
    De l'Empire
    Catholique
    Les fait mentir.

DONAT.

T.C.D.: A College Miscellany (26 May 1938), p. 173.

Poison d'Autrui

O marchandeurs
De grands melheurs,
Braves écouteurs
De tous les pleurs,
Vrais amateurs
De tous les cœurs!
    Le *sens-unique*
    Sans *ralentir*
    De votre nique
    Vous fait mentir.
                NODAT.

2

"CHRISTINE"

CHRISTINE

Bend the black Elms and howls
—Paolo! Francesca!—
Down the steep road the frost wind
Into our teeth, face-cutting, cruelly
Slashing down all but the hurricane lantern
Of will, love-lit and burning still.

The torture of the disappointed months
We tread behind, only the bitter will
To happiness remains against the gale,
Three miles in the vindictive gale.

Then to the cottage come, serious as children.
Chop the sullen wood, light an unwelcoming fire
In the trough between efforts then, sat as men do
On half-climbed mountain, silent and anxious.
Next doors are shut against winds inquisitiveness
And curtains drawn against mocking sleet

This poem, referring to Christine Foster, Conor's first wife, is found in his undergraduate commonplace book. It was written in March 1940. Source: O'Brien papers, University College, Dublin.

Your body naked, beautiful in the curving firelight
Given
And taken.

Oh shout and stand you flames,
Tall candles, triumph taut, ring of the frost,
Joy, holy inexhaustible joy
Tears like bells of Christmas, laughter
Like winter blown from the skies, knife edge
Of ecstasy poised and enduring,
And the blankets thrown from the bed, and clothes
Thrown to four corners, and standing
Flame-roaring bare-bodies, twining to the ceiling.
Earth spurned. Wind cowed.

3

PROFILE:
MR. SEAN MACBRIDE, T.D.

When he laughs, which he does often, his skin, of very good quality parchment, crackles into a complex system of fine folds; the remarkable eyes, prominent and yet recessed, like those of some mad monk of romance, flicker with the persuasions of gaiety: the chuckle of that exotic uvula conspires, with the bandit eyebrows, giving a touch of *diablerie* to what you may be very sure is a most harmless witticism. The total effect is rather impressive and not at all amusing. You do not feel as if you had taken part in an exchange of pleasantries: you feel more as if you had been listening to a band or had been exposed to the action of an unknown ray.

In repose, or in that expression of utter desolation which takes the place of repose, the face is more attractive, if not more reassuring. The great tragic eyes shine out from a skull in which they seem the only living things: the rest of the almost fleshless face with its high forehead and cheek-bones, its thin curved nose, is such that you feel in the presence of an apparition. It is as if one of those death-masks, of Tone or of Emmett, which are to be found in glass cases in certain patriotic houses, were to open its eyes and look out at you.

The contrast between the two faces is, in the strict sense, dramatic:

The Leader, 2 August 1952, pp. 19–20. This piece was anonymous and the authorship was never revealed. In the last sentence, the occupant of the lodge is Noel Hartnett, formerly a very close adherent of Sean MacBride, who later lost the faith. An earlier reference to advice given to Noel Browne on photographic and ecclesiastical subjects relates to a rebuke to Noel Browne for being photographed with the Protestant archbishop of Dublin.

these are the masks of Comedy and Tragedy, and the man who carries them both with such an air could, one imagines, have been a great actor. There are those who say that this is no hypothesis, that he is in fact constantly acting a part: *poseur*, they say, and, most inappropriately, "playboy." This gibe, although it often merely voices the envy of the inarticulate and drab, is not altogether unjust. The professions of law, politics and diplomacy are not conducive to unconditional sincerity. One who brings to these professions, in addition, something of the actor's temperament, and a foreign accent, may be expected to fall occasionally a little short of rugged candour. Mr. MacBride is hardly so often amused, or so affectionate towards his interlocutor, as outward appearances suggest. "Switching on the charm," say his critics sourly, to which his friends might reply—indeed the remark has been attributed to Mr. Con Lehane—that it would be a pity for one who controls so much candle-power not to let the light of his countenance be seen from time to time. Yet, if the Comic mask, with its whole range of social expressions, is assumed, the same is certainly not true of the face in sadness: that is, in reality, not a mask at all, but the face itself. The relevant myth is not that of the Actor, who plays any part at will, but that of the Clown. On a superficial view this comparison seems wild: there is not the faintest suggestion of buffoonery about this distinguished ex-Foreign Minister, on whom the adjective "suave" has been stamped in indelible printer's ink. Yet—apart from the stereotype of the clown who laughs while his heart is breaking—acute observers, who know him well, have seen in that drawn and humourless face an extraordinary resemblance to Charlie Chaplin. Mr. MacBride, like Charlie, looks wistfully at the world: he is full of unrequited loves—for the Six Counties, for journalists, for the Fianna Fail party, for the constituency of Dublin South-West. He often, especially in the Dail, pleads his case, not like the lawyer that he is, but like the tramp, bowler-hatted, twisty-footed, before the circus giant or the haughty maiden. Some of his speeches would indeed have been better if, like Charlie's, they had been confided to the medium of the silent screen. No matter, he implores, he entreats, bankers to break the link with sterling, Orangemen the link with the Crown. The maiden turns her back, the giant lumbers threateningly, the hero breaks into a run. Confronted with bulky grim realities, Charlie is often a sad figure. But there is also a dream-world—O Salon de l'Horloge', O Palais de la Muette!—in which he is a brilliantly successful statesman, elegant, eloquent, strolling with the leaders of Europe; what he is doing is not very clear, but with what distinction he does it! Now he is addressing the Congress of the United States: the representatives of the greatest nation on earth are on their feet denouncing the Partition of Ireland, the television cameras are whirring, it is an unheard-of scene, he is being carried shoulder high by the nine Justices of the Supreme Court along the road to Lincoln's Tomb, he has saved his country! The tramp stirs uneasily on his bench and awakes to the cold winds of Crumlin.

The dream was not, of course, all a dream, nor did the hero always run before the giant; the myth of the Clown does not explain the whole character, but it gives an essential clue. Yet there are many, both friends and enemies, who would find it absurdly irrelevant. Dr. Noel Browne, for instance, who gave prolonged and anxious study to the character, could find nothing pathetic or romantic in it. He saw it, certainly, as "two-faced," and eventually informed the public of the fact, but the two faces which he saw are not those which we have here described, the tragic Clown, with and without his mask. He saw, instead, that figure of melodrama, the cold and deliberate hypocrite, the Machiavellian who assumes a mask of idealism. Politicians have long accused each other of Machiavellism; this is a cliché of invective rather than a contribution to political psychology. But when Dr. Browne said, as he did in his letter of resignation from the Inter-Party Government, that he had had "a bitter experience" of Mr. MacBride's "cruel and authoritarian mind," his words had a more exact ring. They accord, it must be admitted, but ill with the Chaplinesque conception of Mr. MacBride's character, and they fit certain known elements in his career. It is more than plausible that the underground commander, the aggressive cross-examining lawyer, the politician who insists on being known as "the Leader," should be authoritarian and perhaps even apparently cruel. This thin-lipped fanatic whose very laughter is somewhat chilling, who is to his immediate following almost a god, how could we have seen him as a Clown? We may say that we can conceive of a cruel Clown, one who laughs while other peoples' hearts break, that even an authoritarian Chaplain is not quite unimaginable, when one has seen *The Great Dictator*.

The word is like a knell; at any rate it has been so for Mr. MacBride. It was the accusation of dictatorial methods—with the implication that he was aiming at an actual dictatorship—which split and ruined his party, and overthrew the Government to which he belonged. "It is my fervent hope," wrote Dr. Browne in his best-known contribution to English prose, "that the destiny of this country will never be fully placed in your hands because it would, in my view, mean the destuction of all those ideals which are part and parcel of Christian democracy." Leaving aside the philosophical question of whether one can destroy ideals—and whether Mr. MacBride is more efficacious than the gates of Hell—we may say, with Antony, that if it were so, it were a grievous fault. But is it so? There is probably something in the accusation of dictatorial methods. Mr. MacBride was not, as Dr. Browne reminded us, used to democratic politics; it was said of him, probably with justice, that he treated his Civil Servants as if they were members of his party, and the members of his party as if they were Civil Servants. Even this, exasperating though it must have been to all concerned, was probably not so much a "method" as an effect of temperament. Mr. MacBride's charismatic radiations do not affect a wide field, but within a restricted danger area—the danger is to the wits—they are exceedingly intense; most of the people around him were inclined to do what he told them, should the sky fall, which it did. There were, as the world knows, those who revolted. Of Mr. Noel Hartnett it would be too weak to say that he shook off the yoke; he bolted with the yoke between his teeth. Such exploits do not disprove the existence of a dictatorial spirit in Mr. MacBride. True, Captain Cowan did not meet the fate of Captain Roehm, but then Mr. MacBride did not have the power, even if he had the will, to constitute himself, like Hitler, as the Supreme Court of the nation. Certainly the new, purged, party follows its leader with uncritical devotion, unsupported by either talent or numbers. Before the war, the National Socialist Party of Germany published a very glossy book containing portraits of the principal Nazis, with such captions as "a constructive organizer," "the great orator," "the hero of the youth," and so on. Under one portrait, however—that of Hess—the caption read simply "Distinguished by his dog-like fidelity to the Fuehrer." If Clann na Poblachta were so unwise as to publish such a portrait-gallery it would, at least, be saved the expense of having to print more than one caption.

Many good democrats have been dictatorial in their own circle, however, and there is no real evidence that Mr. MacBride wishes anything but well to our democratic state. His main achievement—apart from giving the Fianna Fail Government a short holiday—was to get the Commonwealth Party to take Ireland out of the Commonwealth. The value of that achievement, as Mr. Costello explained, was that it "took the gun out of politics." That is to say that it weakened, and was intended to weaken, the power of the IRA which, if Mr. MacBride was a conspirator, was the only organisation which could have enabled him to seize power. Certainly the organisation which he weakened would have been more use to a plotter than the organisation which he did so much to build up: the Department of External Affairs. One senses somehow that on the Night of the Long Knives, the inhabitants of Iveagh House will manage to be among those who neither knife nor—above all—are knifed. True, he managed, with the aid of General Marshall, to induce these gentlemen to put their fingers into the pies of various other

Departments—pies from which they were hastily withdrawn when Mr. Lemass and Mr. MacEntee came riding back—and he got Mr. Blowick to plant a great deal of Sithca Spruce. He also—and it was not an inconsiderable achievement—got the money for Dr. Browne to build his hospitals, and he seems to have given Dr. Browne a good deal of advice, not all of it on photographic and ecclesiastical subjects. In the sphere of justice—and notoriously the main interest of the plotter—his interventions were aimed at saving men from the gallows. It is reliably told that, at one of the last Cabinet meetings before the election which led to the fall of the Inter-party Government, Mr. MacBride spent many hours of Government time in struggling for the reprieve of a man who had been condemned to death. The young Nero, of course, is said to have wept as he signed a death sentence, but then he did sign it, whereas Mr. MacBride, on this occasion, as so often before, got his man off.

Mr. MacBride is much more like Jan Masaryk than he is like Nero or Hitler or any of those apocalyptic tyrants. He is not a dictator, he is, at worst, one of those through whom dictatorships occur. In such a man the danger to democracy lies not in his strength but in his weakness, and his over-confidence. He thinks he is bridging gulfs that are unbridgeable; he thinks that hard work is a substitute for sound judgment; he thinks he is using people who are really using him. These were the gifts that led to the *debacle*, when he and his young rival, locked in a death-struggle, like Holmes and Dr. Moriarty, rolled together into the political abyss.

What symbol for so complex a man? One thinks, even more than of Chaplin, of Don Quixote. (And, incidentally, how fine it would be to have a film in which Chaplin would be both Quixote and Sancho Panza.) "Quixote" is a term of abuse among the Marxists—worse than "lackey" but better than "bandit"—but we use "Quixote" rightly in a spirit of kindly criticism. The gaunt knight, wistful yet severe, in the dilapidated La Mancha of Roebuck, has been reading tales of chivalry, from Standish O'Grady to Patrick Pearse. He will rescue the fair lady Cathleen Ni Houlihan from the castle Discrimination, where the British giant, Gerrymandering, holds her thrall. The ogre Sterling bars the way with his famous Link, which will have to be snapped. The good fairies from America will help to accomplish this. (They have all been expelled from the State Department, but Quixote does not know this.) He saddles his spavined mare, Poblaclante, and gallops down the drive. But something is missing. He calls aloud for Sancho Panza. But Sancho will never come again. Sancho has locked himself into the lodge.

4

THE MAGIC OF MAURIAC

In 1952 the Nobel Prize for Literature went to François Mauriac, who has, over forty years and in more than twenty novels, written of men and women as answerable to God, guilty in the sight of God, and serving always, willingly or unwillingly, the mysterious purposes of God.

Six years ago this same prize, this European accolade, went to another Frenchman who had, over a longer period and in a greater number of words, shown us men and women learning to rejoice in the idea that they were answerable only to themselves, that they were not guilty at all, and that they served no supernatural purpose.

Mauriac himself was horrified when the Nobel Prize was awarded to André Gide. It was, he thought, a sinister portent that the stricken Europe of today should single out for honor the great immoralist, the experimental anti-Christ. His horror, one imagines, must now be tinged with confusion. The fact that it has been possible to award this prize both to Gide and to Mauriac provokes the mind to grapple with the ambiguities, perhaps the contradictions, that are present in our idea of literature. Some may say that there is really no problem, that both Gide and Mauriac are honored as masters of French prose, without regard to the contradictory messages which they are using their mastery to convey. So, they might argue, one might consistently praise both Saladin and Richard the Lion-Hearted for their military skill, rightly excluding, as irrelevant to this particular subject, the debate of Cross and Crescent. For all I know, this, or something like it, may be the view of the five

Commonweal 58 (15 May 1953), pp. 144–46, 148–50. By "Donat O'Donnell."

judges, appointed by the Norwegian *Storthing*, who make the Nobel award. It would be fitting enough that the spirit of the Parnassians should linger on in the North among those icicles of Thule which they so often used as symbols of the death-like detachment they admired. Sully-Prudhomme, who was, as it happens, the first winner of the Nobel prize, would have seen nothing incongruous in honoring two masters of opposing tendencies: his only doubt would have been whether either of them had the right to a tendency at all.

But in our own time most people, and even most writers, have rejected the Parnassian attitudes. "Art for Art's Sake" is a phrase we treat with suspicion, and that only partly because of its debasement by Metro-Goldwyn-Mayer. The most influential writers of today tell us that literature is committed in the political and social struggle: *la littérature engagée*. Although neither Gide nor Mauriac belonged to the little group which has impressed this slogan upon our consciousness, they would both, I think, have given it some kind of assent. They both were teachers, inculcating different and irreconcilable sets of opinions, and they regarded their teaching, or at any rate the content of their works, as more important than their prose style.

Is there not then, one may say, a detestable dilettantism, a frivolous complacency, in honoring them both? Is it not debasing literature, and humanity, to institute competitions in mere elegance of expression, remaining indifferent to what is being expressed? Is it not like the action of some fatuous Religious Book-of-the-Month Club which might choose successively the Rubaiyat of Omar Khayyam and the New Testament? Worst of all, does not this jaded byzantinism, indifferent to moral values, confirm the judgment of those who speak of the decadence of the West?

Such questions should be asked if only because they force us, with their dangerous misconceptions, to think of what literature really is, of what thing worthy of praise a great novelist like Mauriac actually does. Literature is surely neither an abstract and self-sufficient pattern, as the Parnassians asserted, nor yet just another form of propaganda in favor of the good, or the bad, life. It is the most human, the least pure of the arts, the one that tells us most about ourselves. It is—to use a word that has lately been much misused—our self-criticism, a subtle and continuing process. I say continuing, but of course we have no certainty that it will continue: we have seen of late that in certain conditions literature can become a system of political flattery and fictionalized slogans, and that the word self-criticism, in the same climate, turns into a technical term, meaning forced confession of crude and improbable crimes.

These practices of total politics must lead not merely to a blunting of human conscience, but probably to an actual dulling of consciousness itself; in short, a regression to a lower human type. It has been, on the other hand—and it still is—the glory of our bourgeois culture that it has eventually honored those who have not flattered it. Those who do flatter it are of course more numerous and better paid, but that is not very important; what is important is that the process of self-criticism, the painful movement towards a finer consciousness, still continues.

In that process these two writers, Gide and Mauriac, with their exceptional lucidity and sensibility, have played a great part. Different though their views of the universe are, they have both tried to tell the truth—not such a simple matter as is generally believed—and to provide increasingly delicate and sensitive instruments for recording and expressing it. This is the great common element in their so diverse achievement, and it is this above all that justifies the conferring of the same honor on the two spiritual adversaries.

Mauriac started telling the truth in 1922, and stopped about ten years later for reasons which I will go into in a moment. During that period, when he was in his late thirties and early forties, he gave us nine novels, beginning with *Le Baiser au Lépreux* and ending with *Le Nœud de Vipères*; this group of novels includes his best work and in particular the two splendid peaks of his achievement, *Génitrix*, which appeared in 1924, and *Le Désert de l'Amour* in 1925. The seven novels which have appeared since 1932 are—with one partial exception, *La Pharisienne*—little more than a companionable reminder of a great presence—like the broadcast talks of Mr. E. M. Forster.

I have spoken of ten years during which Mauriac spoke the truth. What was the nature of that truth? It was, in the words of a watchful critic of the twenties: "disturbing and unhealthy;" "bizarre and morbid;" "very pernicious and morally base." These adjectives, describing the best work of one who is now universally esteemed as a great Catholic novelist, fall strangely on our ears. Mauriac was, of course, then, as he is now, a Catholic. But he did not then consider, as he does now, that edification and the avoidance of scandal were primary concerns of the Catholic writer. He even distrusted and disliked—as do most Catholic writers—the very words "Catholic writer" for he knew that his best work as a novelist sprang, not from faith and reason, but from the imagination, a very weak Christian. The Catholic and the writer did not form a dual entity: they were separate and related in a complex and changing manner. For Mauriac at this time imaginative truth was the first, and at his greatest moment the only consideration. "Only fiction does not lie," he wrote, "it opens on the life of man a secret door through which slips in, altogether unchecked, his unknown soul." What then was the nature of the traffic through this secret door, in the days when it was open?

It was a traffic, first of all, between the mind and nature, the natural forces of a given place. Mauriac is a man of Bordeaux and almost all his work—all his best work—is rooted in that hot and sandy region, the land of pines and vines, of sun and storms and forest fires. Here is that forest of symbols of which Baudelaire speaks: here are correlatives of human passion. "Sultry" and "torrid" are adjectives which one now proffers with diffidence: they have been debased by cinema advertisers in order to provide a stimulating explanation for the discontented, bad-tempered or simply vacant expressions of so many films stars. Otherwise one would inevitably apply one or other of them to Mauriac's world, with its electric air and its impending storms of lust and rage and hail and lightning. One of his heroines "believed implicitly," he tells us, in "these stage directions carefully drawn up by the Supreme Being for the lives of each and all of us ... the soil had to be softened by the storm." It would be easy to discount this as a trick, and of course, a trick is sometimes just what it is. A very good critic, Mr. William Empson, has referred to the frequency with which characters in plays look out of windows in hope of observing a "pathetic fallacy." It sounds cynical, but the play in question is "Macbeth" and the pathetic fallacy is the light thickening and the crow making wing to the rooky wood. The process, whether fallacy or metaphor, or both, is a very old one, probably inherent in the conditions of human experience. Our everyday use of a meteorological term, "atmosphere," to describe human relationships, should remind us how deep in our thinking this fallacy goes. It reminds us also that it is not always a fallacy, for the meteorological atmosphere does really affect the emotional atmosphere.

In Mauriac's case, there were several reasons why the process should be an essential part of his imagination and not—except when he became tired and parodied himself—just a trick. He is, like so many religious writers, mainly interested in childhood and youth, and it is natural that the sights and sounds and smells of the Gironde of his boyhood should recur to his mind or should be deliberately invoked. Here a comparison with Proust is possible. *Remembrance of Things Past*, as we know, is organized round certain spasms of involuntary memory: the biscuit soaked in tea, the uneven flag-stones, the red phase from Vinteuil's sonata. Proust deliberately, almost religiously, respected these mental landmarks, and turned the wheel of his great baroque world around them, as his Paris turned around the low hill of the Etoile. In Mauriac there is no such deliberate orientation, no such architecture. Yet when he refers to certain sounds or smells—the song of the cicadas, the smell of burning resin—there is an excitement, a lyricism in his prose, an extra tension in his narrative. It is as if it were really Proust's intermittent God in the machine that was giving these "stage-directions" under which nature seems to take part in the human drama. The two principal characters in *The Desert of Love* know that the impending storm cannot break "until the last bull has died in the arena." That seems to be a magical belief—and Mauriac has been reproached for it—but is it not really a phenomenon of memory?

The truth is, I think, that memory is assisted by magic. I have said that the imagination is a weak Christian but it cannot help, in our culture, being a Christian of sorts. Mauriac's imagination is deeply penetrated by the sense of a divine purpose in all things and consequently of the unity of creation, in which the natural forces not only may, but must, relate themselves to human lives. It is also penetrated—and sometimes seems more deeply so—by the sense of an evil counter-purpose, of diabolic intervention. Most of his stage-directions seem to come from this quarter, and often, as in so many other Catholic writers, as with Bernanos especially, we are left with the impression of a world entirely given over to the powers of evil.

"Thanks to a certain gift of atmosphere," he later wrote in an attempt at justification, "I try to make perceptible, tangible, odorous, the Catholic universe of evil." That sounds well, but its suggestion of purpose is probably false. The picture of the well-meaning author using his "gift of atmosphere" as an instrument for exposing evil does not convince. The imagination, source of all this famous atmosphere, is neither so purposeful nor so well-meaning. But it is true that it is in creating an atmosphere of evil that Mauriac's imagination excels, and that what one might call his respect for evil is characteristically Christian and, specifically, Catholic.

The atheist Gide liked to write of crime and he wrote about it with a curious detached innocence; in his writing horrible crimes happen, but they happen, as it were, without a pedigree; they still belong to the world of newspaper clippings, the *fait divers*, rather than the world of "King Lear" or "Oedipus Rex." Their fragmentary, accidental character seems to me to result from that voluntary, that almost austere, limitation of the imagination which is involved in the act of atheism. For the religious writer, however, who not merely believes but feels that there is a purpose in the universe, it follows necessarily that the presence of evil must inspire awe. In an extreme case like Mauriac it inspires a fascinated horror, a permanent Jansenistic fear and trembling before the

God who permits and punishes sin. For him, as for other religious writers—and one thinks especially of Dostoevsky—evil is not just an accident, or a social by-product, but an ever-present condition and a universal system.

In Mauriac's work, evil expresses itself above all in terms of domination and captivity. Early in his career he told us of his fascination with "the power of minds over other minds which are inferior to them," and this is still the theme of his latest novel *Goligai—The Loved and the Unloved*. Nor is it really only the power of minds—the word in French is the ambiguous *esprits*—but a spiritual power, and an emotional dominance of the whole personality. The context of this phenomenon is usually the family, an institution which is compared to a prison: "the living bars of a family." The archetype of all his novels, so far as this situation is concerned, is *Génitrix* (1924), one of the earliest works of his maturity, and one of the finest he has ever written.

This idea of evil as emotional domination has a great and varied extension in Mauriac's work. It pervades, I think, his whole concept of sexual love, which is the main theme of most of his novels. To love, for his heroes and heroines, is to fall victim to a kind of trick or mirage. He has spoken of the certitude fatal to human happiness "that carnal love is evil, evil which we cannot help committing."

The theological warrant for so unqualified a statement, is, I imagine, slender, but it is never, with Mauriac, a question of theology, so much as of emotional conviction. Why should one *feel* that carnal love is evil—ignoring for the moment the un-Irish assumption that one cannot help committing it?

I believe that the root of the feeling lies in the dread of domination, and in particular the dread and attraction of maternal domination, so terribly expressed in *Génitrix*. Very old and primitive connections of ideas are also at work: notably the fallacies of witchcraft, the theories that the beloved has cast a spell over the lover; that the lover is surrendering his soul, that is, power over himself, to the beloved; that pleasure is an instrument of domination, and cruelty an instrument of emancipation. These old and ignorant ideas still fight a rearguard action in the *Maquis* of our mind, and occasionally supplies are parachuted in to them from the outside. They form an important part of the history of the idea of evil, and they supply a subterranean resonance to the sensuality of the superstitious. There is certainly both sensuality and superstition in Mauriac's novels of the twenties. They are, according to a clerical critic, "steeped in an atmosphere of refined sensuality, that penetrates to the marrow of your bones"—a remark that surely belongs with the finest examples of advertising copy.

This was the origin of the charge of "collusion with evil" which was persistently leveled at Mauriac by Catholic critics, and others, up to 1929. He defended himself as best he could. First, it was the business of the novelist to tell the truth, and, since truth was of God it was impossible in this way to offend God. Basically this arguement is sound, but as he developed it, it ceased to be so. He spoke of "reproducing the modern world as it exists" but in fact, as he well knew, and as his critics told him, he was not doing anything of the kind: his "truth" was subjective and emotional, not scientific. His other defense was that "there are no loves, only one Love." His heroes and heroines, in so far as they really love, love God. He shows them discovering the corrupt and unsatisfactory nature of physical love. "We take the only road we can," says the heroine of Le Désert de l'Amour, "but it doesn't lead towards what we're looking for."

His critics answered that the theory of this was correct, but that his practice was quite different. He said that he regarded carnal love as evil, but he depicted it as seductive. André Gide—and this was apparently the last straw—paid him a perfidious compliment. "The object of your novels," he wrote, "is not so much to bring sinners to Christianity as to remind Christians that there is something on earth besides heaven.... Doubtless if I were more of a Christian I should be less your disciple."

Mauriac himself, in the spring of 1929, came to admit the truth of such criticisms. "I depicted evil with a secret collusion," he admits, "because I was describing attractions which I felt." He now determined to eliminate this characteristic of his work: this determination was the main artistic result of the crisis which is known as his conversion. He now accepted M. Jacques Maritain's doctrine of altitude: that the artist in portraying evil must keep his distance. The old collusion must go; the secret door must be kept shut.

Spiritually this no doubt represented an advance. Intellectually it was a clarification, for there was confusion as well as collusion in these novels. But artistically it represented a defeat. Mauriac had voluntarily accepted a kind of censorship, a permanent internal vigilance committee established in his imaginative world. He could no longer tell the truth as he felt it, for that might be collusion—or, as with the last of his great novels, Le Nœud de Vipères—it might seem to be lack of charity. He hedged himself round with extraneous restrictions until almost everything he wrote—and he still wrote a great deal—seemed touched-up, rearranged and false.

Fortunately, though perhaps rather curiously, he did not withdraw from publication the earlier work, Le Baiser au Lépreux, Génitrix, Le Désert de l'Amour and others in which he now admitted the existence of a certain collusion with evil. Fortunately: for it is by these works, with *Le Nœud de Vipères*, that his reputation will, in the long run, assuredly stand or fall. It will, I believe, stand.

So high a valuation may seem, at first, inconsistent with the language I have used in describing the work of this period. How can work so abounding in "confusion," "collusion," "superstition," "witchcraft" and various kinds of fallacies, be rewarding? If telling the truth is all-important, what kind of truth is hidden at the bottom of this cauldron?

The answer might very nearly be: the whole truth and nothing but the truth. The imaginative artist is, as it were, the only one who attempts the whole paper which the Creator has set us. The scientist attempts only questions of fact, available to measurement: only his conscious mind is relevant to his effort. For the psychoanalyst's patient on his couch, the unconscious alone is important. All of us in our daily lives respond at different times on different levels, now emotionally, now intellectually. No one attempts a total response, in which the whole personality takes part, in which the conscious mind collaborates closely and continuously with the unconscious. No one, that is, except the imaginative artist.

The truth he tells, being total truth, is at one and the same time, in one and the same fable, about everything human—about man's conflict within himself, about his relation to his immediate environment, and to the universe. It is often—if the expression may be used—a twisted and distorted truth—as the truth told by the rings on the section of an oak tree sometimes lies in twistings and shrinkings telling of drought or floods. In the writer these are the twists imparted by unresolved conflicts in the writer himself or in his culture, directly felt by him. They are of an altogether different nature from the twists—neither honorable nor truthful—inflicted by a deliberate censorship or a desire for edification or any other form of propaganda.

It was in this sense, and with such organic distortions, that Mauriac told the truth. The magic let loose in his writing is latent in our minds also—whether as superstition or as intuition—but his merit is to be articulate.

I had a friend once whose mental world lay in a very different climate from Mauriac's. His favorite slogan, from which he seemed to derive great comfort, used to be, "Man is not a fallen angel but a risen ape." I think he would have been impatient with what I have had to say about Mauriac. In particular the idea of man as a prisoner, an emotional captive in a dungeon of guilt and half-perceived relations—that would have annoyed him. Even if it was true, he would argue, "what was the use of it?" Better an inspiring, a liberating picture of man. Better, for instance, Gide's fable "Prometheus badly chained" in which Prometheus, tired of his vulture's eternal nagging, simply turns round and wrings its neck. That is a heroic gesture, but your Mauriac heroes with their guilt-complexes are simply contemptible.

One could answer, I suppose, that there are more ways of killing a vulture than by wringing its neck; you can, for instance, choke it with liver. The light which such a writer as Mauriac brings about the dark and guilty places of the human heart is not what creates these dark and guilty places, nor do they cease to exist when the light is gone; on the contrary. But it is probably best to decline altogether the gambit of "what is the use?"; to forget Sir Arthur Quiller-Couch with his query about any poem: "Will it encourage the crew?" Let the crew sink or swim, if they can only be "encouraged" by jazzing-up the ship's log.

The battered old Parnassian slogan was at any rate better than that, but it would be better still in the revised form: "Art for truth's sake." That is the sole criterion which should ever have been applied—even by himself—to the work of so great a writer as François Mauriac.

5

A Sunday in East Berlin

"The People's Police are on the Watch," declares a slogan at the subway station in the Alexanderplatz, from which I emerged into East Berlin. Beneath the slogan is an exhibit of photographs, with humorous captions in the Berlin dialect, showing the various feats of this famous force which, like the "B Specials" of Belfast, is politically selected and para-military.

There are, however, no People's Police and only two or three civilians to be seen in the great ruined expanse of the Alexanderplatz, in the central section of old Berlin. Quite near the subway there is a bookshop, closed since it is Sunday morning—and a more Sabbatarian Sunday than Belfast ever dreamed of. Marxist classics, translations from the Russian, technical books on athletics, sumptuous works on Czechoslovakian glass and Bulgarian ceramics. All the books are handsomely produced, by the great presses of Leipzig and Dresden, and most of them look beyond the means of the kind of people one sees in the streets.

Along the Leninallee, moving towards Unter den Linden, a few scattered groups of people; for several minutes no wheeled traffic at all. Then five large trucks come by, full of smart well-built Russian troops—normally a rather rare sight in what is often referred to as "the Communist shop window" of East Berlin. There is also a woman in one of the trucks, two women in another—all three plain and stolid, dressed in cotton frocks. Two small cars follow, moving fast, each full of men in dark suits, and each flying the flag of the Democratic Republic. Then

Commonweal, 61 (29 October 1954), pp. 90–91. By "Donat O'Donnell."

no more traffic. This great city—there are a million people in East Berlin, two million in the Western sectors—shows less sign of life, here at its center, than any normal little town of a few thousand.

On the walls of such buildings as are standing in the Leninallee, and in the Marx-Engels Platz to which it leads, are big red streamers with political slogans. *German Youth Unite for Peace; the German Democratic Republic is the Unshakable Bastion of World Peace; Only the Imperialists Stand between You and a Happy Life; End the Fascist Terror in West Berlin.* Smaller posters appeal to Christians and Socialists to support the Peace Movement. Two more Russian trucks cut diagonally across the deserted Marx-Engels Platz and at last disappear down Unter den Linden. Moving in the opposite direction a Russian air force officer on leave passes, followed by his wife and child at a distance of about a yard and a half.

At the corner of Unter den Linden is the first sign of revelry, or the Continental Sunday—a stall with two folding card-tables, on one of which are six bottles of beer, on the other six glasses. There are no chairs and the expected roisterers have not arrived. Further down the famous avenue a Karl Marx Exhibition—housed in a Hohenzollern palace with an effigy of some caracoling Frederick—is doing no better. The doors are open but nobody comes in or out.

Then at last, almost opposite the huge Soviet Embassy—the only modern, and almost the only whole, building in the avenue—the people come in sight. They are entering Unter den Linden in procession from a side street and turning down towards where the Red Flag flaps on the Brandenburger Tor.

Along the route of the procession an excellent public address system carries a speaker's words. He is talking about heroes of the anti-fascist struggle, for this is Anti-Fascist Memorial Day. One of the heroes it seems was President Pieck. President Pieck gets a clap. Comrade Grotewohl, hero and Prime Minister, gets a slightly better clap. "The Russian mother, heroine of the anti-fascist struggle" gets a clap from those near the platform—as comes over the public-address system—but the procession itself is silent on this theme.

The procession, as I follow it towards the Wilhelmstrasse, is rather quiet and seems tired or bored. Here and there a group, or one man, is marching, but most are just walking, some almost shuffling. There is a complete absence of excitement, both in the speaker's voice and in the crowd. No staging, no lights, no bands, no cheers, no salutes.

Most of the crowd are young; the only elderly people I saw were in a rather pathetic contingent, about thirty strong, behind a banner with the inscription "West Berlin." Most of them, also, look "petit-bourgeois", rather than workers; students, civil servants, professional men—in general, people with a little more than their chains to lose. One group walks behind the banner "Juridical Faculty of Humboldt University;" it is followed by a group which apparently consists of the cleaners and messengers of the same university, who are in turn followed by the philosophy students.

Herr Grotewohl, Prime Minister of the Democratic Republic, is now speaking, in the pure clear German of Hanover. His voice is earnest and persuasive, rather than inflammatory, and he attempts hardly any rhetorical effects. His theme is simply that of repeating, amplifying and again repeating the same appeals as are already before his audience's eyes on red streamer-slogans.

One cannot get a sight of the platform without actually joining the procession, for here the People's Police, who must all be concentrated at this spot, form a cordon to screen off the mere sight-seers from moving on with the procession. Otherwise no attempt is made to interfere with the spectators, a few hundred of whom are present; some of them are moving away at this moment in the very middle of Grotewohl's speech; a few little girls are playing, unreproved, a form of tag. Such pressure as may be applied—as is, it may be safely assumed, applied—in connection with these meetings is not in the form of "terror in the streets" as in the early Nazi days. In West Berlin they say, almost certainly with truth, that the Communists, who control virtually all employment, work by vocational pressure. The employees of a given office, the students of a given faculty are given advance notice of such a meeting; their presence or absence is noted by a personnel officer, and the absentees are liable to lose their jobs or their educational opportunities. The organization of the procession under vocational banners, the type of people participating, and their obvious apathy, all tend to confirm this view.

Herr Grotewohl's lecture is coming to an end. He has congratulated the French on their victory for peace in the rejection of EDC and has assured them of German support. He has denounced, but not in tones of any great conviction, the rebirth of fascism in Western Germany. He is confident—it is his peroration—that the movement for peace and democracy will succeed because it is "deeply grounded in the German national character."

Then as the next speaker addresses his German audience entirely in the Russian language the reason for the presence of Soviet troops becomes clear. He is General Gundorow, Special Representative of the Soviet Union, and it is for his protection that the many truck-loads of Russian troops are present. The Russians want no more incidents in their shop window of East Berlin.

6

POETRY, INSPIRATION AND CRITICISM

"He was not an omnivorous devourer of sensations; he did not scour the world for them or pick tit-bits from many times and places. When something caught him, he was its devoted and responsive victim, who sought to extract all that he possibly could from it and was by his very devotion hampered from looking at anything else."

This, on Walter Pater as a critic, is typical of Sir Maurice Bowra's sober and clear appraisals. It is also, I think, a self-criticism, for Sir Maurice is the kind of critic that Pater was not. Omnivorous, in his new book of essays, *Inspiration and Poetry*, he scours the world from Dorset to the Caucasus and from Moscow to Nicaragua; "devours sensations" as different from each other as a medieval Georgian epic can be from the hymns of Hölderlin; ranges in time for his tit-bits from Augustan Rome to the end of the nineteenth century. Unlike Pater, again, he does not seek to extract everything possible from a chosen subject; perhaps he is too sane for that; "sanity" is a favourite word of his. He writes like one who feels that in criticism also there is a margin beyond which it is unprofitable to cultivate, a point at which it is better to push on and work the surface of new territory, leaving the Paters to scratch in the dust-bowl of unanswerable questions. Not, of course, that he is impatient or American in the vulgar sense; few critics have so even a temper, such catholic sympathies, a mind so open or so quick to fill. Simply, with a restraint which is perhaps classical, he is content to act as the introducer of the poets, the sensible and travelled man who knows the city;

Spectator, 8 July 1955, pp. 53, 55–56. Review of *Inspiration and Poetry* by C.M. Bowra, by "Donat O'Donnell."

an unusually alert chorus, enormously well-read and learned in many languages. This kind of critic is much more obviously useful than the "devoted and responsive victim" of the Pater stamp; but he is a teacher. The devoted and responsive is interested primarily in his own relation to the work; he may be confused, obscure, boring, tortuous, but he is sincere in the sense that he is not interested in deceiving anyone, except perhaps himself. The teacher has already settled accounts with the work; he is interested in the relation between himself and his class, in the act of teaching. If he is to hold the interest of his class he must skim and simplify, therefore to some extent betray. A good example, in the present volume, is Sir Maurice Bowra's analysis of an effect of Thomas Hardy's. He makes the sound point that Hardy "supplements a body of simple spoken English with resonant and unusual words of Latin origin and with Anglo-Saxon words which have passed out of currency and have an archaic air." To illustrate this Sir Maurice quotes the lines from Hardy's poem on the loss of the Titanic:

> Steel chambers, late the pyres
> Of her salamandrine fires,
> Cold currents thrid, and turn to rhythmic tidal lyres.
> Over the mirrors meant
> To glass the opulent
> The sea worm crawls—grotesque, slimed, dumb, indifferent.

Sir Maurice's comment on this needs to be quoted in full:

> The contrast is between the proud hopes of those who built the great ship or travelled in it and the cold lifelessness of its present state. He uses his Latin words "salamandrine" and "opulent" to stress the first side of the contrast. Each has a touch of irony. The engines which seemed to flourish like salamanders in the flame are quenched for ever; the mirrors on which the sea-worm now crawls were meant for people whom wealth seemed to protect from any stroke of doom. Against these words of pride, turned with irony to express the huge degree of the catastrophe, Hardy sets his humble words like "thrid" and "slimed" of which the first conveys the inhuman, relentless movement of the water, and the second the absolute difference of the Titanic's present inmates from those for whom it was built.

This is interesting and impressive; to an audience—it was part of a Byron lecture delivered at Nottingham University—it would be very impressive indeed. But the reader, who can reconsider the lines themselves, will soon have less faith in the commentary. The contrast in Hardy is surely neither so clear-cut nor of quite the same kind as Sir

Maurice Bowra suggests. The Latin words are not really symmetrically disposed: "indifferent" applied to the sea-worm is quite as Latin as "opulent" applied to the voyagers, to take only one of several instances. "Rhythmic tidal lyres" are very far from being "humble words" and very far also from suggesting the "cold lifelessness" which Sir Maurice identifies with the present state of the ship; neither the tide nor the sea-worm is lifeless, and the point is surely that their life is "indifferent"—the keyword—to human life, not that there is, or could be, such a thing as an "absolute difference" between the two sets of inmates. The commentary blurs also the curious use of "salamandrine," applied not to the engines, as Sir Maurice implies, but to the fires themselves: a fact which leaves little room for the supposed irony about the quenched pride of fire-resistant engines. In short, the commentary subtly distorts Hardy's meaning by simplifying his contrasts, both of language and of situation, and by coarsening his irony. This distortion is natural, and may even be necessary, in the lecture-room, to convey something like the general sense of a poem, but a criticism which works in such a way can only be loose and approximate: "an approach to" Hardy and others rather than something that actually tries to arrive.

Sir Maurice Bowra rightly reminds us that "there is room in the world for more than one kind of critic, and in general it seems foolish to lay down rigidly what a critic ought to be." His own variety of "approach" criticism makes pleasant reading and has the very considerable merit of introducing us to writers of whom—lacking his formidable linguistic attainments—we should otherwise know nothing. He has the great gift of curiosity, and makes us share something of his pleasure in handling so exotic an object as the mediæval Georgian epic, Shot'ha Rust'hveli's *The Knight in the Tiger's Skin*—even though, as he so truly says, "we cannot enjoy the many felicities of language which its admirers claim for it." He is at his best, however, in discussing writers, like Hölderlin and like Rubén Darío, who belong to the literary traditions which we know but who are, because of language difficulties, less read than they deserve to be. He quotes freely and aptly and gives a translation; often what he quotes is something which, we know, will always remain in our mind even if we never read another line of the author concerned. Thus he tells us of Rubén Darío's poem, *Los Motivos del Lobo*, the story of the wolf of Gubbio, who was converted by the example and preaching of St. Francis but relapsed after a spell of convent life and, when appealed to by the Saint, made his devastating criticism of humanity:

> *Hermanos a hermanos hacían la guerra,*
> *perdían los débiles, ganaban los malos,*

> *hembra y macho eran como perro y perra,*
> *y un buen día todos me dieron de palos.*

> (Brothers made war on brothers,
> the weak lost, the wicked gained,
> woman and man were like bitch and dog,
> and one fine day they all took sticks to me.)

And the wolf takes leave of the Saint with his own version of "So get you gone, von Hügel, though with blessings on your head":

> *Déjame en el monte, déjame en el risco,*
> *déjame existir en mi libertad,*
> *vete a tu convento, hermano Francisco,*
> *sigue tu camino y tu santidad.*

> (Leave me on the mountain, leave me on the cliff,
> leave me to live in my liberty,
> go to your convent, brother Francis,
> follow your way and your sanctity.)

The essays on Pushkin and on Lermontov and that on Dante and Arnaut Daniel—the last the most closely reasoned in the book—are rich in both quotations and information; indeed, curious facts come second only to quotations among the attractions of *Inspiration and Poetry*. One feels a wiser and a better man for knowing that Walter Pater was not invited to the unveiling of the Shelley Memorial at Oxford because "he was not thought quite respectable."

The book takes its title from its opening essay, but it is also suggested that the essays collectively form some sort of inquiry into the working of poetic inspiration. "Sir Maurice Bowra starts," say his publishers, "with a chapter on inspiration and its ways of working in poetical creation. He then looks at some of the problems which this raises, and examines them in individual cases, which vary from [Horace to Rust'hveli] and includes [*sic*] matters so different as [Dante and Daniel, Gil Vicente and Samson Agonistes]." That this claim to a unity of conception is quite misleading (as well as unnecessary) immediately appears from Sir Maurice Bowra's own preface in which he states that the various essays "have indeed been composed for different purposes, often for special occasions, and they cover very various ground." He hopes that the other pieces "are not too distantly related to the subject treated in the first chapter"; in fact, they are related by being (with one exception) about aspects of poetry. The problems of "inspiration"are hardly discussed except in the opening essay. This is not to be regretted, for Sir Maurice Bowra is not at his best among the foggy generalisations which accumulate round such a subject. "There is no doubt of the fact: what the poets have conceived through inspiration is also what we feel to be their most essential and most authentic poetry and we are justified in calling it inspired." And on the following page: "When we say that a poem is inspired we mean that it has an unusual degree of power." The problem is surely to find whether, in fact, the poems or the lines conceived by poets in the "rapturous moments" of "inspiration" are always, or even very often, those which the reader regards as possessing an unusual degree of power. Sir Maurice Bowra assumes that they are, but a critical examination of what evidence we have, from the letters and notebooks of poets, would be more interesting than mere assumptions—even the assumptions of a very learned man who loves poetry. Perhaps he has the noble fault of loving poetry too much; he is certainly very credulous where the assertions of poets are concerned. He tells us, for example, that, for Horace, "poetical inspiration is an occasion for Dionysiac joy," and that Horace takes, us "into the secrets of his poetic being" in his lines about the Bacchic frenzy:

> Euhoe, recenti mens trepidat metu
> plenoque Bacchi pectore turbidum
>   lætatur; Euhoe parce Liber,
>   parce gravi metuende thyrso.

of which he quotes Sir Edward Marsh's translation:

> Still reels my mind with joy and holy fear,
>   Still throbs my heart with presence of the God;
> I faint, I tremble—mighty Liber, hear!
>   Spare me the terrors of thy rod.

With all the great respect which is due to Sir Maurice Bowra in such a matter, it is also possible to feel that Horace was simply putting on some highly traditional airs and that these frigid *vers calculés* are evidence against the very assertion which they make. But Horace is artistically infallible in the eyes of this admirer: "His words, chosen with unfailing care and insight, are always fresh and alluring, and the result never looks laborious."

The criticism which results from "the maximum response which maximum attention can give"—Mr. R.P. Blackmur's well-known

7

THE LOVED ONE

Mr. Waugh, so his publishers tell us, suffered three years ago from a brief attack of hallucinations. He has now, according to the same source, made these "the theme of a light novel which should delight all those who live on the border lines of sanity—rather more than half the inhabitants of the kingdom according to medical figures."

It seems doubtful whether a novel about delusions of persecution —which is what Mr. Pinfold's hallucinations mainly are—will bring un-alloyed pleasure to those whose reason is tottering on its throne. The present reviewer, who has no claim to speak for the British lunatic, found *The Ordeal* moderately interesting, almost entirely unfunny, and a little embarrassing. The first, and probably the best, chapter in this short book is called "Portrait of the Artist in Middle Age." The portrait it presents of Mr. Pinfold seems to be in fact a portrait of Mr. Waugh, painted by no satiric or malevolent hand. "Affectionate, high-spirited and busy in childhood; dissipated and often despairing in youth; sturdy and prosperous in early manhood; he had in middle age degenerated less than many of his contemporaries. He attributed this superiority to his long, lonely, tranquil days at Lychpole, a secluded village some hun-dred miles from London." He had been a good soldier, is a Catholic —with the prefix "Roman"—professes an "idiosyncratic Toryism" and has a short way with intruders into his personal life. (Why, if literate, they need to intrude is not made clear.) He has become physically lazy

Spectator, 19 July 1957, p. 112. Review of *The Ordeal of Gilbert Pinfold* by Evelyn Waugh, by "Donat O'Donnell."

and "corpulent," eats less, drinks more, sleeps less, becomes "decidedly seedy" and is ordered to go on a sea voyage. In his cabin on the ship he begins to hear, through some defect in the wiring as he believes, various strange conversations, at first unrelated—a Bible class, a jazz session— then beginning to take the form of a conspiracy directed at him: he is threatened with a beating, there is a plot to kidnap him. He tries to relate this conspiracy to his fellow passengers—then he begins to hear these passengers talking about him:

> "... He'll commit suicide one of these days, you'll see."
> "I thought he was a Catholic. They aren't allowed to commit suicide, are they?"
> "That wouldn't stop Pinfold. He doesn't really *believe* in his religion, you know. He just pretends to because he thinks it aristocratic. It goes with being Lord of the Manor."
> "There's only one Lychpole in the world, he told the wireless man."
> "Only one Lychpole and Pinfold is its Lord...."
> "Here he is, drunk again. He looks ghastly."
> "A dying man, if ever I saw one."
> "Why doesn't he kill himself?"
> "Give him time. He's doing his best. Drink and drugs. He daren't go to a doctor, of course, for fear he'd be put in a home."
> "Best place for him, I should have thought."
> "Best place for him would be over the side."

For anyone who finds that kind of dialogue funny *The Ordeal of Gilbert Pinfold* will be a feast indeed. Some of Mr. Waugh's admirers will regret that he has chosen to make "a light novel" out of material fundamentally unsuited to such treatment. It may be said that the comic treatment of the grimmest themes—as in *The Loved One*—is precisely where Mr. Waugh excels. That is true when as a satirist he allows himself a free hand—dealing, for example, with the proletariat, Americans, or other beings beyond the range of human sympathy—but not when he is treating sacred subjects, such as himself. Then the mellowness of *Brideshead* blurs the vision and the tone of the satirist, and impairs the cruelty which alone could turn delusions of persecution into comedy. The Waugh of before *Brideshead Revisited* seldom wrote about himself; the Waugh of after *Brideshead* seldom writes about anything else.

8

CAREY BLOOM

On his native soil the Kerry blue is a shaggy blue-black animal, a little short on leg, purposeful and reticent, and a fierce fighter. So was our Kerry blue in Paris, above all shaggy, and we were very proud. The Parisians are exceptionally fond of dogs; they are also inexhaustibly curious about the diversity of the creations of God, or the Supreme Being. For both those reasons our Kerry blue attracted a good deal of attention. It was therefore nothing exceptional when the stout lady, proprietress of the restaurant in the Place Notre-Dame-des-Victoires, came over and asked what it was, as a dog. I told her it was an Irish dog, of a race unknown in France. To this she replied that she had an Irish dog herself, and went and got it. She produced with pride a rather impressive beast, trim and tufted, resembling an exceptionally tough poodle and having about it that suggestion of the sinister which the combination of physical strength and marked elegance always seems to evoke. As the two dogs were introduced I admired the stranger. He was, I confessed, superb as an Irish dog but, I was ashamed to say, I did not recognize the breed. The reply was crushing:

"*Mais, mon pauvre monsieur, c'est une des races les mieux connues de chiens irlandais! C'est un Carey Bloom!*"

There were, she revealed, only three "Carey Blooms" in all Paris: her dog, a bitch in the Avenue Henri Martin, and another dog in the Boulevard Raspail; but in the last case she thought the district cast

Atlantic 202 (November 1958), pp. 142–46, 148. This piece, by "Donat O'Donnell," which is almost entirely autobiographical, refers to events that took place in late 1955.

doubt upon the pedigree. I could have added to the list, but found it too hard to explain that my own dog also was striving, in his woolly way, to be a Carey Bloom.

I got two things out of this encounter: a new name for my dog and a new place to take Irish visitors in Paris. Irish people in Paris, like other visitors, want to plumb the depths of French wickedness and perversity, but it is by no means sure that they all know a depth when they plumb one. The dog of the Place Notre-Dame-des-Victoires was a good answer to this sort of thing. He constituted visible and tangible evidence of French perversity, in a form which any Irish person could understand. "When I look at that dog," said one of the Irish visitors, "I understand the Fall of France." His cup was full when I revealed that the dog had belonged to André Gide, when he lived in the Rue Vaneau. As the beast sneered at them across the café table, my friends found it easy to believe themselves in the presence of a disciple of Gide's. Only that diabolical brain, surely, could have conceived the project of tonsuring a Kerry blue into the semblance of a poodle.

I always meant to survey the field completely, to visit the pedigree bitch of the Avenue Henri Martin and the attainted dog of the Boulevard Raspail, but my newspaper decided otherwise. My new editor felt that the Irish people were not interested in what was happening in Paris; they were interested in what was happening in Donny-carney: I was to come home, quickly.

This raised a difficulty: what about Carey Bloom? It is very easy to bring a dog from Ireland (or England) to France: you just bring it. But to bring a dog back from France to Ireland or England is quite a different matter. You must, to begin with, obtain a license to import a Canine. If you get this you must, on arrival in Ireland, hand over the Canine, in an approved Nose-and-Paw-proof Receptacle, to an approved place of Quarantine, there to be confined for Six Calendar Months, at cost to owner of £2 a week. Then, if the dog is still alive, you can have him. All this is understood to be required to keep the scourge of rabies out of Ireland and, of course, England. The French, however, have a different story.

It became clear that there were three courses possible:

1. To leave Carey Bloom in France.
2. To bring him to Ireland complying with the Regulations.
3. To bring him to Ireland without complying with the Regulations.

The first course I should have favored myself, but it was ruled out by my two small daughters. The second course found no supporters: it would probably kill or at least disable the dog, and it would also cost us more than £50; the sentimentalists and the realists united in rejecting any such policy. It was therefore decided, by elimination, that Course 3 was to be adopted. Carey Bloom was to be smuggled, and I was to do the smuggling.

This was a more formidable and dangerous task than at first appears. In Ireland it is the Department of Agriculture that administers these laws. And it has been said that there are only two forces worth mentioning in Ireland: the Church and the Department of Agriculture. I risked not merely a heavy fine and a jail sentence, but also the loss of my job. Then hope dawned. I didn't have to smuggle Carey Bloom into Ireland at all. England would do. England and Ireland, politically, are fractured, but to the veterinarian they are still one and indivisible. If Carey Bloom were once in England, he could be brought to Ireland without fuss or formality. And even if I were caught smuggling into England, it would be by Englishmen, having broken an English regulation, and possessing therefore a sacred claim on the sympathy of my own countrymen. Even my newspaper would have to back me up; my friends could see to that. If it failed me it would be accused of playing England's game, and then let it look to its circulation!

In good spirits, then, I prepared for the attack. My family went ahead by air, leaving me with the car and Carey Bloom. My last dinner in Paris I took in the Place Notre-Dame-des-Victoires. The stout lady, pleased at what I had done for the reputation of her dog and house, gave me photographs of both. The picture of the dog had been taken at one of our evening gatherings. The dog was seated at a café table, with a hideous expression of intelligence, in the middle of a lively group; he had a glass of Pernod in front of him and four saucers—a surprising number, for he drank very little. On the wall behind, someone had taken care to hang a portrait of M. Gide. To a man facing, perhaps, an English prison on the morrow, it all seemed a little childish, and yet endearing. They put me to bed on the premises.

My start on the following morning was not as early as it should have been, nor my head as clear. It was eight o'clock when, with Carey Bloom upright in the seat beside me, I left Paris by the Porte de Neuilly, on the road to Dieppe. I stopped at Pontoise to consult the local vet. My plans involved putting Carey Bloom in a case, and the case in the boot of the car; anyone who knew Carey Bloom realized that this could hardly be done without assistance, much noise, and perhaps even bloodshed, unless the patient were unconscious.

The vet of Pontoise was large, *sportif*, and *très gentleman*—with crew cut. He was also in full sympathy with my project. The English quarantine laws were a piece of cynical hypocrisy. *La rage canine* was, without doubt, a very terrible disease, but did I know when the last case of it had been notified in France? No? *Eh bien, mon pauvre monsieur*, the last case of *la rage canine* in France occurred in 1910! *Dix ... neuf ... cent ... dix!* Under President Fallières! Had I so much as met anyone who had even heard of President Fallières? No? Well, then!

The vet of Pontoise was striding up and down the room, breathing heavily. I tried to bring him back to the immediate practical aspects of the problem: I had a boat to catch, needed instructions on dog-doping, and the dope itself. "None of that," said the vet, "presents any difficulty. Do you know the real reason for the quarantine regulations? It is that the dog breeders of England fear the French competition—and Dutch competition perhaps a little too—"

"My boat goes," I said, "at 12:30, and if you could give me some pills, something that would work quickly—"

The vet stopped walking and looked me sternly in the eye. "Of course I will give you the pills," he said. "*Ne vous affolez pas. Vous avez largement le temps.*"

I looked at my watch, with gathering hopelessness.

"It is admirably simple," said the vet of Pontoise. "Suppose there is a minister who is an honest man and who says, 'You are breaking my feet with your silly regulations about quarantine for dogs: I will abolish them!' *Vlan!* So what happens? One dog breeder rings up his brother, the governor of the BBC. Another calls his uncle, the editor of the *Times*. A third takes up the phone and says, 'Give me Canterbury 1.'

"So all the hysterical old women of England—that is 40 million out of a total population of 50 million—get together and make some *brouhaha*. They say: Keep out French Diseases! They say: A Vote for Labor Is a Vote for Rabies! Then one day the minister gets up in the House and says the question needs further study, and he sets up a commission of dog breeders' brothers to study it! As for you, monsieur, here are four tablets of Gardenal. Give the animal one not more than half an hour before embarkation; give him the other three on the boat—just put them in his mouth, he'll swallow them. You've nothing at all to worry about—he'll sleep like a woodcutter, and the customs people in England are the same as our own, they never look at anything."

Out in the yard the vet of Pontoise—who refused any payment— took a good look at Carey Bloom. "He could be a nice-looking dog," he said, "if he were properly trimmed."

Having no time for this controversy, I got into the car and prepared to turn into the street.

"Of course," said the vet, "I know that in England they like dogs to be like that. They have the mania of the natural. It is perhaps," he added thoughtfully, "a form of hypocrisy."

As I drove through the Vexin on the road to Dieppe I felt considerably fortified by the vet's remarks. His exposure of the economic basis of the quarantine regulations was convincing enough—allowing for French hyperbole—and it conferred on my own enterprise an agreeable touch of righteousness. I was encouraged, furthermore, by what he had said about the laxity of the customs examination.

It was only in Dieppe itself, driving down to the port, at noon, that the brightness of this vision began to fade. I realized that I was a half hour late, and that the doping of Carey Bloom was going to present certain difficulties. At the port I had two simultaneous problems to solve rapidly: to get the car on board, and to dope Carey Bloom. *En principe*, cars are not accepted at all, unless presented an hour before departure. And it was now—successive officials pointed out—thirty minutes ... twenty minutes ... ten minutes before departure. French officials, once they have logically established the utter impossibility of some course of action, usually like to show that they, being *élite* personalities, can none the less do it, this impossible thing, and the formalities in this case were pushed through with surprising speed. This involved, however, running up many steps and gangways, and the frequent assumption of that air of harassed and apologetic helplessness that, for the French official, is the mark of a deserving member of the public.

In between these interviews I had repeatedly to get back to the car for an even more difficult argument, with Carey Bloom. Carey Bloom is a patient dog, and he did not at all object to my trying to feed him Gardenal. I could put the tablet in his mouth and hold his massive jaws together. He would look at me sadly but uncomplainingly, his eyes deep violet pools under the blue shadow of his shaggy brows. Then, when I let go my hold, Carey Bloom would deposit a white and glistening object on the seat of the car. The ultimate official, who came to the car with the cleared papers, seven minutes before departure time, found me still clutching Carey Bloom's head, the two of us staring at each other fixedly. The official mistook this for a display of Anglo-Saxon sentimentality and disapproved. "You had better get your car on board immediately," he said. "You need not fear seasickness, either for yourself or your dog. The sea is perfectly calm. But hurry in the name of God."

There was clearly now no question of putting Carey Bloom into a suitcase and the suitcase into the boot of the car. That, and the doping, would have to be done on board, at leisure as I hoped. I pushed Carey Bloom onto the floor in front of the seat and covered him with a rug.

The result looked depressingly like a dog covered with a rug. I drove to the ship's side and sat in the car waiting to be hauled aboard. But a face, covered with soft coal, appeared at the window, and spoke:

"You are not, monsieur, by chance a member of the Union of French Stevedores and Port Workers, affiliated to the CGT? No? In that case, monsieur, perhaps you would be good enough to hand me the key of your car, and proceed, yourself, on foot, on board the boat. I will take your place at the wheel and will occupy myself with the loading of your car. You can be tranquil."

I got out, as tranquilly as I could, but I did not proceed on board the boat. I waited. In a remarkably short time the stevedore was out again, jumping up and down and waving long blue-bloused arms. He was not, it seemed, paid to be bitten by dogs.

It was not the Queen of England who ruled in France, and French workers had rights, for which, through their syndicates, they knew how to enforce respect. Other members of the Union of French Stevedores and Port Workers, gathered round, agreed with these views. I was not impressed, because I knew the man had not been bitten. Persons who had been bitten by Carey Bloom stayed bitten; they did not jump up and down in this frivolous manner, conversing about the Rights of Man and of the Citizen. I explained, and demonstrated, that the dog was sage and gentle. As for myself I owed no more allegiance to the Queen of England than they did, being a good Irish Republican. In fact, the dog was there in defiance of an English regulation—a regulation, moreover, which was unfairly aimed at French exports and was devised to protect the private interests of the English four hundred families, including Sir Eden himself. The stevedore, to whom I gave a thousand francs, saw my point of view. He would put car and dog aboard: "Once there you are in England. The sailors are all English and capable of anything. They are all little bourgeois, Calvinists, and police spies."

How right he was I found in a very few minutes, aboard the S.S. *Black Prince*. It was a fine clear day with a dead calm sea, but no sooner had my car been hoisted onto the lower deck, and the French stevedore departed, than a company of Calvinists descended with a huge tarpaulin. Silently, with grim efficiency, they lashed this covering into position over the car, securing it tightly. A small gap remained between the lower edges of the tarpaulin and the deck; as a window of the car was open, air could still penetrate to Carey Bloom. But only air; no question now of the leisurely administration of drugs, no question of a doped dog sleeping quietly in the boot. No possibility of tampering with that tarpaulin without detection, even if I were a skilled tarpaulin-tamperer, which I was not. The seamen might not all be Tory police spies, as the

French stevedore claimed, but they had a look about them of belonging to that class of men who are described as "law-abiding" because they like to see other people getting into trouble.

I made my way to the bar, for a Guinness. The barman, I found with pleasure, was an Irishman, even a Kerryman—Mahoney by name—and therefore by definition indifferent to the law, "our pets," and the public health of England. He heard my story gravely. No, nothing to be done with those seamen. All non-Catholics, mostly Methodists, don't smoke and don't drink, would inform on their own mother. The only help he could give, the Kerryman said, was with the Newhaven dockers. These were a decent crowd, that is to say, mostly Irish, who could be trusted to keep quiet if it was made worth their while. With the help of the dockers I should be able to get the car and dog quietly off the boat and as far as the customs shed. After that I was on my own. He thought the chances were about five to one against my getting through. You would be better off in England poisoning old women, the barman thought, than to be caught smuggling a dog. However, he would do his best for me, and wished me luck.

At Newhaven, the dockers did their part, as arranged through the barman. I drove slowly along the quayside, using one hand to pull the rug back over Carey Bloom. Carey Bloom, normally a very quiet dog, growled and shook the rug off. I pulled it back again, wishing I were in some quiet English watering place, respected by all, happily poisoning old women. Carey Bloom stayed under the rug this time, but shivering and sniffling. I reached the customs shed.

The customs shed (motor vehicles) at Newhaven is a building I now know rather well. It is open at both ends, full of wind and echoes. There are a few officials there, but it is difficult to make them out at first, so still are they in the uncertain light of the great windowless hall. You make them out, however, as you go along. One of them now came forward: the Automobile Association, a gingerhaired man with that touch of slightly furtive affability that marks the man who has one leg in the official world and another in that of private enterprise. He would clear the car papers while the other customs formalities went through; it would only take a few minutes. He took my triptyque and disappeared into the shadows.

Several minutes passed in a silence broken only by an occasional whimper. Then suddenly H.M. Customs was beside me: a friendly fresh-faced man with an outdoor look about him and a perfunctory sort of expression which I liked even better.

"Anything to declare?"

"No, I'm in transit to Ireland—going on to Holyhead tonight."

"Nothing intended for the United Kingdom? No brandy, wine, cigarettes, or perfume?"

"Nothing at all."

"All right, sir, you can carry on."

My car began to move forward as on its own initiative toward the exit of the cavern, toward freedom and success. Its lights shone on a gingerhaired man: the Automobile Association. He waved; I stopped. They were a little slow clearing the papers—the usual man was away—would I mind waiting where I was for a few minutes? By this time H. M. Customs had strolled up, benevolently, a man with time on his hands. I wanted to say that I would like to wait anywhere except where I was, but I had some difficulty in finding suitable words for this thought. I said I would wait. H. M. Customs decided to keep me company. He was a fisherman, and it was his opinion that the best fishing in the world was to be found in Connemara. Or perhaps Donegal. Though Lough Derg, in Limerick, at dapping time was hard to beat.

Bored, Carey Bloom stretched himself under his rug. At least I hoped it was under his rug. I had a hideous feeling that the rug by now had slipped off. But it was impossible to look round. All I could do was to trust to the dim light and try to make intelligent answers about dry-fly fishing in the west of Ireland.

A figure appeared, moving briskly from the direction of the exit. The Automobile Association! The figure came closer. It was not the Automobile Association. It was more of H.M. Customs. More, and older, and nastier.

"Have you cleared this car?" he asked my fisherman friend.

There was a slight Scots edge on his voice, and a singularly unpleasant inflection to it. The remark had an unfortunate effect on Fisherman. He dropped the subject of the May fly on Lough Derg and took a quick look inside the car.

Then his manner changed. "I'm afraid, sir," he said quietly, "I'll have to ask you one further question."

Something told me what that question was going to be.

"Are you carrying any animals in this car, sir?"

"No," I replied firmly.

"Since you declare you are carrying no animals, sir, perhaps you would tell me what that is?"

I looked round, for the first time. Carey Bloom's muzzle and two front paws were resting on the front seat. His shoulders were covered with a tartan rug. He was asleep.

"That," I said, "is my dog."

"Since you admit that is your dog, sir," said the Scot, "how do you explain your previous declaration that you were carrying no animals?"

Clearly he felt that this was a telling piece of cross-examination. Privately I agreed with him, but I decided to go down fighting.

"This dog is being conveyed to Ireland," I said. "In Ireland he will be put in quarantine immediately. I am taking him direct to Holyhead. He will not be let out of the car in England at all. All your previous questions were about what I had for the United Kingdom. I took it that this question was the same. As I had no animals intended for the United Kingdom I thought it was right to answer the question in the negative."

Fisherman's mouth hung open, like that of a Lough Derg trout in dapping time. He was obviously dazzled by this unexpected piece of dialectic. There was a silence.

I was weak enough to break the silence by a conciliatory remark. I should have known better than to make a conciliatory remark to a Scot, but my nerves had been under a strain for some time. "I should prefer to take him to Ireland for quarantine," I said, "but of course, if that would be contrary to your regulations I'm perfectly prepared to put him into quarantine here."

I thought this a fair offer, but it brought out the worst in the Scot.

"You don't seem to r-realize your position," he said grindingly. "It's not a question of what you are *prepared* or not prepared to do. The animal of course, will be impounded, and *may* be committed to quarantine if the authorities are satisfied as to your willingness and ability to pay for his upkeep. Otherwise he will be dest-r-royed. The fact is that you yourself have already committed two very serious offenses: first by importing a dog without a license and second by falsely declaring that you were not carrying animals. On either count you are liable on summary conviction both to a heavy fine and to a p-r-rison sentence of not more than Six Months. I shall now have to report the matter both to the police and to my own superiors. You, sir, will please remain where you are and ensure that that animal does not leave the car until he is officially impounded."

The program for the evening was faithfully observed. The police arrived and took a statement. And later came an overalled contingent with a handcart on which stood a large crate. They looked like something out of Defoe's *Journal of the Plague Year*. To them, not without a twinge, I handed over Carey Bloom. He licked my hand in farewell, but otherwise made no sign. As they wheeled him away, toward imprisonment or death, I saw on the back of his crate a huge sign in yellow characters:

DANGER!

RABIES!

I thought bitterly of President Fallières. I became aware at the same time that a new character, and one having authority, had come on the scene. This was an elderly man, not in uniform but in sports coat and flannels. The old gentleman's general appearance was kindly and paternal, but I could see from his expression that he had Very Little Sympathy for Certain Classes of Offender and that I belonged to one such class.

"I'm afraid," he said, "that in view of what's happened we'll have to put some further questions to you formally. After that we'll have to search your car thoroughly. You see you've already made one false declaration, so you can't expect to receive normal tourist treatment."

He left a moment for this insult to sink in. Then: "Are you carrying any Narcotic Drugs?"

"No."

"Any Plants or Parrots?"

"No."

"Any Arms or Ammunition?"

"No."

"Any *more* animals?"

This was too much.

"Look," I said, "I'm not a professional dog smuggler, or any other kind of smuggler. That dog belongs to my daughters, who are very fond of it. If it had to go into quarantine I wanted to bring it to Ireland. If it were quarantined there they could visit it every day. As it is they won't be able to visit it at all. I'm sorry if I infringed your regulations, and you can go ahead and search my car. You won't find anything."

For the first time since coming to Newhaven I had managed to strike the right note. The old gentleman's manner perceptibly softened. He made no reply, however, until the car had been searched and been found, as I had said, to be free from Narcotic Drugs, Arms, Ammunition, Plants, Parrots, and Other Animals. He addressed me now as a fellow human being, rather than as an individual engaged in a Vile Traffic.

"I can understand your feeling for your Pet," he said. "I have three dogs of my own. But, believe me, it's in the interests of Our Pets themselves to see that these regulations are observed."

He lit a cigarette, for effect. Then quietly: "Have you ever seen a case of rabies?"

"No," I said. "I'm afraid I haven't. You see the last case of rabies in France was in 1910. The year of the Coronation of King George V. That was before I was born."

Balked of his dramatic effect, the old gentleman looked at me thoughtfully. "We don't want to be unnecessarily severe about this," he said. "We should prefer not to have to prosecute, if we can avoid it. I'm quite prepared to accept your story, send the dog to an approved place of quarantine in England, and let you go on your way, without further formality. So if you'll just show me the license from the Eire Department of Agriculture to import the dog into Ireland, we can regard the matter as closed."

The Scot, who had looked depressed during the earlier part of this speech, cheered up at the end perceptibly and unpleasantly. He could obviously see, merely by looking at me, that I possessed no licenses of any kind. He was quite right.

"I didn't have time to get a license," I said. "I was ordered by my employers to come home at very short notice indeed. My first idea was to leave the dog with some French people, who would give it a home for a time, while I made the necessary arrangements in Dublin for its importation. Then at the very last moment, the night before I left, I found that the home was quite unsuitable. I couldn't just abandon the dog, so I decided to take him to Ireland and hand him over for quarantine there. I don't think the Irish authorities, in the circumstances, would have made too many difficulties about there being no license."

The Scot smiled. What *he* thought of my story was quite clear. But his superior, the owner of three dogs, looked puzzled. He would, at least, not condemn me out of hand.

"You say you found this home was unsuitable," he said. "Now just what do you mean by that?"

"Well," I replied, feeling better, "you see, the man who offered to take care of the dog was a Frenchman, a café proprietor. My dog is a Kerry blue—you know the breed, I expect—and this man said he owned a Kerry blue, too. That made me think he would know how to look after my dog, so I agreed to leave it with him. Then, to be on the safe side, I decided to go and have a look at his dog. This is what I found."

I handed over the photograph of the dog of Place Notre-Dame-des-Victoires.

The three customs men studied it. The two Englishmen were visibly affected. They seemed like men peering into an abyss. It was the old gentleman who spoke.

"Do you mean that they give this unfortunate dog ... drink?"

"Pernod," said I quietly. "Then they make him do tricks for the customers."

"Do you know," said the old gentleman, "I wouldn't have believed it, even of the French."

One felt that moral condemnation had reached its ultimate. He examined the picture again for some time, then handed it back.

"I can't condone breaking regulations," he said, "but I must say that if I had to choose between breaking a regulation and leaving my dog with a man like that—well, I might do what you did. I'll recommend no further action. I wish you good luck and you can be sure your dog will be well looked after."

It was the Scot who showed me past the police, to the Automobile Association and freedom. The Automobile Association, in an under-tone, wanted to know what had happened. The Scot told him:

"The gentleman made a false declaration to the customs and was caught in possession of contraband," he said. "He gets off under English law because he once knew a poodle that took to the drink. Good night."

9

Serpents

When Deganawida was leaving the Indians in the Bay of Quinte in Ontario he told the Indian people that they would face a time of great suffering. They would distrust their leaders and the principles of peace of the League, and a great white serpent was to come upon the Iroquois, and that for a time it would intermingle with the Indian people and would be accepted by the Indians, who would treat the serpent as a friend. This serpent would in time become so powerful that it would attempt to destroy the Indian, and the serpent is described as choking the life's blood out of the Indian people.... And he told them that when things looked their darkest a red serpent would come from the north and approach the white serpent which would be terrified, and upon seeing the red serpent he would release the Indian, who would fall to the ground almost like a helpless child, and the white serpent would turn all its attention to the red serpent.... And Deganawida said they [the Indians] would remain neutral in this fight between the white serpent and the red serpent.

Mad Bear, the Tuscarora Indian who related to Edmund Wilson the long allegory which includes the story of the serpents, is one of the leaders of a messianic and nationalist movement which has developed in recent years among the Iroquois "Six Nations" in New York State and Canada, and apparently affects in some degree other Indians in regions as far afield as Florida, Wisconsin and even Arizona. Socially, this

Spectator, 27 May 1960, p. 773. Review of *Apologies to the Iroquois* by Edmund Wilson, by "Donat O'Donnell."

movement draws strength from the resentment created by the impact of industrial society—particularly the physical and legal impacts of great engineering projects, "thruways" and seaways—on the Indian reservations with their ancient treaty-rights, never fully observed and never completely rescinded by the white man. Politically, the movement is strongly affected by the activities of the "newly emerging nations" not only in Asia and Africa but also in Latin America. *Apologies to the Iroquois* contains a photograph of Fidel Castro receiving Mad Bear in Cuba in 1959 and, according to Mr. Wilson, Iroquois nationalists hope that Cuba will sponsor the admission of the Iroquois League to the United Nations. Culturally, the movement is traditionalist and pagan in tendency. The dances and ceremonies of the Longhouse are revived and there are even those—as yet a minority, it seems—who want to return to the Sacrifice of the White Dog. Other sacrifices are not altogether to be excluded. Brigadier Holdridge, a paleface sympathiser with the Indian nationalists, once campaigned in favour of hanging Harry Truman, General Bradley, Cardinal Spellman and John Foster Dulles. We have no means of knowing whether this program appealed to Indians more than to other sections of the population, but the Brigadier recently counselled violence to the Indians specifically: "to resist, with all their power, even to gunfire, if necessary, in defence of their territory."

Apologies to the Iroquois is an extremely interesting, attractive and yet finally unsatisfactory discussion of these questions. The interest and attraction derive from Mr. Wilson's well-known and unflagging powers of observation and description, and especially his watchful respect for individual members of an alien culture: the unsatisfactory character is probably the result of the peculiar requirements of the *New Yorker*, in which most of the material originally appeared. The more obviously irritating characteristics of *New Yorker* reporting—artfully-artless meandering, and an affection for detail above and beyond the call of duty—are certainly not dominant here, but the reader is conscious that something of the kind has been expected, and that something better has been lost by reason of this expectation. "The nationalist movement of the Iroquois," writes Mr. Wilson, "is only one of many recent evidences of a new self-assertion on the part of the Indians. The subject is much too large and complicated even to be outlined here, but ..." No doubt it is large and complicated, and no doubt there is much to be said for Mr. Wilson's method of confining himself to a few tribes and a few concrete problems, rather than indulging in generalisations about Indian movements. Yet as a long description of a dance follows a long account of a lawsuit and these are followed by another lawsuit and another dance, it is possible to feel that room could, after all, have been found, if not for an outline of American Indian nationalism today, at least for something more than the shrewd, tantalising hints scattered through the 300 pages of this volume. Not that there is anything frivolous about either the lawsuits or the dances: it is the slow, restless oscillation from subject to subject, the *New Yorker's ton de bonne compagnie*, that is frivolous. But the white serpent has come to crave this cunning mixture of information and distraction, and even Mr. Wilson must sacrifice to him.

In Mad Bear's allegory there is also a black serpent, who eventually defeats the red and white serpents, and whose victory is the prelude to the return of the Indian messiah, Deganawida, and the restoration of the Indian nation. The culminating moment is already at hand. The big war between the red and white serpents is due to begin in 1960, and as a result of it the United States is to come to an end and a great light will come to the Indian people.

No doubt such fantasies are common to all oppressed peoples—and a people can still feel itself oppressed, even if no one is any longer conscious of oppressing it. Nor is there anything new in what is represented by the red serpent—a sporting flutter on the enemy of one's enemy. "England's difficulty is Ireland's opportunity" was for long the watchword of the most irreconcilable "minority people" in Western Europe. What is probably new, however, is the role of the black serpent—the feeling that a general victory of oppressed non-white peoples is at hand. Mr. Wilson writes:

> They know that they came from the Orient, and they know what has been happening in China. They also know that India has freed herself, that Ghana is now a free state, and that the Algerians are struggling to become one. They have sensed that the white man has been losing his hold and, like the rest of the non-white races, they are sick of his complacency and arrogance. They find this a favourable moment for declaring their national identity because, in view of our righteous professions in relation to the Germans and Russians, they know that, for the first time in history, they are in a position to blackmail us into keeping our agreements and honoring their claims.

Cold war, unlike hot war, has probably more beneficiaries than victims, but it resembles hot war in that those who are most apt to benefit are those who manage to avoid taking part in it. The American Indians, like so many African and Asian peoples—but unlike the people of Tibet—may greatly gain, materially and politically, from the cold war. Agreeable as this is, it is not without its dangers, even for the beneficiaries. All weak peoples are apt to cherish a sense of superior virtue, corresponding to the magnitude of the crimes they have been powerless to commit. This sense, in times of oppression, is a relatively harmless consolation. On the emergence of freedom it becomes a costly delusion. Atavistic practices, being felt to guarantee the tribal distinctness—and therefore superiority—become more cherished than intelligence or even common sense. The reverses brought about by this scale of preferences will in the long run, if there is one, overthrow it; in the short run they are more likely to intensify atavism: "The Sacrifice of the White Dog was not, it seems, enough...."

Logically, the discredit of racism should have done nothing to make primitive animism respectable. In practice the white man's shame does tend to have that effect. The eighteenth century pronounced the Savage noble, in cheerful ignorance of how the Savage behaved; the twentieth century, having had the opportunity to study all varieties of savagery, refuses to pronounce a value-judgment at all. The resources of civilisation have, apparently, become exhausted quicker than Mr. Gladstone would have thought possible. It is only "apparently," of course; the anthropologist who writes as if he thought that the practices of headhunters were no less valuable and no less commendable than the proceedings of the Royal Society is playing a scientific game, which most of his readers understand. But members of the communities studied might be forgiven for taking the game seriously; for reaching the conclusion that Western civilisation, having studied what it wrongly took to be a primitive form of society, had been forced to see that this society was in fact an alternative civilisation, of no less value than that of the declining West. The relativist anthropologists of the twentieth century may be seen in retrospect to have been no less disastrous than the absolutist ethnologists of the last century. For something like the dream which haunts Mad Bear—and no doubt many other Mad Bears in other parts of the world—may very easily come true. The red and white serpents may indeed destroy each other, and the black serpent may inherit the earth. In the perspective of human history this need not be an unmitigated disaster—except for amateurs of a particular pigmentation—provided that the transit of civilisation has already been successfully accomplished. But it will be a pity if the survivors of the human race are in such a mental state—as a result, among other things, of anthropological "respect"—that they fancy their survival to be a result of their persistence in sacrificing dogs.

10

ORWELL LOOKS AT THE WORLD

"I knew that I had a facility with words and a power of facing unpleasant facts, and I felt that this created a sort of private world in which I could get my own back for my failure in everyday life." These words, about himself as a boy, Orwell wrote when he was already near his death; and they are both true and an example of their own truth. Not that objectively Orwell was a failure, at school or in life. But he did feel himself to be a failure; he did want to get his own back; he had the ability to face unpleasant facts and knew that ability to be, in his own carefully chosen word, "a power". In the same sentence he demonstrates his possession of that power by facing two facts about himself: his sense of failure and desire to get his own back. "I am going to tell you some facts about yourself", he says in effect to the left-wing intellectuals who were for long almost his only readers, "but first you must recognise that I face unpleasant facts about myself, and face such facts in person—facts like bullets. These are things that most of you are very little inclined to do. Through my skill with words, and the power which such skill exerts over people like you, I am now going to compel you to face at least some of the facts which you are trying to hide from yourselves and others."

Most of those addressed—perhaps on this page I can say "most of us"—responded to this challenge, I suppose, in one or both of two opposite ways. The first way was to admit that Orwell's criticisms were largely true: that left-wing intellectuals were, too often, intellectually

New Statesman, 26 May 1961, pp. 837–38. Review of *George Orwell* by Richard Rees and *Collected Essays* by George Orwell, by "Donat O'Donnell."

dishonest, selective in their moral indignation, furtive worshippers of power, and startlingly ignorant both of political realities and of the working class. The quantity and quality of this acceptance no doubt varied. You could, for example, accept Orwell's indictment as being true about your friends but not about yourself. Or you could, if you wanted to, drop being a leftist—for motives probably even less admirable than those which had taken you to the left—have your eyes conveniently "opened" by Orwell's fearless honesty. Some of Orwell's American admirers in the Fifties may have been, in reality, more impressed by the arguments of Senator McCarthy than by those of *Animal Farm*, but an Orwellian conversion lent dignity to retreat. There were certainly also, among those clever and anxious people whom Orwell addressed, those who actually enjoyed submitting to the punishment which he inflicted:

> Come fix upon me that accusing eye
> I thirst for accusation.

But the main reason why many intellectuals accepted the truth of Orwell's accusations is that so many of these accusations were true, and the lucidity of Orwell's prose made their truth inescapable. Intellectuals are probably not more dishonest than other people; their resources for self-deception are of course much greater, but then so is their compulsion to self-criticism: greater forces committed on both sides, and the result equally uncertain. But one characteristic which the intellectual must have, or he ceases to be an intellectual at all, is the ability to see when a real point has been made in debate. It was impossible for anyone with that ability not to notice that Orwell kept scoring direct hits. You knew that certain things he said were true, because you winced when you heard them.

There can be little doubt that Orwell did change the minds of quite a few people through whom he changed the minds of many others. He cleared out a great deal of cant, self-deception, and self-righteousness, and in doing so shook the confidence of the English left, perhaps permanently. The right, as everyone knows, paid no attention to him except for the valuable ammunition he was to supply against communism, and retained its own variety of cant, almost undamaged. But the cant of the left, that cant which has so far proved indispensable to the victory of any mass movement, was almost destroyed by Orwell's attacks, which put out of action so much cant-producing machinery in its factories: the minds of left-wing intellectuals. His effect on the English left might be compared to that of Voltaire on the French nobility: he weakened their belief in their own ideology, made them ashamed of their clichés, left them intellectually more scrupulous and more defenceless.

There was, of course, and is, a second way of responding to Orwell's challenge: you could question his impartiality and therefore his right to judge. But Orwell has been accused of being essentially a reactionary writer whose work both "objectively" strengthened, and was intended to strengthen, the existing order. On this view the critique of that order which his works contain is held to be perfunctory, a sort of diversion to draw attention from the real attack, which was directed against the left. In its extreme forms, this accusation is very easy to refute. Anyone who calls Orwell a fascist—and I believe the thing has been done—either knows nothing at all about him or his life. Orwell's life, and the Spanish wound which shortened that life, refuted such absurdities. But if no human type, except perhaps the communist party member, could be more remote from Orwell than is the fascist, it is also true that he is very far indeed from being "progressive".

Sir Richard Rees, in his sympathetic and enlightening book, brings out well the "old-fashioned" side of Orwell—the deep English patriotism, the distaste for machinery and modern psychology, the love of the country, of animals, even the lingering nostalgia for the Edwardian age. These qualities, in Orwell's work, growl in many asides, and growl increasingly often. It is a tory growl: each quality in itself, obviously, is not necessarily tory, but grouped together they do form a tory pattern. It is not surprising that Orwell should have taken pleasure in defending Kipling against leftist criticism (his important essay on Kipling is unaccountably omitted from the present volume of collected essays, the title of which is misleading, as are the claims on its dust jacket). If we add to the list a chivalrous but rather insensitive attitude towards the underdog and a tendency towards self-immolation, what seems to emerge is the character of an English conservative eccentric.

The character is on the whole an attractive one, and has done much to make English life more decent—a favourite word of Orwell's. The limitations of the viewpoint it implies are probably more obvious to foreigners than they are to the English. Orwell seldom wrote about foreigners, except sociologically, and then in a hit-or-miss fashion otherwise unusual with him; he very rarely mentions a foreign writer and has an excessive dislike of foreign words; although he condemns imperialism he dislikes its victims even more. Indeed he sometimes goes beyond dislike; it rises to something like hysteria. In *Shooting an Elephant* he records fantasies about sticking a bayonet into the belly of a sniggering Buddhist priest. This is the kind of fantasy that Orwell himself found sinister in *No Orchids for Miss Blandish*. It is really more disquieting in *Shooting an Elephant*: not that sadistic fantasies are unusual, even in good and gentle men, but that quite unmistakably Orwell was much more likely to have this kind of fantasy about a Burmese than about an Englishman.

I do not suggest that it is morally better to have such fantasies about an Englishman. The point is that if sadistic fantasies are unevenly distributed by race or nationality, the consequences are more likely to be political—and therefore contagious and dangerous—than if they remain purely personal.

Orwell of course was too decent and clear-headed to support any racialist or imperialist programme. The presence in his make-up of the kind of feeling that inspires such programmes led to no more than a certain deadening of his feeling and understanding where most of the population of the world was concerned. He turned towards foreigners, especially Asians, that part of his mind which brooded darkly about sandals, beards and vegetarians. He could not "think himself into the mind" of any kind of foreigner and he seldom tried to do so. He never thought it worth while to imagine seriously what it would be like to belong to a people with a quite different historical experience from that of the English. As far as he considered such matters at all, I think he felt that not to be a product of English history was a sort of moral lapse.

Many people, quite obviously, are not less insular today than Orwell, but no one of comparable intelligence can now attain that degree of insularity—short of being whimsical like Mr. Evelyn Waugh or Mr. Kingsley Amis. During almost all of Orwell's writing career, England was sufficiently central to the world's political and economic life for an Anglocentric view of the world not to be seen as an eccentric one. Since then, the McCarthy years, the "thaw" in Russia, the rise of African nationalism, the Common Market in Europe, the ferment in Latin America, the Russian-American space race, emanations of Communist China and, in a different category, the Suez experiment and its failure have made a world in which much though not all of Orwell's writing must seem, to readers outside these islands, somewhat provincial.

We are near enough now to 1984 to see that the world then, whatever it may be like, will not be very like Orwell's imagining of it. Is it fantastic to see in Orwell's *1984* the reflection of a feeling that a world in which the pre-1914 British way of life had totally passed away must necessarily be a dehumanised world? And is it altogether wrong to see the inhabitants of *Animal Farm* as having points in common, not merely with Soviet Russians, but also with Kipling's lesser breeds generally, as well as with Flory's Burmese who, once the relative decencies of the Raj are gone, must inevitably fall under the obscene domination of their own kind?

To insist on the limitations of Orwell's thought is only to establish the limits within which we admire him. How much there is to admire, how much we owe to him, every page in these collected essays reminds us. That spare, tough prose has not aged; that clear eye sees more than ours do even if there are things which it cannot see through, and which we now can see from the other side in time. What political writer now cares as much as he did, both about what he is writing and about how he is writing it? Subsequent writers who exploded anger seem far off and apathetic compared with this careful writer who tried so hard to keep his judgment and his language from being clouded by an anger as real as Swift's.

11

MY CASE

One evening late in May of this year, Mr. Andrew Cordier, Executive Assistant to the United Nations Secretary-General, telephoned me from New York. I was in my house in Howth, near Dublin. "Mr. Hammarskjöld wants you to go to Elisabethville as his representative. Are you prepared to go?"

I said yes, stipulating only that the invitation should be announced as one to join the Secretariat, without mention of the Congo. I knew the Irish Government, already bearing heavy commitments in the Congo, would be reluctant to see an Irish official assume the unpredictable responsibilities of the UN representative in Katanga.

I would like to think Mr. Hammarskjöld picked me because he had approved my work as a member of the Irish Delegation at the General Assembly over the past five years. Unfortunately there is very little evidence that this was so. Mr. Hammarskjöld had, indeed, approved a statement I had made in one of the Assembly's Congo debates, in which I had resisted a tendency to vote increasingly tough resolutions, and had made the point that what the UN needed was not wider powers on paper, but fuller and more consistent practical, diplomatic and financial support for the Secretariat in carrying out the far-reaching resolutions already voted. Apart from this one intervention, I have no reason to think that the Secretary-General had taken particular note of what I was doing, as a second-ranking member of the delegation of a small country.

Observer, 17 December 1961. This is Part 2. Part 1 was published 10 December 1961.

There were, I believe, two reasons why Mr. Hammarskjöld picked me for the post. The first was that I fell, nationally, within the extremely restricted field of his possible choice. For the trial of strength, or at the very least of nerve, which he knew was coming in Katanga, he wanted someone from a "reliable" country—that is to say a country which was giving unswerving support to the UN.

There are, unfortunately, few "reliable" countries in this sense. Sweden is probably the most conspicuous example, and Mr. Hammarskjöld had chosen a Swede, Dr. Sture Linner, to lead the operation in the Congo. Under the firm leadership of Mr. Frank Aiken, Irish Foreign Minister and head of the Irish delegation to the UN General Assembly since 1957, Ireland had come to be regarded as a "reliable" country. She was not readily amenable to Great Power pressure; she paid her share to the Congo operation, in men and money; she neither clamoured for increasingly drastic resolutions nor covertly obstructed the implementation of resolutions already voted. It was, therefore, natural enough for Mr. Hammarskjöld, having a Swede in Leopoldville, to pick an Irishman for Elisabethville.

The reason he picked this particular Irishman was considerably odder. He happened to have read a book of mine. This book, "Maria Cross," had appeared some years earlier, not under my own name. It had nothing whatever to do with the UN, Africa, politics or diplomacy. It was a collection of critical essays on a group of French and English Catholic writers. Mr. Hammarskjöld was one of the very few people who had read it, and he liked it. This is the reason he picked me, and not some other person from a "reliable" country, to represent the UN in Katanga.

This will seem to many people an eccentric principle of selection; it seemed so to several of my former colleagues on the Thirty-Eighth Floor of the UN building (where the Secretary-General has his offices), if I may judge by the expressions of wary perplexity with which they tended to greet me. Mr. Hammarskjöld thought and felt as much about literature as he did about politics. He believed, with an almost mystical intensity of conviction, that the two fields were really one and required the same qualities. He would not have laughed at the story of Danton, who when Fabre d'Églantine asked him for a job, is said to have made the magnificent reply: *"Vous êtes poète? Alors je vous fais Ministre de la Marine."*

My trouble, in my fleeting contacts with Mr. Hammarskjöld, was that he seldom laughed at anything, and never at anything I considered funny. He had, as a critical fellow-countryman Professor Herbert

Tingsten observed, "a humourless twinkle in his eye." Conversations about literature tend, unless cheerfulness at some point breaks in, to reduce me to uneasy silence, and this was always the effect of Mr. Hammarskjöld's remarks about St-John Perse (whom he had translated), a poet who in any case interests me but little.

As will be gathered, I was not at all close to Mr. Hammarskjöld, but regarded him with immense respect, verging on awe. I saw in him absolute integrity devoted, with bravery and high intelligence, to a noble end. His aim was the creation of a centre of international moral authority, rising out of a chaos of nationalisms and clashing ideologies, to defend the common human cause of peace and justice. He himself, in the eyes of many people, and in my own eyes, incarnated this authority.

His task was almost superhuman, for what exists is international anarchy, and that anarchy is necessarily reflected at the UN itself. Those who most strongly criticise the UN for its confusions and failures are often themselves the cause of these confusions and failures since they pursue, or ask others to pursue, ends that are not compatible with the strengthening of an international moral authority, and the good working of a Secretariat serving that authority. Many Governments, and among them the most powerful, act at the UN as if they were inspired, not by any principle of the Charter, but by some dull and petty conception of short-term interest. That is how they act: they speak, of course, quite otherwise.

The day I left New York for the Congo Mr. Hammarskjöld gave a luncheon in my honour. I gathered that this was a most unusual mark of favour; one falls instinctively into the language of a court when speaking of Mr. Hammarskjöld's existence on the Thirty-Eighth Floor. The other courtiers eyed me as courtiers do eye one another on such occasions. Mr. Hammarskjöld, I remember, became quite cross, and unusually animated, on the subject of Jackie Kennedy. He thought she was getting excessive publicity. She was not, he said, at all good-looking, and it was no good pretending that she was. I found this much better fun, and much more endearing, than our previous talk about St-John Perse.

Mr. Hammarskjöld's jealousy of Jackie Kennedy—for that, amazingly, is what it was—was a bizarre touch of human weakness that brought him somehow within range. I continued to admire him, just this side of idolatry, but for the first time I began to glimpse the possibility that one might, if one knew him better, actually get to like him. That was the last time I saw him alive.

While I was in Elisabethville, up to the last week of Mr. Hammarskjöld's life, the sun of royal favour reached me with increasing warmth. He approved of the way I was setting about my task, and had very much commended, in particular, our action on August 28 when we expelled a considerable number of the foreign officers in Tshombe's army. He used the phrase: "*Il a du cran*"—"He has pluck." I felt excessively pleased with myself.

Then, on September 14, with the fighting going on in Elisabethville, the grim telegrams began to come in from Leopoldville, where Mr. Hammarskjöld had arrived. A cloud had come between me and the sun and I felt cold. I also felt extremely puzzled. That was because I had not yet begun to fathom the personality, or trace the words and actions, of that extraordinary man Mr. Mahmoud Khiari, who appears later in this story.

The train of events that led to the first battle of Elisabethville can be told here in outline only. In the first week of September, Mr. Tshombe and his advisers, with the encouragement of Sir Roy Welensky and Sir Roy's friends in England, had begun their hate campaign and manifestations against the UN and against the so-called "foreign elements" (i.e., non-Katangese Congolese) in Katanga. This campaign, encouraged by the mercenaries who had gone into hiding, and by an important section of the European population, was carried out on the direction of Mr. Tshombe's European-run Sûreté and Ministry of Information. There are many things I do not admire in Mr. Tshombe's administration, but I have acquired a healthy respect for the Katangese propaganda machine.

The object of its activity at this time was twofold. Internally it needed to intimidate the opposition. Katanga is of course completely a police State and no vocal or other opposition is tolerated where Tshombe's writ runs. But a very large number of the African population—probably a majority—detest Tshombe's regime. It was necessary to frighten these people—that is to say practically everyone except the members of Mr. Tshombe's Lunda tribe and the Bayeke tribe of Minister of Interior Mr. Munongo—because, with the departure of so many of the mercenaries, the opposition might come into the open and perhaps destroy the regime. So they had to be frightened, by menaces on the radio, by raids on houses, by beatings, flogging and stabbing.

As a result of this, 25,000 African inhabitants of Elisabethville —mainly, but by no means exclusively, Baluba—had, by September 5, sought the protection of the UN in the neighbourhood of the Swedish camps. It is one of the most remarkable achievements of the Katangese propaganda machine that it has been able to use the existence of the refugees to discredit not the people from whom they fled, but the people who gave them protection.

I warned Tshombe in writing that if he did not immediately desist from these activities the UN might find it necessary to act under Paragraph A.1. of the Resolution of February 21. This is the paragraph that deals with civil war situations and authorises the use of force if necessary in the last resort. Mr. Tshombe told me that no such campaign was in progress and that, in any case, the man responsible for it was the Minister of the Interior, Mr. Munongo, over whom Mr. Tshombe said, as President, he had no control. The campaign went on.

The other aspect of the campaign was directed against the UN. The objects were to show the world pictures of Africans demonstrating hostility to the UN, and to suggest that, as a result of the unwise action of the UN in expelling the foreign officers, Katanga was threatened with grave disaster. So it was, and is, but the people responsible for the disorder were, and are, Tshombe's advisers. The campaign against the UN took the form of violent vituperation on Press and radio, of threats and of organised street manifestations which followed a prescribed form, like a ballet.

Gangs of Lunda and Bayeke youth, the so-called Jenakat, would parade through the streets shepherded by officials of Tshombe's Ministry of Information and carrying banners with slogans prepared by that same Ministry. These youths would be stopped by Tshombe's police at the entrance to the Avenue Fulbert Youlou, where the UN headquarters then was. Tableau with caption: MR. TSHOMBE'S FORCES OF ORDER RESTRAIN ANGRY KATANGESE CROWD FROM ATTACKING UN. Then the police would allow about a dozen of the youths to slip through the cordon: no photographs for this phase of the operation. The youths would then throw rocks through our windows. Caption: ANGRY KATANGESE IN ANTI-UN DEMONSTRATIONS. The police would then fire some shots in the air. Caption: MR. TSHOMBE'S POLICE FIRING IN DEFENCE OF UN HEADQUARTERS.

This was comic enough, although annoying and disconcertingly effective as propaganda. There were, however, signs of worse to come. The incitements were growing in violence, and incitements to murder are not likely to remain without response for long in any part of the Congo, least of all in the particular oasis of peace and order in which we were being pelted with rocks.

We had evidence from two European sources of conspiracies to murder UN officials. On September 9 an attempt was made to arrest

M. Michel Tombelaine, my French deputy, against whom the incitements had been particularly violent. In this situation, I had recommended to my superiors in Leopoldville that, as a result of resistance to our efforts to implement the resolution, a situation had arisen in which firm intervention would again be required. We would have to silence Mr. Tshombe's radio, to arrest the people responsible for the twofold campaigns of murderous incitement, to get out the remaining hidden mercenaries, and to use force if necessary against Mr. Tshombe's gendarmerie. And if we did have to use force we should not desist until the secession of Katanga, source of all these ills and many others, had been ended. I still think that these recommendations were correct. My recommendations, correct though they were, were to be answered favourably, but in a disastrous manner.

On September 10, Mr. Mahmoud Khiari and Mr. Vladimir Fabry arrived in Elisabethville with instructions for General Raja, Commander of UN forces in Katanga, and for myself. Mr. Khiari, a Tunisian, was nominally Head of UN Civilian Operations in the Congo, but Dr. Linner had entrusted, or relinquished, to him great authority in the political field in which he had shown enormous ability. He was mainly responsible for the successful meeting of the Congolese parliament, for the Adoula-Gizenga *rapprochement* and for the emergence of a well-balanced Central Government.

He is a negotiator of extraordinary skill, and his skill had rendered great service to the UN. He had merited the high esteem, and he had also won the confidence, of Mr. Hammarskjöld. We had received our instructions from Mr. Khiari in connection with the operation of August 28 and it seemed entirely natural to accept verbal instructions from him in so important and secret a matter.

I cannot here attempt a portrait of Mahmoud Khiari, but it is necessary to say a few things about him. He is, in the fullest sense of the word, a fabulous man: towering, mysterious, exotic, of vast capacities and not entirely worthy of belief. His only purpose was to bring the UN operation in the Congo to a successful conclusion. I liked him and admired him; I still like and admire him but, knowing what I now know, my admiration is tinged with caution and regret.

Mr. Khiari gave us our instructions in the drawing-room of Les Roches, my residence in Elisabethville. Those present at the main meeting at which the instructions were given included, as well as General Raja and myself, and Mr. Khiari and Mr. Fabry, Colonel Jonas Waern, the Swedish officer commanding South Katanga; Colonel Bjorn Egge, the Norwegian Intelligence Officer; and my deputy, Michel Tombelaine.

The instructions were as follows: to take over the post-office, the radio studio and the transmitter; to raid the Sûreté and Ministry of Information offices; to arrest any European officials found there, and seize their files; and to arrest Godefroid Munongo, the Minister of the Interior; Jean-Baptiste Kibwe, Vice-President and Minister of Finance, and Evariste Kimba, so-called Foreign Minister. Tshombe also was to be arrested if absolutely necessary. Mr. Fabry, who was then Legal Adviser to the O.N.U.C. at Leopoldville, and who was to die in the crash at Ndola, produced from his brief-case *Mandats d'amener*—roughly equivalent to warrants for arrest—for Tshombe, Munongo and the others. These warrants bore the seal of the Central Government.

Strictly from the point of view of the situation in Elisabethville these were sound enough instructions, and the necessity for them arose from Tshombe's resistance, encouraged from the outside, to the implementation of the Security Council resolutions. The trouble was that nobody outside Elisabethville, except Mr. Khiari and Mr. Fabry, seems to have known about the instructions.

When I went to Leopoldville, several weeks after the close of hostilities, I found to my bewilderment that neither General MacKeown nor Mr. Linner knew the instructions I had received. In New York I found that neither Dr. Bunche nor General Rikhye—the Military Adviser—knew about them either. Dr. Bunche believes that Mr. Hammarskjöld did not know about them at all.

Mr. Khiari claims that he had been in personal, direct communication, by a channel unknown to anyone else, with Mr. Hammarskjöld by secret unnumbered telegrams. It may be so; it is probable enough that Mr. Hammarskjöld had begun to see the necessity for some strong action. But it seems unlikely to me now that Mr. Hammarskjöld did know the details—and they were pretty large details, like arresting a "President"—of the instructions given to us. If he did not know them, he was unable to answer Lord Lansdowne, and he flew to Ndola.

I learned of his death over the Telex in the cluttered signals room of UN Headquarters in Elisabethville, among the stolid Canadian sergeants and their pinups from *Playboy* magazine. Outside, someone was mortaring the grounds in an inaccurate and desultory way for headline purposes (KATANGA FIGHTS ON). I cannot honestly say that I immediately felt a deep sense of loss. The recent telegrams had left me too numb for that. What I felt was something of what men have felt in all ages, hearing of the end of a great reign and knowing the succession uncertain.

12

WHITE GODS AND
BLACK AMERICANS

In Accra recently a Nigerian company, under the direction of the brilliant young artist Demas Nwoko, presented a dramatised version, in
Yoruba, of Amos Tutuola's *The Palm-Wine Drinkard*. The highlight of
the evening was "The White Gods", a European couple, as they appear
to a simple West African, interpreted by a very sophisticated West
African. Lank straw-coloured hair hung round their pallid masks; they
seemed all knees and noses, their movements angular, their courtship
bird-like, their voices shrill and sad. They were felt to be benevolent,
in a sense, and powerful, in a sense, but the benevolence and the power
had strayed in different directions, and all this was somehow conveyed
by the movements of these dislocated dolls. The audience before which
these figures mopped and mowed was black and white. The black part
laughed heartily, in frank, spontaneous recognition. As for the white
part, we laughed too, but later and less. It was disconcerting to feel oneself seen in this way: one felt naked, awkward, ruffled. *Les Blancs riaient,
mais jaune*.

And here is James Baldwin describing, in *Another Country*, a white
man dancing with a black girl:

> Ida and Ellis had begun a new dance; or rather, Ida had begun a new cruelty.
> Ida was suddenly dancing as she had probably not danced since her adoles-
> cence, and Ellis was attempting to match her—he could certainly not be said

New Statesman, 1 May 1964, pp. 681–82. Review of *Notes of a Native Son* and *Nobody Knows
My Name* by James Baldwin.

to be leading her now, either. He tried, of course, his square figure swooping and breaking, and his little boy's face trying hard to seem abandoned. And the harder he tried—the *fool*! Cass thought—the more she eluded him, the more savagely she shamed him. He was not on those terms with his body, or with hers, or anyone's body. He moved his buttocks by will, his thighs were merely those of a climber, his feet might have been treading grapes. He did not know what to do with his arms, which stuck out at angles to his body as though they were sectioned and controlled by strings, and also as though they had no communion with his hands—hands which had grasped and taken but never caressed.

Reading this I was instantly both reminded of the White Gods and struck by a contrast. Those arms "sectioned and controlled by strings" are exactly those of the White Gods, but the spirit of the scene is very different. The laughter of the black audience at the White Gods had no more hatred or bitterness than the laughter of an English Edwardian audience at the Dixie Minstrels: some contempt, yes, some affection too, in both cases. In Baldwin's tone there is neither amusement nor affection; there is cold contempt with a touch of something else, either pity or cruelty. True, this white character is a particularly unsympathetic one and he is supposed, at this moment, to be seen through the eyes of a white woman. But she is a white woman invented by James Baldwin and her vision and her tone are characteristically and unmistakably Baldwin's.

It is not surprising that a West African and an American Negro should contemplate the jerky progress of the Caucasian with quite different emotions. The historical experience of the American Negro has been far more bitter; his present, though in absolute economic terms more prosperous, is socially and psychologically much harder to bear. The West African's house is a modest one, but he is master in it; the American Negro lives in the basement of a rich man's house, as a poor relation.

The relationship makes the poverty much more bitter. "That's part of the dilemma of being an American Negro," said James Baldwin in a radio interview,

> that one is a little bit coloured and a little bit white, and not only in physical terms but in the head and in the heart, and there are days when you wonder what your role is in this country and what your future is in it. How precisely are you going to reconcile yourself to your situation here and how are you going to communicate to the vast headless, unthinking cruel white majority:

that you are here, and to be here means that you can't be anywhere else. I could, my own person, leave this country and go to Africa. I could go to China, I could go to Russia, I could go to Cuba, but I'm an American and that's a fact.

It is Baldwin's achievement that he has convinced an important section of his white fellow-countrymen that he "is there". He has not only made them see him, but made them see how *he* sees *them*—a feat which no American Negro writer, not even Richard Wright, had ever before succeeded in performing. His fellow-countrymen had seen him as a specialised abstraction: not seeing "a man" or "another American", but only "a Negro", that is to say a phenomenon about which the most important facts were certain physical characteristics. The presence of these characteristics reduced "him" almost to "it": an object about which one held certain views, possibly even liberal views, and whose movements were restricted to certain grooves, both in the mind and in the city. When this object flew from its groove, when America discovered Baldwin discovering America, the effect was something between that of a clear message from a mind in Outer Space and that of a stinging rebuke from a deaf-mute.

It was not that other American Negroes, from the late and great W. E. B. Du Bois to Richard Wright, had not written, and written well, about the Negro situation. What Baldwin did was to shift the ground, to talk about *American* situations, human situations in America. He threw away the placards of the "literature of protest"; he tells us in *Nobody Knows My Name* how he did that and how he had to quarrel with Richard Wright about it. He wrote without flattery, either of the white people or—what was harder—of his own people. The hatred and fear of whites which had inevitably marked his youth dissolved into his imagination, leaving his consciousness unusually clear, his tone calm and casual. "What White people have to do," he said, "is to try to find out in their own hearts why it was necessary to have a nigger in the first place, because I'm not a nigger, I'm a man, but if you think I'm a nigger it means you need it. Why?"

If white Americans—and other whites—are having to give increasing attention to this question, this is obviously not just because of Baldwin, or any other writer. But it is Baldwin who made this question explicit in this particular way, not thundering at injustice but probing for the roots of a sickness. He has made white men listen to him and simply because of this—so deep is the alienation of "black" from "white"America—he has made some Negroes suspicious of him. Their suspicions have been summarised for them by another important American Negro writer, Julian Mayfield—who himself admires Baldwin—in these words:

> There must be something wrong with Baldwin because his books are on the best-seller list and his articles appear in prestige, mass-circulation magazines. Worst yet, he's always on television giving his opinion about this or that; and although I usually say "hear, hear" to his ideas, tell me—since when did Mr. Charlie White Man Boss become so interested in the opinion of any black man but an Uncle Tom? And why should Baldwin be writing about "queers" all the time when there are so many more important things to concern Negro writers?

If Baldwin is a "queer" Uncle Tom, he must be a very queer Uncle Tom indeed. He told his New York television audience, for example, in May 1963, that he would have trouble convincing his nephew to go to Cuba "to liberate the Cubans in the name of a government which now says it is doing everything which it can do but cannot liberate me." Mr. Mayfield rightly stresses—in relation to the role of spokesman for his people which has been almost forced on Baldwin—the importance of an article which Baldwin contributed to the *New York Times Magazine* in March 1961 and which is now reprinted in *Nobody Knows My Name* under a new title, "East River Downtown". This article was about the violent demonstration which a group of American Negroes staged in the gallery of the UN Security Council, after the news of the murder of Lumumba. Some prominent American Negroes were shocked at this behaviour, and Dr Ralph Bunche made himself their spokesman; James Baldwin spoke up for other, and much more numerous, Negroes. At a time when the newspapers made "communist-inspired" the prescribed epithet for the demonstration, Baldwin condemned "the American assumption that the Negro is so contented with his lot here that only the cynical agents of a foreign power can rouse him to protest." And he told the readers of the *New York Times*—not at all accustomed to such thoughts—that a young American Negro today will not "settle for Jim Crow in Miami" when he can "feast at the welcome-table in Havana".

It is true, and it is significant, both for Baldwin's hostile critics and for his friends, that when he has made his point about Miami and Havana he adds the words: "These are extremely unattractive facts ..." Thus discreetly, and without loss of dignity, he intimates to his reader that he is not a communist, and that—at the least—he would wish to be a loyal American. (In his earlier writings he uses "we" in speaking of Americans generally, both black and white. I have not noticed this pro-

noun, thus used, in his later work.) Such words are passwords, the minimum guarantee without which his voice could not be so widely heard;
the fact that he can give, and has given, this password is what makes him
distrusted by some, like Mr. Mayfield's querist, among the Negro Left.
In a community whose "leaders" have so often turned into the tools of
its oppressors, it is natural enough that people should worry about
Mr. Baldwin, lest he too be "got at"; that there should be a sharp intake
of breath every time he is heard from, or heard about, at a meeting organised by the Congress for Cultural Freedom. Yet because Uncle Tom
is an anti-communist, it does not follow that Mr. Baldwin, to be justified, must be a communist, or pretend to be a communist, or even sed-
ulously refrain from letting it be known that he is not a communist. He
could not follow such lines without ceasing to be himself, without losing
what one of his angrier critics, with perhaps unconscious felicity, called
his "excruciating detachment".

Why should he write so much about homosexuals instead of the "so
many other important things to concern Negro writers"? He writes, of
course, about what is important *to him*, not about what should interest
"Negro writers" as a class, and he has denied that he belongs to such a
class: "I am a writer. I am not a Negro writer." In the same sense
Mauriac denied being "a Catholic novelist", gave scandal to Catholics
by writing about sex and money; Yeats, although a good Irish nationalist, could not pretend that he found gerrymandering in County
Fermanagh more interesting than sex and magic. Yet Mauriac remained
a Catholic, Yeats an Irishman and Baldwin a Negro. When Baldwin
writes about homosexuals he writes with a Negro's sense of another
"outlawry", and also, it seems, with some sense of release at a transpo-
sition of values: escape into a world where the colour of a man's skin is
less important—in reality, not just in theory—than another attribute, in
this case a particular sexual bent. It is not as simple as that—exploitation
of black boys by white homosexuals is one of Baldwin's themes—but in
general homosexuality, in Baldwin's work as in Proust's, is felt to provide an alternative set of hierarchies and values to those of the larger
society. Proust felt torn by this; Baldwin is less torn because, by the
nature of his situation, he cannot feel himself to be a part of the white,
heterosexual Anglo-Saxon Protestant culture under which—not
in which—he grew up.

Even Baldwin's harsher critics among American Negroes show some
affection and admiration for him. The respected left-wing intellectual
Negro quarterly *Freedomways* devotes some space to him regularly
—many of my quotations are taken from its pages—and its contributors
oscillate between rebuke and applause. If a reviewer finds Baldwin's

13

NEO-COLONIALISM

For Mr. Brian Crozier—as for many conservative and some liberal writers—neo-colonialism is a communist bogey, successfully used to foment anti-Western feelings in the ex-colonies. He "traces", according to the blurb, "the theory of neo-colonialism back to its unmistakably communist sources." He tells us in his first chapter that

> the contrast between communist theory and practice, and between Western performance and Leninist predictions, was embarrassing to the communists. Something had to be done about it—not by deeds, which might be costly, but by words, which cost less but were often deadly. That was how "neo-colonialism" came to be born. The unknown back-room genius in the Kremlin who coined the term deserves high praise, for it was ingenious and has proved highly successful in that it has been accepted uncritically by many non-communist nationalists in the emerging countries.

In the second chapter we learn that the Soviet government had reason to congratulate itself because—*inter alia*—"Dr Nkrumah's representative at the United Nations", Mr. Quaison-Sackey, had told the General Assembly on 5 April 1958:

> By neo-colonialism we mean the practice of granting a sort of independence with the concealed intention of making the liberated country a client-state,

New Statesman, 29 January 1965, pp. 154–56. Review of *Neo-Colonialism* by Brian Crozier.

and controlling it effectively by means other than political ones. What has happened in the Congo is an example.

One would expect some evidence for the theory that the concept and term "neo-colonialism" were deliberately invented in the Kremlin and then palmed off on the unsuspecting Africans. We get no evidence from Mr. Crozier, except—in relation to the concept—for some references to Lenin on economic imperialism, and Krushchev on the necessity for economic as well as political independence. The claim that the Soviet Union launched the *word* "neo-colonialism" remains altogether unsupported. The present reviewer has some evidence for believing that it is untrue. Having taken a desultory interest for some years past in the origin of this term, I asked the late Professor I.I. Potekhin—then the leading Soviet specialist on the political aspects of African affairs—about Soviet usage of it. He told me that the term was "not one of ours"; that he personally deprecated its use as often loose and unscientific; that he did not use it himself but that it had recently—this was early in 1964—become part of accepted terminology in Soviet writing because of its wide acceptance in Africa and Asia. By this account, if anyone "palmed off" anything on anyone else, it was the Africans on the Russians and not *vice versa*. It is possible, of course, that Potekhin was misleading me, and that the Russians, having injected this poison into the underdeveloped blood-stream, now leave it to do its foul work while proclaiming their own innocence. I find, however, no reason, either in Mr. Crozier's pages or elsewhere, to doubt Potekhin's word.

The earliest use of the word cited by Mr. Crozier is not from a Russian but from a Ghanaian source and it happens to be misdated. Mr. Quaison-Sackey could not, in April 1958, have cited to the General Assembly "what has happened in the Congo" as an example of "the practice of granting a sort of independence", and this for several reasons. The Congo was not granted *any* sort of independence until mid-1960; Mr. Quaison-Sackey did not become the representative of Ghana at the UN until June 1959; and the General Assembly was not sitting in April 1958. Mr. Quaison-Sackey's statement on neo-colonialism appears to date from the Congo debates following the events of July 1960, by which time the word "neo-colonialist" was being used rather widely.

It would be a useful assignment for a doctoral dissertation to do what Mr. Crozier claims to do and trace the origin and development of the term and theory of neo-colonialism. The student who goes to work on this task will, I believe, find richer material in French than in Russian or in English-language publications. The earliest use of the word I know of myself is in *L'Humanité*—and I make a present of this to Mr. Crozier—in 1924, but not with the present connotation: it refers to German demands for the return of the lost colonies. In its present sense I believe it to be a post-war growth, referring first to the various French efforts to create facades representing democracy etc. in North Africa; and later to the various facades of mock-independence created, from 1960 on, in Francophone sub-Saharan Africa.

Certainly the realities which combine to give the word "neo-colonialism" its power—the many forms of contrast between a formal "democracy" or "independence" and the real power in the hands of the old rulers—have been more blatant in the adapted French Empire than elsewhere. Here writers like Mr. Crozier miss an essential point: it is not, primarily, a question of Russian or other propaganda creating illusions through the use of such a term; propaganda will not achieve widespread international success unless it presents a good means of giving expression to suppressed realities. It is the force of the realities, not the cunning of the agitator, which gives power to the word. The citizen of Madagascar, as he walked in "his" capital along the Avenue of Independence from the statue of Joan of Arc to that of General Gallieni (with the inscription "Pacifier of Madagascar"), had plenty of reasons, and not only symbolic ones, for feeling that something funny had happened to the word "independence". When he—and those like him in the two Congos or Gabon or the Cameroons, or indeed in many other places, like Northern Nigeria or Nicaragua—heard about "neo-colonialism" they were ripe for the use of the word, because it referred to realities which were important to them, and on which the standard political lexicon of "their" press and parliament was dumb.

The term "neo-colonialist" is—as Mr. Roger Murray has pointed out to me—"operational" rather than analytic: that is to say, it is used flexibly, as a fighting word, and therefore often loosely and variably, and sometimes wildly. But however it may be used, its effectiveness is in proportion to the *local* realities against which it is used and tested. And whatever Western writers may say, it will ultimately be the peoples of Asia and Africa and Latin America who will, in the light of their experience, determine the success of the neo-colonialist critique. Mr. Crozier betrays, in many turns of speech, his deep-rooted inability to grasp this. About the Northern Rhodesian Copperbelt, he says:

> It may be objected that even today, only a small number of Africans are working side by side with their European colleagues on equal terms. This, however, is of less interest than the *trend* towards Africanisation of the higher grades.

Of less interest to whom?

The pivot of neo-colonialism is the puppet. Many Western liberals, whether because of their charitable disposition or for other reasons, have difficulty in seeing puppets, or at least in making out the strings. Mr. Crozier—whom I take to be a sort of right-wing liberal—is no exception. For him that most grotesque of puppets, the Abbé Fulbert Youlou, of Brazzaville, cannot have been a puppet because the French did not intervene to save him in 1963. Yet surely one discards puppets when they can no longer serve their purpose—as Bao Dai and many another were dropped and as Tshombe will be dropped. It is true that, since human beings are not automatons, no political puppet is ever altogether and exclusively just that. Ulbricht is not *just* a puppet; neither was Laval; nor Ngo Dinh Diem, nor Tshombe. All could, or can, demur to this, or jib at that; all pursued, or pursue, some ends of their own; all, quite possibly, had or have some idea that they were, or are, serving the true interests of their own people. Nonetheless, the most important facts about such people remain that they are put into power, and kept in power, by foreign influence and that if that influence is withdrawn, or turned against them, they fall. Youlou fell because the French no longer thought him worth supporting; M'ba of Gabon, whom they *did* think worth supporting against similar internal pressure, is still there, as are many other similar worthies. The fate of Ngo Dinh Diem is not, as Mr. Crozier suggests, a proof that the unfortunate man was never a puppet, but a reminder that politicians who belong objectively to the puppet class are wiser not to attempt to go on the legitimate stage.

In the course of his defence of the roles of the mining companies and of French policies in Africa and British policies in South-East Asia, Mr. Crozier emphasises certain facts the truth of which no one, I believe, will challenge. The mining companies *have* invested a great deal of money in Africa, the French *are* spending a lot on "aid", Malaysia was not *solely* a British creation. But there is nothing in any of these arguments to convince anyone who is seriously troubled by the realities aimed at in the word "neo-colonialism". The anti-neo-colonialist asks: who are the true beneficiaries of all these investments and aids and ingenious federal contraptions? Mr. Crozier does his best but does not really answer such questions.

He is indeed honest enough to be gingerly about some of the answers: he does not make any large claims for the benefits which 70 years of Belgian and other investments have conferred upon the people of the Congo. But his enthusiasm for French "aid" in Africa will surprise many who have visited some of the territories in question. Neither in the prosperous European streets of Abidjan, nor in the desolate bush of

Dahomey, Niger and Upper Volta does one see much sign of forms of aid benefiting the mass of the indigenous population. One can see in Abidjan a number of Frenchmen, and a smaller but sufficient number of black pro-French politicians, who are obviously doing well out of the high Common Market prices for *robusta* coffee and other African commodities; the African population of the city, and of the developed plantation area around it, seems, if anything, less well off than that of neighbouring territories which do not enjoy such benefits as should result from guaranteed high prices and other forms of metropolitan generosity.

On Malaysia, of which I have no first-hand knowledge, I read Mr. Crozier's fairly detailed account with interest and considerable scepticism. The scepticism increased where he told his readers about the UN investigating mission which arrived in Borneo in mid-August and found itself able, by mid-September, to be "in no doubt about the wishes of Sabah and Sarawak" (Mr. Crozier). These wishes were said to be in favour of Malaysia and, as it happened, Malaysia was proclaimed a sovereign state on the day following the publication of the commission's report. It would have been proclaimed in any case, but the commission's blessing was nice to have.

> The team was headed by an American, Mr. Laurence Michelmore; its other members were nationals of Czechoslovakia, Brazil, Argentina, Ghana, Ceylon, Pakistan, Jordan and Japan. This seemed a careful blend of diverse tendencies. By no stretch of the imagination could it be considered in advance as biased in favour of British "imperialism".

Nobody, not even the British, is now supposed to be in favour of British "imperialism", but any UN hand (doing his sums in private as distinct from orating for purposes of edification) would read off that composition as follows: "five safe American votes, one British vote, one communist, two mavericks. Safe American majority of five to four: safe Anglo-American majority (if Britain and America agree) of six to three. With an Anglo-American rift a real split in the commission, but an American majority; with Anglo-American agreement, a safe two-thirds, and a possibility of attracting the mavericks."

"In the event," says Mr. Crozier, "the UN report was a sweeping vindication of the British and Malayan contention that the peoples of Sabah and Sarawak knew what Malaysia was about and wanted it." Few who have experience of the workings of the UN would doubt that, for a commission with this composition, working in these circumstances, the peoples of Sabah and Sarawak might well be found to know and want what the Americans deemed it expedient to have them know and want, by the deadline of 16 September. This does not, of course, necessarily mean that they wanted to be incorporated in Indonesia; it is quite possible they did not, but the character, composition and conditions of working of the UN commission are not such as to make its report "a sweeping vindication" of the opposite theory.

Mr. Crozier minimises Britain's responsibilities for the creation of Malaysia:

> The Tunku's conversion [to the Malaysian idea] was rather sudden and had nothing to do with Britain ... I have said enough already to show that Malaysia was not, in any sense, a British—that is neo-colonialist—plot ... The neo-colonialist charge does not stand up to objective scrutiny.

It is quite possible that much of the Indonesian anti-neo-colonialist case would not stand up to objective scrutiny, if it got it, but Mr. Crozier's large assumptions and unsupported assertions are far from constituting such a scrutiny.

Few will dispute Mr. Crozier's conclusion that the relationship between the newly independent countries and the former imperial powers ought to be a "fruitful relationship of cooperation in the path of human betterment". But many people in the newly independent countries feel that if a fair proportion of the "fruits" are to go to those countries, and if it is the "humans" of those countries—and not other "humans"—who are going to be "bettered", then they had better make their voices heard on how the wealth and power of the underdeveloped world are being distributed. In doing so they have found the word "neo-colonialism" a useful one; the fact that people like Mr. Crozier deprecate the use of the word will not discredit it among them—on the contrary.

thought they might win. It was the same Yeats, strongly drawn to fascism, but no lover of hopeless causes.

In April 1934 he was still advocating "force, marching men" to "break the reign of the mob", but professing, somewhat disingenuously, that "no such party" as would undertake this work had yet appeared. By August 1934—when the party for which he had in fact written the songs was on the verge of public disintegration—he had found that that party "neither could nor would" do what he proposed for it. This, it will be noted, does not amount to a disavowal of the programme of "force, marching men" to "break the reign of the mob". The irony and detachment of the poem "The Church and the State" belong to the period after the final break-up of the Blueshirt movement.

Comment on the question of Yeats's attitude to fascism has been bedevilled by the assumption that a great poet must be, even in politics, "a nice guy". If this be assumed then it follows that, as Yeats obviously was a great poet, he cannot *really* have favoured fascism, which is obviously not a nice cause. Thus the critic or biographer is led to postulate a "true Yeats", so that Yeats's recorded words and actions of fascist character must have been perpetrated by some bogus person with the same name and outward appearance. If one drops the assumption, about poets having always to be nice in politics, then the puzzle disappears, and we see, I believe, that Yeats the man was as near to being a fascist as his situation and the conditions of his own country permitted. His unstinted admiration had gone to Kevin O'Higgins, the most ruthless "strong man" of his time in Ireland, and he linked his admiration explicitly to his rejoicing at the rise of fascism in Europe—and this at the very beginning, within a few weeks of the March on Rome. Ten years later, after Hitler had moved to the centre of the political stage in Europe, Yeats was trying to create a movement in Ireland which would be overtly fascist in language, costume, behaviour and intent. He turned his back on this movement when it began to fail, not before. Would the irony and detachment of this phase of disillusion have lasted if a more effective fascist leader and movement had later emerged? One may doubt it. Many in Germany who were "disillusioned" by the failure of the Kapp putsch and the beer-cellar putsch were speedily "reillusioned" when Hitler succeeded—and "disillusioned" again when he lost the war.

Post-war writers, touching with embarrassment on Yeats's pro-fascist opinions, have tended to treat these as a curious aberration of an idealistic but ill-informed poet. In fact, such opinions were quite usual in the Irish Protestant middle class to which Yeats belonged (as well as in other middle classes) in the Twenties and Thirties. The *Irish Times*, spokesman of that class, aroused no protest from its readers when it hailed Hitler (4 March 1933) as "Europe's standard bearer against Muscovite terrorism", and its references to Mussolini were as consistently admiring as those to Soviet Russia were consistently damning. But the limiting factor on the pro-fascist tendencies of the *Irish Times* and the Irish Protestant middle class generally was the pull of loyalty to Britain—a factor which did not apply, or applied only with great ambivalence, in the case of Yeats. Mr. T. R. Henn is quite right when he says that Yeats was "not alone in believing at that moment of history, that the discipline of fascist theory might impose order upon a disintegrating world." I cannot follow Mr. Henn, however, to his conclusion that "nothing could be further from Yeats's mind" than fascism's "violent and suppressive practice". "Force, marching men" and the victory in civil war of "the skilful, riding their machines as did the feudal knights their armoured horses" (*On the Boiler*) surely belong to the domain of violent and suppressive practice.

Just as one school is led to claim that the pro-fascist Yeats was not the "true" Yeats, so another tries to believe that the fascism to which Yeats was drawn was not a "true" fascism. Several critics have assured us that he was drawn not really to fascism but to some idealised aristocracy of 18th-century stamp. "In all fairness," writes Dr Vivian Mercier, "we should allow that his views were closer to Hamilton's or even to Jefferson's than they were to Mussolini's." As far as political theory is concerned this is probably correct—although the name of Swift would seem more relevant than those of Hamilton or Jefferson. But it ignores one important reality: that Yeats was interested in contemporary politics and that he was a contemporary, not of Swift's or Jefferson's, but of Mussolini's. He had, in any case, the assurance of his friend Ezra Pound that the Duce was translating Jeffersonian ideas into 20th-century terms. He would certainly have preferred something more strictly aristocratic than fascism, but since he was living in the 20th century he was attracted to fascism as the best available form of anti-democratic theory and practice.

George Orwell, though critical, and up to a point percipient, about Yeats's tendencies, thought that Yeats misunderstood what an authoritarian society would be like. Such a society, Orwell pointed out, "will not be ruled by noblemen with Van Dyck faces, but by anonymous millionaires, shiny-bottomed bureaucrats and murderous gangsters." This implies a degree of innocence in Yeats which cannot reasonably be postulated. O'Higgins and O'Duffy were not Duke Ercole and Guidobaldo, and Yeats had considerable experience of practical politics, both in the Nineties and in the early Twenties. "In the last 40 years," wrote J. M. Hone in the year of Yeats's death, "there was never a period in which his countrymen did not regard him as a public figure." When he thought of rule by an élite, it was a possible élite, resembling in many ways the nominated members of the Senate in which he had sat. Its membership—bankers, organisers, ex-officers—would correspond roughly to what Orwell, in more emotive language, describes. Nor should it be assumed—as Orwell with his "murderous gangsters" seems to imply—that the sensitive nature of the poet would necessarily be revolted by the methods of rule of an authoritarian state. Yeats—unlike, say, his brother, or Lady Gregory—was not, in politics, a very squeamish person. "Seventy-seven executions" did not repel him; on the contrary, they made him admire O'Higgins all the more. At least one of his associates of the early Thirties might have been described as a "murderous gangster".

It is true that neither Yeats nor anyone else during Yeats's lifetime knew what horrors fascism would be capable of. But the many who, like Yeats, were drawn to fascism at this time knew, and seemed to have little difficulty in accepting, or at least making allowances for, much of what had already been done and continued to be done. "The Prussian police," wrote the *Irish Times* in an editorial of February 1933, "have been authorised by Herr Hitler's Minister to shoot communists ... on sight." The same editorial ended with the words: "Naturally the earlier phases of this renascence are crude, but Germany is finding her feet after a long period of political ineptitude."

Yeats read the newspapers; he also read, as Hone records, several books on Fascist Italy and Nazi Germany. If, then, he was attracted to the dominant movements in these countries, and if he supported a movement in his own country whose resemblances to these Continental movements he liked to stress, it cannot be contended that he did so in ignorance of such "crude" practices as the *Irish Times* described. It is true that the Blueshirts did not even try to go to anything like the lengths of their Continental models. It is also true that, unlike the case of their models, the communists whom the Blueshirts were fighting were, in Ireland, largely imaginary.

Some writers—notably Professor D.T. Torchiana in his well-documented study *W.B. Yeats, Jonathan Swift and Liberty*—have insisted that, in spite of Yeats's authoritarian and fascist leanings, he was essentially a friend of liberty. "Both Swift and Yeats," Torchiana concludes, "served human liberty." The senses in which this is true for Yeats are important but clearly limited. He defended the liberty of the artist, consistently. In politics, true to his duality, he defended the liberty of Ireland against English domination, and the liberty of his own caste—and sometimes, by extension, of others—against clerical domination. Often these liberties overlapped, and the cause of artist and aristocrat became the same; often his resistance to "clerical" authoritarianism makes him appear a liberal. But his objection to clerical authoritarianism is not the liberal's objection to *all* authoritarianism. On the contrary, he favours "a despotism of the educated classes" and in the search for this is drawn towards fascism. It is true that fascism was not in reality a despotism of the educated classes, but it was a form of despotism which the educated classes in the Twenties and Thirties showed a disposition to settle for—a disposition proportionate to the apparent threat, in their country, of communism or "anarchy". In assessing Yeats's pro-fascist opinions, there is no need to regard these as so extraordinary that he must either not have been himself or not have known what he was about.

Yet, in challenging the assumption that Yeats's pro-fascism was either not "truly Yeats" or not "truly pro-fascist", one must not overlook the intermittent character of his pro-fascism and of all his political activity. If his pro-fascism was real, his irony and caution were real too, and his phases of detachment not less real than his phases of political commitment. The long phase of nationalist commitment (1887–1903) was followed by a long phase (1903–1916) of detachment from almost all practical politics (except those to which the theatre exposed him), by a critique of Irish nationalist politics, and by the formation of an aristocratic attitude which did not find practical political expression until after 1916 when he reentered Irish politics on the right, in the Free State Senate. After clerical pressures had made the Senate uncongenial to him and had extruded him from it, he withdrew again from active politics (1928–33), only returning when a situation propitious to fascism seemed to present itself. When O'Duffy's Irish fascists failed ignominiously he turned away from politics again, though not forever: in the last two years of his life politics flared up again. And always, in the long phases of withdrawal, he tended to write of all politics with a kind of contempt, a plague-on-both-your-houses air. ("Contempt for politics" is of course a characteristic conservative stance.)

Yeats's "manic" phases of political activity were no less real or important than the "depressive" phases which followed them. And the options of the "manic" phases were not haphazard or middle-of-the-road. They were either anti-English or—in Irish politics—aristocratic and, from the time fascism had appeared, distinctly pro-fascist. At the end, in the last two years, as we shall see, these two elements were beginning to combine.

It was Yeats's misfortune as a politician, and his good fortune as a poet, that his political opportunities or temptations were few and far between. Irish politics in their normal run have not, since the introduction of universal suffrage, been receptive to poets, aristocrats or Protestants. It is only in rare conjunctures, times of great national stress and division, that an Irish party is likely to find room for such exotics, for in such times, men welcome an ally with a name and voice. Such moments of excitement and emotion, which offered opportunities, were also the moments which most stirred the poet. Such times were the Parnell split of 1891 and the Sinn Fein split of 1920/22. The abortive fascist movement of 1933 seemed to be, but was not, the opening of another profound fissure in Irish political life.

In the first two cases, the world of Irish politics proved, when "normalcy" had returned, no place for the poet. In the third case the poet retired from a political movement which had lost momentum. It is fairly safe to say that, if it had succeeded, it would have dropped him or forced him out: not through any great aversion on his part from thugs in coloured shirts, but because an Irish fascism, to have any chance of staying in power, would necessarily have to become an intensely clerical fascism. In fact, the successor movement to the Blueshirts—the Christian Front—was a noisily Catholic clerical-fascist movement. This was a kind of fascism—perhaps the only kind—which Yeats could not accept, or tolerate, since his authoritarian view of life derived ultimately from his concept of the caste to which he belonged, and the distinguishing mark of that caste was its Protestantism.

In the political writings of his last two years the two elements in his politics—the "Irish" and the "Protestant" elements—entered into a new set of relations. The "Irish" element became more vocal than it had been since 1916 and the "Protestant" element was obliged to break finally with the traditional right wing in Irish politics. Anti-English feeling, long dormant in Yeats, became increasingly pronounced in the period 1937/9. A series of poems—"Roger Casement", "The Ghost of Roger Casement", "The O'Rahilly", "Come Gather round me Parnellites"—both expressed and did much to rekindle the old pride in Irish nationalism which the cynicism that followed the Civil War had dulled. The Casement poems especially had a powerful anti-English charge:

> O what has made that suddent noise?
> What on the threshold stands?
> It never crossed the sea because
> John Bull and the sea are friends;

But this is not the old sea
Nor this the old seashore.
What gave that roar of mockery,
That roar in the sea's roar?
The ghost of Roger Casement
Is beating on the door.

No Irishman, reading these lines on the eve of the Second World War, had forgotten that Casement had been hanged, as well as "morally assassinated", for trying, in 1916, to bring help to Ireland from Germany. And some Irishmen, at least, must have reflected that if the sea was no longer the old sea, which had been friends with John Bull, the reason for this might be that the nation from which Casement had tried to bring help now possessed a powerful air force. Potentially, "The Ghost of Roger Casement" was as explosive as *Cathleen ni Houlihan*.

Just at this time Yeats was writing to Ethel Mannin that, while he liked neither side in Spain, and did not want to see his old leader O'Duffy—now fighting for Franco—return to Ireland with enhanced prestige to "the Catholic front", he was attracted by the thought that a fascist victory would weaken England.

> I am an old Fenian and I think the old Fenian in me would rejoice if a fascist nation or government controlled Spain because that would weaken the British empire, force England to be civil to India and loosen the hand of English finance in the far East of which I hear occasionally. But this is mere instinct. A thing I would never act on. Then I have a horror of modern politics—I see nothing but the manipulation of popular enthusiasm by false news—a horror that has been deepened in these last weeks by the Casement business. My ballad on that subject has had success.

The success of the ballad was mainly among those who had been Yeats's political enemies and against whom he had conspired—De Valera's party. It was in De Valera's paper, the *Irish Press*, that the ballad appeared. There were adequate reasons for a degree of reconciliation between Yeats and his former foes. First, from Yeats's point of view, the events of the early Thirties had shown that, if there was a "strong man" in Irish politics, it was not O'Duffy but De Valera. Second, five years of De Valera's government had dissipated the theory—once cherished by Yeats's former political friends—that De Valera meant communism. Third, De Valera was the main barrier against what Yeats then saw

—with considerable justice—as a rising tide of clericalist power, a tide which threatened all that Yeats had built in Ireland:

> I am convinced that if the Spanish war goes on or if [it] ceases and O'Duffy's volunteers return heroes, my "pagan" institutions, the Theatre, the Academy, will be fighting for their lives against combined Gaelic and Catholic bigotry. A friar or monk has already threatened us with mob violence.

In the same letter, Yeats noted how De Valera had carried in Parliament, against a pro-Franco opposition, a measure to stop Irish volunteers from going to Spain.

The fourth reason for a rapprochement with De Valera's party is more complex. Just as Yeats's own mind was hopelessly divided about the Spanish War—the authoritarian and Anglophobe in him desiring a Franco victory, the Irish anti-clerical dreading the results—so the party of his former friends was also in confusion. But their confusion was almost the mirror-image, the inversion, of his. They wanted, or said they wanted, a Franco victory, on Catholic grounds. But also as the party of the Anglo-Irish treaty, the "Commonwealth Party", they contained the most "pro-British" elements in Irish life: the people who in the event of Britain's going to war, would try to see to it that Ireland came in on Britain's side.

De Valera at this time was engaged, with the Chamberlain government, in the negotiations which led to the return of the Irish ports, which the Treaty had retained under British control. Without the return of these ports Ireland's neutrality in the coming war, which it was De Valera's policy to ensure, would scarcely have been practical politics. Yeats—who, as Frank O'Connor has told us, in his last years admired and defended De Valera—puts his name and influence explicitly behind the recovery of the ports, implicitly but clearly behind a policy of neutrality.

From the point of view of De Valera party, Yeats's tentative overtures—for such I believe, they were—would have presented some advantages. The patriotic poems undoubtedly struck a genuinely responsive note among most Irish people: their appearance in De Valera's newspaper was helpful, especially at this time, in Ireland; the prestige—by now great—of Yeats's name in England would be helpful there in relation to the ports and to neutrality. Yet, while there were reasons on both sides for some degree of rapprochement, it may be doubted whether this would ever have become close or warm. Irish political life between the wars had been too bitter for that. De Valera's memory has not the reputation of being short or inaccurate. Yeats's activities in 1922/23 and in 1933 would have been quite fresh in De Valera's mind. It is believed also that he had read, with distaste and distress, the lines:

> Had De Valera eaten Parnell's heart
> No loose-lipped demagogue had won the day,
> No civil rancour torn the land apart.

Real reconciliation had to wait for the next generation. After the war Yeats's son, Michael, joined De Valera's party and became a senator.

The two main currents in Yeats's active politics—his Anglophobe Irish nationalism and his authoritarianism—necessarily converged in the years immediately before the war, thrusting him in the direction of desiring the victory of the fascist powers. The doctrine of John O'Leary, to whose school Yeats always claimed to belong, was Tone's doctrine: that "England's difficulty is Ireland's opportunity." The caution and scepticism which were also permanent features of Yeats's personality worked, together with his repulsion from Irish clerical fascism, to prevent him from being carried too far by Tone and O'Leary. But an underlying wish found voice at this time, when the prestige and authority of England were lower than they had been for centuries, in an increasingly anti-English tone, in verse and prose and in his conversation. This did not happen without a violent inner struggle. "The 'Irishry'," he wrote in *A General Introduction for My Work* (1937),

have preserved their ancient "deposit" through wars which, during the 16th and 17th centuries, became wars of extermination; no people, Lecky said at the opening of his *Ireland in the 18th Century*, have undergone greater persecution nor did that persecution altogether cease up to our own day. No people hate as we do in whom that past is always alive, there are moments when hatred poisons my life and I accuse myself of effeminacy because I have not given it adequate expression. It is not enough to have put it into the mouth of a rambling peasant poet. Then I remind myself that though mine is the first English marriage I know of in the direct line, all my family names are English and that I owe my soul to Shakespeare, to Spenser and to Blake, perhaps to William Morris, and to the English language in which I think, speak and write, that everything I love has come to me through English; my hatred tortures me with love, my love with hate. I am like the Tibetan monk who dreams at his initiation that he is eaten by a wild beast and learns on waking that he himself is eater and eaten. This is Irish hatred and solitude, the hatred of human life that made Swift write *Gulliver* and the epitaph upon his tomb, that can still make us wag between extremes and doubt our sanity.

On the Boiler, written the following year, assumes—without however being altogether explicit about it—that the fascist powers are winning and England is in contemptible decline. "The fascist countries," he writes in the section "Tomorrow's Revolution", "know that civilisation has reached a crisis, and found their eloquence upon that knowledge." The only fault he has to find with them is that "perhaps from dread of attack" they encourage large families. He assumes in "Ireland after the Revolution" that "some tragic crisis shall so alter Europe and all opinion that the Irish government will teach the great majority of its schoolchildren nothing but"—a list of manual and menial occupations follows.

At the time when this was written, the "tragic crisis" many expected was that which was to lead Pétain's France to adopt somewhat similar educational policies. It is hard to resist the conclusion that Yeats, when writing this, expected, and hoped, that Ireland "after the revolution" would be a sort of satellite of a fascist-dominated Europe. As regards England his contempt, in this year of Munich, is unqualified and savage. After saying some hard things about King George V he concludes "Ireland after the Revolution" with the words:

> The Irish mind has still, in country rapscallion or in Bernard Shaw, an ancient cold, explosive detonating impartiality. The English mind, excited by its newspaper proprietors and its schoolmasters, has turned into a bed-hot harlot.

Dorothy Wellesley, who was troubled by his increasingly anti-British attitude in the last years of his life, made a shrewd comment:

> Why then, in the 20th century and when the Irish are freed from their oppressors the English, does he despise and dislike us increasingly? Because he dislikes the stuffed lion and admires the ranting, roaring oppressors.

During Yeats's life the English government gave him a Civil List pension and offered him a knighthood which he refused. The Athenaeum Club gave him the signal honour of a special election. Since his death, the British Council has presented him to the world as one of England's glories. There is therefore some irony in the thought that there was something in him that would have taken considerable pleasure—though not without a respectful backward glance at Shakespeare—in seeing England occupied by the Nazis, the Royal

Family exiled, and the Mother of Parliaments torn down. Meanwhile in Ireland one would have expected to see him at least a cautious participant, or ornament, in a collaborationist regime. It is probably fortunate for his future reputation, and especially his standing with the British Council, that he died in January 1939 before the political momentum of his last years could carry him any farther than *On the Boiler*.

How can those of us who loathe such politics continue, not merely to admire but to love the poetry, and perhaps most of all the poems with a political bearing? An important part of the answer is supplied by the poet himself in a note on "Leda and the Swan":

> I wrote "Leda and the Swan" because the editor of a political review asked me for a poem. I thought "After the individualist, demagogic movement founded by Hobbes [*sic*] and popularised by the Encyclopaedists and the French revolution, we have a soil so exhausted that it cannot grow that crop again for centuries." Then I thought "Nothing is now possible but some movement from above preceded by some violent annunciation." My fancy began to play with Leda and the Swan for metaphor, and I began this poem; but as I wrote, bird and lady took such possession of the scene that all politics went out of it, and my friend tells me that his "conservative readers would misunderstand the poem".

They would have been puzzled, certainly.

Very little seems to be known—and perhaps little can be known—of how this process of transformation works. How can that patter of Mussolini prose "produce" such a poem? How can that political ugly duckling be turned into this glorious Swan? It is in a sense like the transmutation, in "Easter 1916", of those whom Yeats had thought of as commonplace people:

> All changed, changed utterly:
> A terrible beauty is born.

Is the connection then between the politics and the poetry only trivial and superficial? There is, I think, a deeper connection: if the political prose and the poetry are thought of, not as "substance" and "metaphor", or "content" and "style", but as cognate expressions of a fundamental force, anterior to both politics and poetry.

That force was, I suggest, Yeats's profound and tragic intuitive—and intelligent—awareness, in his maturity and old age, of what the First World War had set loose, of what was already moving towards Hitler and the Second World War. That he is conscious of the danger a letter shows as early as 1923: "Unless Europe takes to war again and starts new telepathic streams of violence and cruelty." But the poetry is already responding to the telepathic streams as early as 1920, when he wrote "The Second Coming":

> Things fall apart; the centre cannot hold;
> Mere anarchy is loosed upon the world.

Years afterwards, just before the Spanish War, he drew Ethel Mannin's attention to this poem:

> If you have my poems by you look up a poem called "The Second Coming".
> It was written more than 16 or 17 years ago and foretold what is happening.
> I have written of the same thing again and again since.

The words "violence", "hatred" and "fanaticism" became keywords in Yeats's poetry. He often uses them in condemnation of the Left in Irish politics—the politics of Constance Markievicz and of Maud Gonne. But he is also increasingly conscious of these same forces in himself:

> I carry from my mother's womb
> A fanatic heart.

The "fanatic heart", an unusual capacity for hatred and an unusual experience of it, probably made him more sensitive and more responsive to the "telepathic waves" coming from Europe than other writers in English seem to have been. The forces in him that responded to the hatred, cruelty and violence welling up in Europe produced the prophetic image of "The Second Coming" and the last part of "Nineteen Hundred and Nineteen".

It may be objected that "Nineteen Hundred and Nineteen" and "The Second Coming" were written not about the coming of fascism but about the Anglo-Irish War and the Black and Tans. The distinction is less than absolute: the Black and Tans were in fact an early manifestation of an outlook and methods which the Nazis were later to perfect. The *Freikorps* on the Polish-German border were at this time trying to do exactly what the Black and Tans were doing in Ireland and the *Freikorps* were the direct and proudly acknowledged predecessors of Hitler's Nazis. There is even a direct link between the Black and Tans and the Nazis in the person of Lord Haw-Haw, who fought for the

British government in the first movement and was hanged by it for his work in the second. Bruno Brehm, one of Hitler's novelists, made the assassination by Irish revolutionaries of Sir Henry Wilson—the principal exponent of intensified Black and Tan measures in Ireland—symbolic of the tragic confrontation of hero and submen. Wilson was to the Irish as Hitler was to Jews and Bolsheviks.

In a *General Introduction to My Work* Yeats made specific the connection between his own hatred and what was happening in Europe:

> When I stand upon O'Connell Bridge in the half-light and notice that discordant architecture, all those electric signs, where modern heterogeneity has taken physical form, a vague hatred comes up out of my own dark and I am certain that wherever in Europe there are minds strong enough to lead others the same vague hatred arises; in four or five or in less generations this hatred will have issued in violence and imposed some kind of rule of kindred. I cannot know the nature of that rule, for its opposite fills the light; all I can do to bring it nearer is to intensify my hatred.

By the time the *General Introduction* was written, fascist power and "rule of kindred" were already in full swing: the length of time—"four or five generations"—is odd and perhaps calculated: it brings to mind the retrospective "commentaries" on the songs for O'Duffy. The paragraph itself may be taken as a kind of retrospective commentary on "The Second Coming".

In "The Second Coming" the poet, perhaps from the foretaste of the Black and Tans, augured the still more terrible things that were to come. The sort of "premonitory" intuition present in "The Second Coming" and in other poems necessarily affected Yeats in his ordinary life as well as in his poetry. Yeats the manager, the senator, the politician, stands in a diplomatic relation to these intimations of power. His references to fascism, though sometimes mildly critical, are never hostile, almost always respectful, often admiring, and this especially in years of fascist victories: 1922, 1933 and 1938. Some reasons for this have already been suggested; it might be added that for Yeats a bandwagon had the same high degree of attraction that it has for other political mortals:

> Processions that lack high stilts have
> nothing that catches the eye.

If a Marxist, believing that history is going in a given direction, thinks it right to give it a good shove in the way it is going, it is natural enough that one who, like Yeats, feels that it is going in the opposite direction should accompany it that way with, if not a shove, at least a cautious tilt. In the poetry, however, the raw intimations of what is impending —the "telepathic waves of violence and fear"—make themselves known, not in the form of calculated practical deductions, but in the attempt to reveal, through metaphoric insight, what is actually happening and even, in a broad sense, what is about to happen. The poet, like the lady, is

> so caught up,
> So mastered by the brute blood of the air,

that he does indeed take on the knowledge of what is happening with the power to make it known. The political man had his cautious understanding with fascism, the diplomatic relation to a great force: the poet conveyed the nature of the force, the dimension of the tragedy. The impurities of this long and extraordinary life went into its devious and sometimes sinister political theories and activities. The purity and integrity—including the truth about politics as Yeats apprehended it—are in the poetry concentrated in metaphors of such power that they thrust aside all calculated intent: bird and lady take possession of the scene.

15

A LONG ENGAGEMENT

It is a triangular affair: Sartre, Beauvoir, History. The second is in love with the first; the first with the third; the third not at all. *Force of Circumstance*, the third long volume of Simone de Beauvoir's huge autobiography is the story of the saddest and most ironic phase of this relationship: from the liberation of France to the liberation of Algeria. The first chapter begins with the words, "We were liberated. In the streets the children were singing:

> *Nous ne les reverrons plus*
> *C'est fini ils sont foutus ...*"

The last chapter greets another victory—peace in Algeria—in a different tone: "For seven years we had desired this victory; it came too late to console us for the price it had cost." What they had learned in the meantime was that the children were wrong to believe that "we shall never see them again; that even the distinction between 'us' and 'them' was not, as it had seemed, absolute." Not only had Frenchmen done in Algeria the same things that Germans had done in France: worse still the French people generally had responded to its knowledge of such things with the same indifference as the German people had shown.

New York Review of Books, 20 May 1965, pp. 4–5. Review of *Force of Circumstance* by Simone de Beauvoir.

The crimes he [Servan-Schreiber] described should have had some effect on public opinion: Arabs shot down "for the fun of it," prisoners brutally murdered, villages burned, mass executions, etc. No one turned a hair ... [Another] narrative—hanging, beating, torture—was read out in stony silence: not one gasp of surprise or disgust: everyone knew already. My heart froze inside me as I once again faced this truth: everyone knew and didn't give a damn, or else approved.

Sartre and Simone de Beauvoir were among the few who did give a damn, and who spoke out at a time when more moralizing writers, including Camus, were silent. Camus's silence was not—as one might perhaps infer from *La Chute* that it was—part of a general refusal to condemn or to be indignant, an achievement of political quietism. Camus publicly condemned—as Sartre also did—the Russian aggression in Hungary, and Camus did so in terms of intense moral indignation. This silence on Algeria—about which he knew so much more than he did about Hungary—can hardly be interpreted except in terms of a specific evaluation of the Algerian situation. The fact that he never —neither in an imaginative work nor in an essay—revealed what that evaluation was, leaves a great enigma in the life of this brilliant and haunted novelist and writer.

In *Force of Circumstance*—as also in *The Mandarins* but in a different way—Madame de Beauvoir is preoccupied by this enigma, and in general by the ambiguously symbolic contrast between Sartre and Camus. She tends to interpret this contrast in the sense of different relations to history. For Camus, according to Madame de Beauvoir, "History was a threat to his individuality and he refused to bow to it" ".... to treat the occupation as the symbol of a natural calamity was merely another means of escaping from History and the real problems". ".... At one moment forced to yield to History, he attempted as soon as possible to secede from it; sensitive to men's suffering he imputed it to Nature. Sartre had labored since 1940 to repudiate idealism, to wrench himself away from his original individualism, to live in History ..."

This language is hard to decipher; one does not really bow to History, or yield to it, escape from it or secede from it, and living in it is not really a matter of choice, or something that one need labor to achieve. Nor is the "History" repudiated by Camus and accepted by Sartre exactly the Marxist construct, still less the allegorical entity which is held to validate the decisions of contemporary Communist Parties. History, in the latter sense, has been rejected by Sartre and Beauvoir as often as it was by Camus. What seems to be involved is the view that the relation of the writer to this historical process should be explicit and continuous, that the writer has a responsibility to comment, to play the role of Chorus to history, but more boldly than the classical Chorus and with some hope in influencing the action. In practice that is the role which Sartre and Madame de Beauvoir have played in France, and their comments, like those of the ancient Chorus, are based on long-held moral assumptions—that cruelty and lying are wrong, whatever the cause and whatever the provocation. This is the "Kantian-priestly" and "Quaker-vegetarian" outlook, so savagely rejected by Trotsky, that ill-rewarded devotee of history. Sartre, and with him Madame de Beauvoir, use the proud language of the servants of History, but have never attained their military morality. Madame de Beauvoir, in *Force of Circumstance*, speaks as if she bowed to history, and yielded to it, but in fact her book is one long refusal to bow or yield, a protest against seventeen years of real history—with its multiplicity of conflicting lies and cruelties—by a compassionate woman, an inveterate moralizer.

If anyone bowed, it was Camus. If he rejected the language of history and spoke in terms which suggested an old-fashioned idealism and moralism, he was in practice on better terms with real history—the history of his place and time—than Sartre was. The anti-idealist could not stifle his moral protest; the idealist talking of other things quietly acquiesced in those of the bloody realities of history that were nearest to him. The accepted stereotype of the Sartre-Camus contrast—a stereotype which derives mainly, strangely enough, from the contrast between Dubreuilh and Henri in Madame de Beauvoir's *Les Mandarins*—depicts Sartre as the ruthless "means-for-ends" man confronting in Camus the man of moral values, near-Commisar against near-Yogi. This is accurate enough as a description of Sartre-language and Camus-language; as a guide to characters and behavior it is wholly misleading.

In *Force of Circumstance* Madame de Beauvoir firmly repudiates the notion that *Les Mandarins* was a *roman à clef*: "Henri, whatever people have said, is not Camus; not at all. He is young, he has dark hair, he runs a newspaper, the resemblance stops there. As for Dubreuilh ... authoritarian, tenacious, closed, unemotional and unsociable, somber even in his moments of gaiety, he could scarcely be more different from Sartre." Henri is more herself than he is Camus: "The joy of existence, the gaiety of activity, the pleasure of writing, all those I bestowed on Henri. He resembles me at least as much as Anne does, perhaps more."

The repudiation is both excessive and revealing. It is excessive because, for example, the resemblance between Henri and Camus obviously does *not* stop where she now says it stops. For Camus had, and had in her eyes, also those attractive qualities—"joy of existence," etc.—

which, as she says, she possessed herself and "bestowed" on Henri. In *Force of Circumstance* she is, for adequate reasons, severe about Camus's later years, but in referring to his death she evokes once again, in moving language, the young man he had been:

> It wasn't the fifty-year-old man who'd just died I was mourning: not that just man without justice, so arrogant and touchy behind his stern mask, who had been struck out of my heart when he gave his approval to the crimes of France: it was the companion of our hopeful years, whose open face laughed and smiled so easily, the young ambitious writer, wild to enjoy life, its triumphs and comradeship, friendship, love and happiness.

Those who identified Camus with Henri were not, then, so wildly wrong. As for Dubreuilh, a reader may feel—as I do—that, while that rather grim figure may be as its creator tells us, quite unlike the "real" Sartre, it is such a Sartre as might be created by some of the suppressed feelings of one whose life has been dominated by loyalty to Sartre, and by a relation which has been both less and more than marriage. "There has," she says at the beginning of the epilogue to *Force of Circumstance*, "been one undoubted success in my life: my relationship with Sartre." The reader of *Force of Circumstance* is likely to accept this, and yet to feel that this success, like others, has not been achieved without sacrifices. There is an intellectual sacrifice, surely, in agreeing to share successively all those elaborate and highly personal constructions in which Sartre has sought to accommodate himself with History. There might well be an emotional sacrifice, for a woman, in conforming to Sartre's ideas of liberty in personal relationships. In *Force of Circumstance* the love-affairs, as well as the drinking parties, seem both resolute and sad. Something else, too, has been sacrificed: style. Sartre writes with immense vigor, stamina, and resource, but also with a deliberate carelessness, a Jansenist rejection of elegance. There is no time for queasiness about *le mot juste*: History is knocking at the door. Madame de Beauvoir has in practice followed Sartre in rejecting the pursuit of a phantom precision, and in assuming the duty of prompt and copious utterance. "The only alternative," she says speaking of her diaries, "would be to pay real attention to how one writes things down and I haven't time." She probably means this only of her diaries, not of her novels, essays, and autobiographies, but in fact she everywhere gives the impression of writing at great length because she lacks the time to write otherwise. Yet this is not the way she wants to write, nor, it seems, the way she thinks she writes. In a surprising passage in the epilogue she says,

Words without doubt, universal, eternal, presence of all in each, are the only transcendent power I recognize and am affected by: they vibrate in my mouth, and with them I can communicate with humanity. They wrench tears, night, death itself from the moment, from contingency, and then transfigure them. Perhaps the most profound desire I entertain today is that people should repeat in silence certain words that I have been the first to link together.

Unfortunately this desire is not very likely to be fulfilled. Madame de Beauvoir's words can be respected for many qualities: integrity, courage, decency, pertinacity, a certain shrewdness, a flair for intellectual and moral dilemmas, an explicit and anguished sharing in the conscience and consciousness of our time. These qualities make many of her books important and interesting, but I doubt if anyone will ever wish to remember a line she wrote. She belongs too much to Sartre to be able to write like one who believed in Yeats's

Words alone are certain good

—far fewer words, be it noted, than she took to say the same thing. Of the three writers—Sartre, Camus, Beauvoir—the only one who lives by his style is Camus, who became, like many other stylists, increasingly unscrupulous, arrogant, and irresponsible. Madame de Beauvoir loyally accepted the responsibility she owed, through Sartre, to history, and the austerities which go with such responsibility. But we know now that there is in her that which, left to itself, would reject History for Literature. It was this that produced, in Henri of *Les Mandarins*, a fusion of her own personality with that of Camus. One reason why history is different—for both good and ill—from History is that men and women have unplumbed resourcefulness in circumventing the idols they themselves create.

16

THE NEUROSIS OF COLONIALISM

Frantz Fanon was an exceptionally brave and honest man; he was also exceptional in his love and respect for the oppressed. He demonstrated these qualities by his professional work as a psychiatrist in Blida, Algeria, by throwing in his lot with the FLN and by his writing. As a writer, he is distinguished by his passionate seriousness and his frequent, penetrating insights. He is neither an easy nor a systematic writer; one feels that his writing is wrung from him by his experience. *The Wretched of the Earth* is not so much a tract or essay as a series of intellectual explosions. Experience detonates an idea; hardly has the dust settled before another idea, equally unsettling, goes up. There are almost no transitions; he writes in the implicit belief that history itself provides the element of continuity in his book, as he moves from reflections on violence in the anticolonial struggles to the deceptions of decolonization, from that to national consciousness and culture, and finally to the mental hospital in Blida: "The truth is that colonialism in its essence, was already beginning to show itself as a great recruiter for the psychiatric hospitals."

Yet Fanon's book has an unchanging central figure: that of "the colonized": *le colonisé.* (The present translator, in an understandable anxiety to avoid a clumsy word in English has rendered *le colonisé* as "the native," but Fanon did not write *indigène;* the native is not the same as the colonized, because the native was there before the colony.)

Nation 200 (21 June 1965), pp. 674–76. Review of *The Wretched of the Earth* by Frantz Fanon.

Who is *le colonisé*? He is any man who has been brought up in one of the poor regions of the world, under the domination, covert or overt, of people from the rich regions. Most of *les colonisés* are non-white—like Frantz Fanon himself, who was a Negro from Martinique—and *les colonisés* form the majority of the population of the globe. The colonized is a product of the colonial system: "The settler (*colon*) and the colonized are old acquaintances. As a matter of fact the settler is right when he makes the claim that he knows 'them.' It is the settler who *made* and *continues to make* the colonized." (Fanon's italics.)

This idea—which is true in certain regions, times and situations—became almost an obsession with Fanon. There are times when he writes as if the colonial experience brought into being an entirely new kind of being, all of whose characteristics derive from colonialism. Even tribal warfare is a product of colonialism: "Collective self-destruction in tribal warfare is one of the means by which the muscular tension of the colonized releases itself." There is an element of truth in this: under co-lonialism and especially under settler rule—Fanon never adequately distinguishes between these two phenomena—the black man, say, will often want to hit a white man, but finds it much safer to hit another black man, and derives some relief from doing so. Nor is it necessarily a question of blacks and whites: witness the shillelagh fights of 18th-century Ireland, which gave the word *donnybrook* to the English lan-guage for "a scene of uproar, disorder and free fighting" (O.E.D.). This was before the Irish got down to the more notable achievement of add-ing the word *boycott* to the English language. It is a reasonable hypoth-esis that donnybrook was in part a *spontaneous* response to settler rule, just as boycott was the beginning of successful *organized* response to the same rule. But this is not the whole truth; for the Irish and the Africans were fighting each other before the foreigners came.

Violence is not, as Fanon often seems to suggest, a creation of coloni-alism. On the contrary, colonialism is a form of violence: a form devel-oped by the most tightly organized and most effectively violent human societies. The British and the Ashanti, the Belgians and the Bayeke, were alike in that they all wanted power and loot, and used force to get them; the British and the Belgians, disposing of more force, got more power and loot, and the Ashanti and Bayeke became *les colonisés* along with their former subjects, the pre-colonial *colonisés*. As far as violence and power are concerned, colonialism introduced no new principles into Africa, merely the more effective application of existing principles.

In this respect, it seems to me that Fanon overrates the originality of colonialism. He is also inclined, I think, to exaggerate its effects and underrate the degree of continuity which exists between pre-colonial and post-colonial Africa. All African phenomena—even dancing—are to him functions of colonialism: "The relaxation of the colonized is just this muscular orgy, during which the keenest aggression, the most immediate violence, are canalized, transformed, conjured away.... These disintegrations of personality, these doublings and dissolutions discharge a basic economic function in the stability of the colonized world." It is curious to find Fanon, of all people, falling into the kind of wild anthropological generalization characteristic of an earlier generation of European observers. In order to establish the correctness of his diagnosis of the dance, it would be necessary to show that orgiastic dancing of the kind described did not exist before the coming of the colonizers—that the Australian Corroboree, for example, sprang into existence only after the First Fleet sailed into Botany Bay in 1788. I wonder whether any anthropologist would subscribe to this thesis. (It is attested, however, that the Australian aborigines did use the Corroboree to express their feelings about the settlers; to that extent Fanon's theory is justified.) It would also be necessary to account for the survival, through the colonial period, of so much dancing of a quite different character from that described—gay and flirtatious dances of the Fanti, grave and ceremonious dances of the Dagomba.

The truth is that *le colonisé* is far less uniform a person than Fanon's French-instilled taste for generalization leads him to suggest. There are people whose colonial experience has been such that they have become culturally part of the metropolis—though a rather special part. Fanon's own Antillais belong to this group, as do almost all the intellectuals of the French tropical colonies. In extreme cases—like those of the Antillais and the Creoles of Sierra Leone—this has been accompanied for years by a sense of actually being French or British and a nearly complete divorce from pre-colonial culture and traditions. In other cases—as in Africa between the forest belt and the Sahara—large populations continued their traditional way of life, hardly touched by the colonial experience. Others have been more deeply affected, but without at all losing their sense of national identity or feeling the slightest temptation to "be" French or British. Colonial rule was often too brief to penetrate the psyche as thoroughly as Fanon assumes. Thus in Ashanti the present Asantehene, Prempeh II, born in Kumasi when it was the capital of the independent Ashanti kingdom, now keeps state in Kumasi, which is the second city of independent Ghana. And young Ashantis have been brought up to believe that Ashanti was never conquered at all—and behave with the assurance of men who so believe. Yet they too are among *les colonisés*.

The value of *The Wretched of the Earth* does not lie in its often fanciful generalizations but in its relation to direct experience, in the perspective of the Algerian revolution. We are only too liable to look at the poor world through rich-world spectacles, and to be unconscious that there can be other ways of looking at it. Fanon forces his readers to see the Algerian revolution—and by analogy other contemporary revolutions— from the viewpoint of the rebels. This is not the viewpoint of the European liberal, sympathetic to the aims of the revolution, but deploring its excesses and seeking a nonviolent way out. It is not even the viewpoint of a French sympathizer with the revolution like Sartre, whose introduction to this volume is mainly preoccupied with France's guilt. Fanon preaches violence, including violence against civilians, as a legitimate resource of the oppressed.

The French established and maintained their rule in Algeria by violence, including violence against civilians; the conquered have the right to use equivalent violence to end that rule; they will rightly refuse to allow their conquerors to instruct them on what forms of violence are to be considered legitimate. Fanon here touches a raw nerve in his Western readers. One of the forms of violence frequently practiced by Algerian rebels was the murder and mutilation of settlers, including women and children. Fanon shows that, as regards the women and children, A.L.N. commanders tried to discourage such acts; they did not always succeed; Fanon neither condones, nor explicitly condemns, the murder and mutilation of women and children: many will regard him as implicitly condoning such acts, and if silence is condonation they are right. Before we cry out in horror at this, we might do well to consider what we ourselves implicitly condone or have condoned, by our silence. The peasants who did these things acted in accordance with a certain logic: the logic of war. They believed that the more atrocities could be perpetrated against settler families and the more horrible these atrocities were, the sooner the settlers would begin to leave the country and the sooner the war would be over—bringing safety to the women and children of the peasants. This peasant logic is in all essentials the same as that applied by the very civilized James B. Conant when he advised that the best target for the first atomic bomb would be a war plant "employing a large number of workers and closely surrounded by workers' houses." Those who can permit themselves the luxury of being advised by people like James B. Conant have murdered and mutilated, and are continuing to murder and mutilate, in Vietnam and elsewhere, far more children than the Algerian peasants ever did. But we do not call it murder when it is done from the air. And we do not feel so bad about it when the children are not white.

Fanon's position essentially is that all crimes committed by both sides in the Algerian War derive from the basic crime of a rule imposed and maintained by violence, and inaccessible to any appeal save that of violence. On the plane of generalities, I think Fanon is right. Yet personal responsibility, on both sides, inescapably remained, as the astonishing Algerian psychiatric case histories which conclude the book show. A young A.L.N. soldier who killed a settler's wife becomes obsessed by a double image combining his own mother with the disembowled European woman. A French policeman, whose daily work is the torturing of Algerian suspects, takes to torturing his own wife and children, and asks Fanon to cure him of this—that is to say, of torturing his wife and children. "This man was well aware that all his troubles were caused by the sort of work he did in the interrogation rooms, although he tried to throw the whole responsibility for this work on to 'the situation.' As he had no intention—it would make no sense—of stopping torturing (he would have had to resign if he did) he asked me straight out to help him to torture Algerian patriots without remorse, without behavioral disturbances, in all serenity."

Feeling unable to supply such services, Fanon left the French-run mental hospital in 1956 and devoted the brief remainder of his life to the cause of Algerian freedom. He did not live long enough to see an independent Algeria. He did see other independent African states and writes about post-independence problems without illusions. He is skeptical about African unity, one-party states, the cult of the leader. He noted—no later than in 1961—that despite "the sonorous affirmations about the unity of the continent," African unity "was sinking into evanescence." As for the one-party state, it was "the modern form of bourgeois dictatorship, without mask, make-up or scruples, cynical." Here again we may note the excessive tendency to generalize; the one-party states are not all alike, or all averse from masks and make-up; bourgeois dictatorships can be assured without a one-party state as every Nigerian knows.

About leaders also he does not fear to generalize, and he hits hard: "Before independence the leader generally incarnated the aspirations of the people; independence, political liberty, national dignity. But after independence, far from incarnating in a concrete way the needs of the people, far from promoting the real dignity of the people ... the leader will reveal his inner function: that of being the chairman of that great company composed of greedy profiteers which is the national bourgeoisie."

After independence, as before it, Frantz Fanon remained a champion of the people and a harsh and fearless critic of their rulers.

17

NKRUMAH — THE MAN I KNEW

As Tim Healy said of Parnell, Kwame Nkrumah was a splendid comedian. This made talking to him difficult because he always registered too much, as if his expression—of amusement, concern, indignation or sheer sincerity—had to be sufficiently vehement to carry conviction to many people over a wide area. When I left his presence I used to feel, among other things, a sort of spiritual crick in my neck, as if I had been watching a movie from a position too close to the screen.

In public, however, his performances were superb. About the time I came to Ghana, he ceased to address mass meetings—because of the bomb attempts and deaths among his audiences—so that I never saw him in full exercise of the art that brought him to power. I did, however, have several opportunities to admire the staging of his Parliamentary appearances: his personal herald literally chanting his praises from afar off; his eight "linguists" with their gold-headed staves; the gallery of crowned chiefs each with his *single* linguist; the Parliamentarians like slightly eccentric Roman Senators in their multi-coloured togas; the Speaker and the Mace and a Speech from the Throne delivered by an actual ruling monarch.

RESPONSIVE AUDIENCE

The audience was responsive, but responsive as to a performance, not

Observer, 27 February 1966.

as to a political exhortation. They rather resembled those Italian soldiers of the First World War whose commander charged over the top waving his sword while the men remained in the trench shouting *Bravo Bravissimo*.

Three times in successive years I have heard Nkrumah warn his Parliament that assets illegally held abroad must be repatriated, but that if they were repatriated by a given date—which changed, of course, each year—the holders would not be penalised. And three times I have heard the whole Parliament of Ghana rock with laughter at this droll idea. Instead of palling by repetition, this particular gag actually became more farcical with each passing year.

The farce, of course, was really a tragedy. The wealthiest and best-equipped of African countries saw its assets running out and its legislators treat Ghana's economic plight, its laws and its leader's "solemn warning" as all together constituting one huge joke. Worse still, the man who less than a decade before had stood for the hopes of Ghanaians and of millions of other Africans seemed to be privy to this most practical of jokes.

His dream had been a great one, his belief in his mission was strong, his talents many; his actual achievements were considerable—the Volta Dam and the smelter, a great expansion of the educational system, and an extraordinary effervescence of building, some of it useful. How did he decline into the position implied by those scenes in Parliament—that of equivocal chairman of a corrupt and cynical oligarchy?

The trouble was that he was an actor who could write his own notices, and he then read them and believed them. Reality receded to a great distance; the wish and the thought became one. It was agreeable that there should be no contradiction between service to the people and a life of ostentation, so there was no such contradiction.

THE PROFITEERS

The theory that when the money ran out there would be none left ceased to carry conviction. The kind of civil servant who advised that large sums should not be spent on new importations of tractors—as long as the batch imported six months before still lay in the port area with tyres and batteries flat—came to be regarded as a stumbling block in the path of Ghana's economic development. The climate of a court set in: the faces of those who were closest to the presence grew grave and guarded like those of priests.

The profiteers of the private sector, and also those of the public sector, talked socialism because that was the language of the court.

"Socialism," said Mr. Krobo Edusei, the Minister for Agriculture, "does not mean that if you have made a lot of money you can't keep it." As a proposition about the socialism of Nkrumah's Ghana this was entirely valid. What was practised in the name of socialism ceased to seem important: what was important was that the word "socialism" should be frequently and energetically implied together with the word Nkrumah.

This was the basis of Nkrumah's quarrel with the university, which was said not to be "inculcating socialism." What this meant was that the university was not obliging its students to repeat slogans flattering to the Government, in the language in which such slogans had to be composed, that of "socialism."

Some socialists at the university misinterpreted this situation. Some students and faculty members started a discussion group called Marxist Forum. After several successful meetings—one of them addressed by Malcolm X—it was suddenly announced that the forum had changed its name. It was now the Nkrumah Forum; some of the original members quietly dropped out.

Prices went up; wage demands were held up by the Convention People's Party's trade union oligarchs. Christiansborg Castle was made over at great cost into a Presidential residence; another Presidential palace stood on the Akwapin Scarp overlooking the Accra Plain; a new palace of African unity was added last year at a cost estimated at between £3-£4 million.

REAL ACHIEVEMENTS

Yet before the contract with reality broke down, Nkrumah's Government had its real achievements; even Northern Ghana, poor though it is, contrasts favourably with corresponding regions of the neighbouring countries—more schools, more dispensaries.

I am being pursued in the New York Press at the moment by a don who reproaches me for not acknowledging what he calls "the fact" that Nkrumah was a fascist. He was no more fascist than he was a socialist. He was not cruel, or militaristic, or racist. He took over the British colonial structure, which was essentially authoritarian like all colonial systems, and retained the powers of past Governors, including the power to replace troublesome chiefs and detain fractious citizens. There was nothing novel about these things; what was novel—and objectionable to the *Daily Telegraph*—was that it was an African who was doing them.

18

THE EMBERS OF EASTER

A blow delivered against the British imperialist bourgeoisie in Ireland has a hundred times more political significance than a blow of equal weight would have in Asia and Africa ... The dialectics of history are such that small nations, powerless as an independent factor in the struggle against imperialism, play a part as one of the ferments, one of the bacilli, which facilitate the entry into the arena of the *real* power against imperialism, namely the social proletariat ... The misfortune of the Irish is that they rose prematurely, when the European revolt of the proletariat had not yet matured.

Lenin

All rebellion is infectious, and that is why Lenin praised the Easter Rising in Dublin. But in 1916 the conditions for a spread of the infection were far less favourable than they were to become two years later. In 1916 "Pearse read the Proclamation of the Republic, pale and cold of face, to an indifferent crowd and 'a few thin perfunctory cheers'" (Desmond Ryan). Because of Eoin MacNeill's Countermanding Order the Irish Volunteers did not rise as a body; only a few hundred men came out at the orders of Pearse and Connolly and fought for a week in Dublin; the executions of the leaders changed the political climate of the country, and eventually led to a second phase of fighting, but only after the victory of the Allies, in changed conditions which deprived rebellion in Ireland of much of its potential international significance.

Irish Times, 7 April 1966.

In April 1918 the British Government moved to impose conscription on Ireland. In Parliament the Irish Nationalist Party—moderate, constitutional and hitherto in support of the war effort—opposed this measure, described as "a declaration of war against Ireland", and on its being carried, left the House of Commons "to organize resistance in Ireland". A one-day general strike took place on 23 April. If the Easter Rising of 1916 had not already taken place, and if Clarke, Pearse, Connolly and other leaders had been alive and watching for their opportunity, they would surely have taken it at this time—a vastly better opportunity than they had at Easter 1916 when the only provocation they could muster was the famous "Castle document", a paper listing various aggressive measures allegedly intended by the British authorities, and almost certainly concocted by the rebels themselves. In 1918 the provocation was real and serious, and the country united against it. It is reasonable to assume that in these conditions the revolutionary leaders could have brought about insurrection, not of a few hundred men in Dublin, but of several thousand throughout most of the country. The consequences of such an event, in the conditions of 1918, would certainly have been far more serious than in 1916, and might conceivably have significantly diverted the course of world history.

First of all, Britain would have had to send troops in considerable numbers to Ireland. An Irish rebellion *with mass support*—which the 1916 Rising lacked, and which one in 1918 would probably have had—would have turned to a guerrilla and the effort to suppress a guerrilla always ties up disproportionately large numbers of troops. General Macready had forty battalions in Ireland in 1920; in 1918 forty battalions could not easily be spared. Whatever the number of troops that could be made available, however, the British Government would have had to adopt the same methods of terrorism as they did at the time of the Black and Tans; indeed the fewer the troops available for suppressing a rebellion, the greater the need for terrorism becomes.

If the British Government had had to use terrorist methods in Ireland in the spring and summer of 1918, it is overwhelmingly probable that there would have been mutinies and desertions among the Irish troops on the Western Front. These troops, by reason of their situation, would have had little sympathy with the original "anti-conscription" movement, but the application of terror, affecting their own towns and villages, would have speedily altered their mood—in much the same way as the execution of the 1916 leaders did change the mood of the Irish people.

What would have been the effect of wide-spread mutinies among the Irish in the British Army in the summer of 1918? Certainly there would have been little or no sympathy with the Irish *as Irish*: most English people habitually regarding the sufferings of the Irish as both imaginary and richly merited. But in 1918, uniform was more conspicuous than nationality, and the actions of a mutineer would speak louder than his accent. By 1918 mass-mutiny had taken Russia clean out of the war; the French Army had been seriously shaken by the mutinies of 1917; the morale of the British Army, like that of all the belligerents by now, was low; the senseless slaughter looked as if it would go on forever. These were conditions favourable to the spread of a mutiny started by Irish troops, throughout the British Army. A British mutiny would almost certainly have spread to the French Army, which had already been on the verge of mutiny, and it might—though this is more doubtful—have spread to the German Army. This would have been the pre-condition of "the European revolt of the proletariat" which Lenin expected. Never again, certainly, were the conditions for such a revolt to be so near fulfilment as they were in the first half of 1918. Explosive forces capable of destroying the older order—the rule of the classes and castes who brought the world to war in 1914—had accumulated by 1918. A spark was needed to set them off; that spark might have been provided by an Irish Rising in April 1918. In Connolly's metaphor, the "pin in the hands of a child" would then indeed have "pierced the heart of a giant"—the giant of the European capitalist order.

The premature character of the Rising—as it now appears in the light of the much more favourable conditions which developed later—may not, then, have been just the "misfortune of the Irish" as Lenin supposed. It may have been the misfortune of all who hoped, like Lenin, to see "the European revolt of the proletariat". It may also have been the misfortune of those who were to die in the Second World War.

Historical speculation is often called futile, because it is of its nature unverifiable. I think it may have its uses in this particular context because it may help us to understand what Connolly and Lenin hoped for and how what they hoped for might have been achieved. Speculation is not futile if it helps us to reconstruct the *possible* universe which great men strove to bring into being. We are only too liable to regard our being in the universe of "how it actually turned out" as conferring on us some kind of advantage in retrospect. The advantage is illusory; our knowledge of "how it actually turned out" is in reality a block to our comprehension of a historical figure in action; his primary characteristic is precisely the lack of that knowledge which distinguishes us. If he had that knowledge he would not act as he did; he might not act at all; he might despair and die.

If Pearse and Connolly could have had a foresight of the Ireland of 1966 would they have gone with that high courage to certain death? We should be wary against answering the question too quickly. It is all too easy to disparage the achievements of ordinary mortals by contrasting them with the visions of heroes. As Pearse read the noble words of the Proclamation of the Republic to those few rows of listless Dublin faces he must have been aware of the gap between the Ireland of his ideals and the Ireland of any plausible reality. Connolly, with the bitter experience behind him of the defeat of the Dublin workers in 1913, can hardly have underestimated the obstacles in the way of the fulfilment of his hopes. It may well be that what would most surprise Pearse and Connolly about 1966 would be the spectacle of Dublin as the capital of a sovereign state, with the soldiers in green doing honour to their memory. Both men, and Connolly especially, would have been pleased at the appearance of the Dubliners: healthier, better fed, better dressed, better housed.

A closer look would bring its inevitable disappointments. That sovereign state is not quite as good, or as sovereign, as it looks from O'Connell Street. The fact that Eastern Ulster still belongs to Britain would hardly come as a complete surprise—especially to Connolly who knew his Belfast. What would come as a painful surprise would be the ease with which this partition is accepted, the fact that nobody anywhere, by any means, is seriously trying to bring about the political reunification of the country. Their own official political heirs, having talked for years about "rousing the conscience of the world" about this problem, have now decided to give the world's conscience a rest. This change first became clearly defined on Ireland's entry into the United Nations, which created an embarrassing opportunity of *really* bringing Ireland's case to world attention. It had been quite safe to raise the problem at the Council of Europe, in Strasbourg, because one could be sure that nobody there would pay any attention. But a resolution in the General Assembly of the United Nations could run the risk of attracting support. The communist countries would support it, and so would a number of anti-colonialist countries. This would be very embarrassing. The Church would not like the communist support. The British would be seriously annoyed, not just amused as in Strasbourg. And the Americans would be much more annoyed, because the tabling of such a resolution would lead to pressure on the administration from Irish-American voters, and the consequent necessity either to offend an ally or alienate a group of voters—or do a little of both, by abstaining. Now those who claim political descent from Pearse and Connolly attach theoretical importance to the reunification of the country, but they attach practical importance to good relations with the Church, the British and the Americans. They had talked about presenting Ireland's case to the world. On entering the United Nations they had to put up or shut up, so they shut up. The antipartition movement was dropped, at first tacitly, later explicitly by Lemass.

Now in bourgeois, bread-and-butter terms, this makes perfectly sound sense. But in terms of the revolutionary tradition—the tradition of Tone and Pearse and Connolly—it constitutes betrayal. It was indeed the primary misfortune of the Irish State that from the very beginning its existence constituted a violation of the principles of its founders. This contradiction had, I believe, a strong, still unexplored, effect on the psychology of my generation, those who are roughly coeval with the State. The Irish nationalist tradition is a very strong one and permeates the personality of those who are brought up in it. From within this tradition the partition of the country seems not a wrong—which is an empty rhetorical expression—but just wrong, as a picture hung in a certain way is wrong, causing vague but persistent feelings of perplexity and dissatisfaction. For a time these feelings were allayed by our elders' intimations that the division of the country—or of the nation as we thought and said—was just a temporary hitch; the March of the Nation had been interrupted for a while, but would shortly be resumed. I doubt whether we fully believed this, but we found it a more comfortable concept than the alternative: the thought that Irish history, in the sense in which we had understood it, had come to an ignominious end. For a time also we could find comfort in a theory often found in association with the "interrupted march". This was the theory that a certain set of politicians had "sold the pass" but that another set of politicians, being true patriots, would recover the pass. In songs special emphasis would be given to lines like:

> Ere her faithless sons betrayed her ...

The supporters of the second, more patriotic, set of politicians had a spirited little song, casting scorn on the very existence of our truncated state:

> God save the Southern part of Ireland
> Three-quarters of a nation once again!

Those whose supporters sang this song were sincere and were patriots. Some had preferred to fight a civil war rather than accept partition; so much did this then matter, which no longer matters to anyone. When these politicians came into office they found that, whatever they might once have sung, three-quarters of a nation was what they were stuck with. So were we. But our dissatisfaction was deepened by the long-continued effort to keep alive the illusion that something was being done about the reunification of the country. Our paradoxical discovery, at the very moment of entering the United Nations, that Ireland was not going to be united had at least the merit of ending a period of pretence.

The Civil War itself is usually blamed for the blight of cynicism and disgust which settled on "free Ireland". The real cause is, I believe, the cause of the Civil War itself: the conflict between loyalties and realities, the intolerable knowledge that the Republic proclaimed by Pearse and Connolly was not attainable. Yeats wrote:

> Fail, and that history turns into rubbish,
> All that great past to a trouble of fools.

My generation grew into the chilling knowledge that we had failed, that our history had turned into rubbish, our past to "a trouble of fools". With this feeling it is not surprising that the constant public praise for the ideals of Pearse and Connolly should have produced in us bafflement rather than enthusiasm. We were bred to be patriotic, only to find that there was nothing to be patriotic about; we were republicans of a republic that wasn't there. Small wonder that Pearse's vision of an Ireland "not free merely but Gaelic as well" did not convince us. In Pearse's sense, Ireland was not free; why should it be Gaelic, which was a much more unlikely condition?

Pearse died, not for an island, or part of an island, but for a nation: an entity with a distinct culture, based on its own language. The nation for which he died never came to life. Culturally, Ireland remained a region, or rather two regions, of the English-speaking world. The distinguishing characteristic of the descendants of the Gaels was no longer language but religion, and the territorial division of the island between these people and the children of the Scottish settlers in Ulster was the slightly distorted expression of a long-standing spiritual division which men like Tone and Pearse lived and died to close. Such men do not live or die in vain, but the State established by their followers was itself the expression of the failure of their hopes. Pearse's hopes for a bilingual nation, spiritually nourished by the genius of the Irish language and by its ancient literature, were also doomed to disappointment, even so far as concerned the "three quarters of a nation". The Irish language survived among a few thousand people in the Western seaboard. Thousands of other people, from the rest of Ireland, did visit these Irish-speaking districts—as a direct result of the Gaelic revival movement—and many of them derived benefit from this. The movement was successful insofar as it enriched a considerable number of lives—and enriched also that perpetual and universal profiteer, the English language. But Irish people generally did not become bilingual, and English remained solidly established as the language both of the home and of business. Most Irish people read English, very often the English of those special editions of the English Sunday newspapers which, in order to placate the Irish censorship, replace their habitual and domestic columns of smut by articles about Lourdes and the Holy Father.

This curious phenomenon reflects the basic situation: that the Irish State is culturally part of Britain, distinguished from the rest of the archipelago so far mainly by its practice of a puritanical form of the Roman Catholic religion and by marked deference to ecclesiastical authority.

Irish became, officially, the first language of the country. It is the language of the Constitution in that, in the event of a conflict between the Irish text and the English, the Irish form shall prevail. This may be the only case in the world in which mistranslation has power to change the original meaning of the text translated, for the Irish form which "shall be deemed to prevail" is generally believed to be a translation from the English text which shall be deemed to be prevailed over in the event of its having been mistranslated. The greatest tragedy about the creation of a State on the basis of ideals impossible to attain was the release sought through national fantasy. When the answer to Pearse's "not free merely but Gaelic as well" turned out to be "75 per cent. free and 0.6 per cent. Gaelic" it proved impossible for Pearse's followers either to accept these figures or to alter the realities they represent. A desperate game of let's pretend followed: Ireland *is* Gaelic—is not Gaelic the first official language? Ireland *is* free—does not the Constitution declare that the national territory consists of the whole island and its territorial seas? The realistic, as distinct from the fantastic, provisions of the Constitution are in force "pending the reintegration of the national territory". Such reintegration, always unlikely, is made much more unlikely by the existence of a Constitution enacted by a small majority of the Catholic three-quarters of a nation, recognizing "the special position" of the Catholic Church, couched in language inspired by Catholic theology and purporting to bind the Protestant majority in Northern Ireland who were never consulted about the matter at all.

These propositions struck an answering chord in the bosom of the Irish lunatic ... Gaelic! *Bás do'n Bhéarla* is chalked on a wall: *death to the English language!* Free! *"Six divisions, sixty minutes, six counties"* read a poster. And a few who were not lunatics, but brave and logical young men went to their death for Pearse's Republic, in whose attainability they had been allowed and even encouraged to believe. They saw clearly that the national territory was not being integrated by semantic exercises; they tried force, sanctioned as they believed by the example of Pearse and Connolly, and they died for the fantasy of a United Ireland at the hands of one or other of the governments which rule the Ireland of reality. The Government in Dublin continued to propagate the fantasy while punishing those who acted on it.

The strange thing is that the politicians who acted in this way were not hypocrites. There was even in their proceedings a desperate kind of honesty. They had proved their genuine devotion to the ideals of Pearse and Connolly by risking their lives for them and they were determined never to betray them. The effort not to betray ideals which were unattainable led not merely them, but most of the rest of us with them, into impossible positions. The present writer blushes to recall that at one time he devoted a considerable part of his professional activity, as a member of the Department of External Affairs, to what was known as "anti-partition". The only positive result of this activity, as far as I was concerned, was that it led me to discover the cavernous inanities of "anti-partition" and of Government propaganda generally. Nominally, the object of this activity was to convince others—Ulstermen, Englishmen, Americans, and even more bemused persons of other nationalities—of the propriety and expedience of reuniting Ireland. Actually the object was to console ourselves for the rubbish that our history had turned into. We consoled ourselves by reiterating, to our own satisfaction, the classic arguments for a free and united Ireland and by demonstrating, likewise to our own satisfaction, the perfidy of our enemies. Even more important, we consoled ourselves by the very fact of our activity, with the illusion that we were doing something to repair the irreparable. The illusory nature of our activity came home to me when I suggested that it might not be a good idea to treat Ulstermen to exactly the same propaganda as Americans were being given. I was quickly and firmly given to understand that the correct "statement of the case" had been made once and for all in a repulsive and expensive pamphlet called *Ireland's Right to Unity*—and that all that was required was to get this artifact into as many hands as possible throughout the world. The document was in fact written by an old Sinn Feiner for other old Sinn Feiners; it made them feel good and they did not trouble to imagine what effect it might have on its hypothetical foreign readers. I once brought this set of phenomena to the attention of Professor C. Northcote Parkinson, who then framed the following Law:

Propaganda begins, and ends, at home.

What I did not realize at the time—possibly because it would not have been comfortable to realize it—was that all this pseudo-activity had a practical, and somewhat sinister function. It enabled the State to punish with a good conscience, the young men in the Irish Republican Army. Partition must be ended certainly but there was a right and a wrong way to end partition. The wrong way was by raiding barracks in Ulster. The right way was by sending bundles of booklets to Bootle.

To such a sorry state had Pearse's Republic dwindled by the 1950's. This was the result, not of the wickedness or incompetence of a particular set of men, but of two sets of pressures—the pressures of reality itself, and those resulting from the inability of idealists to accept that reality. Functionally the pseudo-activity of "anti-partition" helped to deaden the pain of the dawning of reality. That grey and humdrum dawn has now arrived.

"Formerly I considered the separation of Ireland from England impossible", wrote Marx to Engels in 1867. "I now consider it inevitable, although after the separation may come federation." In its broad lines what Marx foresaw has come about. Not only has Mr. Lemass's Government left the solution of partition to the day when Captain O'Neill and his followers embrace Mr. De Valera's Constitution—an event likely to occur simultaneously with the Conversion of the Jews—but this Government has also proposed that the three-quarters of a nation which it controls should be treated as part of the United Kingdom for trading purposes.

In Africa the funeral ceremonies of a Chief may be held many years after his death. In Dublin this year, were held the funeral ceremonies of the Republic proclaimed fifty years ago.

The national objective of Pearse and Connolly is now finally, and necessarily, buried. The cultural objective of Pearse, a fully bilingual Ireland, is being tacitly abandoned. Have the social objectives of James Connolly, or even those of Pearse, fared any better? At first sight the answer seems to be an emphatic no. Connolly was a revolutionary socialist, who won Lenin's approval, and who would have approved Lenin's revolution. The Republic Connolly wanted was a Workers'

Republic, in which the workers of Belfast would have played an important part. As things have turned out, both parts of Ireland are firmly in bourgeois control, and no significant labour movement has emerged. The *Irish Independent*—which, after the Easter Rising, continued to call for more executions until it got Connolly—is still the main organ of the Catholic bourgeoisie and still the most popular newspaper in that part of the country which this year commemorates the Easter Rising. Naturally, it ran a commemoration supplement. The Labour Party in this three-quarters-of-a-nation has been dominated for years by dismal poltroons, on the lines of O'Casey's Uncle Payther. Connolly is venerated as a martyr, and labour leaders sometimes pay homage to his ideals, without specifying what these ideals were, and always compensating for the reference by some allusion establishing the speaker's religious orthodoxy, and if possible Connolly's also. The Northern Ireland Labour Party is even more remote from Connolly, as it is a respectable offshoot of the respectable British Labour Party whose leaders, like the respectable labour leaders of Connolly's own time, are prepared to support imperialist wars provided that they are allowed to call them by some other name.

Ireland has progressed, it is true, both economically and socially since 1916; in fifty years it would be odd and depressing if it had not. Increased prosperity has been due primarily to improved living standards in Europe generally and secondarily, in recent years, to the rise of a sort of meritocracy, of able administrators both in the State services and in public and private concerns. For this, as well as for the establishment and maintenance of solid conventions of political democracy (with some partial exceptions in Northern Ireland), and for a high level of financial integrity in the conduct of public affairs, Irish people have a good deal to be thankful for, as compared with most other people in the world. And in fairness it must be admitted that much of the credit for these real achievements belongs to those very politicians whose operations in the realms of fantasy I discussed earlier.

Yet much remains to be done, as politicians are in the habit of saying when compelled to allude to the failures and disasters of their period in office. The greatest failure, which would have dismayed Pearse and Connolly equally, was the long failure to reform the Irish educational system. "The education system here", wrote Pearse, "was designed by our masters in order to make us willing, or at least manageable, slaves." The system referred to by Pearse long remained in all essentials intact, as the educational system of a Republic which honoured Pearse's memory and had to forget what he said. The reason for this is that "our masters", who designed the system, comprised not only the British ruling class—of whom Pearse was thinking—but also the Irish Bishops, who in such matters long remained our masters. This system placed primary education in the control of school managers who, as far as concerns the needs of most of the population, are the Catholic clergy. A recent official report, *Investment in Education*, disclosed that about one-third of primary school leavers (at age fourteen) "left full-time education"; of these, 28 per cent. passed the primary certificate, 10 per cent. were absent, 8 per cent. failed and of the remainder there was no trace. Thus more than half these children left without having reached, in the language of the report, "what is considered a minimum level of education". "This",—as Senator Owen Sheehy-Skeffington, the most vocal and courageous critic of the system, has pointed out—"is what causes so many of our young Irishmen and women to go ill-equipped to England and to be employed there, all too often, as 'hewers of wood and drawers of water'."

The most pathetic feature of this system is that its worst victims are its stoutest defenders. In a newspaper a correspondent challenges anyone to deny that "all the small schools of rural Ireland have poured forth the very best scholars". And in the same letter, shocked by Senator Skeffington's temerity in answering back to a Bishop, this correspondent makes the following pronouncement: "The Senator's talk on education, his unscrupulous expressions and vile outbursts on such a distinguished Churchman does (*sic*) nothing as far as I can see but make a mockery of education." It is visible that somebody has made a mockery of education, but it is simpler to assume that the mockery has been made by the Bishops, who had control over the educational system, rather than by Senator Skeffington, who had no such control.

We have no cause, in this anniversary year, for self-congratulation. But we should not abandon ourselves either to that cynicism which is the obverse of our hypocrisy. Nor should we take refuge, as some are now doing, in blaming "the old men" for what has gone wrong. Much of what went wrong was inevitable, like the division of the country. For the rest we are all responsible, in the degree to which we co-operated in nonsense, or failed to expose it, or quietly acquiesced in the injustice being systematically practised against the children of the poor in Ireland. Civil Servants like myself, for example, by taking part in the fantastic activities of "anti-partition" incurred their share of the responsibility; so did the Civil Servants who took part in the parallel activities of a Department of Education whose main function was to ensure that the control of education stayed out of its hands. The clergy at large, especially but not exclusively the Catholic clergy, have their share of the

responsibility, and members of the Hierarchy have a share in proportion to their power—and in a few notorious cases, also in proportion to
their truculence and bombast. And the heaviest share of all is borne by
those laymen, both politicians and voters, in whom the very thought of
a hypothetical clerical rebuke induced a chronic mental cringe.

The action of 1916 was not a programme: it was a challenge, to conscience and to courage. The fact that the national, cultural and social
objectives which Pearse and Connolly had in mind have not proved attainable in Ireland does not enable us to evade the challenge of their
action, or of their words. Pearse's words on education still reverberate
in the current controversies and seem at last to be beginning to have
practical effect. There were also for a while signs that the government
which claims descent from Pearse and Connolly had not entirely forgotten that Connolly regarded the Easter Rising not just as an Irish rising against England but as a blow against capitalist imperialism—the
idea of the "pin in the hands of a child". Nothing very dramatic along
these lines could be expected from today's bourgeois republic but, for
a time, there appeared to be a realization that it would not be seemly for
the heirs of Connolly simply to follow blindly, at the United Nations,
the directives of that power which has inherited Britain's role as the
centre of capitalist imperialism, with its systems of indirect rule in Latin
America, South-East Asia and parts of Africa, and its counter-revolutionary policies directed against the People's Republic of China. For a
time, therefore—from 1957 to 1960—Ireland's representatives—or
three-quarters representatives—strove to maintain an independent
stance at the United Nations in the annual vote about continuing to seat
Chiang Kai-Shek's delegation as representing China: that is always the
substance; the forms vary according to expediency. For a few years the
Irish Delegation held out on this issue, and some related issues, declining the State Department "whip". The realities of life at the United
Nations are such that even this modest display of independence earned
Ireland considerable respect in the General Assembly. It even seemed
possible at one stage that Ireland might have something distinct and
useful to say in relation to revolution in the under-developed world, and
the attitude of the advanced world towards revolution. These hopes
were to fade. In 1961, when the late Adlai Stevenson produced a new
procedural device for keeping Chiang Kai-Shek in the seat, the Irish
Government—which had tied itself into semantic knots in the endeav-
our to defend its "China policy" against clerical and other pressure at
home—thankfully availed itself of the Stevenson gimmick in order to
jettison its "China policy"; shortly afterwards, though not immediately,

the rest of the independent line was jettisoned. For practical purposes, Ireland now became a safe Western vote: that is to say a vote on which the rulers of the advanced, capitalist countries could count, in all important questions, for the support of policies deemed appropriate in the defence of their international interests. (When they are split, as at Suez, the safe votes go to the strongest, the USA.) This transition was unnoticed at home, partly because the new policy continued to be expressed in the language of the old one—very much in the spirit of the Constitution of 1937—and partly because Irish public opinion, like public opinion in other countries, is hopelessly confused about the significance of UN proceedings. But for persons in the habit of following these proceedings attentively the undramatic but perceptible change in Ireland's voting pattern from 1961 on had a chilling significance, finally confirmed when in 1965 the one-time "independent" voted, along with the other satellites, for the continued exclusion of the government of the people of China from China's seat and the continuance in that seat of a delegation representative of American policy in Asia. The significance of this realignment was that, as far as official foreign policy was concerned, the last embers of the 1916 spirit had expired.

It is not, however, primarily a question of official policy; there was nothing official about the Easter Rising, from any point of view an entirely unauthorized undertaking. Connolly's writings speak not to Governments but to men and women, Irish and other. There is no need to lose oneself in speculations about what Connolly would have done had he lived. We need not believe those Communist writers who insist that Connolly would have followed the Party line from NEP to the rift with China, welcoming on the way the purges, the pact with Hitler, and the crushing of the Hungarian revolt. We need not believe, either, those anti-Communists who suggest that Connolly, delighted with the peaceful liquidation of the Western forms of imperialism, would have seen with dismay the appearance of a far more terrible form of imperialism rising from the ashes of the Revolution Betrayed. We have no need of hypothetical Connollies, tailored to the requirements of someone's propaganda. We have Connolly's writings, and the record of his acts. The sense of these is the sense of the revolutionary movements in the underdeveloped world today. His writings reflect not only immense strength of character but also high intelligence; these are not the qualities that are required to swallow the American, and American-satellite, line on these revolutionary movements—that they are "master-minded" from Moscow or Peking, that those who oppose them are the real anti-imperialists etc. From Connolly's writings it is not easy to imagine him accepting the thesis that the armed Vietnamese peasants are the imperialists and that the American marines, who are killing them and poisoning the rice-fields around them, are saving Vietnam from imperialism. Nor need we suppose that he would be as easily swayed as are his supposed heirs by the thought that the Vietnamese guerrillas, being either communists or Buddhists or both, quite possibly do not go to Mass.

It is quite proper and fitting that Dublin should have held commemoration in 1966; some Dubliners will have reflected, during the commemoration, on such themes as these, and on how the spirit of Easter 1916 may be at work in the wide world around them.

19

THE HOMER WATT LECTURE

I

It is hardly probable that there will be many people at the P.E.N. Congress who warmly support Dante as a Ghibelline, but are indifferent to the *Divine Comedy*; who admire Milton's work as Cromwell's Latin Secretary, but care nothing for *Paradise Lost*; who prefer to think of Tolstoy as the champion of the Dukhobors, rather than as the author of *War and Peace*; who are interested in Yeats not as a lyric poet, but as the theoretician of the Irish Blueshirts.

It follows that if the members of the congress are content to discuss the question on the level on which it is posed they *must* answer it as follows: "We read the classics not because their authors took a stand in a contemporary conflict, but rather because they illuminate the spirit of man."

The question is designed to elicit that answer, and that only; though presented as an investigatory question it is in fact a rhetorical one. Indeed the whole definition of the topic is rhetorical beginning with its title, "The Writer as Public Figure." For most 20th-century intellectuals the idea of a "public figure" is distasteful, associated with pomposity and falsity. Victor Hugo could see himself with entire approbation as a

The Homer Watt Lecture at New York University was delivered by Conor on 19 May 1966. A version of it was published in *Book Week*, 12 June 1966. The version published here is the one that Conor originally submitted to *Book Week*, which, for reasons of space, shortened it.

public man, but no important writer since his day has been able to accept such a role without at least some degree of irony and even disgust. Yeats could be half-indulgent, half-mocking to himself in his Senatorial capacity:

> A sixty-year-old smiling public man.

For a later generation, that of Auden, the mockery had sharpened:

> Private faces in public places
> Are wiser and nicer
> Than public faces in private places.

Nothing that has happened since then has taken the edge off these words. "The Writer as Public Figure," therefore, is a title calculated to evoke a concern, which the following definition fans into alarm. The Dr. Jekyll of the congress's general theme, "the writer as independent spirit," is here shown in danger of turning into Mr. Hyde, "the writer as public figure." On the advice of those equivocal apparitions, Simple Humanitarianism and Rigorous Ideology, the writer "dons"—ominous hieratic words—a *persona*. This fateful action tempts him to forget his true love, Creative Impulse. He is now fit for anything. He may emerge as a Ghibelline, a Roundhead, a Dukhobor, a Blueshirt, or a person who rejects an invitation to a garden-party at the White House.

I suspect that the last avatar might prove the most disturbing of all, for it seems to me that the topic is defined in such a way as to recommend to the congress the following proposition: Writers should not take stands in contemporary conflicts—such as the war in Viet Nam—because if they do, their true creative impulse may suffer, and they may neglect their proper work of illuminating the spirit of man.

For some reason this proposition calls to mind Hilaire Belloc's lines about the Llama:

> The Llama is a woolly sort of fleecy, hairy goat
> With an indolent expression and an undulating throat
> Like an unsuccessful literary man.

Perhaps it is that those literary men who will have the least difficulty in assenting to the proposition implied in the P.E.N. program are those who most resemble Belloc's Llama, obviously not a combative quadruped. But those who have in fact most illuminated the human spirit have not been of this stamp. On the contrary, they have had a high propensity—as we shall see later—to take stands in contemporary conflicts. Julian Benda suggested that this was a novel phenomenon and said that generally in the past "the men of thought or the honest men remained strangers to political passions." In justifying this generalization, Benda gave politics as narrow, and passions as pejorative, a meaning as possible. His aphorism, however, is remembered after his qualifications are forgotten and serves the ends of those who, for one reason or another, wish to save the writer from his politics. The writer, not necessarily for the same ends, often seems to concur, as Yeats so often did, in the aftermath of some exhaustive political bout:

> I never bade you go
> To Moscow or to Rome
> Renounce that drudgery
> Call the Muses home.

It cannot be claimed, however, that Yeats was "a stranger to political passions"—even in Benda's pejorative sense—nor can it be claimed, however repugnant many of us may find some of Yeat's political involvements, that he was not a man of thought or an honest man. This in itself does not shake Benda's thesis: his point was that a rot had set in at the end of the last century, and that writers who in the past had been "strangers to political passions" were today liable to be distracted or debauched by them. This thesis is obviously attractive to those who like to evoke, in order to deprecate, the image of The Writer as a Public Figure.

Those who are thus attracted are not necessarily those who would have attracted Benda. Sir Denis Brogan, for example, praised the magazine *Encounter* for its struggle against *la trahison des clercs*—Benda's title, covering his attack on writers of talent who made themselves spokesmen and propagandists for political causes. Readers of this article, invoking Benda's name to praise *Encounter*, may have been left with the impression that Benda, Sir Denis, and *Encounter* were all, in the same sense, enemies of political commitment. Now Benda was a liberal—which is after all also a political designation—and his passionate and brilliant attack on Barrès, Maurras, and the French right-wing intellectuals generally was, among other things, "a stand in a contemporary conflict." But he made it clear at the same time that he was equally prepared to defend the liberal position against attacks from the left, if these came in equal force, which they did not at the time and place in which he was writing—France in the late '20s. Liberals of this kind tend to be more popular in retrospect than they are during the "contemporary conflicts" into which they are drawn. The liberalism of the magazine *Encounter* and of Sir Denis Brogan has been of a different kind, more congenial to the prevailing power structures. Indeed, the magazine *Encounter* has had such a central position in the intellectual life of the English-speaking world in the second half of the 20th century, and such a mediating role between the writer and the capitalist power structure that it deserves, in the present context, our particular attention. *Encounter* publicly disclaimed having a political line but in fact it had one—the divergence here between declaration and practice would scarcely have won Benda's approval.

Its political line—unmistakeably reflected in its successive issues, especially the earlier ones—was mainly that of combating left-wing influence, especially Communist influence, in intellectual circles. An important part of this line was the inculcation of uniformly favorable attitudes in Britain towards American policies and practices. Writers in Britain and America were encouraged thereby to accommodate themselves and their readers to the demands of the power structure in their countries. More important even than that, writers living under the subordinate power structure, Britain, were encouraged to accommodate themselves and their readers to the demands of the superior power structure, that of the United States. Thus an awkward transition was skillfully bridged. I referred to some of these phenomena in an article on *Encounter* in the *New Statesman* about two years ago. Since then some new light has been shed on the subject by the *New York Times*. "The CIA," according to the *New York Times*, "has supported anti-communist but liberal organizations such as the Congress for Cultural Freedom and some of their newspapers and magazines. *Encounter* magazine was for a long time—though it is not now—one of the indirect beneficiaries of CIA funds." (April 27, 1966) A number of young British writers of moderate talent and adequate ambition co-operated actively in this anti-Communist but liberal program. Some of these were progressive tories; more were moderate socialists, on the right wing of the British Labor Party. If, today, that Party, in the throes of its success, seems too largely anaesthetized to issues on which its traditions should make it sensitive—such as Viet Nam—this is due, not entirely to humdrum economic motives, relevant though these are, but also to an effective cultural and political penetration, of which *Encounter* was the spearhead. Similar penetrations took place elsewhere—for example in France, through *Encounter*'s sister, *Preuves*, though with less success—and in the underdeveloped countries and among minority groups. The vocal agents of this penetration are not important in themselves, as writers: collectively they have importance, as belonging to that great category which President Eisenhower—a neglected stylist—defined: "the men of thoughtful mien."

In a skillfully-executed politico-cultural operation of the *Encounter* type, the writing specifically required by the power structure was done by people who, as writers, were of the third or fourth rank but who were, as the Belgians used to say about Moise Tshombe, *compréhensifs*, that is, they could take a hint. One or two of them were also highly competent in public relations. But the beauty of the operation, in every sense, was that other writers of the first rank, who had no interest at all in serving the power structure, were induced to do so unwittingly. Over the years the magazine, shrewdly edited, adequately financed and efficiently distributed, attracted many writers who hardly noticed, or did not think it important, that this forum was not quite an open forum, that its political acoustics were a little odd, that the sonorities at the Eastern end were of a quite different character from the western ones. Thus writers of high achievement and complete integrity were led unconsciously to validate, through their collaboration, the more purposeful activities of lesser writers who in turn were engaged in a sustained and consistent political activity in the interests—and as it now appears at the expense—of the power structure in Washington. It is of course quite possible to claim that, for the survival of all that is best in our civilization, the writer *ought* to serve these interests. But that is not the claim that is made by Sir Denis Brogan or—in different but similar contexts—by the neo-liberals who frame certain documents for consideration by bodies like the Congress for Cultural Freedom and International P.E.N. The claim actually made in these quarters is that the writer should beware of involvement in politics. Given the actual political commitment of *Encounter*, and its associated bodies, this can only be interpreted as advice, coming ultimately from the Western power structure, to the writer to keep out of *left-wing* politics. And, of course, conservatives have long used "politics" in this restrictive and contemptuous sense, as the words of *God Save the King* remind us.

The words of the hymn *Ev'rybody talks about Heaven ain't goin' there* are clearly sound doctrine. I suggest that it is equally sound to assume that everybody who advises the writer to keep out of politics ain't necessarily keeping out of politics himself. Indeed such people are often much more political—in the sense of pursuing political ends by the most effective means, including ruses—than are those writers whom they chide for political words, actions, and gestures.

II

All power is exercised through words: even the crassest form of military power depends on the word of command. The writer—he who has power over the written word—is therefore potentially a threat to the lines of communication of political, social, religious, and economic power. Sometimes this has been acutely felt—as in 18th-century France, 19th-century Russia, the Communist world, South Africa, and some underdeveloped countries—Nigeria and Ghana. Sometimes it is only fitfully and dimly apprehended, as in the western world at present. And writers themselves have responded in very different ways to the existence of this challenge or opportunity. Some rejected it altogether, turning their backs contemptuously on the world of politics and power. Despite the suggestion of Benda and his followers, this group is both relatively small and relatively novel. Before the 19th century even those writers, such as Montaigne and Goethe, who appear most indifferent to power, had usually served it in some fashion. The genuinely apolitical writer—of whom Mallarmé is perhaps the purest example—is a modern and Western phenomenon. At the opposite extreme, the worshippers of power are also a small and modern group—Nietzsche and the political Nietzscheans—Barrès, Maurras—of whom Benda complained. Another small and modern group might be called the dreaders—those in whom the thought and spectacle of power induces a mixture of repulsion and fascination—Buechner, Kafka, and Orwell.

Much larger and very much more ancient is the broad category of those who have been positively interested in politics and power, either practically or imaginatively or both. This includes the thin but long and distinguished line of the "wielders"—those supreme political leaders who have also been masters of the written word—from Caesar to de Gaulle and Mao Tse-tung. A larger group, also represented in many ages is that of the servants and sharers, those writers who have been actively involved in political service or struggle: this line goes from Thucydides to André Malraux; it includes Cicero, Dante, Machiavelli, Milton, and Swift. Then there is the group of students and analysts— some of whom were also servants and sharers, for these groupings are not exclusive: Thucydides again, Tacitus, Machiavelli, Hobbes, Burke, Marx, Balzac, Tocqueville. There are the tappers—those who drew on the politics of power for imaginative material: Shakespeare, Pushkin, Yeats, Proust. But the largest and most ancient of all is the great group of the preceptors and correctors—those who in all ages have sought to instruct and admonish the wielders of power—either generally, or in particular, or aiming at the particular through the general—and also to instruct and admonish the community about the nature and limitations of power. It is not enough to say that this function is very ancient, for it lies at the very roots of our Judaeo-Hellenic culture, and of other cultures also. It was a function of the Hebrew prophets, and of the

Greek dramatists: of Socrates and Plato, of the Chinese sages and Church fathers. Among later writers who exercised it were Bunyan, Pascal, Swift, Voltaire, Rousseau, Byron, Shelley, Blake, Hugo, Marx and Engels, Dickens, Dostoevsky, Ibsen, Gorki; in our own time Pasternak, Twardowski, Milosz, Orwell, Sartre, Richard Wright, James Baldwin, Frantz Fanon.

It is hardly legitimate, when one considers the earlier names on those lists to claim that the later names have deviated from something we are to regard as "the true function" of the artist. It is true—and platitudinous—that the specific controversies in which ancient writers were involved no longer seem very relevant to us. But the intellectual, imaginative, and moral energy which impelled them into these controversies are not irrelevant to us. Even the direct fruits of such controversies are often more relevant than we assume. The blow which Pascal struck in the *Provincial Letters* is not a musty episode in a forgotten quarrel: it is a living encouragement to all men everywhere who have to struggle against entrenched intellectual dishonesty now. Nor do energies thus expended by these men represent time lost to their proper creative activity—hours which they ought to have spent in a back room piling up more linage of immortal verse. On the contrary, the shock of struggle reverberates in their work itself and adds to its power. Yeats himself might have gone the way of the Rhymers Club—as once looked possible—had he not been drawn into the passions and disillusions of Irish politics.

Those who today advocate political quietism for the contemporary Western writer tend to do so by narrowing the separate concepts of "writers" and of "politics" so as to enlarge the gap between them. The writer is contracted into the "pure artist"—much purer than most writers, except for the symbolists and post-symbolists, have actually been. "Politics" in turn is narrowed, as Benda tends to narrow it, into the slavish following of a party line. If these contractions are accepted, the view that "the writer cannot be a politician" follows of itself. But one may reasonably refuse to accept these contractions. A more normal, and less mystical, idea of the writer would be that of a person who uses the written word with unusual skill and impact—whether as novelist, poet, historian, dramatist, journalist, or otherwise. And a more normal definition of politics would embrace all forms of political activity from extreme left to extreme right, from the maverick to the sound party man. And on the definitions it becomes clear that it is not only absurd but dangerous to rule that writers should keep out of politics.

It is dangerous because the widespread acceptance of such a rule would mean that writers possessed of autonomy, integrity, and freedom to choose would keep out of politics, which would thereby be left the exclusive province of the hacks, subsidized by the controllers of the power structure. Worse still, within the "anti-Communist but liberal" culture for which the Western power structure has provided material support, the apolitical writers would in fact be playing an unconscious, and therefore inappropriate political role—that of liberal decoy-ducks—in a system of which the business end was subsidized anti-Communism. To that condition doctrines of political quietism have lulled certain gifted writers in our day.

The point is not, of course, that writers are always right, or even left, in politics. The political views of the greatest poet of this century might be called, at best, eccentric. The point is that if writers as a class are in-duced to believe that politics is not their business—and many of them were so induced in the 1950s and after—the political life of the commu-nity generally is impoverished and becomes more easily depraved. Concentrated, institutional power—in politics, in the army, in the econ-omy—needs the challenge and stimulus and correction of criticism. It may be uninformed criticism, as power usually claims, but then there is the possibility of informing it. The community-at-large also needs to be enlightened about the nature and workings of the power structure and the implication of its politics. This can be best accomplished by full dis-cussion in which uncowed and unbought persons participate. All these are commonplace of liberalism. They are not however compatible with that "anti-Communist but liberal" position which warns the writer against political involvement. For that advice, if taken, would mean the withdrawal from the political process of those who are by definition best qualified to contribute to free discussion: the most articulate among the most intelligent.

The tendency in recent years has been for writers to awaken from their apolitical catalepsy. The read-ins and teach-ins are I think a sign of returning political health, to be welcomed even irrespective of their immediate content, vital though that is. These things have a wider meaning. They mean that modern minds are recapturing an old knowl-edge—that power is too important to be left to the specialists in power, that writers, in virtue of their character and skill, and of the most an-cient and justly honored traditions of their craft, belong in politics, not only as citizens, but as profession.

20

ENCOUNTER RETORTS

The "Column" section of the August *Encounter* is mainly devoted to an attack on "the Joe McCarthy of politico-cultural criticism"—myself—for an article which appeared in this journal three years ago, and for a lecture I gave to the alumni of New York University last May (which was reprinted in part in the *Washington Post*). The personal vituperation which fills so much of the section was to be expected, and most of it may be ignored. It includes, however, one falsification of fact which—since the writer (signing himself "R") elaborates it with much sarcasm and portentousness—might as well be demolished here. "R" asserts that "he once described his own political activities on behalf of the United Nations in Katanga as those of 'a Machiavelli of Peace'." I never described my own activities in Katanga or elsewhere in these or similar terms: the passage from *To Katanga and Back* on which "R" presumably relies relates to Hammarskjold.

In the *New Statesman* article, I presented the view that *Encounter*, while claiming to have no "line" has in fact consistently followed an anti-communist line, in close accord with the foreign policy of the United States. That article was published at a time when *Encounter* was still subsidised by the Congress for Cultural Freedom. The contentions

This essay was set in type for publication in the *New Statesman* during the summer of 1966, but was subsequently killed under threat of a libel action by the editors of *Encounter*. Their specific objection was to the last paragraph which quotes the *New York Times*. The piece was written in reply to the *Encounter* piece that resulted in Conor's entering a libel action against *Encounter*, which resulted in a printed apology, a donation to a designated charity, and costs. Source: O'Brien Papers, University College, Dublin.

in it rested, not on any assertion that the magazine was indirectly financed by the CIA—for no such assertion had then been made—but on the observation that its political articles were heavily weighted against the Soviet Union and communism, and that its sensitivity to acts of oppression was a specific sensitivity to communist acts of oppression.

In the lecture this year I indicated that I found credible—and consistent with the phenomena which I had observed earlier—a statement which appeared in the *New York Times* last April about *Encounter* and the CIA. The *Encounter* columnist expresses at length his indignation about this. He does not, however, find room to quote the "passing sentence", as he calls it, in which the *New York Times* team of correspondents, examining the activities of the American Central Intelligence Agency, referred to *Encounter*. The London *Times* omitted this sentence from its reprint of the *New York Times* article: "R" finds this omission "significant" and I agree with him. The position therefore now is that the British public, which is currently being invited by *Encounter* to form a strong opinion about this matter, is not informed either by the *Times* or by *Encounter* or—so far as I know—by other organs of its own press, of what the *New York Times* actually said. If the matter is important—as *Encounter* seems to believe and as I believe myself—it is in the public interest that this deficiency should be remedied.

The third *New York Times* CIA article (28 April 1966), having stated that the CIA was "said to be behind the efforts of several foundations that sponsor the travel of social scientists in the communist world," and had supported "through similar channels ... anti-communist but liberal organisations of intellectuals such as the Congress for Cultural Freedom and some of their newspapers and magazines," went on to say—and this is the "passing sentence":

> *Encounter* magazine, a well-known anticommunist intellectual monthly with editions in Spanish and German as well as in English, was for a long time —though it is not now—one of the indirect beneficiaries of CIA funds through arrangements that have never been publicly explained.

The text is from the international edition of the paper.

Denials followed. Four eminent American intellectuals—J.K. Galbraith, George Kennan, Robert Oppenheimer and Arthur Schlesinger —wrote to affirm *inter alia* that "an examination of the record of the Congress, its magazines and its other activities will, we believe, convince the most sceptical that the Congress has had no loyalty except an unswerving commitment to cultural freedom." The *New York Times* printed this letter without comment under the heading "Cultural

Freedom Congress Praised" (International Edition, 9 May). On the following day the *Encounter* letter appeared—a long one signed by Stephen Spender, Melvin J. Lasky and Irving Kristol and datelined "New York, May 9". This letter stated that *Encounter*'s small annual publishing deficit was, until two years ago, met by the Congress for Cultural Freedom in Paris; that the Congress funds were derived from various foundations, all of which were "publicly listed in the official directories, with their officers duly named, their activities described"; and that the signatories "knew of no 'indirect' benefactions". It inquired whether the *New York Times* wanted "the reader to infer that the editorial content or that the past or present editors of *Encounter* were in any way influenced by the CIA." After a tribute to the integrity of those connected with *Encounter*, the signatories pointed out a factual error—the incorrect assertion about German and Spanish editions—and, in the international edition of the paper a serious typographical error (the nature of which they did not specify) and a garbling of two sentences "which makes your report sound even more suggestive than it was." They concluded by pointing out that *Encounter* is now financed by Halmsworth's *Mirror* group, and they again emphasised its independence.

To this is appended the following editorial note, here reproduced in full. "The *New York Times*, in mentioning *Encounter*, did not say or intend to suggest that the editors of the magazine knew of any indirect benefactions or that its contributors had ever been propagandists for the CIA. On the contrary, *Encounter* is known as a distinguished international opinion."

It will be observed that this is not a retraction: "R" calls it a repudiation of the damaging implications of the original story. This we may allow, not without some perplexity. If we combine the central elements of the original story—which have not been withdrawn—with the subsequent editorial clarifications, the official position of the *New York Times* appears to be the following: *Encounter* is a distinguished international anti-communist journal of independent opinion, which was for a long time—but is not now—an indirect beneficiary of CIA funds, without this, however, carrying any implication that the editors knew of such benefactions or that its contributors had ever been propagandists for the CIA. If this description were to be carried on *Encounter*'s masthead, I for one would not feel it necessary to discuss the matter further.

21

Burke, Marx, and History

The spectre haunting Europe in *The Communist Manifesto* (1848), and haunting the world today, walks for the first time in the pages of Burke:

> Out of the tomb of the murdered monarchy in France has arisen a vast, tremendous, unformed spectre, in a far more terrifick guise than any which ever yet have overpowered the imagination, and subdued the fortitude of man. Going straight forward to its end, unappalled by peril, unchecked by remorse, despising all common maxims and all common means, that hideous phantom overpowered those who could not believe it was possible she could at all exist except on the principles, which habit rather than nature had persuaded them were necessary to their own particular welfare, and to their own ordinary modes of action (*Letters on a Regicide Peace*, 1796).

I do not know whether Marx was familiar with this passage; he did know some of Burke's writings and quotes from them, both in his despatches to the *New York Daily Tribune* and in *Capital*. In one of his *Daily Tribune* despatches in which he finds a quotation from Burke useful to buttress an argument, he calls Burke "the man whom both Parties in England consider to be the model of the British Statesman" (*New York Daily Tribune*, December 1855). In *Capital* he calls him "the celebrated sophist and sycophant" (*Werke*, Berlin ed. 23, p. 34) and also "the execrable political cant-monger Edmund Burke" (*Werke*, 23, p. 788).

This was a lecture given at the University of Chicago, 1 December 1966. Source: O'Brien Papers, New York University Archives.

There is of course no contradiction. From Marx's point of view it was inevitable that the man regarded by both parties in England as the model of a British statesman should be a sophist, sycophant and cantmonger. He concedes to Burke, however, "one thing" which distinguishes him from his successors—talent. We know Marx to have been familiar with Burke's *Letter to a Noble Lord* (1796) which he quotes in *Lord John Russell* (1855) and refers to in *Capital*. To Burke's writings on the French Revolution, Marx refers only in general terms, saying that "in the pay of English oligarchy Burke played the Romantic against the French Revolution just as, when in the pay of the North-American colonies at the beginning of the American troubles, he played the Liberal". It is a harsh interpretation, and in considerable part a misleading one, but it is clearly based on something more than a nodding acquaintance with Burke's life and writings. We may, I think, infer the same from the apparent ease with which he finds an appropriate quotation from Burke when he finds it necessary to attack the house of Russell. The fact that he does not cite Burke's major counter-revolutionary writings—the *Reflections on the Revolution in France* (1790) and the *Letters on a Regicide Peace* (1796) cannot be taken as indicating that he did not know them. Marx quoted only that which was useful to him, and it is not surprising that he should not have drawn on these particular works. These writings of course strongly influenced, and are held to have been, the model for the German Conservative-Romantics, whose dominance at the beginning of the 1840's after the accession of Friederich Wilhelm IV, closed the door on the young Marx's hopes of an academic career.

Whether Marx knew the spectre passages from Burke—as I think probable—or whether he did not, the likenesses are close between its content and aspects of Marx's writing. The spectral imagery—to which both Burke and Marx were inordinately given—is of less importance than the substance. The picture of the revolutionary party will remind a modern reader much less of the French Revolutionary leadership of 1796 than of the determination of a Marxist party, the form of determination which the Communist Manifesto was intended to kindle, and did kindle:

"Going straight forward to its end, unappalled by peril, unchecked by remorse, despising all common maxims and all common means...." Even more striking is the picture of the possessing classes: "... those who could not believe it was possible she could at all exist except on the principles which habit rather than nature had persuaded them were necessary to their own particular welfare, and to their own ordinary modes of action".

Scarcely in other terms does Isaiah Berlin summarize the intellectual limitations of the bourgeoisie in the view of the young Marx:

> The bourgeoisie which wishes not to alter [the world] but to preserve the status quo, acts and thinks in terms of concepts which, being products of a given stage in its development, themselves serve, whatever they pretend to be, as instruments of its temporary preservation.

Both writers see the possessing classes as potentially the victims of ways of thought developed for their preservation as classes, but unsuited to meet direct and determined revolutionary challenge: the "ordinary modes of action" are "instruments of temporary preservation". In their different camps both Burke and Marx seek to awaken the classes they champion. Burke, in ordinary circumstances a friend to habit, now warns the possessing classes of the need for not ordinary but extraordinary modes of action: for the poor, however, he sees and counsels the advantages of prejudice and superstition—terms which, with characteristic pugnacity, he seeks to bring into favourable use. Marx, for his part, while satisfied with the socially-formed intellectual limitations of the bourgeoisie, tries to liberate the proletariat from the bourgeois intellectual assumptions it has acquired to its own class doctrine. The corresponding phenomenon, from Burke's point of view, is the acquisition by members of the ruling class—like the Duke of Bedford—of liberal, reformist theories, natural enough to "ability without property", but strictly suicidal for "property without ability". The eloquence and fury with which such people are attacked in the *Letter to a Noble Lord* obviously impressed Marx, who attacked in a similar spirit, though in more cumbrous language, those whom he regarded as the unconcious carriers of bourgeois ideology among the proletariat.

The revolution which Burke feared is not of course identical with Marx's Communist revolution, but has much essential in common with it, and in some ways more in common with it than with the actual French Revolution of Burke's day. Burke would have been likely to see in the principles of the Communist revolution the emergence in even purer form of all that he most detested in the contemporary revolution whose progress he watched with horror and fascination in France, and sought with eloquence and skill to check in England. The spirit of total, radical innovation; the overthrow of all prescriptive rights; confiscation of property; destruction of the church, the nobility, the family, of tradition, veneration, the ancestors, the nation—this is the catalogue of all that Burke dreaded in his darkest moments, and every item in it he would have discovered in Marxism. In the personality of Marx himself he would have seen incarnated that energy which he regarded as most dangerous to ordered society: the energy of ability without property. In Engels he would have seen a prime representative of a category whose activities he found both noxious and incomprehensible: the category of the men of property who encouraged the spread of principles inimical to the rights of property—a sort of bourgeois Duke of Bedford made more noxious by the possession also of energy and talent.

Like Burke, Marx and Engels long and anxiously scrutinised the French Revolution, seeking in its course the secret of the future development of European and world politics. Like his, their imagination was deeply penetrated by the energies which the Revolution let loose, deeply impressed by the contrast between the scale of these events and the routine of politics in a world that hoped the Revolution could be ignored, or treated as a purely local event, isolated in space or time. Like him they looked through the political surface of the Revolution towards its economic and social substance: Burke provides, in the *Reflections* and elsewhere, some of the best examples of that aristocratic critique of the bourgeoisie, to which the *Communist Manifesto* allows a provisional and sardonic welcome. Burke and Marx both sought to understand the revolutionary principles at work in France—Burke in order to stop them from spreading, and to destroy the nucleus of infection; Marx in order to hasten the victory of a new revolution, bringing with it the triumph of all that for Burke had been most hateful—though not of that which had been most contemptible—in the old one.

The great revolutions of our own time, those of Russia and China, came, under Marxist leadership, in lands which had never known an equivalent of the French Revolution. France itself, and those other Western countries most exposed to the Enlightenment, and—like Britain and the United States—least resistant to those principles of political democracy which Burke abhorred, are also among the least revolutionary in the world today. The country which was the fulcrum of counter-revolution in his day—the country to whose Empress he turned in admiration—was to become for our time that nucleus of revolutionary infection which France was for his. We have lived to see Russia itself, through revolutionary force, superseded by a power which had clung even longer than Russia to the ancestral ways, which had furnished the supreme example in the world of long adherence to a social contract in the form that Burke conceived it—"a partnership not only between those who are living but between those who are living, those who are dead and those who are to be born".

It would be vain, I believe, to try to relate Burke's philosophy of history to Marx's; it is not on this ground that their resemblances lie.

Burke was a practical politician—sometimes it is true an impractical one, but always with practical intent. He proclaimed—and increasingly in the counter-revolutionary phase of his last years—his distaste for abstract, metaphysical speculation. Although he probably over-stated this distaste for polemical reasons—to mark his position the more sharply from that of the French constitution-makers, with their unbounded assertions of confidence in Reason—such efforts in his writings can hardly be made to yield a coherent system of their own. With the exception of his two earliest works—one of which is generally accepted as ironic—all his writing is political pleading, much of it necessarily compressed by the limitations of the spokesman of a party; until his last years when he felt himself to be politically alone. But it is precisely at this time, when he is personally most free in his speaking and writing, that he shows himself most opposed to abstraction and systematization. If the ageing Burke had arrived at some new system, or original formulation, he would have been bound, on his own professed principles, to suppress it, since what the age needed was not any form of adherence to a tried and tested system. His own personal position—that is to say his Irish Catholic family background, combined with that conformity to the Church of England which was indispensable for any kind of career in his day—made it difficult for him to describe exactly what that tried and tested system was. In his correspondence he speaks of himself as being "attached to Christianity at large: much from conviction, more from affection" (Corr. VI, p. 215; 26 January, 1791). By "Christianity at large" he seems to have meant those tenets and traditions which were common to the Roman Catholicism and to the Church of England. (Certainly by the time he wrote these words in 1791 he already held the Dissenters and their peculiar tenets and their political tendencies in marked aversion.) His approval of the Church of England is specifically political: "I think that Church harmonizes with our civil constitution." But in France, and in Ireland, it was to Roman Catholicism he looked as to the source of social stability. His position then was broadly traditional, but also pragmatic; it was far from that of an idelogically-minded reactionary like Joseph de Maistre who—though he greatly admired Burke—felt that Anglicanism was absurd, since it was absurd to believe that there had been a special Incarnation for the English. Burke shrugged off such points; he detested what he called "the spirit of polemical theology"; he had seen it at work in Ireland. What he liked to use, and did use, was an appeal to a consensus of gentlemen—men of education and property—based on a common, though not necessarily precise—or rather necessarily not precise—recollection of a common Christian education; this required, in the XVIIIth century, a certain blurring of the dogmatic, the miraculous and the controversial elements in traditional theologies. A pious and at the same time politic vagueness about fundamentals—leaving the security of assumed common ground—is as much part of Burke as are genuine warmth of feeling, splendour of language and, when it serves, piercing political insight. He did not aim at the reputation of a systematic thinker. To Philip Francis's strictures on the draft of the *Reflections* he replied: "The composition you say is loose and I am quite content it should be since I never intended it should be otherwise".

Burke's writings were known surprisingly soon on the Continent, especially in Germany. One of his earliest works, *A philosophical Enquiry into the Origins of the Sublime and the Beautiful* (1756) was being annotated by Lessing as early as the following year and both Herder and Lessing planned to translate it. The *Reflections* were translated in 1794 by Friedrich von Gentz, later to be a significant political figure in his own right and secretary to the Congress of Vienna. Through his effect on Gentz, F.J. Stehl and others, Burke did enter into the intellectual inheritance of the German-speaking world with which Marx grew up; as the first important intellectual champion of the counter-revolution, he belonged indeed in the intellectual Pantheon of the German ruling class in the post-revolutionary epoch. The young Marx does not appear, however, to have paid any attention to Burke; the first reference I find in the collected works is in 1853—in the London years—and the quotation seems to be at second hand. The reasons why the young Marx should have shown no interest in Burke—even no hostile interest—are obvious. Burke's intellectual heirs in Marx's youth—people like Friedrich-Julius Stahl—were so far to the young man's right as to seem beneath his contempt. His quarrels were with those nearer to him; he was what would now be called a worser: the nearer a man's opinions were to one's own, assuming them not to be identical, the worse they are. But even if Burke's position had been nearer he could still have had little interest for Marx at this stage. Like the whole English tradition, in the eyes of the Germans, Burke was deficient in what Engels called "the sense of theory"—Lessing himself had deplored his lack of system—and it was theory, in Hegel and his successors, that absorbed the interest of the young Marx.

The differences in relation to theory and system correspond to national traditions; they also correspond, however, to political needs. For Burke, the defender of the status quo, systematization was neither necessary nor desirable; he saw established order in society as menaced by the kind of order which theorizing seeks to establish. He valued above all things the web of unexamined prejudices which held together a society with steep gradations in property and rank. These beliefs—which could be called an ideology—though that is not his language—he sees as historically-formed and therefore not susceptible of merely intellectual rearrangement. On the contrary his concern is to impress on the principal beneficiaries of the existing society how precious to them are the habitual ways, and how dangerous it is to allow theorists to tamper with them. Marx, seeing essentially the same phenomena from exactly the opposite point of view, must reach the opposite conclusion. He sees just as well as Burke the importance and the sense of historically formed beliefs and attitudes which help to keep the dispossessed in their place. For his revolutionary ends it is as imperative to get rid of these beliefs and attitudes as it is for Burke, for his conservative ends, to protect them. Religion, deference to one's superiors, resignation, respect for established institutions, being historically formed, need no invention. But to offer an alternative system of beliefs and attitudes does require analysis, synthesis, a sustained theoretical effort. Burke in eschewing theory, and Marx in developing it, are both equally logical, granted their opposed intentions.

In 1852, facing the failure of his high hopes for revolution in his own time, Marx wrote a sentence which might almost have come from the pen of Burke: "Men make their own history, but they do not make it just as they please; they do not make it under circumstances chosen by themselves, but under circumstances directly encountered, given and transmitted from the past". And he added, as if feeling for the first time the full weight of the Burkian partnership: "The tradition of all the dead generations weighs like a nightmare on the brain of the living" (*18th Brumaire of Louis Bonaparte*, 1853). It may not be entirely a coincidence, as a result of changed environment, that it is shortly after this time that we find Marx's first references to Burke.

In our century, the idea of using Burke to cast out Marx has occurred from time to time to some conservative writers. A.V. Dicey, in 1918, seems to have been the first to hit upon the expedient of substituting "Russia" for "France" in a number of Burke's counter-revolutionary writings. More recently, and especially since the appearance of Mr. Ross Hoffman's *Burke's Politics* in 1949, more subtle variations have been played on this theme. For a time, a right-wing periodical even carried a *Burke Newsletter* as a regular feature. Fortunately the effort proved to be too much of a strain: one cannot continue very long pretending that this country's relation to Russia and China now is essentially identical to England's relation, as Burke conceived it, to France in the 1790's. Nor is Burke's language, addressed to gentlemen, appropriate to the needs of right-wing movements in conditions of universal suffrage.

Perhaps the most enduring achievement of this group has been the mis-placed and rash contempt for Burke which it has engendered among people who have not read him—or have read only a few purple patches—but who dislike his modern sponsors. Here a comment of Harold Laski's is relevant: "There is no wise man in politics with an important decision to make", said Laski, "who would not do well to refresh his mind by discussion with Burke's mind". Laski here, surely, places the emphasis where it belongs, not on the acceptance of a body of doctrine, but on contact with a mind. And this is as relevant to Marx as it is to Burke. The order which Burke defended has passed away, yet what replaced it is not the antagonist he feared. Marx's revolution has not come from the class and from the cities in which he expected; his teachings are active today, not among the working class of the most advanced countries, but among a class which he viewed with deep suspicion—the peasantry—and a class which he both despised and feared—the so-called lumpen proletariat, and in countries whose historic role he regarded as inevitably subordinate. It is not surprising that these thinkers of the eighteenth and the nineteenth centuries should not be serviceable as guides to the conditions of the twentieth. Yet the fundamental social realities with which they were at grips are still with us: tribe and class; and their insights into them are still relevant to our thinking about a world in which these realities are now differently disposed. But above all, the manner and intensity of their coming to grips has meaning for us—the example of intelligence fired by passion. We have now become used to separating the two, and to assuming that passion serves only to blind intelligence. Burke saw differently. With an intuition which derives perhaps from a potentially revolutionary element in his character—an element perceived by his astute adversary, Mary Wollstonecraft, and detectable in the *Letter to a Noble Lord*, in some of his writings on Ireland, and in the confidences of his son, Richard—he recognised, with foreboding, in his revolutionary adversaries, that combination of qualities which mark his own writing and all great writing and action: "I have a good opinion", he wrote, "of the general abilities of the Jacobins: not that I suppose them better born than others; but strong passions awaken the faculties: they suffer not a particle of the man to be lost" (First *Letter on a Regicide Peace*).

Both Marx and Burke were "better born", in Burke's sense, than others; in them strong passions awoke mighty faculties: not a particle is lost.

22

TWO-FACED CATHLEEN

"We know from our literary histories," writes Mr. Thompson, "that there was a movement called the Irish Literary Renaissance and that Yeats was at its head. We know from our political histories that there is now a Republic of Ireland because of a nationalistic movement that, militarily, began with the insurrection of Easter Week, 1916. But what do these two movements have to do with one another?"

It is an interesting question. Unfortunately Mr. Thompson is hardly qualified to answer it, because he has little understanding of either of the movements whose interaction he has undertaken to study. For the "nationalistic movement" this is clear even from what he thinks he knows from his "political histories." The Irish Republican movement did *not* begin, militarily or otherwise, with the insurrection of Easter Week, 1916: it began, ideologically, no later than Wolfe Tone, and militarily no later than the Rebellion of 1798. No one was more conscious of this fact than the men of 1916 themselves. The proclamation of the Republic was not a beginning, and not presented as a beginning: it was, and was presented as, the latest and the most momentous in a long series of revolutionary acts which made up the Irish nationalist tradition. Yeats himself clearly saw the significance of conscious revolutionary continuity when he wrote, in "Sixteen Dead Men":

New York Review of Books, 29 June 1967, pp. 19–21. Review of *The Imagination of an Insurrection: Dublin, Easter 1916: A Study of an Ideological Movement* by William Irwin Thompson.

How could you dream they'd listen
That have an ear alone
For these new comrades they have found,
Lord Edward and Wolfe Tone ...

Recognition of the large, plain fact that 1916 was *not* a beginning would disarrange Mr. Thompson's thesis—there having been no Irish Literary Renaissance to speak of in the days of Tone and Emmet—but I do not think it is for that reason that he ignores it. His scholarship is quite honest; only deficient in any feeling for his subject. He is saturated in that easy contempt for other people's nationalism, which is the prerogative of nations so powerful that they take their own nationalist assumptions for universal truths. Connolly and Pearse according to him "shared the common futility of being nationalists." It is a defensible view, but one which, if adopted, leaves little of interest to be said about Connolly and Pearse. If one held, for example, that "Washington and Jefferson shared the common futility of being nationalists" one might be wise not to devote one's time to writing about the American Revolution. In writing what he calls "a cultural study of ... [an] ideological movement," Mr. Thompson is fatally handicapped by his breezy contempt for the force that made the movement move.

In writing about the Literary Renaissance—which interests him more—Mr. Thompson is differently, but again fatally, incapacitated. He writes horribly. It is true that some who are considered excellent critics also write horribly, but their contortions are a kind of anguished groping, while the quality in Mr. Thompson's writing which makes us wince is the opposite: a jaunty insensitiveness. His Yeats was "riding the bandwagon with Maud Gonne," "a pretty ideologue of the Nineties": with her this Yeats "tagged along" and found himself "out on a limb." It is not the slang that matters, but the lack of feeling that it reveals when used in this context. We are still conscious of this when the writer assumes a judicial air to tell us that Joseph Plunkett's poetry was "baroque and chryselephantine"; that "Never a disciple of Pater, A.E.'s sense of beauty was based upon intense consciousness of moral responsibility" and—crushing verdict—that "A.E. never mastered English prose."

Mr. Thompson has "read up" his two subjects reasonably well, and when he follows his authorities—which he does not always do—and when his authorities happen to be right—which is not always the case— his summary accounts of various aspects of the Irish national and literary movements will be of some use to readers for whom these subjects have the charm of novelty. Similarly the précis of the plot of *The Plough and the Stars* (which takes up fifteen of his twenty-five pages on O'Casey) will doubtless interest persons who were in some way debarred from reading or seeing that interesting play. Otherwise, *The Imagination of an Insurrection* has, in this reviewer's opinion, little to recommend it. Not only does the treatment of the two movements in themselves fail by reason of lack of sympathy and sensitivity, but the attempt to relate the movements turns out to involve no more than an energetic assertion of the proposition that imagination has a place in history. "History often repeats itself, but imagination must always be more flexible than factual knowledge to see that history never repeats a pattern in the same way." This ponderous revelation, attained on the penultimate page, is not even true: nothing is less likely than "factual knowledge" to suggest that history ever "repeats a pattern in the same way."

> Did that play of mine send out
> Certain men the English shot?

There can be no sure answer to the question that troubled Yeats on his deathbed. *Cathleen Ní Houlihan* (1902) did powerfully affect "certain men" who took part in the Rising of 1916. One of them has recorded that for him and his friends the play was "almost a sacrament." Yet it could not have had this effect if it had not touched a "stock response": those who were so powerfully moved by this appeal to romantic nationalism, were already romantic nationalists, already drawn toward sacrificial exaltation. There may well have been "certain men" who were moved by *Cathleen Ní Houlihan* at a crucial moment in their young lives; men who here contracted the infection that was to kill some of them in Easter Week, 1916. But it is overwhelmingly likely that, if their resistance to the revolutionary infection was so low that they succumbed to *Cathleen Ní Houlihan* they would have been fatally infected by something else, between 1902 and 1916, even if *Cathleen Ní Houlihan* had never been written, and if Yeats and Maud Gonne had never existed. It is certain that the leaders of the Rising—Tom Clarke and Pearse and Connolly—were there quite independently of even the most patriotic manifestations of the Irish Literary Renaissance. The real "literature of the Rising" was not that of Yeats and Synge and Lady Gregory: it was Wolfe Tone's *Autobiography*; it was *Speeches from the Dock* and especially Robert Emmet's speech; it was the patriotic verse of Thomas Davis, "Speranza" (Oscar Wilde's mother) and Fanny Parnell; it was John Mitchell's *Jail Journal*; it was Sullivan's *God Save Ireland* and Ingram's

Who Fears to Speak of '98? The writings of the Irish Literary Renaissance had positive and political impact only when they inscribed themselves clearly within this tradition, as with *Cathleen Ní Houlihan* or with Lady Gregory's *Rising of the Moon.* These are hardly the works for which lovers of literature in other lands have interested themselves in the Irish Literary Renaissance. The trouble with discussion of "literature and revolution" is always that the literature which most interests the literary is different from the literature which most interests the revolutionary.

The Irish Revolution would have happened—to the extent that it did happen—even if the great Irish writers of the first part of the century had never existed. It could be contended with some force that the greatest work of the Irish writers is entirely independent of the Irish revolutionary movement. Joyce early turned his back on all Dublin's chatter, religious, literary, and revolutionary; Synge, in the classical aristocratic manner, preferred the unspoiled peasantry of the Gaelic West to the politicized *babus* of the urban lower-middle classes and the trade unions—who made the revolution; even in Yeats's case, his greatest poetry was written, not in the bliss-was-it-in-that-dawn period, but in the Twenties and Thirties, in the doldrums of disillusion, when Irishmen felt as Frenchmen did after the overthrow of another tyranny:

> *Que la République était belle—*
> *sous l'Empire!*

Yet the chatter on which Joyce turned his back continued to fill his head: Synge's turning towards the Gaelic world was part of a general quickening of interest in that world, which was in turn a part of the revolutionary ferments; Yeats's mind, in old age even more than before, was preoccupied and exalted by the politics of the past and of the present, by revolution and counter-revolution. In and around the Abbey Theatre, a center both of literary and political excitement, the two movements did interact, in a puzzled and intermittent way, sometimes in sympathy, more often bickering. Though the bickering was more conspicuous, I feel that the sympathy was more fundamental. The bickering came from the demands of the political leadership that the theater should serve immediate and obvious propaganda needs—and the resistance of Yeats and Lady Gregory to these demands. The sympathy stemmed from a common quest for identity; a common rejection of bourgeois materialism (what Mr. Thompson calls "a rejection of civilization"); a common romanticism; a common conviction that Ireland had something of importance to offer to the world, and a common feeling that something exciting was afoot. In this last respect, the two movements did help each other. The theater's refusal to make propaganda on demand for the revolutionaries itself made good propaganda—for the theater. And the existence of a theater which refused to make propaganda on demand was itself, in the longer term, good propaganda for the revolutionary cause: the Ireland which claimed to have so much to give to the world did indeed have something to offer, and did have men who were prepared to defend that something. Though each movement could have existed without the other, though each often ignored or scorned the other, each also acquired from the other a heightened sense of tragedy—and later of tragi-comedy.

When did it all end? There is a rather widely held opinion that "the influence of the Irish Catholic clergy," asserted after political independence and through the Censorship, put an end to the Irish literary movement. This opinion is congenial to those who dislike the Catholic clergy (often for adequate reasons) and also to those who are quick to perceive the futility of other people's nationalism. As an explanation, however, it does not work. The influence of the Catholic clergy, in Ireland's social and educational life, was quite as formidable—and in some ways more formidable—before independence as after. The reality of censorship—in schools and colleges and municipal libraries and in the life of the countryside and the small towns generally—had existed long before independence. The State censorship, when established in 1928, was notoriously incompetent and eccentric, and such efforts at censorship, when not backed by a powerful apparatus of terror, have normally—as in Tsarist Russia—served to stimulate rather than repress literary creation. What really happened was that the exalting sense of Ireland's exceptional destiny which had existed before 1922 simply faded into the sheer ordinariness of a paternal, pettifogging, fairly decent little Republic. The dreams of the founders were unattainable. It wasn't going to be a Workers' Republic, as Connolly hoped, or a Gaelic-speaking one, as Pearse hoped, or a united one, as all the revolutionaries had hoped and assumed. The North was lost for good; the leftwing extremism flickered and died in the Thirties; so did the rightwing extremism of the Blueshirts. A melancholy sanctity prevailed. Yeats hated it but, as Mr. Thompson would say, "he tagged along," finding himself, to his surprise, publishing a poem in De Valera's *Irish Press* and defending De Valera's policy of neutrality.

There is a tension and excitement, which can be creative, in the struggle to be free from something obvious like British Imperialism or Tsarist autocracy or white supremacy. The kind of partial victory and partial defeat which must be the only outcome of such a struggle must lead to a period of perplexity and bitterness, not exalting to the minds of the young. For Ireland that "post-independence" period may be thought of as ending about 1966, the fiftieth anniversary of the 1916 Rising. There are signs that the period now beginning, dominated by those who are too young to be directly affected by either the illusions or the disillusions of the first half of the century, may prove in some ways—socially and institutionally rather than nationally—not less bitter than the Twenties and Thirties. There are some grounds for hoping that these new strains may prove more productive, both in politics and in literature, than was the time of disappointed liberty.

23

IN QUEST OF UNCLE TOM

Travel books are never about the places and people they are supposed to be about, but about the differences between these and the places and people the writer knows best, and about what these differences mean to the writer. For the native of the place, however, the things that he and his relations have in common with neighboring peoples and with other men generally are not less important than the things that separate them. The traveler's account, based on a catalogue of differences and ignoring the common, must therefore seem wrong to the native. This will always be so, unless the native is already rapt in the vision of himself as the foreigner sees him, a fascinating, inimitable, inscrutable concentration of qualities unique even if sometimes repulsive. Romanticism, egoism, and masochism aiding, some Irishmen, like some Jews, have attained that sinister condition described by Claudel: *la quiétude incestueuse de l'âme assise sur sa différence essentielle.*

The stage Irishman, as Mr. Pritchett correctly observes, does exist. He might have added that the "house" for the stage Irishman has always consisted largely, though not entirely, of foreigners, and that this is why off-stage Irishmen have often so hotly resented the stage variety, as a combination of traitor and ambulant forgery, self-framed to corroborate the vision of the foreigner and to answer his need. For the stage Irishman this is part of the fun. He baits his respectable fellow-countrymen by playing on their secret fear that, deep down, this

New York Review of Books, 14 September 1967, pp. 10–11. Review of *Dublin: A Portrait* by V.S. Pritchett and *Irish Journal* by Heinrich Böll.

is how they really are. He baits the foreigner, both by overacting the part prescribed for him, and by direct and crude insult, made admissible by the mask. And above all he baits himself, even to death, as did Brendan Behan, the greatest of his kind.

For a minority people, the question of what and how they seem to others is often of more pressing importance than the more difficult question of what and how they actually are. A hostile stereotype can be literally lethal, under certain conditions. Even a mildly unfavorable account can be a form of isolation, a sort of trap. On the other hand a favorable account can seem to be a kind of freedom: the connotations of the label have become that much more favorable. One can breathe that much more easily.

An Irish reader of these two books will be interested not so much in what they may reveal about the Irish as in what they reveal about the English and about the Germans: What qualities, in the life of a small, peripheral, and largely pre-industrial people, at present seem significant to intelligent middle-class observers from populous and heavily industrialized countries? Today—to judge from these books and the general tone of much recent press comment by journalists—the central significant quality is that of gentleness. The excellent photographs by Evelyn Hofer—which will make anyone who loves the city want to acquire *Dublin: A Portrait*—are rich in this quality: so rich that after a while the cumulative effect becomes a little cloying. The serenity of an eighteenth-century façade; the wistful faces of two children; the Chamber of the Dáil, without its denizens and with its prayer; a pub lounge at a quiet hour, with few and placid customers; a Veteran of the Rising, musing on the past, black homburg on his head, dog at his feet, umbrella by his side; an evening landscape, a touching, trusting seamstress; an affable brewer on a soft rug; a pensive lawyer and—the last picture in the book—a sad and serene portrait of two pale sisters, clad in some dark material in a vesperal light. There is even a portrait of Mr. Patrick Kavanagh, the poet, wearing, at least over the upper part of his rugged features, a gentle expression, which is not the one most familiar to his fellow citizens.

As for Herr Heinrich Böll, an understandable revulsion from the manners and customs of his fellow-countrymen has led him to idealize everything that is most wishy-washy in the Ireland he thinks he has seen: "we floated"—this is "in a no-man's-land, between dream and memory" through which Herr Böll in his *Irish Journal* all too frequently drifts—"through the gate to Trinity College, but this great grey place was uninhabited save for a pale young girl who sat weeping on the library steps, her bright green hat in her hand, waiting for her sweetheart or mourning his loss." (If this was really memory, and not dream, it is more probable, give the apparent time of year, that the young woman had been unable to keep up with her guided tour because the cobbles hurt her feet.)

Mr. Pritchett, of course, is another matter. He knows Ireland much better than most outsiders do and as a critic, both penetrating and sympathetic, he usually knows how much credit to place in various "let's pretend" Irelands engendered by the expectation of foreigners upon the chronic tendency of ex-slaves to "play up." (The answer is always, of course, "some credit" since the "let's pretend" Irelands have by now also become a part of the reality.) Mr. Pritchett's account can be recommended, though with some reservations, to any visitor to Ireland. He is a wise and urbane guide, and his account is rather better balanced, and certainly more pertinent to the visitor's needs, than the jagged commentaries of the local inhabitants are likely to be. The local inhabitants will, of course, pick holes and, perhaps in order to appease their spirits, Mr. Pritchett has made a considerable number of small errors. He has *Finnegan's Wake* for the ballad, which is right, but keeps the apostrophe for the book, which is wrong—and to the Joycean a scandal; Merriman and not "Berryman" is the author of *The Midnight Court* and Arland, not "Aarland", Ussher the author of *The Face and Mind of Ireland*; the list could be extended.

What is more important, and what is likely to escape most readers of the book, is that Mr. Pritchett, ecumenical though he sounds and no doubt is, does on the whole share the outlook, on recent Irish history and politics, of a particular section of the Irish people: those middle-class Dubliners who favored the Anglo-Irish treaty of 1921. This was a world in which Protestant ex-Unionists, ex-"Castle" Catholics, former pillars of the Irish Parliamentary Party, and moderate Sinn Feiners made up Dublin "society" in the aftermath of the Irish Civil War. Mr. Pritchett first visited Dublin under their auspices, and his quite legitimate sympathy with them sometimes leads him into an unwary confidence in them as sources of information. Their ideas and Mr. Pritchett's own can mingle, in the narrative of an eminent literary critic who disdains historiography, in a way which disguises important aspects of Irish history:

> In the first flush of political power the Catholic majority created a Catholic Peasant state which was well on the way to becoming as exclusive as the Spanish. A sweeping censorship of books was soon established; the Senate, in which many distinguished Protestants had a voice, was abolished; and re-

placed eventually by a body far less distinguished; there is no divorce and birth control is legally non-existent.

This lacks chronology and precision. The specifically "Catholic" legislation—on divorce, censorship, and contraception—was passed by the first Government of the State, a Government which Mr. Pritchett elsewhere eulogizes. The old Senate was abolished by the second Government—that of Eamon de Valera, for reasons which had nothing to do with the voices of distinguished Protestants, and had a great deal to do with Fascism, a subject which Mr. Pritchett here overlooks. After the De Valera Government came to power, a section of the "intelligence and property of the country" adopted in 1933–34 the style and symbols of Fascism. "They have the Blackshirts in Italy," said one of their advocates, "they have Brownshirts in Germany and now we have the Blueshirts in Ireland." The De Valera Government, determined not to go the way of other democratic governments in Europe, introduced a measure to make the Blueshirts illegal: the Wearing of Uniforms Bill. The old Senate, which had "House of Lords" powers and was designed to serve similar purposes, threw out the Wearing of Uniforms Bill. Several of the Senators were actually wearing the Blue Shirt. On the following day, Mr. de Valera introduced in the Dáil (House of Commons) his measure for the abolition of the Senate. Mr. Pritchett's account here folds out of sight a significant chapter of modern Irish history. His index does not mention the Blueshirts or their leader, General O'Duffy, nor do the photographs include a portrait of the most interesting Irish face extant: that of Eamon de Valera. There is however a fine definition of the source of Mr. de Valera's appeal:

> It is (I think) the dour and passionate grammarian of unchanging mind who has captivated a people within whose lively voices one instantly recognizes the pervading tone of the melancholy pedant.

Since Irish history is part of Mr. Pritchett's theme, and since Irish history is no more gentle than that of any other conquered people, his text fortunately cannot be as oppressively gentle as the accompanying photographs or as the Teuto-Celtic Twilight of Herr Böll. Yet he too, as in the case of the Blueshirts, tends to obfuscate contention; he was captivated as he tells us, by the "purity and languor" of the Dublin air, and this spell still lingers in his pages, reinforced by all those creepily beautiful photographs.

The Western mind, craving a respite from social strife, finds something congenial in contemplating the prospect of Ireland today, and in contemplating it mentally transforms the prospect into something more congenial still. Irish people, in their contacts with their neighbors, will find the new image more helpful than the old "brawling" image—still dear to the *New Yorker*—but both images are extrapolations and exaggerations of observed fact. Irish resignation and gentleness—like the Irish brawling which is an attempt to escape from them—are among the facts of Irish life. The gentleness of the people does give a pleasant quality to life in Ireland, especially for the middle class, who as elsewhere are much less gentle than the common people; hence, possibly, the expression "gentleman," like "Eumenides" for the Furies. The gentle resignation of many Irish people, especially women, and especially people who stay in Ireland, is largely due to the Faith—that is to say to the instruction, tone, and social policy of the Church. But the Church is changing, and attitudes to the Church are changing too. The combination of the *aggiornamento* with more secular forces of modernization has already brought about, within the past year or so, major and liberal changes in the structure of Irish education. Will gentle resignation, as a marked characteristic of the Irish, survive such changes? A visitor like Herr Böll—who puffs and snorts with ecstasy while he wallows in this Irish characteristic—naturally laments any signs of progress. In the most abominable passage in his ghastly little book, this man actually deplores the introduction of "the Pill" to Ireland. The untold misery that the Church's teaching on contraception, combined with an unquestioning faith and the poverty of the land, have meant to so many thousands of Irish homes, means nothing to this literary tourist, in comparison with the faintest threat to the proper lukewarm temperature of his bath in other people's resignation.

Uncle Tom has become hard to find of late, and I fear that people have started coming to Ireland to look for him. I think they will eventually be disappointed. The Irish people, despite their numerous historical, social, educational, and dogmatic misfortunes, are still alive and, with any luck, will yet be kicking. The amateurs of the submissive will then have to seek their quarry elsewhere. I should add that I don't really include among these Mr. Pritchett, upon whom, I am afraid, some of my indignation with Herr Böll has splashed over.

24

INSIDE BIAFRA

If you wish to enter Biafra otherwise than in the wake of the Federal Nigerian troops, you must do so clandestinely by special aircraft or overland through Cameroun. To the south, it is effectively blockaded by sea; in the north and west it is invested by Federal forces: only on the east has this unrecognised republic of 14 million people—including two million refugees who fled there after the massacres in the Northern Region of an estimated 30,000 easterners last year—had some access to the outside world.

On 22 September, with two American academic colleagues, I entered Biafra through Cameroun. The approach itself made clear the peril in which Biafra stood. The road which constitutes the sole civil access to this beleaguered population—a population more numerous than that of the entire Congo—is a mere track, almost impassable now at the end of the rainy season, and quite impassable for anything less well adapted than a Land-Rover. There is an Air Cameroun service from Douala to Mamfe in Western Cameroun—the jumping-off point for Biafra—but it operates on Fridays and Saturdays and we arrived on Tuesday. So we went by road, which took us 12 hours, mostly of jolting, sliding and searches by the Camerounian gendarmerie.

At the Inland Hotel, Mamfe—a typical colonial rest-house—we could hear Enugu Radio for the first time with its slogan, "Save Biafra for the free world." The Biafrans were still clinging to the anachronistic belief that since the Soviet Union—mechanically identifying Biafra

Observer, 8 October 1967.

with Katanga—had given some military help to the Federal Government, the West, or at least the United States, would have to come to the rescue of Biafra. As regards Britain, the Biafran Government had given up hope: the radio reported various prominent Biafrans as abjuring British titles and returning British decorations, because of Britain's military aid to the Federal Government. None the less, it was to the West generally—the US, West Germany, France and even Portugal—that Biafrans still looked.

From our fellow-guests at Mamfe, it was clear that Biafran affection for the West was not uniformly reciprocated. An American correspondent on his way out—I believe he was the last correspondent to leave Biafra, and certainly we met none there—was disgusted with the inefficiency with which the war was being conducted: 250 white mercenaries, in his opinion, would soon "clean up the mess." A Dutchman, whose business in the mid-west had closed down for lack of outlets while Biafran forces held that region, celebrated with shining eyes the news of the Federal recapture of Benin.

The notion cherished by some left-wing writers that Western business interests inspired the secession of Biafra—as the Union Minière inspired the tactical secession of Katanga—is without foundation. Most Western businessmen have left the area, their business at a standstill because of the blockade. And of the few that remained, those that we met were avid for news of Federal victory, bringing "business as usual" once more in sight. The implications of such a victory for the Ibos did not move them.

A German Air Cameroun pilot, who had had much contact with businessmen leaving the Eastern Region on the Mamfe-Douala flight, corroborated our impression that dislike of Ibos is prevalent among this class. When asked why, he tapped his head. "Too much up there," he said. This verdict is at the root of the tragedy of the Ibos. The nineteenth-century doctrine of "the educated native ... curse of the West Coast" is no longer openly uttered, but it still weighs heavily on human lives.

The reason why the Federation of Nigeria has such a powerful appeal to certain minds is that it was, and is, a device for keeping the educated African in his place, under the control of the dignified rulers of the North.

At Mamfe we were met, eventually, by a Biafran Government Land-Rover. My colleagues (Professors Stanley Diamond and Audrey Chapman), in the immediate aftermath of the 1966 massacres in the North, had helped to set up a committee for Biafran refugees, and this was the body on whose behalf we were visiting the area. We were known to be sympathetic to the Biafran cause, in the sense that we shared, and still share, a belief that the conquest of the Eastern Region by the North, in the name of federation, would be a great human disaster. We were received in Biafra, therefore, as friends and were guests of the Biafran Government during our stay.

Beyond Mamfe the road forks, at a place called Three Corners. From this point the better road into Biafra (or Nigeria) bears north, through a place called Ikom. As Federal troops were reported to be there, we took the other and worse road through Ikang to Calabar —Calabar is a "minority" region; the provincial administrator is a non-Ibo and an anthropologist.

It is sometimes suggested that antagonism between Ibo and non-Ibo inside Biafra is more or less equivalent to the hostility between Hausa and Ibo in Nigeria, so that if it is wrong for Eastern Nigeria to be dominated by the North, it is equally wrong for non-Ibos to be dominated by Ibos inside Eastern Nigeria. An attempt is even made to present the Federal troops as liberating the minorities from Ibo oppression. This, however, is not plausible, since the organisers of the Northern massacres did not generally distinguish between all the peoples of the East. The only Southerners spared were those who had Western (Yoruba) tribal markings.

We met a number of non-Ibos—three of them provincial administrators. Several of them had complaints about Ibos, but the character of the complaints—job-discrimination, unfair local allocation of regional funds, etc.—pointed to differences on a scale not to be compared with the gulf which has opened between the populations of North and East. I saw nothing to suggest that, if the East were left alone, its population could not live together on as reasonable terms as do the populations of the United Kingdom, which has also its minority problems, although the English are at least as apt as the Ibos could be to ignore their existence.

Descending from the ferry at Oron, across the river from Calabar, we had our first unescorted encounter with Biafran popular vigilance. Biafra's small Army—before the war Easterners formed a very small part of the Nigerian Army—is supplemented by a large militia, hastily recruited and miscellaneously armed; and by a corps of civil defenders, enthusiastic boys and girls, equipped with only symbolic weapons, such as wooden guns. Check-points are usually manned by a few militia and police, enthusiastically aided by defenders.

These parties work in an egalitarian "People's Army" style and they are invariably suspicious about European strangers. This is not only because of British and Russian arms aid to Lagos: we also found that it was very widely believed that expatriates from the University of Zaria had helped to plan the massacres in the North. We did not believe this, but that was not the point: the people who questioned us and searched our luggage believe it.

We produced papers: "Don't waste my time," said the militiaman, pushing us into an enclosure, where many others awaited questioning. A young Ibo woman, a graduate student who was with us, was shocked by this discourtesy. "Wicked," she said. "They used to be too good, you know, but now they are wicked soldiers." Underneath the disapproval there was pride and underneath the pride something else: sadness or doubt.

We stayed a week in Biafra, mostly at Enugu—where we stayed in the empty half-lit grandeur of the Presidential hotel. We had two long interviews with the military governor, Colonel Ojukwu, bearded and slightly stooped, obviously under extreme tension but master of himself. He gave a long and lucid analysis of the events leading up to the present situation. He spoke in a very low voice, with studied understatement. Of Britain he spoke with a kind of baffled affection—he seemed to be the most pro-British person in Biafra. He could not, however, see any acceptable solution, except one that would be secured by Biafran determination and fighting strength.

Would he be willing to accept a cease-fire? Yes, in principle, but the blockade would have to be suspended, and Federal forces withdrawn from Biafran soil. Would he be prepared to withdraw his own forces from the Mid-West? He could not, he felt, abandon the Ibo region, the Eastern part of the Mid-West, to the mercy of the Northern troops. He was prepared, as he has often explained, to accept a Customs union, and all practicable forms of technical and economic co-operation. He knew, however, that this was not enough and that his adversaries hoped to impose their own terms on a defeated Biafra. He still hoped to hold them off, but he clearly knew that the situation was grave. The day we first saw him was the day of the execution of Victor Banjo and other officers convicted—on what appear to be sound grounds—of intelligence with the enemy.

The effect of this news, as it spread through Biafra, was alarming. Ibos are not traditionally disposed to deference—which is one of the reasons why they are so disliked—and the Ibo soldier is unusually apt to question an order. I heard a junior officer speak of the treachery and incompetence of the "so-called higher ranks." Everywhere at the checkpoints, as we travelled between Enugu, Port Harcourt and Calabar, we saw evidence of a popular tendency to ignore constituted authority, suspected of faint-heartedness and treachery. It was essentially the same response—though so far more mildly expressed—as that of the Jacobin patriots of 1791–93, on learning of defeats and the treasons of generals. For no traveller can mistake it: this is a popular and patriotic war, waged by people who feel that their survival is quite literally at stake. It is not "Ojukwu's war" as the Federal leader General Gowon appears to imagine.

It is possible that the State of Biafra may be crushed out of existence by the numerically superior and better armed Federal troops, with their limitless access to outside support, as compared with that pathetic "lifeline" through Mamfe and Ekang. What is certain, however, is that a nation has been born and will in some form endure. There is a reality about the birth of Biafra, in blood and confusion, that there never was about all those ceremonial haulings-down of flags, in which the colonial authorities handed over symbols of power to selected orators and other dignitaries.

The Biafrans have been forced to stand alone, in the wreckage of a Federation which does not want them but does want the resources of their territory.

Potentially, in resources and skills and human energy, they are probably the richest nation in tropical Africa. The obstacles to their development are political and military. If some of the brightest hopes of Africa are not to be buried in the debris of the Federation, Britain has a responsibility to use its influence towards a cessation of hostilities (including blockade) and towards negotiations based on the principle of a much looser association of the component parts of the old Federation.

The day before we left Enugu the shelling began. People were afraid, not of the shelling itself—which did little damage—but because it implied the nearness of Federal troops, whom they regarded as their tormentors and the murderers of their kin. This is what the apparently benign concept of Federation has come to mean for the majority of the population of the Federation's most developed region.

25

STUDENT UNREST

Universities and colleges in the United States have been very unevenly
affected by student unrest. There are colleges—like Bucknoll in
Western Pennsylvania—that are so free from student radicalism that
they can with impunity confer honorary degrees on people like Hubert
Humphrey. At the other extreme, on the national spectrum, is San
Francisco State College which has been living for nearly two years in a
state of permanent revolution. Universities which have become known
for the radicalism of their student bodies—like Berkeley, Wisconsin and
Columbia, as well as San Francisco State—may have little enough in
common otherwise and no one fully understands the conditions in
which dissatisfaction may suddenly explode into violence.

Despite its great size—about 42,000 students—New York University, where I work, has so far experienced very little violence, either by students or by police. This is in part due to its geographical
location; it does not, as Columbia does, border on Harlem. It also
possesses, as Columbia did not, an administration which generally
thought it was to remain accessible to students and to make timely concessions: effective student control of dormitory and social facilities,
some student participation in university government, and the creation
of a Martin Luther King Institute for Black Studies, with the creation
of additional scholarships for black students. Anti-war demonstrations
were also handled with deliberate delicacy. When last year students,
with some support from the faculty, hindered Dow Chemical—which

Irish Times, 10 March 1969.

manufactures napalm—from recruiting on campus, no substantial disciplinary action was taken.

Those students who were concerned with obtaining changes from and in the university were reasonably satisfied with the progress obtained in these respects. Other students—a minority, but an important minority, of the radical minority—believing that disruption of the universities could be the prologue to the disruption of the system as a whole, and to social revolution in America, could obviously not be disarmed by any university concessions or reforms, which they necessarily considered as token and manipulative. For such students the use of direct action involving violence and forcing the university administration into punitive measures, thereby "radicalising" larger sections of students, is logical.

Whether violence does or does not break out on any campus depends to a considerable extent on whether the students who profess these beliefs actually believe in them to the point of running serious risks. Some months ago, a lecture given in Washington square by the South Vietnamese observer at the UN provided a test case, both for confrontation-minded students and for the university administration and faculty. For the students, the South Vietnamese observer was an ideal target, not only because of the loathing which his regime and the war it lives on inspire in great numbers of students, but also because an attack on him, and a disruption of his meeting, would have the merit—in the eyes of the extreme group—of separating off liberals from radicals at a point and on an issue favourable to the radicals.

Liberals were in principle committed to the principle that while they deplored what the observer had to say, they would defend (to a rather hypothetical death) his right to say it. Radicals, on the other hand—and not just the most extreme faction of these—would hold that since the observer was no more than the symbol and front for organised lethal violence applied daily by the Government of the United States to the small Asian people, which the observer falsely pretended to represent, the use of a modicum of force to prevent the delivery of his apologia for violence would be justifiable; and it would be hypocritical—and in practice collusive with imperialism—to uphold his right to be heard. Many who rejected this argument on principle only did so with reluctance, and not without sympathy for the students, who did in fact disrupt the meeting and poured water over the observer.

The arguments of liberals of strict and undivided observance was however fortified when the same students went on from the wrecked Vietnam meeting—"dizzy with success", as Joe Stalin used to say—to break up a meeting being addressed elsewhere in the building by James

Reston, the Washington correspondent of the *New York Times*. Reston had, in fact, hedged on the war and other subjects, and close student questioning of him would have been in order. By breaking up his meeting, however, these students showed that they were prepared to deny a hearing, not just to a symbolic personage like a representative of South Vietnam or South Africa, but to anyone with whose opinions they did not agree. As the number of persons with whom they did agree was small indeed, this opened up a rather dismal practical prospect—even apart from the basic issue of principle—for the university.

The question now agitating the university concerns what disciplinary action should be taken against those concerned, and how it should be taken. The first relevant disciplinary hearing took place this week. The debate around this hearing hinged on the question of whether the hearing should be open or closed. A University Senate rule passed last year—in conditions of incipient turbulence—lays down that such hearings should be held in private, without admitting any members of the faculty or students, unless directly affected. A number of members of the faculty—including the present writer—hold that, where the disciplinary hearings have political associations, all members of the faculty and students are, in present circumstances, directly affected. We argued therefore that open hearings should be held, that if attempts are made to disrupt these hearings the disrupters should be removed, and that only if the behaviour of the student public is such that the open hearing become impossible should closed hearings be resorted to. Faced with this demand, the administration fell back on a rather unhappy compromise: faculty and students—apart from those "directly affected," in a narrowly constituted sense—would be excluded from the hearings themselves, but the proceedings would be televised for the university community, on closed-circuit, and screened for simultaneous viewing in the Loeb Student Centre. As "private proceedings" are not normally televised, this concession made nonsense of the administration's claim to be governed by a Senate rule which it had no power to change, while at the same time it did not appease the critics, who pointed out that television could be turned off, which was in practice done.

Faculty members calling for open hearings decided to go to the place of hearing at the time of its opening at one o'clock last Thursday, and there to request admission. These faculty members were identified as the "radical group," although in fact their position on this matter was a liberal one. (They were not defending any "right" to disrupt meetings or hearings.) The title liberal was, however, reserved for another faculty group, which proceeded, very separately, to the same spot, and which might more accurately have been distinguished as "humanitarian."

Their very respectable position was that they did not agree either with the students who would demonstrate in support of the student on trial, or with their "radical" colleagues, requesting admission to the hearings, but that if the proceedings should, as at Columbia, culminate in the use of force by the police, they wished to be present, strive to avert violence and, if necessary, share the fate of their colleagues and students.

In practice, nothing very dramatic happened on this particular occasion. About 500 students, mostly belonging to Students for a Democratic Society, converged on the place of hearings, using the slogans : "Open it up or shut it down" (with reference to the hearings), "Work, study, get ahead, kill" (a terse summary of the role in which they believe their society has cast them and which they reject), and finally and more inscrutably, "Law and order."

Outside the hearing centre was a police barrier, manned by a small number of patrolmen on foot. In reserve were mounted and helmeted police. We requested admission and were refused by a gentleman in plainclothes, who wore an armband marked "Faculty" and looked like a policeman. He identified himself as a member of the Law School. A few of the students began to shout abuse at the police in a rather half-hearted way: "Government by pigs" could be heard, and an occasional "Oink, oink." The police, to whom these witticisms were obviously not new, looked bored rather than irritated. No violence of any kind occurred, although a speech by an S.D.S. organisor—not a student at New York University—hinted that violence of some unspecified kind might later be used under some unspecified conditions.

The student on trial came out, having made a prepared statement to his judges and having indicated that he would take no further part in the proceedings. The radical students then walked off with him to the student centre, where other students, in slightly smaller number and of a less radical tinge, were watching the continued proceedings on closed-circuit television. The setting and atmosphere were that of a newsreel cinema. The radical student leaders summoned the television audience to join them in a march of protest round the University. None of the viewers moved. There were cries of "Shut up" and "Get out." After a while the radicals withdrew. (Among those who stayed I noticed one of the most extreme radicals of last year.)

The tribunal has not yet delivered its sentence. If it is a severe one more vigorous demonstrations, but probably not much larger ones, are to be expected. "We are living on a volcano," said a senior member of the administration privately. He added, more suprisingly, that the pressure of student radicalism, however unreasonable it might sometimes be, was essential to the healthy growth of universities at this time.

The debate continues.

26

BIAFRA REVISITED

I

On Easter Sunday I paid my second visit to Biafra. The first visit had been eighteen months before, in the third month of the Nigerian War, September 1967.[1] Then we had come in overland, by Land Rover from Mamfe in Cameroun, to Calabar: we—then as now I traveled with Stanley Diamond, Professor of Anthropology at the New School for Social Research in New York—had interviewed the Biafran leader Colonel Ojukwu in Enugu, and had visited Port Harcourt and Onitsha, where we crossed the Niger Bridge into the section of the Mid-West region then held by Biafran forces. Enugu fell within a few days of our visit; shortly afterward the land route of access was cut. Biafran forces evacuated the Mid-West and destroyed the Niger Bridge. Later Onitsha fell, after a stubborn defense. In the South Port Harcourt and Calabar were lost. What is left of Biafra, territorially, is now accessible only by air.

We traveled there by way of Lisbon, Angola, and the Portuguese island of São Tomé. The jet flight from Lisbon to Luanda takes nine hours: Portuguese Airlines must fly around the bulge of Africa, instead of taking the much shorter trans-Saharan route. The flight from Luanda to São Tomé takes two hours, in a twin-propeller Fokker, which makes the journey only once a week, if weather conditions are suitable. In this approach one gains a sense of Biafra's isolation, not merely physical but political. The Portuguese lifeline is itself under

New York Review of Books, 22 May 1969, pp. 15–23, 26–27.

pressure of boycott, and its use, vitally indispensable as it is, entails political disadvantage for the Biafrans. It's a lifeline to whose existence the states of the Organization for African Unity are opposed in principle.

The level of prosperity in Portuguese São Tomé is perceptibly higher than on any part of the West African continental coast. Military and police are not nearly as conspicuous here as we saw them to be in Angola, nor are there any other signs of an emergency. Profound peace appears to reign here; even the boasts of an inter-racial society are not without all foundation. We watched the Good Friday procession in which about a thousand of the faithful followed, with candles in their hands, the coffin of Christ and the statue of his mourning mother. The crowd was made up of both blacks and whites, and many shades in between. It would be only too easy for a paleo-colonialist to draw a moving contrast between this apparent peace and harmony and the horrors which two kinds of independence have brought to nearby Nigeria. (To be effective the contrast would have to be confined, on the Portuguese side, to São Tomé: the names of Angola and Mozambique carry with them the reminder of the horrors of persistence in colonialism.)

In a little São Tomé restaurant we asked a young Biafran, who had been living in São Tomé for three months, what he thought of the Portuguese system. He showed signs of embarrassment at the question: he was hardly in a position to criticize his hosts. Finally he said that the system, though "paternalist," was probably all right for the São Tomé people, who were living in the nineteenth century, or maybe the eighteenth. As for him, he was homesick and wanted to get back to Biafra as soon as possible. Without any self-consciousness or heroics he made it clear that the idea of living at peace under any kind of colonialism, as compared with having to fight for independence, was not even a temptation for him.

The Joint Church Aid relief flights from São Tomé to the improvised air strip at Uli in Biafra are operated, on alternate nights, by the World Council of Churches and by the Catholic organization, Caritas Internationalis. We had a reasonable claim to be permitted to use these flights: Stanley Diamond and I are both trustees of the American Biafra Relief Services Foundation, which has raised over two million dollars for relief and rehabilitation in Biafra. Part of the object of our journey was to see the use which the Biafran Committee, which operated the various medical and other projects sponsored by the Foundation, was making of the funds and supplies.

We were, however, also known as sympathizers with Biafra's political claim to a separate existence, and the World Council people, one of whom did not conceal his perhaps understandable distaste for semi-political cargo, could not find room for us on "their night." Finally we went in, in a C97, along with ten tons of salt, on a Caritas flight, the night of the 2,000th relief flight from São Tomé. Between twenty-five and thirty flights a night (and sometimes more) were being operated, carrying about 250 tons of food and medical supplies each night.

Each pilot did two or three flights a night; only the "two-flight" ones carried passengers. The pilots coming off duty were celebrating the 2,000 in modest quantities of Portuguese champagne. They had earned it, the strain of flying the São Tomé-Uli run regularly must be considerable. Apart from the occasional hazards of Nigerian bombing and anti-aircraft fire (and that of Biafran anti-aircraft mistaking its target) there is the permanent and probably more serious hazard of having to use a very busy "airport"—which is little more than a stretch of road—with the use of lights kept to the barest minimum. Uli is receiving not only from São Tomé but also from Cotonou, Santa Isabel, and Libreville. At the busiest hours, landings and take-offs seem to occur in uninterrupted series, while an unbroken line of lightless Biafran trucks moves up to receive the cargoes and take them away. The speed, efficiency, and order of this improvised and delicate operation are really astonishing.

Our own flight was uneventful, if salty. We were met by our host, Dr. Fabian Udekwu, formerly Professor of Surgery at Ibadan and organizer of the Biafran Relief Services Association, who took us in his car the two-hour journey to the provincial capital, Umuahia. He was already a refugee twice over; once from Ibadan, after the murder of General Ironsi, later from northern Biafra after the entry of Federal troops. He had just thought himself on the verge of becoming a refugee for the third time; the fall of Umuahia, where he worked, had been feared. What principally distressed him about that was the thought of having to abandon Queen Elizabeth hospital in Umuahia, with the new extensions which he had just made with the help of the Foundation: "It would have been a sword through my heart," he said. The Biafran forces had repelled the Nigerian drive, recaptured the village of Uzuakoli sixteen miles west of Umuahia, and seized some armored vehicles.

The battle of Umuahia had been fought on Good Friday: this was Easter Sunday morning; for the moment Umuahia seemed safe. (After we left, Umuahia fell, on April 24; the hospital is now in Nigerian hands.) It was about three in the morning. In several places files of women with burdens on their heads were moving along the sides of the road. Some women, Dr. Udekwu said, preferred to go to market early these days: the bombing. He talked of other things: of his years of sur-

gical work in Chicago, at the Cook County Hospital; the experience he
had acquired there with gun-shot wounds was now of service to him. He
spoke of Harold Wilson, in tones of wonder: "That man sits in London
and says he knows what's best *for me*! And he's never even *been* here!"

Biafra, when we saw it by day, had a very different aspect from that
which we had seen on our previous visit, in September 1967. It was not
(as we had feared) that there were many visible signs of famine. The terrible conditions of August and September 1968—when people, mainly
children, were dying of malnutrition at the rate of between five and six
thousand a day—have been checked, as a result of the relief airlift. At
present, relief workers estimate that perhaps one hundred people die in
this way each day, mainly in the immediate war zone. We saw the red-
dish hair and other signs of the kwashiorkor disease among children
(caused by protein deficiency) rather more often, but not startlingly
more often, than one sees such cases in West Africa in peacetime.
Otherwise the people we saw (outside the hospitals), including most
of the children, looked fairly well fed (though appearances may be
deceptive).

Even an appearance of relatively good health is an astounding,
though precarious achievement. There are now more than 700,000
people living in schools that have been converted into refugee camps,
and a far greater number of refugees—estimated by the Biafra
Rehabilitation Commission at about 5 million—have been absorbed in
the villages, under the extraordinarily elastic hospitality of the "extended family" relationship, or at the request of the Biafran government. The food airlifted to Uli by the Church organizations and Red
Cross is collected by Biafran trucks nightly and carried to the camps and
to the over-populated villages. In every village a nutritional clinic or
feeding center has been set up, administered by the village under the
sponsorship of one of the relief agencies: the relief agencies supply the
protein for the refugees, while the carbohydrates, fats, and vegetables
are supplied by the host villages. In addition every available source of
local protein is tapped: villagers and refugees alike eat rats, mice, liz-
ards, snails, caterpillars, and grasshoppers. Famine—as Biafra knew it in
1968—is being held at bay for the moment, but only just. Most camp-
dwellers have only one meal a day, and many refugees still receive less
than 1200 calories a day.[2] Many relief workers fear that the "protein
famine" of 1968 may be followed in 1969 by an even more disastrous
carbohydrate famine, before which an airlift would be powerless because of the bulk of the supplies required.

Biafran doctors and scientists—a very important and influential group of people in wartime Biafra—do not fully share the apprehensions of the foreign relief workers. They believe that the Biafran people themselves, through the "Land Army" and the more and more intensive cultivation of their soil—of which we saw evidence everywhere, along the country roads and on every available patch of ground in the town of Umuahia itself—not only can remain self-sufficient in carbohydrates but can in time become less dependent on outside aid in protein also.

They believe for example that Biafra can re-establish its poultry industry; if the relief agencies will provide the necessary day-old chicks and seed corn, the Biafrans think they can do the rest. Outside relief workers—some of them at least—are skeptical about this claim. They may be right; I am incompetent to express an opinion on this question. The Biafran doctors and scientists with whom I spoke were as qualified and as visibly competent and dedicated as the relief-workers, and it would be their own people who would suffer if they were wrong. Is it possible that the old European reluctance to admit that Africans have any capacity to look after their own affairs may be at work here unconsciously—despite the tangible proofs of ingenuity which the Biafrans have given?

One would think that people who have proved their ability to produce their own petrol and keep a road-transport and distribution system running efficiently under conditions of staggering difficulty might also know how to raise chickens. Yet one also hesitates to discount the opinion of people without whose efforts famine would actually be raging throughout Biafra now. The Biafrans are deeply conscious of this, and their differences of opinion with some relief workers are moderately and discreetly expressed. Nor can the "carbohydrate famine" danger be dismissed as unreal, in conditions where an area already as densely populated as the Nile valley has had to accommodate an influx of refugees doubling its original population.

The Goodell Report took the danger of a carbohydrate famine extremely seriously, and predicted a shortage of 730 calories per person per day during the four-month period April-July 1969. It may be that the Biafrans are under-estimating the danger, in their entirely unprecedented situation. Their commitment to their cause might tend to have this effect: it is possible also that the element of ingenuity in the Biafran character may be accompanied by an excessive optimism about what ingenuity may accomplish.

The phrase "the Biafran character" may surprise, Biafra being such a new entity. I use "Biafran" about people who regard themselves as

Biafrans, and about these only. Most of these people, but not all, are Ibos; the non-Ibos among them may not all be friendly to the Ibos—some of them speak sourly, in the presence of Ibos and otherwise, about Ibo attitudes to minorities in the past—but they share common values with Ibos and tend to pride themselves on the same qualities: egalitarian manners, thirst for education, commercial enterprise, self-reliance, and technical ingenuity. Hostile critics—who dominate Nigeria outside Biafra—would add arrogance, unscrupulousness, and rapacity to the list of Biafran characteristics, but generally admit the more positive qualities—as making the negative ones all the more dangerous. However it may be assessed, "the Biafran character" is a real thing.[3]

I do not know how many, among the "minority peoples"—Ibibio, Efik, Ijaw, and others—regard themselves as Biafrans. There are certainly a good many—as Biafrans themselves admit—fighting on the other side. In the present Biafran territory, among the educated "elite"—in whose company visitors to Biafra are likely to find themselves most of the time—the proportion of minority people is high, and their Biafran sentiment strong. It is hard to guess the proportion among the population generally, but there are certainly many non-Ibos among the non-elite. One member of the party with which we traveled was "a minority," and several times greeted people from his own village—people obviously not belonging to the Establishment—in the villages through which we passed; if this was a staged performance the people involved were consummate actors, and planted with a verisimilitude attainable only by a director of genius.

The Goodell Report estimates that 40 percent of the minority groups belonging to areas now occupied by Federal troops are now in Biafran held territory. Neither the figure nor the exact reasons for this particular movement of population would be easy to verify at present. In any case the only ultimately satisfactory solution to this vexed question of minority allegiance seems to be that proposed by Colonel Ojukwu: an internationality supervised plebiscite among the various communities (after the cessation of hostilities) on the question of whether they want to belong to Nigeria or Biafra.

The change which stuck me most, between Year One and Year Two, was in the relation of "popular" to "elite" elements. In the period after the fall of the Mid-West, and just before the fall of Enugu, there were signs everywhere of a sort of Jacobin spirit, combining exacerbated patriotism with intense suspicion of treachery: a suspicion directed in particular at Biafrans with official credentials. Mixed groups of police, soldiers, and militia then manned the innumerable road-blocks, with little regard for rank among their own number. They had no respect for official cars, and a disconcerting spontaneity in the manipulation of lethal weapons.

With respect to crisis, Easter 1969 was a comparable period: once again the capital was in imminent danger of falling. But the atmosphere was very different. Along the main roads, the road-blocks, considerably less frequent, were manned by disciplined police: along the side roads by civil defense workers, also disciplined: everywhere, when Dr. Udekwu gave his credentials ("State House") he was greeted in a friendly or respectful manner. There was no trace of vigilantism.

I record the change as a fact. How is it to be interpreted? Does it imply a decline in popular support for the Biafran cause? One European woman I talked to, who knew the villages through her relief work, was inclined to think so. Women in particular, she thought, were war-weary: recently, for the first time, she had heard the question asked: Might not the price be too high? She admitted, however, that support for Colonel Ojukwu continued strong: this seemed to qualify the question about the price.

My own observation, limited as it was, suggested that the people continued to support the cause and the war no less strongly than before, though in a different mood. For about forty miles, during a journey from near Awka to Umuahia, we had to follow behind a military convoy of five trucks. In every village we passed through, the people greeted the soldiers, sometimes cheering them, more often exchanging chaff; there were laughter and smiles. At a hospital, one of our group produced a tape recorder and the walking wounded—about twenty-five of them—gathered round to sing the war songs of Biafra. They were very young; they had been in action with their light weapons, short of ammunition, against a heavily armed, copiously supplied, and vastly more numerous enemy. They would soon be going back into action, under the same conditions. It would have been hard not to be moved and impressed by their singing.

The mood had changed. The soldiers and people had suffered greatly. Senator Goodell's Biafra Study Mission estimated that about 1½ million people died in Biafra in the twelve months ending February 1969, "from famine and associated causes of death." Many of the survivors—the nearly 6 million refugees estimated by the Biafran Rehabilitation Commission—have lost almost everything they possessed. All are suffering from acute shortage of almost all commodities, from extremely high prices, and from numerous other privations, including a two-year hiatus in education. The daily air-raids, although they have caused far fewer deaths than hunger and disease have caused, add considerably to the nervous strain, as they are entirely indiscriminate and may strike anywhere in any village, at any daylight hour. Figures of military casualties are hard to obtain, but the hospitals are full of badly wounded soldiers.

It was not surprising that the exuberance of 1967 had gone. But the suspicion so prevalent in that period had gone too. It seemed to me that the people had greater confidence in their leaders; no doubt it was clear that anyone who wished to "sell out" would probably have done so already. The people also seemed to know what they were up against: a long war if they were to be able to survive as a nation. The new mood, as far as we could analyze it, seemed to be one of chastened determination.

When we got back from Awka to Umuahia on Easter Monday evening, we found that the compound in which we had been staying—a former agricultural research station a few miles from Umuahia—had been strafed in our absence by four Migs. One of the houses hit had been that of our host, Dr. Udekwu (who had accompanied us on our trip). A projectile had gone through his bedroom, and under his bed, at a level of about six inches from the floor, leaving a hole six inches in diameter in both walls. It had passed through a cupboard destroying two tins of Vim, a detergent. He told us that when he was at home on such occasions it was under his bed that he habitually took cover. We told him we had saved his life, through the necessity of escorting us. He refused to be grateful, being too angry about his Vim.

The compound attacked in this way by low-flying aircraft is not near any military target.

II

When we met Colonel Ojukwu on the morning of Easter Tuesday, we found him calmer and apparently more confident than when we had met him last in Enugu eighteen months before. Yet his analysis of the situation was a forbidding one. Militarily, the vast disproportion between the equipment of his troops and that of the Nigerians had been lessened, but only slightly. The Biafrans for the moment had adequate ammunition for their rifles and light automatic weapons. They had no heavy weapons, other than certain home-made devices; no armored cars other than a few which they had captured from the enemy; no military aircraft at all. Their enemies were well provided by Britain and the Soviet Union with all these resources.

Nor did Colonel Ojukwu underestimate the fighting spirit of Federal troops. "Hausa troops," he said, "would always die rather than surrender." Mixed groups of Hausa, Yoruba, and people from the Rivers state had fought tenaciously, especially, we gathered, in defense of Owerri, where they had been encircled. (Owerri held out for some time after this, but its recapture by Biafran forces was confirmed by foreign correspondents on 27 April. It is a more important center than Umuahia, captured by Federal troops a few days before.) It was true that certain groups—he mentioned the Tivs—had been virtually eliminated from the fight, true also that the Biafran soldiers, fighting in defense of their homeland, were superior to their adversaries, man for man. He thought that this would show itself even more clearly if, instead of having to defend fixed positions like Umuahia, they were fighting a fully guerrilla war in the bush. But he agreed that the loss of Umuahia would be a heavy blow for political rather than military reasons.

Politically, he thought it would be folly to put much trust either in the hope of any imminent crack in the coalition of other Nigerian peoples against Biafra, or in the Organization for African Unity and its then approaching Monrovia Conference. The coalition might break down some day, but the only safe assumption was that it would hold together for the present. Among the OAU states there was a good deal of popular sympathy with Biafra but—apart from the Arab and Islamic factors—several governments which might otherwise be helpful were under economic pressure from Britain and sometimes elsewhere to support the Lagos position. He would send a delegation to Monrovia, so that Biafra's case would not go unstated, but he would not go there himself. He hoped for some new recognitions in addition to the four African states which already recognize Biafra—Gabon, Ivory Coast, Tanzania, and Zambia—yet he was obviously not counting on numerous or quick conversions.

In most respects, the picture presented by Colonel Ojukwu could hardly have been bleaker. His confidence, obvious in his demeanor, was based on his conviction of the unity, tenacity, and ingenuity of his people defending their heartland. He thought it would be a long war and that the institutions and ideology necessary to sustain it to a successful conclusion had not yet fully emerged. He spoke of what he called "the Biafran revolution" and said that the present Biafran government had evolved, somewhat to every one's surprise, into a civilian government of which he was a part. Now, when he spoke of the soldiers, he said he never quite knew whether to say "we" or "they." I noticed that his tone, when he said the word "civilian," altogether lacked that professional note of contempt which so many African officers have acquired from their instructors. (This account of Colonel Ojukwu's conversation is the record of the impressions of an attentive listener: although Colonel Ojukwu knew that we would be writing about our visit we were not interviewing him as journalists and took no notes.)

What is the future of the Biafrans of today if their territory is completely over-run by Federal troops? What form could a Biafran state take if Biafrans successfully hold off the Federal troops? Which result — Federal victory or Biafran survival—is desirable from the point of view of African independence and development?

As regards the first question, I found that the fears of total genocide—the systematic obliteration of all Ibos and minority peoples taking "the Ibo side"—which were horribly real in 1967—had to some extent diminished. Under certain commanders and in certain places—at Calabar, for example, under Benjamin Adekunle—Federal troops had engaged in systematic genocide; in other places, other commanders had refrained from this. Biafrans now know that large numbers of Ibos are at least surviving—for the present anyway—under Federal rule. Present fears are less dramatic than in the past, but equally real and pervasive. Surrender would put Biafrans at the mercy of people who had massacred their brothers both in the North and in various places inside the Eastern Region. Though few are even willing to speculate on what might happen if Biafra were completely overrun, some feel that the present relatively restrained treatment of Ibos remaining in many occupied areas may be influenced by the present relatively high level of international concern about the situation, and Nigeria's need to retain British support and not alienate the United States. Federal victory, removing or greatly weakening these protective factors, would create a new situation in which mass murder might easily be repeated—e.g., in the form of collective reprisals after individual acts of resistance.

But even on the most favorable hypothesis Biafrans consider themselves doomed, if defeated, to a life of second- or third-class citizenship in a state in which their energies and capacities would be denied proportionate outlets. "They would tell us to shut up," said one educated Biafran. He said he would rather die than have to shut up when he was told. His past record proved that he meant what he said.

An elite attitude? Perhaps; but it would be unwise to assume that it does not go much deeper. The gap between an educated African and the members of his extended family in the villages is sometimes exaggerated by European observers, and the use of the term "African elite" as a device for ignoring and expunging the opinions of Africans who happen not to be more uneducated than ourselves is rather too frequent among us, especially on the Left. (In practice it means that *all* Africans can be ignored as the opinion of the uneducated is necessarily uninformed.) In the case of Biafra, there can be no doubt that discrimination against Ibos in education and employment would be felt as a social and economic injury not to the elite only but to all the villages. It is not altogether surprising, then, that even relieved of some of their fears of imminent mass genocide, the Biafrans still feel they are engaged in a struggle for survival as the kind of people they are.

The question of what form a generally recognized Biafran state might take depends of course on whether a Federal government can eventually be obliged, either by stalemate and exhaustion or by a tilt of the military situation in favor of Biafra—e.g., as a result of a French decision to supply military aid on a considerable scale instead of the present thin trickle of light arms and ammunition—to accept the existence of *any* Biafran state. In this event, Colonel Ojukwu's proposal for internationally supervised plebescites in the minority areas would become relevant. If both sides were prepared to implement this in good faith, and to agree to the necessary movements of population—including the return of the Ibo-speaking population which formed the majority in Port Harcourt— then this could provide a hopeful basis for a stable solution. With Port Harcourt under its control, Biafra would be able to receive supplies by ship. Both sides, after a protracted experience of the vicissitudes of war, might well take care to avoid a new outbreak. On the other hand, Nigeria's acceptance of a landlocked Biafra, within something like the present military periphery, could only provide a breathing space: it is clear that if Biafrans saw what they considered a favorable opportunity for recovering Port Harcourt and access to the sea, they would run great risks to take it.

If Federal claims about the allegiance of minority peoples are correct, the plebiscites would cause Biafra to lose large areas of the former Eastern Region, including much of the oil-rich territory. A settlement on plebiscitary lines, whether with a fully independent Biafra or under some form of confederal arrangement, would be a genuine compromise between the original Biafran claims and the original Nigerian position. The exact nature of the difficulties which might be involved in carrying it out cannot be predicted in advance of the results of the plebescites, but it should be possible to combine Biafran access to Port Harcourt with the principle of minority self-determination. Should the plebiscites result in a "Biafran vote" in the Ibo heartland, and in Port Harcourt, with a "Nigerian vote" in a territory separating Port Harcourt from the heartland, it should be possible to meet the difficulty through a scheme of compensated resettlement of population, moving pro-Biafrans from Nigerian territory, and vice versa, and linking Port Harcourt territorially with the heartland. Large-scale resettlements of villages have been carried out quite smoothly elsewhere in Africa—e.g., in Ghana in the Volta settlement program. It is not of great significance that the new movements of people would be across a political line still to be created, since by definition any communities affected would be remaining in (or moving into) the political entity in which they felt they belonged.

To many observers—including the present writer—such an outcome seems far more desirable than either the continuation of the war or the subjugation of all of Biafra by the Federal forces. There are also many, however, who sincerely consider such a result unthinkable in principle, since it would involve the recognition of a secession and undermine the integrity of African states. Thus a friend of mine—at present teaching in an East African University—writes in part as follows:

> As for Ojukwu, I don't any more support secession in Nigeria than I would in the USA: (a) it won't work and (b) it isn't progressive. The future lies with nations, not tribes, and the longer people think otherwise the longer they serve to perpetuate the injury [of colonialism and white supremacism].

"The future lies with nations, not tribes...." Perhaps. But is Nigeria a nation? And are the Biafrans—as defined in the earlier part of this essay—a tribe? Are even the Ibo-speaking people—all 9 million of them—to be tagged as a tribe, politically fit only for amalgamation in a nationhood which they must be deemed to share with those who have massacred them? By what standards are strips of territory, like Dahomey and Togo (one of which is represented in the other by the French), to be considered nations worthy of condemning the concept of nationhood for which Biafrans have fought for nearly two years? In what way has Cameroun, whose national anthem includes the stirring line, *"Peu à peu nous sortons de la sauvagerie,"* yet earned the right to be regarded as a nation?

The answer of course is that colonization, followed by de-colonization, has resulted in certain political entities and not others. It is hoped that it is in conformity with these entities, and not otherwise, that the sense of nationhood will develop. This is reasonable as a hope and as a goal. It is also true that in fact a sense of nationhood, transcending tribal divisions, has often arisen and developed within the old colonial frontiers *against* the old colonial rulers. It is also entirely reasonable and legitimate that the new states should resist attempts by the former metropolitan power, or other outside interests, to manipulate their territories and resources, by re-annexing them under a secessionist front, as happened in Katanga.

But what happens when the attempt to build a nation within the old colonial frontiers visibly and tragically breaks down as it did in Nigeria? What happens when a numerous, spirited, and gifted people, finding by grim experience that its members cannot live in security throughout the territory of which it is supposed to be a part, takes its destiny into its own hands? Must we say that because the aspirations of this people are not reconcilable with the territorial system sanctioned at Berlin, and its extensions under de-colonization, this people must be defined as a tribe and crushed in the name of nationhood? Kenneth Kaunda in Zambia and Julius Nyerere in Tanzania at any rate do not think so.

"We accepted the boundaries we inherited from colonialism," said the Government of Tanzania in recognizing the Republic of Biafra,

and within them we each worked out for ourselves the constitutional and other arrangements which we felt to be appropriate to the most essential function of a state—that is the safeguarding of life and liberty for its inhabitants.... But when the machinery of the state, and the powers of the Government, are turned against a whole group of the society on grounds of racial, tribal, or religious prejudice, then the victims have the right to take back the powers they have surrendered, and to defend themselves.... In such a case the people have the right to create another instrument for their protection—in other words, to create another state.

The curious thing is that those who most insist on the sacrosanct character of the present "national-territories" are often the most acutely aware that many of the "nations" which they champion are in fact gliding rapidly not toward nationhood, but from a neo-colonial into a paleo-colonial condition. My anti-Biafran friend refers to the African country in which he finds himself at present as "the most repressive, aggressive and depressive place I've known." His wife details what he means, describing the returning arrogance of white supremacists. I myself saw this tendency at work immediately after my departure from Biafra when I landed in Cotonou, the capital of the independent and sovereign state of Dahomey. There, in the bar of the Croix du Sud Hotel—clientele entirely white at the time—a customer addressed the barman as follows: "Come on, Felix, you mess of a black ass, where's your sister?" Eight years or so ago, when "independence" was new, his white companions would have shushed him and hurried him home; this time they just laughed; it was "all right now." There are some African countries where such conduct would be inconceivable because Africans are really, and not merely nominally, running their own affairs.

One of these is certainly Biafra. Indeed in all tropical Africa, Biafra is probably the clearest case of a country where Africans, and only

Africans, are in charge. It is strange and sad that people who are sincerely and passionately devoted to the cause of Africa should recognize the numerous Dahomey-type façades and deny recognition to a genuinely heroic African independence struggle occurring before their eyes in Biafra. They not merely admit, of course, but strongly affirm the need for revolutionary change in the African states, but stipulate that such change must occur within the present boundaries: revolution is good but secession is bad. Yet there is really no more—indeed there is considerably less—reason to suppose that the forces of change will be more respectful of African boundaries than they have been of European ones. It is not to be expected that indigenous forces making for change will everywhere and always be confined within the boundaries which were laid down, without any regard for any indigenous forces at all, at Berlin and in other European capitals.

Biafra could almost certainly survive were it not for the relatively large military support given by Britain and the Soviet Union to Lagos as compared with the thin trickle of arms Biafra has managed to secure from elsewhere. Thus the subjugation of Biafra, if it should occur, would be yet another achievement of external technology and fire-power on African soil, and not in any way a vindication of the internal coherence of an African state. It would also provide the occasion for a smothering of African creativity and talent on a scale and in a manner never attempted by colonial powers directly. The survival of Biafra, on the other hand, would be a victory for African courage, endurance, and skill, and an opportunity for the further development of African creativity.

III

An end to fund-raising for Biafran relief is among the demands of Negro student demonstrators at the Samuel J. Tilden High School in the East Flatbush section of Brooklyn.

Asked why the demonstrators opposed aid to starving children of the secessionist province of Nigeria, a member of the school's Afro-American club explained:

"We black nationalists support Nigeria."

New York Times, April 24, 1969

In Biafra at Easter I had seen young Africans, probably about the same age as those who demonstrated at the Tilden High School, preparing to go back to the front and singing the war songs of their black nation: Biafra. The news item, combined with this experience, forced me to think about the reasons why Biafra seems to be either invisible or obnoxious to so many black Americans (though by no means to all). It was not the first time the question had occurred to me. Now it presented itself more insistently. Because of past experiences of my own, it was mainly by way of "the Katanga parallel" that black American suspicion or hostility in relation to Biafra had reached me: "You were against the secession of Katanga. Why are you *for* the secession of Biafra?" I have tried to explain that the cases were not parallel. Katanga had been a case of foreign intervention, not of genuine secession, as the chronology made clear:

10th July, 1960: seizure of Elisabethville, capital of Katanga, by Belgian paratroops.

11th July, 1960: Moïse Tshombe in the presence of the Belgian paratroop commander, Major Weber, declares the "independence" of Katanga.

The Katangese "patriots" were almost all Europeans and the pro-Katanga blacks were their employees. In any case the secession of Katanga was never anything but a maneuver for the recapture of the resources of the whole of the Congo: "We must rebuild the Congo, starting from Elisabethville," as Baron Rothschild said.

The Biafra case was entirely different. The element of military intervention by the former metropolitan power in support of secession was absent. The former metropolitan power was in fact supplying the armament for the destruction of Biafra. The movement for Biafran independence was a spontaneous movement representing more than 9 million Africans. Local European interests came down strongly against it. The British oil interests—the local equivalent to Katanga's Union Minière—did nothing to instigate secession, and opposed it even before Biafra declared the nationalization of its oil resources. Neo-colonialism is quite impartial about slogans, methods, principles, and doctrines, and uses whatever serves its turn: support for temporary "secession" in Katanga and for "unity" in Nigeria sounded different but served the same purpose: European capitalist control over the resources of Africa. The British Government in 1961 had considered the use of force against Katanga "unthinkable." From 1967 to 1969 the British Government—a different one but animated by the same desire to protect British financial interests—supported the use of force against Biafra and supplied the Lagos Government with the means to destroy Biafra.

Black students would listen politely to this line of argument, and even take it into consideration, but they were seldom convinced. The reasons for the anti-Biafran feeling lay deeper than the "Katanga parallel," though they were related to it. The Tilden student demonstrator put it in a nutshell when he said: "We black nationalists support Nigeria." He quite simply and naturally saw Nigeria as a black nation: one of the largest and most populous of black nations, and for long one of the most admired. The attainment of independence by the African states had been an important factor in the resurgence of black America. These states were called "nations" and anything that put the nationhood of any of them in question seemed to belittle the achievement of independence. The idea that nationhood in Africa might have to assert itself in other ways than within the frontiers of colonization and de-colonization opened up too long and confusing a perspective to be readily acceptable.

The simple fact that Nigeria is no more a nation than Austria/ Hungary or the Ottoman Empire—those "prison-houses of peoples"— is hard to assimilate, because the idea of the sovereignty, solidity, and full nationhood of the existing African states—not of some putative future ones—has been felt as a vitally necessary element in the morale of black Americans in their struggle against a white racist society. The Nigerian civil war evokes images of that depressing Africa of "warring tribes" from which the old slavers, in their more moralistic moments, used to claim to have rescued the blacks of America.

This situation causes many blacks to be highly suspicious of the motives of white sympathy with Biafra, and much less suspicious about the motives for the materially far more significant white support for Nigeria. There is a suspicion that white sympathy with Biafra is a mask for anti-black feelings, hostility to the existence of black states, pleasure in thinking of oneself as Lady Bountiful and in having "them" depend on "us" as against "their own kind," concentration of interest on a spectacle of "African savagery" in the conduct of the Federal troops, and so on. I do not myself believe that elements of this kind enter to any significant degree into the motives of those who are in any way really active in helping or supporting Biafra. I do not doubt however that all of these kinds of *schadenfreude* are present among the reactions of white audiences generally to news and pictures of the war in Nigeria. In any case, it is impossible for most blacks, knowing what they do of the white society in which they live, to imagine that white sympathy for Biafra could be anything other than hypocritical and loaded with hostility.

There are other factors at work, reinforcing the basic impulse to resist something which is felt as a threat to black nationhood. There are for example the "Moslem" and "Portuguese" factors. For Black Muslims, of course, the Biafrans are just brainwashed Christians, predictably ranged against the twin forces of Islam and black nationality. In this quarter the Biafran case may not even be argued. *Muhammad Speaks* recently (11th and 18th April) carried a long article based on a tape-recorded interview with the present writer in which it carefully and accurately printed everything of any significance I had said, except what I had to say about Biafra.

But the Moslem factor in the Biafran conflict may well affect more black Americans than those who belong to the nation of Islam. The Moslem "image" is a powerful one and if it has captivated many romantically minded Europeans it is not surprising that it should appeal to many black Americans, through its association with indigenous dignity and imperviousness to Europeanization. The negative side of the Arab impact on sub-Saharan Africa is little known, and white references to it are suspect—quite legitimately indeed: the pretext invoked by Leopold II for grabbing the Congo was "liberation" from the Arab slave trade.

The Portuguese factor is for some a clincher. Since the Portuguese, the oppressors of Angola and Mozambique, the last unrepentantly and openly colonialist power, are "supporting" Biafra, can anyone doubt that African nationalists should support Nigeria? Portuguese support appears in practice to be limited to allowing Biafran planes to use facilities in Portuguese-held territory, Bissau and São Tomé. This Portuguese "assistance"—provided I believe on a commercial basis—is in no way comparable, as a practical element in the military situation, to the copious flow of military supplies from Britain and the Soviet Union to Lagos. São Tomé is important as a source of civilian relief, not of arms.

Nor indeed is French aid to Biafra—consisting so far of a trickle of small arms and ammunition—comparable with the Soviet military aircraft and British armored cars and artillery—and now, it seems, tanks— which are available to Lagos. But the British and Soviet supplies become invisible as they go to what is thought of as a black nation, while the French and Portuguese aid seems disproportionately important because it is seen as aid for secession and "tribalism." The habit of referring to the Ibo-speaking peoples—more numerous than many European nations, including my own—as "a tribe" does them immense harm. Once Nigeria is seen as a nation and Biafra as a tribe, the verdict against Biafra is delivered with certainty, as at the Tilden High School.

We all tend to think in analogies and stereotypes about situations of which we have no direct experience. The white grid of analogies and stereotypes about Africa has served to promote racist arrogance among whites inside and outside Africa. Now another historically formed grid—powerfully affected by the necessity of dismantling the white one—stands between many black Americans and a realization of what Biafra means.

The Biafrans have been trying to break this grid down, and the recent visit to this country of Chinua Achebe, probably the most distinguished living African novelist, must have made a significant impression. Of the two best-known writers of the old Nigeria—and perhaps of all Africa—one, Achebe, is a convinced Biafran patriot, and the other, the playwright Wole Soyinka (a Yoruba), is a prisoner in Northern Nigeria, after having sought to bring about a cease-fire. No one seriously interested in African literature, in its relation to African social and political life, can have failed to ponder the meaning of the choices and fates of these two men.

The war continues with varying fortunes, Federal hopes that the fall of Umuahia might mean the end of Biafran resistance were dashed by the Biafran recapture of Owerri a few days later. The attitudes of black Americans as well as of others may change as the realities of Biafra's stubborn fight become more clear. It would help if representatives of black organizations in this country—not just Negroes chosen by the American government—would visit both Biafra and Nigeria, on a fact-finding mission.[4] If they did so the most skeptical would, I believe, soon see where it is that the flame of African independence burns most brightly, and why it is that Biafrans and their friends believe that the name of Odumegwu Ojukwu deserves to stand in African history with that of Patrice Lumumba as a symbol of African endurance, courage, and patriotism.

NOTES

1 See *New York Review*, December 21, 1967.
2 I am indebted here to two reports, available only in mimeographed form—"History of the Relief Programme to Biafra," by Rev. Anthony Byrne (São Tomé, 10 December, 1968) and "Biafran Refugees: Problems of Disease, Prevention and Medical Care" by Dr. Chukuedu Nwokolo (Biafran Rehabilitation Commission, January, 1969)—as well as to the report of Senator Goodell's Biafra Study Mission (United States *Congressional Record*: Senate, 25 February, 1969). The Goodell report contains a detailed study of the relief situation and much other information. It should be read by all concerned with the question of Biafra.
3 I do not mean by this that, even among those who "choose Biafra," all inter-ethnic suspicions have disappeared. A paper, "Tribalism in Biafra: Symptoms and Cures," read by Professor Eyo B. E. Ndem at a seminar at Government College, Umuahia, on 29th March, 1969, discusses with considerable frankness anti-Ibo attitudes prevalent

among minority groups both "before the revolution" and "lying dormant" since then. Professor Ndem is himself a member of a minority group, and is a convinced Biafran. His view is that although "group-hate in Biafra" never reached the destructive intensity which it reached "in Nigeria," it remains a danger and needs to be combated by various conscious efforts including the encouragement of inter-marriage (which already takes place among some groups, e.g., Ibos and Ibibio in Calabar).

4 I tried myself to visit Nigeria as well as Biafra but it was made plain to me that I would not be a particularly welcome visitor. As what I wished to visit in Nigeria was not so much Lagos as the Federally held area of the old Eastern Region, I needed assurances of Nigerian official cooperation. These were not forthcoming either from Nigerian diplomats here or from Chief Ehahoro, who was here at the time.

27

Camus, Algeria, and "The Fall"

Camus's political writings on the Algerian war are collected in *Actuelles III (Chroniques Algériennes)* which he published in 1958. It is a depressing volume. The manner, in the post-1945 essays, is not so much that of Camus as that of the moderate bourgeois French journalism of the period: categorical and resonant in tone, equivocal in substance.

> The Arab personality will be recognized by the French personality but in order for that to happen, France must exist. "You must choose your side," cry the haters. Oh I have chosen it! I have chosen my country. I have chosen the Algeria of justice in which French and Arabs will associate freely!

He had one concrete idea during this early part of the war—that of a "truce for civilians." He went to Algeria in January 1956 and presented this idea at a public meeting. The proposal was badly received. Camus was attacked by the Europeans, largely ignored by the Moslems. An informant of Albert Memmi spoke of his disappointment at Camus's "sweet sister" speech.

The dual crisis of the autumn of 1956—Suez and Hungary—brought a closer assimilation of Camus's position to that of the French right-of-center. He supported the Hungarian rebels—as did Sartre—but, unlike Sartre, drew "European" lessons from their action: "in spite of the dramatic bankruptcy of the traditional movements and ideals of the left, the real Europe exists united in justice and in liberty, confronting all tyrannies."[1] In relation to Suez, the only violence which he condemned

New York Review of Books, 9 October 1969, pp. 6, 8, 10–12.

was that of the language of Marshall Bulganin.[2] In a message to French students on Hungary he acclaimed "that violent and pure force which drives men and peoples to claim the honor of living upright."[3] At the same time, he believed that as a result of the lesson of Hungary, "We will be less tempted to overwhelm our own nation, and it alone, under the weight of its historic sins. We will be more careful—without ceasing to demand from her all the justice of which she is capable—about her survival and her liberty."[4]

The France whose survival was in question was a France which included Algeria: thus the rightness of the Hungarian rebellion provided a reason for putting down the Algerian one. In respect of methods, his position remained humane: torture was "as contemptible in Algiers as in Budapest."[5] Hope nonetheless resided exclusively in the Western camp:

> The defects of the West are numberless, its crimes and its faults real. But in the last analysis, let us not forget that we are the only people who hold that power of improvement and emancipation which resided in the genius of freedom (*le libre génie*).[6]

Despite his revulsion from the methods of the repression, his position was necessarily one of support for repression, since he consistently opposed negotiation with the actual leaders of the rebellion, the FLN. In 1955 he had proposed an Algerian round table without the FLN, and in 1958 in the Foreword to his *Chroniques Algériennes (Actuelles III)*, he points out that negotiation with the FLN would lead to "the independence of Algeria controlled by the most implacable military leaders of the insurrection, that is to say, the eviction of 1,200,000 Europeans of Algeria and the humiliation of millions of Frenchmen, with the risks involved in the humiliation."

He makes it clear that he rejects this independence, and therefore the negotiation. The rejection of negotiation is basic and necessarily implies support for the substance, if not for the details of the methods, of the French Government's policy of pacification. The actual political formulas proposed by Camus in 1958 have to be situated in the light of this: they are formulas of a type frequently canvassed and varied by French governments at this period, designed to help the process of pacification—through the isolation of the FLN—and capable of execution only after the suppression of the FLN, if at all.

Thus the regime of "free association" which he foresaw required French military victory over the insurgents. After that he aspired to the extension of democratic rights to the Arab population, but the results of the democratic process could be overruled from France. The French Government was urged to announce:

> One: that it is disposed to give full justice to the Arab people of Algeria and to liberate it from the colonial system; two: that it will make no concession on the question of the rights of the French of Algeria; three: that it cannot accept that the justice which it will consent to render should signify for the French nation the prelude for a sort of historic death and for the West the risk of an encirclement which would lead to the kadarization of Europe and the isolation of America.[7]

Camus's position in the Fifties was one of extreme intellectual and emotional difficulty and tension. He had written about freedom, justice, violence, and revolt in abstract terms and asserted principles which he presented as of both fundamental importance and universal application. He never altogether abandoned this language and he continued to write about politics in the tone of a severe moralist. Yet his actual positions were political and partisan. The violence of the Hungarian rebels and of the Anglo-French expedition in Egypt raised no problems. It was violence "on the right side": precisely the logic he had rejected, on grounds of a rigorous morality, in relation to revolutionary violence. Freedom was an absolute for the Hungarians and their violence in asserting their will "to stand upright" was "pure." The violence of the Algerian Arabs, who thought that they were making the same claim, was "inexcusable" and the nature and degree of the freedom to be accorded to them was a matter to be decided by France, in the light of its own strategic needs—a plea which was irrelevant when made by Russia.

He remained in fact a Frenchman of Algeria and what seemed to be the increasingly right wing positions of his later years were latent in his earlier silences. The only public statement of Camus on the subject of the Algerian war that has the ring of complete candor is one that he made in Sweden in December 1957 just after he had received the Nobel Prize: "I have always condemned terror. I must also condemn a terrorism which operates blindly, in the streets of Algiers for example, and which one day may strike my mother or my family. I believe in justice but I will defend my mother before justice."[8]

The defense of his mother required support for the French army's pacification of Algeria. It is only in the light of this situation, with all its conflicts and ironies, that one can understand Camus's last and perhaps his best novel, *La Chute (The Fall)*.

La Chute began as a story for *L'Exil et le Royaume*, and is marked by some of the same preoccupations as the stories in that collection. The place of exile is Holland, the setting a dock-side bar. The story is cast in the form of a monologue; the narrator is Jean-Baptiste Clamence, once a lawyer, now describing himself as "a penitent judge" (*juge pénitent*).[9] Clamence's style is elaborate and ceremonious. "I see you gag at that imperfect subjunctive. I must confess my weakness for that form and for fine language in general." One of the reproaches that had stung Camus most at the time of the publication of *L'Homme Révolté* was that of excessive elegance in style: in the person of Clamence he gives this tendency full rein, while partly parodying it, and taunts his adversaries. He diagnoses that his interlocutor is a bourgeois: but a "refined bourgeois! To gag over imperfect subjunctives indeed proves your culture twice over since you recognize them in the first place and then since they irritate you."

The setting, like so much in *L'Exil et le Royaume*, is dreamlike: "Holland is a dream, sir. A dream of gold and smoke. More smoky by day and more gold by night. Did you notice that the concentric canals of Amsterdam are like the circles of hell? A bourgeois hell, naturally, peopled with bad dreams."

Clamence tells of his life in Paris, as a lawyer: "I specialized in noble causes.... I had my heart on my sleeve. You would have really thought that justice slept with me every night." He abounded in small courtesies, was generous, lived a full life:

> I succeeded in loving at the same time women and justice, which is not easy. I went in for sports and fine arts.... I was made to have a body, hence that harmony in me, that easy mastery which people felt and which helped them to live, they sometimes told me. In truth, through being a man, with so much plenitude and simplicity, I became a little bit of a superman.

One day when coming back from court after making "a brilliant improvisation ... on the hardness of heart of our ruling class," Clamence was crossing the Pont des Arts when he heard a laugh behind him, looked around and saw no one there: "The laugh had nothing mysterious about it. It was a good laugh, friendly...." That evening when Clamence saw his face in the bathroom mirror "it seemed to me that my smile was double."

He tells of another incident which altered his picture of himself. Getting out of his car to remonstrate with a stalled motorcyclist who refuses to move and uses abusive language, he is hit in the face by a pedestrian who takes the side of the motorcyclist. Behind his car, a line of traffic starts to honk horns. He returns to his car and drives off while the pedestrian taunts him with cowardice: "After having been struck in public without reacting, it was no longer possible for me to caress that beautiful image of myself." He dreams of revenge: "The truth is that every intelligent man dreams of being a gangster and of ruling over society through violence alone. As that is not as easy as you might think by reading certain kinds of novels, one generally relies on politics and runs to the cruellest party. What does it matter after all to humiliate one's mind if in that way you can succeed in dominating everybody? I discovered in myself sweet dreams of oppression."

He tells of a kind of love affair. He learns that a woman with whom he had once slept had told a third party that he was not much good. He takes care to recapture this woman, dominate her, and mortify her: "Until the day when in the violent disorder of a painful and constrained pleasure, she rendered homage aloud to what enslaved her. On that day I started to get farther away from her, since I had forgotten her."

Then he tells of his "essential discovery": Crossing the Pont Royal in Paris one night in November, three years before the evening when he heard the laugh, he sees a young woman leaning over the parapet. After passing her, he hears the noise of a body falling into the water. He stops without turning round. He hears a cry repeated several times, going down the river and then ceasing. He listens for a while, then walks off with short steps in the rain: "I informed nobody."

His relations with his friends change: "My fellows ceased to be in my eyes the respectful audience I was used to. The circle of which I was the center broke and they placed themselves in a single row, as on a courthouse bench.... Yes they were there as before but they were laughing.... The whole universe started laughing around me."

Clamence is pursued by a ridiculous thought: "One could not die without having confessed all one's lies. Not to God or one of his representatives. I was above that as you may imagine. No—to confess it to men, to a friend or a woman one loved for example." He cherishes such projects as jostling blind men in the street, bursting the tires of invalid chairs, and slapping infants in the subway: "The very word justice threw me into strange furies."

One day on a transatlantic liner he sees a black spot on the ocean. He looks away, his heart beating. When he looks back the black spot has disappeared. It bobs up again, a piece of flotsam.

> Yet I had not been able to look at it. I had thought immediately of a drowned person. I understood then, with acceptance, as one resigns oneself to an idea whose truth one has known for a long time, that that cry which years before had rung out on the Seine behind me had not ceased, carried by the river to-

wards the waters of the Channel, to make its way in the world across the vast space of the ocean and that it had waited for me until this day when I met it again. I understood also that it would continue to wait for me on the seas and on the rivers—everywhere where might be found the bitter water of my baptism. Even here, tell me, are we not on the water?

He speaks of the guilt of Jesus for the deaths of the Innocents: "That sadness which you can make out in all his acts. Was it not the incurable melancholy of one who heard throughout the nights the voice of Rachel, groaning over her little ones and refusing all consolation? The cry rose in the night. Rachel called her children, killed for him, and he was living."

He realizes that he is again pleading a case. He is half-advocate, half-prophet: "After all, that's what I am, taking asylum in a wilderness of stone, of fog and stagnant water. An empty prophet for a mediocre time. Elijah without a Messiah. Crammed with fever and alcohol, my back stuck to this mildewed door, my finger lifted towards a lowering sky, covering with curses lawless men who cannot bear any judgment."

He takes to his bed suffering from "swamp fever, I think, which I picked up when I was Pope." This was during the war, in North Africa when Clamence had been neutral between the opposing parties, and subsequently interned by the Germans. A fellow prisoner proposes that they should choose from among themselves a new Pope who would live among the suffering people: "'Who among us,' he said 'has the most weaknesses?' By way of a joke I raised my finger, and was the only one who did. 'Good. Jean-Baptiste will do.'" He exercises his pontificate for a few weeks, his main problem being the distribution of water in the camp. He gives up after drinking the water of a dying comrade: "Persuading myself that the others needed me more than they did the man who was going to die anyway, and that I should keep myself alive for them. This is the way, my friend, that empires and churches are born, under the sun of death."

He explains how he carried on his new profession of penitent judge, by the practice of public confession:

I mix together what concerns me and what has to do with other people. I take common characteristics, experiences which we have suffered together, weaknesses which we share, good manners, present-day man in short, as he rages in me and in others. With all that, I make a portrait which is one of everybody and nobody. A mask in short, quite like a carnival, one recognizable and simplified, one in front of which you say: "I think I've met that fellow somewhere." When the portrait is finished, like this evening, I show it with an air of grief: "That, alas, is what I am." The indictment is finished. But at the same moment the portrait which I show to my contemporaries becomes a mirror.

He confesses that he is in possession of the stolen panel, *The Just Judges*, from van Eyck's *The Mystic Lamb*. He thinks his interlocutor may be a policeman, and invites him to make an arrest. This interlocutor is, however, like himself, a lawyer, they are "of the same race." Clamence addresses to him the last words of *La Chute*:

> Tell me, I beg you, what happened to you one evening on the banks of the Seine and how you succeeded in never risking your life. Say to yourself the words which for years have not ceased to ring out during my nights and which I will say at last through your mouth: "Young girl, throw yourself in the water again, so that I can have a second chance to save us both." A second chance, eh? What a rash suggestion! Supposing, sir, we were to be taken at our word, we'd have to carry out our promise. Brrrrr! The water is so cold! But don't worry. It's too late now. It will always be too late—luckily!

Roger Quilliot rightly warns that to try "to identify Camus with Clamence would be as gross an error as to insist on mixing him up with Tarrou."

An American critic, Emmet Parker, says that "Jean-Baptiste Clamence, rather than being a modern John the Baptist, Clamens (*sic*) in Deserto, as many critics have thought, comes near to being a satirical portrait of left-wing intellectuals as Camus saw them, lost in the nihilistic desert of 20th century ideologies, led astray by their own systematic abstractions."[10]

Even though the novel contains, as M. Quilliot has established, many echoes of the Sartre/Camus controversy, and not a few jibes at the Sartre position, it would be a serious error, and a belittling one, to take Clamence as a kind of caricature of "Sartre and other progressive intellectuals." Clamence himself surely gives the clue when he says: "I mix together what concerns me and what has to do with others." It is a "game of mirrors" as Camus himself said. It is inconceivable that Camus, the Saint Just of 1944, "the godless saint" of post-Liberation youth, could have devised the character of the penitent judge without his irony being aimed at himself as well as others. The book is not "satirical" in any ordinary sense; its irony is wry and painful, its tone that of the *examen de conscience* which stands in the background of the French moralistic tradition to which Camus consciously belonged.

La Chute is not a caricature but a probing of man's nature as known to Camus through his own experience: Clamence is certainly not Camus but is the arrangement of mirrors through which Camus inspects that experience and causes it to be reflected. Nor can the specifically Christian, or pre-Christian, elements in La Chute—so clearly signaled both in the title and in the name of the narrator-protagonist—be glossed over. Under the surface of irony and occasional blasphemy, La Chute is profoundly Christian in its confessional form, in its imagery, and above all in its pervasive message that it is only through the full recognition of our sinful nature that we can hope for grace. Grace does not, it is true, arrive and the novel ends on what is apparently a pessimistic note. Yet the name of the narrator—that of the forerunner—hints, however teasingly, at the possibility of a sequel.[11]

La Chute belongs to the same cycle as the stories in L'Exil et le Royaume, although it was not finished until later. Its preoccupation should, I think, be related to those of the stories in that collection, to Camus's sense of isolation after the publication of L'Homme Révolté, and especially to his sense of exile resulting from the developing tragedy in his own country. The isolation and the exile are of course connected, because it was Camus's position in relation to Algeria, and therefore to other colonial situations, which marked him off from the political positions of the Sartre circle.

I believe that La Chute, the only one of Camus's novels which is not set in Algeria, is the one in which Algeria is most painfully present. Amsterdam is not only an anti-Algeria, a sunless, foggy place of exile; it is also a limbo: "You know then that Dante accepts the existence of angels who were neutral in the quarrel between God and Satan. And he puts them in limbo, a sort of ante-chamber of his hell. We are in the ante-chamber, my friend."

It is not, I think, fanciful to relate this concept of limbo to Camus's position on the struggle in his native Algeria. Torn between justice and his mother, Camus was drawn into a long hesitation which seemed to many like neutrality. Eventually, with the decision to put his mother first, he came by 1958 to support everything that was fundamental in the French Government's position. At the time of writing La Chute, and even later, his position seemed indecisive and unsatisfactory to both communities in Algeria. Naturally the community that resented this most was his own: that of the Europeans, who showed him clearly what they thought in January, 1956.

This seems to me to cast some light on the call and the laugh in La Chute. Daru in L'hôte was doubly summoned: the policeman, Balducci, called on him to convey the prisoner to the nearest town. The prisoner called him to help the rebels: "Viens avec nous." Daru does not follow either call and is left in isolation: essentially Camus's position. I believe that in *La Chute*—a much more complex work than *L'hôte*—these two calls were pressing on Camus's consciousness at this time and fused at a deep level into one: the voice of Rachel calling her children. Clamence's paralysis on the bridge corresponds to that of his creator before the conflicting calls of what he had thought of as his country. The laughter which follows him, which "put things in their proper places," is provoked by the discrepancy between what he had been saying and how he behaves. He who had talked so much of justice must now abjure such language, since there is something he prefers to justice. The emergence of the ironical *juge pénitent* prepared the way for a different view of life, more conservative and more organic.

Essentially, Camus is beginning to take the side of his own tribe against the abstract entities. He is heeding that call which reached him most deeply, thus taking an ironic distance from those universals which had hitherto dominated his language. Perhaps for this reason there is a curious sense of liberation about *La Chute* as compared with the stories in *L'Exil et le Royaume*. The manner of the short stories is generally flat and grating, suggestive of painful effort. In *La Chute* on the other hand, beneath the bitter irony there is a return of that undertone of elation which we find in *L'Étranger* and *La Peste*. It is doubtful whether lyricism and irony were ever before so combined as they are in Clamence's narrative. The circles of hell are also a sort of circus, with Clamence as the master showman, virtuoso in the manipulation of mirrors and in a patter which constantly amalgamates the ridiculous and the sublime.

On February 13, 1960 Albert Camus was killed in a car accident at a place called Le Grand Frossard. He was forty-seven. *La Chute*, which implied a renewal, remained his last word.

Probably no European writer of his time left so deep a mark on the imagination, and at the same time on the moral and political consciousness, of his own generation, and of the next. He was intensely European because he belonged to the frontier of Europe and was aware of a threat. The threat also beckoned to him. He refused, but not without a struggle.

No other writer, not even Conrad, is more representative of the Western consciousness, and conscience, in its relation to the non-Western world. The inner drama of his work is the development of this relation, under increasing pressure and in increasing anguish.

Many articles and commentators identified Camus as the just man. In this they were unjust to him, perhaps even more so than Madame de

Beauvoir when she wrote of him as "that just man without justice" (*ce juste sans justice*). Both verdicts shrink the dimensions of the tragedy. He was above all an artist and his primary and most enduring concern was not with justice but with artistic truth. Yet the artistic truth of the novelist, dramatist, and essayist has social and political implications, and is a form of justice.

In *L'Étranger*, artistic truth was contrasted with, and placed above, forms of justice in society. In *La Peste*, artistic truth joins, through a basic human integrity, an ideal of social and political justice. But *La Chute* breaks up that marriage: artistic truth here reveals justice as a complex and self-flattering illusion.

In historical terms, the ideal of revolutionary justice which was appropriate to a Frenchman under the Occupation (*La Peste*) was no longer appropriate to a Frenchman involved in France's position in the postwar world, and especially not to a Frenchman of Algeria (*La Chute*). Both artistic truth and justice had their social and cultural habitat. Camus was a creation of French history, French culture, and French education, and all the more intensely French because of the insecurity of the frontier. He liked to express himself in universal terms: that too was a French tradition. He could not divest himself of his Frenchness; he could not betray his mother; if France in Algeria was unjust, then it was justice that had to go, yielding place to irony. Rieux and Tarrou made way for Jean-Baptiste Clamence.

Camus's basic dilemma is that of all intellectuals in the advanced countries in their relations to the poor countries, but with the difference that he felt the dilemma much more acutely and faced the implications of the choice he made, in *la Chute*, with unmatched imaginative integrity. Not every intellectual has to make the same final choice, but each must realize how much he is a product of the culture of the advanced world, and how much there is that will pull him, among the "Algerias" of the future, toward Camus's "fall." One may still feel it to be a fall indeed, a great personal tragedy, and a defeat for a generation: a defeat most decisive when unacknowledged. One may feel—as the present writer does—that Sartre and Jeanson were right, and that Camus's voice added to theirs instead of turned against them, would have rallied opinion more decisively and earlier against imperialist wars, not only in Algeria but also in Indochina-Vietnam and elsewhere. One may experience horror at the sight of the moral capital of *La Peste* being drawn on in support of the values of the Cold War and colonial war.

Yet we must recognize that it was to Camus, not to Sartre, that the choice was presented in a personal and agonizing form: that Sartre's choice, even if it was the right one, came relatively easily,[12] whereas Camus's choice, wrong as we may think it politically, issued out of the depths of his whole life history. Politically, Camus and his tribe, the Europeans of Algeria, were casualties of the postwar period. Imaginatively Camus both flinched from the realities of his position as a Frenchman of Algeria, and also explored with increasing subtlety and honesty the nature and consequences of his flinching. The moralist talks himself out of existence in the terrible, hollow, public rhetoric of these last years. At a different, much quieter level, the serious explorations of the mature artist have hardly begun when they are suddenly cut short by senseless accidental death.

Among those who mourned him in all the world's great cities and some other places, there were many who still thought of him as the just man, the Godless saint. Others, who could no longer think of him in this way, mourned mainly for the artist, and for what might still have been. The paradox and torment of his political development presented themselves to us no longer as conscious choices but as the conditions of the life of the artist: conditions in which *La Chute* represented an heroic achievement. He left us at last the tone, the smile, and the half-promise of Jean-Baptiste Clamence: and also the mirror.

NOTES

1 *Franc-Tireur*, November 10, 1956: Quilliot, *Camus, Essais*, p. 1780. The general edition of Camus's works used in the present essay is the *Oeuvres Complètes*, Paris: Bibliothèque de la Pléiade (Gallimard): I. *Théâtre, récits, nouvelles*; II. *Essais*, edited by Roger Quilliot, 1965.

2 *Tempo Presente/Demain*, February, 1957: *Essais*, p. 1763.

3 Message to a meeting of French students, November 23, 1956: *Essais*, p. 1781.

4 *Ibid.*

5 *Discours de la Salle Wagram*, March 5, 1957: *Essais*, p. 1783.

6 *Ibid.*

7 *Algérie 1958* in *Chroniques Algériennes (Actuelles III)*.

8 Stockholm interview, December 14, 1957: *Essais*, pp. 1881–2.

9 This is probably a reference to the penitent orders of friars, who both do penance themselves and suggest penance to others.

10 Emmett Parker, *Albert Camus: The Artist in the Arena*, University of Wisconsin, 1955, p. 160.

11 When in a review in *The Spectator* of the English version of *The Fall*, I stressed its Christian tendency, Camus wrote to his English publisher, Hamish Hamilton, confirming that this approach to the novel was sound.

12 "Relatively" must be stressed. Sartre's choice may have been easy subjectively, but it involved the risk of his life.

28

HOLY WAR

I

In Northern Ireland many well-informed people will tell you that it is
an illusion to believe that the struggle is a religious one. Unionists, who
are almost all Protestants, will assure you that their opponents, who are
almost all Catholics, are the objects of distrust not because of their faith,
but because of their political allegiance, which has generally gone, not
to the British Crown and to what Unionists like to call the Constitution
of Northern Ireland, but to the idea of an Irish nation. Surprisingly,
some high Catholic ecclesiastics are in general agreement with this
view: the real trouble, they think, is not between Protestant and
Catholic as such, but between Unionist and Nationalist; it just so happens that the Catholics tend or have tended to be Nationalists; they are
oppressed not for their faith but for their politics.

These are the positions of Conservatives, both Protestant and
Catholic. But on the Left there prevails an equal conviction of the essential irrelevance of the sectarian factor. The issue is "only apparently"
a religious one: it is basically a distorted form of class war. Landlords
and industrialists have deliberately promoted religious strife in their
own economic interest. Sections of the working class have become
dupes of this propaganda. Protestant workers have been encouraged to
look to their economic exploiters as their political and religious leaders.
And, in a smaller way, Catholic workers have been encouraged to look

New York Review of Books, 6 November 1969, pp. 9–16.

to other exploiters—the weak but not quite insignificant Catholic bourgeoisie—as their protectors against an oppression that they mistakenly see as principally sectarian in character.

In fact—the argument runs—the bourgeoisie and land-owning classes are the sole beneficiaries of the religious antagonism, and the working classes are the dupes of the contrasting emblems behind which they march in July and August. The whole religious issue, I was informed by a student activist in Queen's University, Belfast, last November, "is just a red herring."

Certainly what is going on is not a simple case of religious war: there has probably never been a simple case of religious war. Ulster Protestants do not dislike Catholics simply because of their submission to the Pope and their devotion to the Virgin Mary. They also dislike them for political reasons. But the politics and the theology are inseparably intertwined. The Nationalists, after all, believe in an Irish nation which should be expressed in an all-Ireland state, which would have a Catholic majority. And the Nationalists are almost all Catholics. Protestants/Unionists believe that the effect of the fulfilment of Catholic/Nationalist aspirations would place them under Catholic domination. This view was crisply expressed in the nineteenth-century Unionist slogan: *Home Rule means Rome Rule*. It was a slogan of immense power because it asserted in memorable words what to most Ulster Protestants seemed an unanswerable reason for opposing the nationalist demand.

Thus the dichotomy which some respectable conservative thinkers, both Protestant and Catholic, seek to establish between the "political" and "religious" issues is artificial, and cannot account for the treatment of Catholics/Nationalists by Protestants/Unionists in Northern Ireland. Such an invention obviously must answer a need. For some laymen I think the need is for an image (of the Province, of oneself) which will be, if not altogether respectable, at least modern: "We are not really living in the Middle Ages. So this is not a religious war; it is political. Twentieth century!"

For some Churchmen, I think the dichotomy may be more important. For all of them it helps to exculpate "religion" generally, in a situation for which "religion" seems on the face of it to bear some share of the blame. It enables some among the Protestant clergy to forget the generations during which the Ulster Protestant mind was formed by the sacred oratory of men like Roaring Hanna and many other spiritual ancestors of Ian Paisley: the same men who both systematically inflamed hatred of Papists, and supplied theological backing for the political re-sistance to nationalist demands. And it helps some Catholic clergy to leave out of consideration how much credibility the use of the influence of the Catholic hierarchy in the Republic of Ireland may have added to the old slogan about "Rome Rule." For bishops as well as for generals, "politics" and "the politicians" often supply useful scapegoats.

Class analysis of the origins and structure of religious antagonisms in Northern Ireland is another matter. It is certain that the ruling classes, and especially the landlord class, did in the past exploit and inflame re-ligious bigotry—most directly, Protestant bigotry. The critical period was in the Twenties and Thirties of the last century. The struggle for Catholic Emancipation in what was the United Kingdom of Great Britain and Ireland, and Tory resistance to that measure, revived the ap-prehension about Popery. The Catholic Emancipation Act was passed in 1829, but it was not until after the Reform Act of 1832, with its er-osion of landlord power and threat of further erosion, that the landed aristocracy threw its collective weight behind an anti-Papist move-ment—the Orange Order—which had originally drawn its strength from small Protestant farmers.[1]

At a great meeting at Hillsborough in County Down in 1834 the leaders of the Ulster aristocracy, led by the Marquess of Donegal and Londonderry, heard the great Presbyterian orator, Henry Cooke, pro-claim the unity of Protestants in a common cause. The cause included the repeal of both Catholic Emancipation and the Reform Act. Cooke was successful in driving out the "Arian" radicals from the Presbyterian church, and in securing that the conservative interests which had always dominated the Church of Ireland (Anglican) should henceforth domi-nate also the Presbyterians and Ulster Protestantism in general. Cooke was not himself an Orangeman, but he is rightly regarded as a principal architect of the victory of Orangeism.[2]

Henceforward, and up to our own time, the Orange Order and its as-sociated institutions have formed a popular politico-religious move-ment, under aristocratic and business leadership. This movement, or condition, has dominated the life of Eastern Ulster—what is now Northern Ireland—for more than a hundred years. From 1912 on, it prevented the Home Rule Bill from being extended to what is now Northern Ireland; and it has provided, through the Unionist Party, the parliamentary majority and the government of Northern Ireland for an unbroken period of almost fifty years, since 1920—the year in which King George V solemnly opened the Parliament of Northern Ireland at Stormont near Belfast. The United Kingdom Parliament retained control of finance, foreign affairs, defense, and other matters—and also, ultimately, the power to abolish the subordinate Parliament which it had created. But in local government, including police, Stormont had the power over the six counties of Northern Ireland. The first Prime Minister, Lord Craigavon, spoke of Stormont as "a Protestant Parliament for a Protestant people." Catholics—a permanent minority—regarded themselves as kidnapped into a condition of second-class citizens. The Irish Free State (later the Republic) denied the democratic legitimacy of the partition of the island.

Politically, economically, and socially the most obvious beneficiary of this history has been the landowning aristocracy. In the rest of Ireland that class has disappeared from the scene as a result of the successful nineteenth-century agrarian agitation of the Land League. But Protestant Ulster remained so loyal, not only to the Crown and the Reformation, but also to the landlord class, that, at the height of the agrarian agitation in 1880, Orange laborers were imported from Ulster to district Mayo under British armed guard to harvest the crops of Captain Boycott, who had been ostracized by anti-landlord forces.[3] Almost all the Prime Ministers of Northern Ireland so far have been drawn from the landlord class: all have been closely associated with that class and have had its support, including the current Prime Minister, Francis Chichester-Clark, descendant of an English seventeenth century Lord Deputy of Ireland.

Industrial employers also benefited from aristocratic rule, for the sharp religious divisions among the working class retarded the trade union movement. With a few notable exceptions they have supported the Unionist Party and its aristocratic leaders, and have contributed to the Orange Order. The upper classes in England also played an important part in the development of sectarian hate in Ulster. From the time when the Liberal Party declared for Home Rule, in 1866, up to 1914, the Tories systematically exploited Protestant bigotry in Ulster. Rudyard Kipling, the bard of imperialism, deliberately struck this note in the great Home Rule crisis just before the First World War.

> We know the hells declared
> For such as serve not Rome
> The terror, threats and dread
> In market, hearth and field—
> We know when all is said
> We perish if we yield.

Yet the class-interpretation of the religious antagonism can be, and often is, over-simplified. In modern times the ruling classes have exploited and exacerbated this antagonism, but they did not create it: it exists independently of them. Indeed when, alarmed by its excesses, important sections of the ruling class have tried to cool down these feelings, they have been defeated by them, as was the case with Captain O'Neill, the previous Prime Minister, who tried to give Northern Ireland a more liberal image, favored a relatively conciliatory approach to Catholics, and fell because of this. No analysis of the Northern Ireland situation which is content to dismiss the religious issues as "a red herring" is of any value as analysis, although it may have its uses in political controversy.

Basically, religious affiliation was and is socially, economically, and politically significant, for it distinguishes, with very few exceptions, the natives and their children from the seventeenth-century settlers and their children. The British Crown, in the post-Reformation period, naturally favored the settlement of loyal Protestants,[4] and the dispossession of natives, whose support of the Counter-Reformation was necessarily a form of rebellion: politics and religion were inseparable from the start.

The Protestant settlers, Scottish and English, were the gainers, the Catholic natives the losers: antagonistic collective interests and loyalties were established immediately. The natives were dispossessed, but not exterminated nor assimilated nor converted to Protestantism. Their Catholicism became the badge of their identity and of their defiance. After the destruction of the Gaelic social order by the end of the seventeenth century and the substitution of English for the Gaelic language—a process completed by the mid-nineteenth century in most of the country—the Catholic Church became almost the sole form of the social cohesion of the native people.

The area of Protestant settlement—as distinct from ascendancy or domination—never spread out effectively beyond that Northeastern corner of Ireland which is closest to Scotland, where most of the settlers came from. The Ulster Protestants held a bridge-head, were aware of a menace, cherished the military virtues: they came, in many ways, to resemble the Afrikaaners in their *laager*. Twice during the seventeenth-century wars native revolt seemed near to success. The victory of William of Orange in 1690 ended that period of turmoil and danger, gave the settlers security of possession, and led to the codification of Protestant/settler domination in a carefully institutionalized caste-system: the Penal Laws, applicable throughout Ireland. These resembled various "white supremacy" codes quite closely, except that the victims of the codes could "pass" by abjuring their religion. Some did, and merged into the population of settler origin: the bulk of the natives remained Catholic.

When the Orange Order (in Belfast and elsewhere) and the Apprentice Boys (in Derry) commemorate the victories of 1690, as they do each year in elaborate ceremonies, the message they are conveying is that of their determination to hold for Protestants in Northern Ireland as much as possible of the privileged status which their ancestors won under William of Orange. These are not, as outside observers so easily suppose, comically archaic occasions. The symbols are historical, the iconography old-fashioned, but the message is for the here and now. The ritual is one of annual renewal of a stylized act of dominance: "We are your superiors: we know you hate this demonstration of that fact: we dare you to do something about it; if you don't, you ratify your own inferior status." That is what the drums say.

When these rituals can be performed without danger of disruption, Northern Ireland is quiet: the natives are deemed to accept their status. They have no means of changing it by ordinary democratic process. They are a minority—one third of the population within Northern Ireland. By definition: since in 1920 the borders of that entity were drawn as a result of decisions taken by the Ulster Unionist leadership with the support of the English Tories, in such a way as to include the maximum territory containing an absolutely safe Protestant majority. The Catholics combine the disadvantage of minority status with the frightening qualities with which a suppressed *majority* is usually invested; for Catholics are in a large majority in the island of Ireland as a whole. They are also in a majority in certain parts of Northern Ireland itself, and notably in the second city of the area: Derry.[5]

Derry is of special importance. It was the principal center of Protestant resistance at the end of the seventeenth-century struggle. Its siege by King James's Catholic army is symbolic of the Catholic siege which Ulster Protestant militants feel they are still withstanding. And it never fell. Derry's "No Surrender" has become the slogan of Ulster Unionism. Derry is near the border: a majority of its population, being Catholic, are believed to be only too willing to surrender it to the Republic.[6] So the Unionist government based in Stormont, using powers conferred on it by London, gerrymandered Derry in such a way that a city with a two-to-one Catholic majority has a City Council with a two-to-one *Protestant* majority. This council has consistently used its power to uphold the privileged position of Protestants in jobs, in housing, in relations with the police, and in other ways. Catholics in Northern Ireland generally are a depressed minority. The Apprentice

Boys,[7] on their annual triumphal circuit on the walls of the city, toss pennies down from the walls into the poverty of Derry's great Bogside ghetto.

In August, the Bogsiders, by disrupting that ceremony, and by successfully resisting police efforts to restore the order which the ceremony represents, shook the bases of the whole system throughout Northern Ireland. The Protestant militants of Belfast, for whom a Protestant force known as the "B Specials" provides armed leadership, sought to restore the balance in their own way, intimidating the local Catholic minority by threats, arson, and shooting. The B Specials are nominally police reservists, exclusively Protestant in composition, and traditionally drawn from the most vigilant anti-Catholic section. Their activities were mainly responsible for the British government's decision to depart from their long-established policy of leaving Stormont to run the internal affairs of the territory in its own way, without intervention or even question from British Parliament, to which the Stormont government owes its existence.

The events of August abolished non-intervention. The British Army, always present in the area, but hitherto completely uninvolved in its internal affairs, was hurriedly given the main responsibility for the maintenance of order in the most troubled districts. Stormont's police were placed under army control and kept out of the principal Catholic districts. The B Specials were required to check their weapons into military armories: it was strongly hinted that the force would gradually be "phased out."

The nature of a sectarian rule which had existed for fifty years suddenly surfaced before a shocked British and international public. The demand for reform in Northern Ireland has acquired a force which it never possessed before. The Cameron Commission—established before the August troubles—published a report which showed that Catholics had been the victims of systematic discrimination in local government franchise, in housing, in jobs, and in relations with the police. All this had long been notorious but the official status of the Commission Report meant that it could no longer be ignored or denied. The Northern Ireland government promised reforms; the British government promised that the reforms would have to be real.

The most pressing of these reforms—and the most alarming to Protestant-supremacy extremists—is the establishment of a police force not imbued with the Protestant-supremacy ideal. This would mean reforming the Royal Ulster Constabulary and completely disbanding the

B Specials. It is against implementation of police reform especially, and in defense of Protestant supremacy generally, that Protestant extremists are now fighting in Belfast. The fact that these "pro-British" people are now skirmishing against the British Army, which is at present defending the "anti-British," is only superficially paradoxical. (Though perhaps sufficiently so for most outsiders.)

Ulster Protestant loyalty since the seventeenth century has been that conditional Whig loyalty of attachment to the Protestant succession. A man is loyal to the Crown so long as it is a Protestant Crown and so long as its servants behave accordingly. If these servants behave in ways which are not clearly Protestant—by the strict standards of the Protestant militants in Belfast's Shankill Road—then they are traitors. Asquith was regarded by most Ulster Protestants in that light in 1912 and Wilson is so regarded by some Protestants today. This lesson of conditional loyalty also is incalculated by the annual rituals I have already mentioned. Each year on Derry's wall they burn the effigy of one Lundy, the governor who was so loyal to the Crown that he tried to deliver the city to the legitimate but Catholic King James. A "Lundy" is a synonym for a traitor and also for one who fraternizes with Papists or favors concessions to them.

The present situation is transitional, complex, and messy. Where once an apparently monolithic and eternal Unionist regime completely controlled the region, today there are numerous separate focuses of power. There is the British Government, which could, if it so decided, use its parliamentary majority to revoke Stormont's powers altogether. There is Stormont, by-passed in vital functions of law-enforcement, badly damaged and yet a force to be reckoned with, because it is fairly representative of the Protestant majority in the area. There are controlling groups in the semi-insurgent Catholic ghettos, areas which are necessarily self-policing, since they are protected by the army from the Stormont police.

These groups have varying degrees of cohesion: fairly high in Derry, fairly low in Belfast. There are Protestant groups, Paisleyites and others, some of them with considerable territorial authority in certain areas (such as the Shankill Road in Belfast). And finally there is the army, responsible to the Queen's government in London, but obliged to take part in tricky day-to-day negotiations with Stormont officials, and with local associations of Catholics and Protestants. The army is also, as the official phrase goes, "in support of the civil power." But where exactly is the civil power? Is it in London or in Stormont? No definite answer can be given to that question and until it can be given there will be no end to even the present phase of the troubles of Northern Ireland.

II

The disruption of the ritual in Bogside ghetto in Derry last August was the culmination of a series of actions which began, or at least acquired perceptible momentum, in October 1968, the month of the first major civil rights demonstrations. The Civil Rights Movement, which greatly accelerated this process, if it did not set it in motion, never of course conceived itself as a movement of "Catholics against Protestants." There were Protestants among its members, and among its leaders. Its main focus initially was in Queen's University, Belfast—a mainly Protestant institution—where it drew on the support of the students affected by the student protest movement in other countries.

The movement had, and has, liberal and radical wings. The liberals wished to get rid of sectarian injustices and anomalies, and thereby make the region as like as possible to other parts of the United Kingdom. The radicals agreed with enough of this program to enter a common movement, but they wanted to use the struggle as an instrument of social education and social transformation. Eamonn McCann and Bernadette Devlin, militant radical leaders, sought to bring it home to both Catholic and Protestant workers that they had a common class enemy, against whom it was in their interest to join forces.

What happened was that Catholics, in considerable number, rallied to the support of a movement which looked as if it was making headway in the direction of securing equal citizenship for them. Protestants, whatever their class, did not rally to it in any significant number. Some of them attacked it violently, as at the village of Burntollet, where non-violent civil rights marchers were stoned by organized Protestant extremists last January.[8] The majority of Protestants simply held aloof, expressing a general distaste for trouble-makers, and bracketing the civil-rights marchers with those who stoned them.

The Civil Rights movement grew, in numbers and in confidence. But it grew as a large but loosely coordinated movement of *Catholics*. Civil Rights leaders were dismayed. I heard Bernadette Devlin this summer, speaking at Strabane, upbraid her almost entirely Catholic audience for their sectarianism. They applauded her fervently. She was, and is, despite herself, the most inspiring leader the cause of the Catholics in the North has had. Instead of leading a class struggle, as she hoped, she has become the inspiration of an oppressed and partly insurgent *caste*, the descendants of the dispossessed native inhabitants (to which caste she of course belongs).

Is this because the Protestant workers, who would not heed the call to make common cause with Catholic workers, are dupes of their bosses? As I indicated at the beginning I doubt the adequacy of this explanation. A system of caste-privilege creates beneficiaries of its own, who are much more numerous than the category of employers and landlords. There are solid satisfactions: a Protestant in Ulster has a better chance of a job, of promotion, of a house, of success generally, by being a Protestant. When he is told that if he will combine with Catholic members of his own class he can bring into being a society in which there are jobs and houses for all, under better conditions, he is not impressed. He will now work with Catholic fellow-workers for limited objectives, in the Trade Union movement—which has so far been remarkably successful in keeping sectarian violence out of the shipyards and factories—but he will not cooperate with them politically.

This may show him lacking in political faith, or in generosity, but it does not, I think, necessarily show him to be deceived as to where his present interests lie. The society, for which he is asked to starve and run certain risks, the society in which there will be jobs and houses for all, is a hypothetical future society. The society in which he is living, and in which his children are growing up, not only confers tangible relative advantages on him, but also confers a benefit which is nonetheless real for being intangible: the sense of superior status, annually confirmed by the right to participate in triumphal ritual. To know that this status is challenged only adds zest to its enjoyment, so long as the challenge is unsuccessful.

Some years ago a bright fourteen-year-old at a good Protestant school in Belfast—in both parts of Ireland most schools are "Catholic" or "Protestant"—was set an apparently simple, but in the context enigmatic, subject: "Ireland." The problem here is that, since there is a *Northern Ireland*, there must be an Ireland, to which one in some sense belongs, yet from the rest of which one is divided. One may well not be quite sure, at fourteen, how this is supposed to work. The schoolboy said he enjoyed living in Ireland because of the beautiful scenery and "mebbe because I get satisfaction out of having an enemy in the South."

He was not alone in this, and the enemy is not only in the South.

Appeals to class solidarity, addressed to members of the dominant caste, meet with little response, not because Northern Protestant workers are exceptionally obtuse or gullible, or the Ulster ruling class exceptionally cunning, but because most members of a privileged caste enjoy

and value their caste privileges more than they enjoy or value association with the subordinate caste, or than anything which they consider
themselves likely to attain through such associations.

If this assessment is correct, it follows that the destruction of caste
privileges in Northern Ireland must *precede* any serious progress toward
class solidarity, and toward non-sectarian politics. And in fact, though
not in explicit form, it is at the destruction of caste privileges—in the
franchise, in housing and jobs, and otherwise—that the most effective
manifestations of the Civil Rights Movement have been directed. The
courage, determination, and ingenuity of the movement, and the degree
of mass support it received from the subordinate caste, have disrupted
the established system, to the extent that it seems safe to prophesy that
caste subordination in anything like its old thoroughness can never be
restored throughout the territory.

This degree of success is primarily and directly due to the Civil Rights
Movement in Northern Ireland itself. But it could not have been
achieved had Northern Ireland been an isolated unit. If the Northern
government, resting securely on the support of the majority in the area,
had been free to act with the ruthlessness the Orange Right desires, the
civil rights movement, supported by a minority which is economically
weak and—should it come to serious fighting—heavily out-gunned,
could hardly have achieved any significant success in this generation.
The fate of the civil disobedience movement in the South African
townships is relevant. No wonder that William Craig (former Minister
for Home Affairs) and some others dream of a Unilateral Declaration
of Independence (U.D.I.) by Ulster. But Northern Ireland is not a remote dominion like Rhodesia: it is a part of the United Kingdom, not
only juridically, but economically, and, to some extent, administratively
and socially. And also militarily: Ian Smith received before U.D.I. a
British assurance that British troops would not be used in Rhodesia:
Chichester-Clark received the troops. U.D.I. is not in the cards—except
as the dream of a small but active and at present violent Protestant
minority.

The Protestant majority's relation to Britain is matched in several
ways by the Catholic minority's relation to the Republic. In both cases
there is a strong basic feeling of solidarity: "our kith and kin," "our
own." In both cases also there is an element of distrust in the relationship. Ulster Protestants remember that England nearly let them down
in 1912. The fear is lively that England may be really letting them down
now. Catholics in Northern Ireland feel that their coreligionists and
compatriots in the Twenty-Six Counties let them down in 1921 by ac-

cepting the Treaty which left them in bondage, while the rest of the country moved to freedom. They also feel—with justice—that the Dublin Government took very little interest in their subsequent fate, up to the point when the events of August 1969 touched the sluggish conscience of the—relatively—rich and free relations.

The governments in London and Dublin have, of course, both long known of the undemocratic and sectarian character of the Northern Ireland internal regime. As far as the Dublin government was concerned, there was rather little it could do about the situation. Even its occasional utterances on the subject emerged in muffled form, since it adhered to the principle that abolishing the partition of Ireland—not the treatment of the minority—was the real issue. When those to whom the propaganda on these lines was directed learned that partition was supported by a majority in the North, they tended to lose interest in the quetion as a whole. The quite real and serious grievances of the minority were buried in the wreckage of anti-partition propaganda.

London, unlike Dublin, had the power actually to do something about the situation. Until very recently, however, it had not the will to do so. For the Tories, the Ulster Unionists were their allies, and the providers of a small, but marginally significant, group of the safest of safe Tory seats at Westminster. The Labour Party remembered the part which Irish issues had played in the destruction of the Liberals in the period between 1912 and 1922, and seemed determined not to be caught in the same way. The Attlee Government, in 1949, through the Ireland Act, not merely confirmed the partition, but provided the parliament at Stormont with a veto on any revision of the boundary.

The progress of the Civil Rights Movement, the violence with which it was met, and the violence also of some of its supporters, made it impossible to continue to turn a blind eye to the situation. People who saw the pictures wanted to know the story. Ordinary Englishmen were surprised and troubled to learn, among other things, that the institutions of the United Kingdom included an armed force of sectarian fanatics. English comments on the institutions of Northern Ireland came—for the first time on any considerable scale—to resemble those of the American Northern press on the institutions of the South. And the British Government's response, in using British troops to protect Catholics in Derry and Belfast resembled, in its nature and in its implications, President Eisenhower's decision to send Federal troops to Little Rock.

As in the case of Little Rock, there were international factors to be considered. Intervention from the Republic was never probable, but was a possibility in certain circumstances. Derry is only twelve miles from the border. If the Royal Ulster Constabulary had been given a free hand in the Bogside—British troops remaining aloof—and if there had then been serious bloodshed, the pressure on the Irish government to send in forces to protect the Bogside would have been heavy.

Technically this would have been an invasion of the United Kingdom. Militarily, London would hardly regard this as a serious threat. But the effect on international politics would have been—and the existing situation was already—serious enough. Relations with the United States would be adversely affected if an Irish-American vote were to be resuscitated as a significant anti-British factor, comparable to the Jewish vote during Ernest Bevin's conduct of affairs in Palestine. In the circumstances, it was not surprising that Mr. Wilson decided that Northern Ireland's affairs were too serious to be left to the government of Northern Ireland. It is also significant that the Tory party, Stormont's friends and godparents, have so far refrained from fundamental or vehement criticism of Mr. Wilson's action.

It is, one may hope, the beginning of the end of the institutionalized caste system. But it is, at best, only the beginning. The institutions are threatened but they remain in being. The most obnoxious of them—the B Specials—has not yet been disbanded or disarmed. Stiffening resistance to change is to be feared: the Unionists who wish to preserve the essentials of the existing system will do their best to stall until the next British election, hoping for a Tory victory and the easing of the pressure on them. There are certainly other Unionists who probably hope that the Labour government will force their hands and finish the job of reform. In Northern Ireland, as in the American South, businessmen, concerned for the image of the region and of their products, diverge from the die-hard segregationists when trouble has become serious. These Northern businessmen are now afraid of passions which in the past they helped to excite but whose present manifestations go beyond their control.

Not only Northern Ireland but the peoples of both islands are involved in these events. The nature of their involvement is blurred by the legalisms of nationality. London says it is no business of Dublin's but a purely internal affair of the United Kingdom (whose full title includes the words "of Great Britain and Northern Ireland").

In mid-August, I was a member of a delegation of the Irish Labour Party (an opposition party in the Dublin Parliament) which went to London to urge on members of the British Labour government the incompatibility of the character of the Northern regime with basic principles accepted by the Labour movement generally, and to call for the abolition of its Special Constabulary. (We were operating—and continue to operate—on the principle that the Labour movement in both parts of Ireland, in close touch with the Labour movement in Britain, offers the best hope both of shortening the present period of violence, arising from the crumbling of the institutionalized class system, and of building decent relations between the communities, especially between Catholic and Protestant workers.)

We were received—most courteously and in many ways helpfully—at the Foreign Office, by Lord Chalfont. Mr. Patrick Devlin, M.P. for the Falls Road area of Belfast—storm center of the recent troubles—wished to accompany us, but this could not be allowed. We were a Foreign Affair, Mr. Devlin a Home Affair. Correct procedure legally, yet a subtle confusion of the human realities. To Mr. Devlin—and to the Catholics of Belfast whom he represented—Lord Chalfont and his colleagues were much more "foreign" than we were. The British Government knew this to be true, but it was not an aspect of reality that it felt able to entertain.

Similarly, the Dublin Government, although it knows that the Protestant majority in Northern Ireland prefers to look to London rather than to Dublin, habitually flinches from this aspect of reality. Mr. Jack Lynch, the head of the Irish government, has recognized the existence of that majority, and has renounced any intention of coercing it. In that he is supported by all parties in the Dublin parliament. Yet his government engages in propaganda intended (at least nominally) to convince world opinion that the partition of Ireland is wrong. What good it will do to convince world opinion of this, if the Northern majority is not convinced, is not clear—since coercion is ruled out, as it is, not only by declarations of policy, but by the realities of the situation.

It would be well for Dublin and London to recognize mutually one another's involvement in the situation, not as constituting mere meddlesomeness, but as a function of the historically formed traditions and allegiances of the two communities which have to live together in Northern Ireland—and in Ireland, and in the archipelago. In Northern Ireland, the smaller of these communities has been oppressed by the larger, and has now served notice of its determination to refuse to continue to be oppressed. It deserves support, and it needs it—from London, from Dublin, and from, among others, the American public.

This is not the same as asking (for example) American support for the reunification of Ireland. That kind of support can only increase tensions, by confirming Protestant suspicions of an international conspiracy to place them under Catholic domination. (Or Communist domination, which militant Ulster Protestants take to be much the same thing. The romantic illusions of some sections of the international extreme left about the nature of the Northern "revolution" and the "new society behind the barricades" have encouraged this local confusion. The internationalists eliminate the religious factor, but the local situation puts it back in and even injects it into the supposed activities of the internationalists.)

Support for equality of rights and the abolition of Stormont's institutionalized caste system is another matter. Its destruction would be a human achievement of more than merely local significance. What we call "racism" is a habit of mind and will which can exploit religion as it exploits pigmentation. In Northern Ireland now there is a chance of breaking, or at least loosening, the grip of this habit. It is of course the existence of the chance, and of the attempt, which stirs up the more violent outward manifestations of religious racism. In a long-term perspective these are signs not of a strengthening of this force, but of the weakening of the institutions. How strong the force itself still is anyone can find who will take a slow walk through Bogside, or within the walls of Derry, or in Belfast down the Falls Road or along the Shankill.

Notes

1 According to the official Orange historian, R. M. Sibbett, the members of the first Orange Lodge at Loughgall, County Armagh in 1795, "almost all ... belonged to the humblest classes ... weavers and small farmers. The gentry stood aloof." (*A History of Orangism in Ireland and Throughout the Empire*, Belfast.) Referring to the subsequent "conversion" of the gentry, Sibbett reflects that "Time and enlightenment produced wonderful effects."

2 See a useful recent work, *Holy War in Belfast* by Andrew Boyd (Anvil Books, Tralee, Ireland; paperback). In the French Revolutionary period many radical Presbyterians made common cause with Catholics in Wolfe Tone's movement of the United Irishmen and in the rebellion of 1798. The actual course of the rebellion included anti-Protestant atrocities by Catholic insurgents in the South. Its thorough suppression and the subsequent general reaction disrupted this always precarious alliance. Governmental concessions to Presbyterians and the work of Cooke completed the process of bringing the Presbyterian body into the camp of conservative Protestant loyalism—the Orange system.

3 This inadvertently publicized the effectiveness of the practice of ostracism and conferred a curious kind of immortality on Captain Boycott's name.

4 Edmund Spenser, himself a settler, noted Machiavelli's recommendation of the introduction of settlers as the best means of securing possession of a conquered province (*View of the State of Ireland*).

5 Alias Londonderry. There is a great pother about nomenclature, even about the name of the political entity in question. Unionists like to call it "Ulster," Nationalists "The

Six Counties." I use "Northern Ireland" here because it is the official designation even though geographically misleading. Ulster is the name of the old province—nine counties, three of which are in the Republic (Eire, Ireland). I use it adjectivally for Ulster Protestants, who will not object.

6 Many observers have even held that, as social services are now considerably better in the United Kingdom than in the Republic, and as so many Derry Catholics are on welfare, they would, if given a choice, remain with the United Kingdom. But if economic interest were always the sole determinant the population in question would be now Protestant, as would the population of the Republic, and the problem would not arise.

7 They are not, of course, boys but men. Their name commemorates the exploit of the Protestant apprentices who, against the wishes of the governor of the city, closed the gates against King James.

8 See *Burntollet*, by James Egan and Vincent McCormack (L.R.S. Publishers, London, 1969), p. 28.

29

AMERICA FIRST OR VARIETIES OF AMERICOCENTRISM

I was a resident in the United States from 1965 to the early summer of this year, when I returned to Ireland to live, and I still hold—though not for much longer—the little green card of the resident alien.

Coming back here to speak at this gathering, I was told at the American Embassy in Dublin that I did not require a visa; I could come in on my little green card. When I presented myself at Immigration at Kennedy airport, I had to explain why, though technically a resident alien, I had become, as it were, more alien than resident. The officers who questioned me were gentle and polite with, in their manner, an indefinable compound of the baffled, the compassionate and the faintly alarmed. It reminded me of something which I could not for the moment place. Then I got it—I came from a Catholic country, and the manner of these Immigration officers reminded me, in its full range, of a sympathetic Catholic priest trying to find out why someone has stopped going to mass.

It also reminded me, this manner, of something else: of the demeanor of some of my American left-wing friends—of whom I love, I am glad to say, a great many—when I told them this Spring that I was resigning from New York University and going back to Ireland to run in politics. Now the Immigration officers and these friends were very unlike in other ways. The Immigration officers were, I believe, patriotic Americans in a traditional and unquestioning way. My friends were all,

Address given to the National Emergency Civil Liberties Committee annual banquet, 12 December 1969. Source: O'Brien Papers, New York University Archives.

in different ways, in revolt against the forces that dominate America today. The first group would sincerely regard the second as anti-American. Yet the two groups have more in common than they know. They are both in the grip of an Americocentrism of which they are not fully conscious. All members of the first group approved of foreigners loving America; the members of the second approve of foreigners hating America. The concept that there are many millions of foreigners who never think of America at all—and many who never even heard of it—would strike most members of both groups as unlikely, suspect and generally unsatisfactory.

It is true that people may be, and are, affected by American imperialism without knowing much, or perhaps anything, about either America or imperialism. Most people are affected in some way by American wealth and power; the whole population of the planet is affected by it in the broad sense that these things exist and by the knowledge of their existence. Many are affected more directly, through the exploitation of the resources of their country by American capital and technology, and through the manipulation of their governments and their social and political life by agents of American corporations and of the American government. And some are affected in the most direct possible way—by the massive use against them of America's apparatus of violence for the supposed protection of the people whom it destroys, as in Vietnam.

There has been, so far as I know, no adequate and satisfactory study of the relation of America's wealth and power to the economic, social and political life of the rest of the world. Establishment, academic approaches to this question are normally concerned, consciously or unconsciously, with minimizing, or exorcising, the concept of America as an imperialist power. One can have so-called political "area studies" of places which are in fact under American indirect rule, and these area studies can simply ignore that fact, and write in terms of Russian or Chinese attempts to find a foothold in countries which are misleadingly presented as genuinely independent. Scholarship of this kind is in fact a part of the phenomenon which suppresses from view a part of imperialism. It is a form of academic activity which still continues, but has had to be conducted with somewhat more subtlety and discretion in recent years, with the increasing consciousness of the degree to which the intellectual and academic communities have been manipulated by the great corporations, and by government agencies like the CIA serving the same corporate interests.

Yet, the task of analyzing American imperialism, its native possibilities and limits—a task understandably neglected by the academies, at least as far as published works are concerned—has not been carried out by the left either. The left has always suffered from a tendency to let its agitation get mixed up with its analysis. It also suffers from its own curiously intense pieties: from a desire to see contemporary realities as much as possible through the eyes of certain past thinkers, and from pedantic ridigity about the modification of established categories. Today, particularly, it is affected for both good and evil, by the greatest show of youthful revolutionary romanticism that has been known since 1848, and by the forms of rhetoric to which that gives rise—including the competition between forms of black and white revolutionary rhetoric.

These tendencies, especially when combined with unconscious Americocentrism, are calculated to obscure the actual relations between America and the rest of the world. Young American revolutionaries see everything that happens in the world in terms of US imperialism and the fight against it. Here I want to refer to an important and influential manifesto, which many of you, no doubt, know—the pamphlet "You Don't Need a Weatherman to Know How the Wind Blows." The manifesto is remarkable in several ways, and I shall come back to it later. For the moment, I want to consider only its presentation of America's place in the world, of which the core is the following:

> Every other empire and petty dictator is in the long run dependent on US imperialism, which has unified, allied with, and defended all of the reactionary forces of the whole world. Thus, in considering every other force or phenomenon, from Soviet imperialism or Israeli imperialism to "workers struggle" in France or Czechoslovakia, we determine who are our friends and who are our enemies according to whether they help US imperialism or fight to defeat it.

Quoting Lin Piao and Che Guevara, the writers argue for the inevitability of "two, three, many Vietnams, and of the over-extension of US imperialism, and thereby its destruction." Through this process, it is believed that the revolution in America itself will have been made by the people of the entire world.

This pamphlet, though its arguments are well presented and often acute in relation to what its authors know best—the present situation of this country's youth—is not singled out here just as a specimen of socialist analysis; there are obviously many more sophisticated analyses in existence. Its impact is a double one: it represents the current, or more or less current, world-view of many of the most serious, courageous and determined young people in this country, and it is distorted to the point of fantasy.

The United States is *not* the sole purveyor of oppression and aggression in the world, nor has it "unified" all other reactionary forces. Neither the Soviet Union, nor imperialist actions by the Soviet Government, are "dependent on US imperialism"—in the long run or otherwise. "The people of the entire world," thrown *en bloc* into the struggle against American power, are not united in any such struggle, and can be united only if the United States insists on making them so. There is no certainty, and no inevitability, about the idea of multiple Vietnams and over-extension—although many potential future Vietnams exist—Thailand, the Phillipines, Latin America, and elsewhere.

The bourgeoisie also learn from Marxism as one of the most acute Marxists of the century, Antonio Gramsci, pointed out in *The Modern Prince*, and they also learn from an even more copious and relevant repertoire: that of their own mistakes. One Vietnam makes others rather less likely than not. The interdependence or exploitation symbiosis of the United States and the poor world is grossly overstated in the whole theory. If all of Africa were wiped out, the American economy would not be seriously shaken, and if all the United States were wiped out, the populations of Africa would neither be much better nor much worse off, nor otherwise greatly affected by the news.

Lin Piao's identification of the advanced countries with "the cities" of the Chinese revolution to be starved into submission by the "countryside" of the underdeveloped world is surely one of the least sound analogies ever to be widely quoted with outright approval. These supposed "cities" are actually exporting grain in quantity to the supposed "countryside." The unsoundness of this key analogy, coming from one of the key figures—this system of thought—spotlights the weakness of the system generally and of its predictions of the inevitable.

It is not true at all, as the manifesto claims, that the relative affluence existing in the United States is now dependent upon the labor and natural resources of the Vietnamese, the Angolans, the Bolivians and the rest of the peoples of the third world. It would be true to say that this relative affluence was achieved in the past by the spoliation of other peoples, by the African slave trade and the genocide of the Red Indian, but it is not true that it depends now, to anything but a marginal extent, on the labor and resources of the third world. Nor is the margin decisive: the United States is not visibly worse off economically for the loss of China, and would be distinctly better off without Vietnam. America is neither dependent *today* on the third world nor capable of being revolutionized by anything that happens there—unless it is something America itself decides to do. Those in America who are counting on the revolution in America being made by the "people of the world" are counting on something that is not going to happen.

"We determine," says the manifesto, "who are our friends and who are our enemies according to whether they help us imperialism or help to defeat it!" We determine according to our predetermined system whether the Ibo or the Hausa, the Belfast Catholic or Protestant, the Moslem or the Hindu, the Arab or the Kurd, is friend or enemy, though not one of them, in relation to the struggles between the pairs, is giving a thought to "us" or to us imperialism, though the hostilities between them antedate the coming into existence of the United States.

This form of thought is almost a sub-society of imperialism, a standing-on-its-head of the old "indirect aggression" theory. Just as, for the United States government, if a foreign State was friendly to the United States, the peoples oppressed by it were automatically suspect of communism and deserved what they got.

So in this world-view, if a State is hostile or even judged to be potentially or "objectively" hostile to the United States, then peoples oppressed by it are enemies of the revolution, and deserve what *they* get. These are two faces of Americocentrism. Another and more reasonable one is also possible: "Violence is the only way of ensuring a hearing for moderation." The saying is not, obviously, one from Mao or Che: it is by the nineteenth-century Irish agrarian agitator, William O'Brien. As it has been attributed to me by Miss Hannah Arendt, I may perhaps claim the patent rights for the present century.

The saying may, in certain circumstances, be true. Now obviously the last thing most of the young revolutionaries of today might seem to want is to ensure a hearing for moderation. That, nonetheless, is what they may succeed in doing and they are aware of this. It is *one* of the possibilities. It is really more probable than the achievement of their actual programme, dependent as that is on an understanding of the world. It is about on the same level, in respect of probability, as the chance that their activities may help—only help—to bring into being some new American form of fascism. The dialectics of non-violence, violence, reform and repression are still insufficiently understood. In my own land, we have had experience of one form of interplay of these forces. The Civil Rights movement in Northern Ireland was modelled, consciously, on the civil rights movement in this country—especially, in the beginning, on the forms which the American civil rights movement took in the early years of this decade in the South. The situations were in some ways comparable. The United Kingdom of Great Britain and Northern Ireland—to give it its full title—is a kind of federal system, within which the political entity of Northern Ireland enjoys limited autonomy, a kind of states' rights. As in the case of the American South, the main function of the local autonomy is to provide cover for a local caste system, the Catholics being the blacks in Northern Ireland. Northern Ireland, like Dixie, is potentially vulnerable to protest, in that ultimate power is in the hands of people who cannot overtly condone or back the use of force in defense of the local caste system. This civil rights movement began as a strictly non-violent one: civil rights workers were pelted with rocks, thrown into jail, beaten by the police, without resistance or retaliation. That was in January of this year near Derry and elsewhere. By August of this year, civil rights people and the people of the Catholic ghetto, in Derry itself, used force to break up a traditional procession of their oppressors—which symbolizes the subjection of the Catholics—and successfully defended their ghetto against the police by the use of petrol bombs. In Belfast, armed defenders of Protestant supremacy started shooting Catholics and burning their homes. The British Government, in a decision strikingly similar to Eisenhower's decision to send federal troops to Little Rock, sent in British troops, with the primary object of preventing a massacre of Catholics. In the wake of these events appeared the Cameron and Thant reports, officially acknowledging for the first time the notorious facts pertaining to the second-class citizenship of Catholics in the area, and the maintenance of an institutionalized caste system through an armed sectarian police. Legislation is following, intended to ensure equality of rights.

"No bombs, no rights" read a local headline. There is no doubt that the young people of the Civil Rights movement with backing from older people had achieved first through non-violent, symbolic protest, and then through the use of a degree of violence, far more than their elders had achieved in two generations of argument and minority voting. It is also true that the cost was high, and probably not yet paid in full, and that the outcome might, and probably would, have been different had Northern Ireland—like Dixie and unlike, say, South Africa— not been a sub-system, legally open to intervention from outside. Nonetheless, the achievement remains real, and notable. In this case, violence did indeed assure a hearing for moderation, which, in the absence of violence, had gone unheard for nearly fifty years.

The Northern Ireland demonstrators were following—at their own pace, in their own way, in their own peculiar situation—an American example. And that example was set in the course of a struggle within America itself. Paradoxically, what is most important for the world outside is not what attitudes you take towards that world, but what happens domestically, inside your own society. Americocentrism, understood in *that* way, makes the soundest of good sense. You can neither export nor import revolution. Your government, it is true, can and does export varieties of counter-revolution, but these are fragile and temporary precisely in the degree to which they require American support. Conversely, a revolution which can be defeated by your Central Intelligence Agency cannot be a very serious revolution. Military intervention is, of course, quite another matter.

It is quite true that, granted the horror and misery of most of the world, advice to concentrate on the internal problems of your own society, so rich as a totality, may seem callous. Many of those most concerned about the world are also those most concerned about life here. Yet, this country being what it is, the most urgent priority, by far, lies here. As long as your society remains dominated by racist values, as it is still now, as long as it is securely in the grip of the capitalist ethic of the devil take the hindmost, as long as it tolerates within itself such great regions of blight and poverty, which as a society it has ample means to heal—so long will anything that it offers to give to the rest of the world be blighted too, whether it be aid or advice. The thing of most real value that America has given to the world in this decade has been something not designed for export: the examples of Americans fighting against American abuses in America. Foremost among American abuses of course have been those policies which have squandered America's wealth on an infamous war in Vietnam, instead of using it for the solution of America's problems in her own cities.

It is obvious that the only hope of changing this society lies in its young people, both black and white. The *impetus* must come from there. But what *direction* the impetus will actually take—a question quite distinct from that of the direction planned—depends to a very great extent on older people, on the generations mainly represented in this room. American society will not change its ways unless the younger generation is sufficiently militant, in sufficient numbers, to force it to do so. And if that necessary intensity and quantity of militancy are present, then some violence will inevitably be involved, at least at the fringes of the movement. Much will depend then on whether those millions of middle-class Americans who now oppose racism and the Vietnam war will continue to do so, will stand firm, or will allow themselves to be scared off by the violence of the left, and the predictably greater violence of the right, into that officially approved condition, the silence of the majority. If that happens, some new form of fascism is likely to be the outcome. If so, it will be the fruit, as before, *not only* of the violence of the young, but also of the timidity and collusion of their elders with the status quo.

My own approach to this is necessarily that of an outsider. Since the advice I give you is essentially to mind your own business, it is logical that I have, up to a point, decided to mind mine, by going back to my own country and there pitting myself against various picturesque local editions of the poor man's Spiro T. Agnew. In these circumstances, it is perhaps not very consistent that I should be addressing you at all: Leonard Boudin must bear the blame for writing me. As an outsider, I felt it most useful to concentrate on your relations with the outside world, and in what seemed to be some dangerous illusions about that outside world. In doing so I concentrated on those aspects of a recent manifesto—the *Weatherman*—which seemed to me to exemplify those illusions. But now I should like to recommend any of you who may not have read the pamphlet in question to read it carefully not for its advice about the world in general but for what it says about America. I speak to those of you who, like myself, were born about the same time as the October Revolution of 1917, and who are not standing up very well either. Read it, this revolutionary manifesto—I shall not try to summarize it—bearing in mind that your reactions in reading it, and in hearing things like it, and in hearing the reactions of your contemporaries to it, are likely to be of considerable significance in the future of this country, and of the world.

Communication between the generations is still possible, not on the basis of flattery, patronage or acquiescence or nonsense, but on the basis of a limited agenda, limited and common objectives. Few, in our generation, are likely to share the militancy and Messianic hopes of the young revolutionaries, and if we don't we should make that clear as we should also make clear the distrust which experience has probably instilled in us for all neat, systematic and precise predictive formulations in politics. This should not rule out work for common short-term and long-term objectives. Could, for example, the present police persecution of the Black Panthers, and what looks very like concerted police terrorism against members of that movement, suggest a common objective at present? Are there means for people, who are non-violent, to make their presence felt against racist terrorism, ordered by this society in the name of law enforcement? Would the Panthers welcome cooperation of that kind and in what forms, and if so will it be forthcoming?

These questions I must leave to you, to black and white Americans, or I overstep the line I set myself as an outsider.

If anything can be done along these lines, however, I should like to support it in any way I can as an ex-resident alien perennial visitor, potential American and sometime fringe participant in your struggle.

Violence is inscribed by the past and present of this society, into its future also. To what extent it will open a hearing for moderation in terms of the promotion of major social change and to what extent it will simply open a way for violent repression depends in some degree on you and especially on the quality of the interaction between those young and middle-aged black and white Americans who have in common a perception and detestation of racism and imperialism and a desire, however loosely formulated, to work together to defeat these forces in America first.

I hope you will forgive me if I have seemed to lecture you. It is a stance which it is rather hard for a lecturer to avoid. In any case it is really not in that spirit that I have wanted to talk to you, but one of respect to an association whose members and friends bore the brunt of reaction in the past decade and in this one are likely to be called to do so again in the decade that is about to open—and most especially those whom we all so rightly have honored this evening. You have struggled against those forces in America which oppress much of the outside world too. That struggle conducted by Americans inside America and primarily for America is the work and the example which the world most needs from America.

30

THE GENTLE NIETZSCHEANS

Nietzsche, it is usually held, was purely a man of thought and letters, and he was certainly never involved in practical politics: his political thought is generally considered to come a long way, in importance, after his contributions to psychology, German prose, and the critique of ethics.

Such classifications have their uses, especially for librarians, but it may also be useful to ignore them. All writing that we know—even the writing of Samuel Beckett—is a form of social communication, a cryptic signaling going on in society and history. And this signaling is not going along a narrow channel, as the old New Criticism would perhaps have preferred.

It does not usually work, even among strong and trained intelligences, through the concentration of maximum attention on a series of texts—that is training or discipline at best; it may also be a game or a refuge. But the real creative and destructive process of communication goes on in jumps, and crisscross jumps at that. Each mind and each age take from the messages what they can absorb and feel they need, and in this process it is irrelevant whether the signaler or the receiver is classified as politician, poet or philosophical writer.

Machiavelli was more important for Nietzsche than were the "purer" men of letters of the sixteenth century. Nietzsche, and later Burke, and an idealized picture of Renaissance Italy were more important in the development of Yeats's imagination than were any of the poets of those places and times. A few lines of poetry, the selected aphorisms of a re-

New York Review of Books, 5 November 1970, pp. 12–16.

tired man of letters, may liberate the demon of a charismatic political leader. The whole imaginative and intellectual life of a culture is one interacting field of force.

It is necessary to emphasize this particularly in the case of Nietzsche because people have gone to great pains to insulate Nietzsche, to isolate him from the culture in which he has been so potent a force. There is, we are told, a legitimate way of understanding Nietzsche, and also illegitimate ways which twist his true meaning. The key to the legitimate way is a spiritual one. When Nietzsche praises, as he so often does, war and cruelty, we are told we must understand him as calling for spiritual struggle and a stern mastery over the self.

Remarks which cannot, on the face of them, be easily interpreted in that way may be attributed to the author's taste for the provocative and the paradoxical, or may be described as not consonant with the general tenor of the work as a whole, which in turn is always presented in the most spiritual way. The Nietzsche who emerges from this kind of treatment is an essentially benign schoolmaster whose astringent and sometimes frightening quips conceal a heart of gold and a strenuous urge to improve the spiritual and moral condition of his pupils.

I cannot say exactly how prevalent this version of Nietzsche is in England; it is certainly influential. I do know that it is almost completely dominant in America, where nearly all the Nietzsche texts generally available in English are translated, introduced, and annotated by Professor Walter Kaufmann of Princeton, a noted Nietzsche scholar, who also happens, as far as interpretation is concerned, to be the king of the gentle Nietzscheans.

The gentle Nietzscheans start out, properly enough, by demolishing the fiercer caricatures of Nietzsche. There are two sets of these caricatures, unfavorable and favorable, and they resemble each other closely. The unfavorable one is the Nietzsche of allied war propaganda in the two world wars. This might be summed up in the language of a headline in a Boston paper in 1940. I quote from memory: GERMAN AGGRESSION DUE TO MAD PHILOSOPHER, CATHOLIC WOMEN TOLD. The Nietzsche presented to the Catholic women of Boston and other similar audiences was distorted by being presented as a German nationalist and—especially in the Second World War—a crude anti-Semite.

There was naturally an emphasis on the more frightening of his sayings, leaving out of consideration anything that might tend to mitigate these. The superman and the blond beast were both taken as representing the Germans. Now the Nazis on their side, in adopting Nietzsche as their precursor, took over to a great extent the Nietzsche of allied

First World War propaganda, with the difference, of course, that for them the idea of a blond bestial Germanic superman had favorable connotations.

The gentle Nietzscheans were able to point out correctly that Nietzsche was not a nationalist, that he seldom wrote of Germany and the Germans with anything but mockery, that his blond beast was without specific nationality and that his superman was to transcend all such petty matters as nationality. Finally, they argued that, far from being an anti-Semite, Nietzsche was outspoken in his contempt for the anti-Semitic screamers of his own day: one of his last recorded sayings, as his mind finally gave way, was "I am having all the anti-Semites shot."

So far, so good: The gentle Nietzscheans go on from there to argue that Nietzsche was "thoroughly opposed to all proto-Nazism" and that Nazi writers can cite him "only at the price of incredible misquotation and exegetical acrobatics" (Kaufmann). I shall come back to this.

Nietzsche's work, which coincides roughly with the decade of the 1880s, at the end of which period he became incurably mad, consists of essays, aphorisms, and the long rhapsodic fable *Thus Spake Zarathustra*. His most perfected form at least for those who have no taste for Germanic lyric playfulness is the aphorism, a form which of course tends to paradox and hyperbole. Contradictions did not worry him greatly, although I think that most of his contradictions are in fact superficial. His psychological insights were profound; they not only anticipate Freud but did much to make Freud possible. Ernest Jones recalls that Freud several times said of Nietzsche that "he had a more penetrating knowledge of himself than any man who ever lived or was likely to live."

The following aphorism would probably be identified by most people as either Freudian or post-Freudian.

> I have done that, says my memory. I could not have done that, says my pride, and remains inexorable. My memory yields.

The aphorism is in fact from Nietzsche's *Beyond Good and Evil*, written in 1885. Freud liked to say that he "tried to read Nietzsche," "gave up studying" him, or "avoided" him. In fact, no one can try to read Nietzsche without absorbing quite a lot, and no one like Freud could have succeeded in avoiding Nietzsche by the turn of the century. It is no exaggeration to say that there was hardly an important mind in Europe in the first half of this century that was not deeply marked by Nietzsche. Some other minds, that seemed at first quite unimportant, were marked also.

The insights were profound in their formulation, by preference explosive. Burke would certainly have classed Nietzsche, with deep disapproval, with those who "exploited the marvellous" giving rise to "new and unlooked for strokes in politics and morals." Machiavelli was in fact a precursor of Nietzsche. The gentle Nietzscheans do not like this: Professor Kaufmann is on the watch. Nietzsche, he says, "refers to [Machiavelli] very infrequently, and there seems no good reason for linking their names as is sometimes done" (Glossary of *Twilight of the Idols*). The references may be infrequent—Nietzsche is as jealous as Freud was about his really quite safe reputation for originality—but they are not insignificant. The category of thinkers about whom Nietzsche was enthusiastic is very small indeed, and the Machiavelli of *The Prince* is high among them. Consider this from *Beyond Good and Evil*:

> Machiavelli in his *Principe* lets us breathe the dry thin air of Florence and cannot resist presenting the most serious matters in an ungovernable allegrissimo—perhaps not without a malicious artist's inkling of the antithesis he is venturing on: thoughts that are long, difficult, hard and dangerous—in a tempo of galloping along in the best and most playful high spirits.

Really, praise of this order hardly has to be frequent to justify a linking of names! Of this order, but above all of this type. For no one who reads Nietzsche at all could fail, one would think, to miss the point here: the adjectives he lavishes on Machiavelli—difficult, hard, dangerous, playful—are not only his terms of highest praise but, by no coincidence, *those he likes to apply to his own work*. I don't think there is any other writer, with the possible exception of Dostoevsky—a late discovery—about whom Nietzsche writes with such enthusiasm and sense of identification. Identification is strong indeed when the hero of one's hero becomes one's own hero.

It is unlikely, I think, that a nineteenth-century German would pick out Cesare Borgia as a heroic archetype, as Nietzsche does, had it not been for Machiavelli. Here again the gentle Nietzscheans are on hand with the disinfectant. Nietzsche's treatment of Borgia "invites misunderstanding" we are told, but the invitation should be declined. Nietzsche called Borgia "a beast of prey" and "a tropical monster" and "these are not terms of approbation." No doubt they are not for Professor Kaufmann. But for Nietzsche? Let us leave the question in suspense for a moment.

You will recall the opinion of those American scholars who held that Burke's great achievement was "to close the Machiavellian schism between politics and morality." As I have argued elsewhere, Burke did not in fact close the schism; he allowed for its continuing existence in "dreadful exigencies." The thinker who closes it is Nietzsche, and he does so, not by restoring the dominion of morality over politics as those scholars imagined Burke to have done, but by letting loose the forces of Machiavellian politics to the destruction of the traditional Judeo-Christian morality.

For Machiavelli, cruelty and lying are still evils, but evils which rulers must sometimes practice, and whose use they must learn. For Nietzsche, cruelty and lying are necessary to healthy life and the vigor of their exercise by a ruler is not an exception but an inherent part of the ruler's superiority, by which he liberates himself from the traditional slave morality and prefigures the Superman. The schism is closed.

The idea of the *Umwertung des Wertes*, the revaluation or transvaluation of values, is at the heart of Nietzsche's system. The recurrent theme is that our culture has been poisoned by the Jews with the poison of the Gospels. The Jews, a strong and pure race but outnumbered, needed, for their own protection and survival, to infect the Gentiles with an ethic of pity and other moral inhibitions. The Gospels carried this infection, and it continues to work even in minds which reject the supernatural aspects of Christianity—in such forms as democracy, socialism, and a reluctance to destroy defective human beings. The reversal of values effected by the Jews must be re-reversed, permitting the emergence of a morality and order of the strong, the subordination of the inferior, and the elimination of the unfit.

Primarily this is to be a moral and spiritual revolution: the gentle Nietzscheans emphasize this. But it also requires, and this they avoid recognizing, a political revolution: democracy and socialism are political concepts and their antithesis must also be political. The Nietzschean aphorism implies a strong executive, a prince. Nietzsche often writes with legislative intent, as in this passage from his posthumous MSS, which were collected under the title *The Will to Power*:

> Society, the great trustee of life, is responsible to life itself for every miscarried life—it also has to pay for such lives: consequently it ought to prevent them. In numerous cases, society ought to prevent procreation: to this end, it may hold in readiness, without regard to descent, rank or spirit, the most rigorous means of constraint, deprivation of freedom, in certain circumstances, castration.

"No philosopher," wrote Nietzsche, "will be in any doubt as to the type of perfection in politics: that is Machiavellianism. But

Machiavellianism *pur, sans mélange, cru, vert, dans toute sa force, dans toute son âpreté* is superhuman, divine, transcendental, it will never be achieved by man, at most approximated."

The bourgeois states of his own day were poor approximations or dilutions: even Bismarck was not Machiavellian enough. Yet Nietzsche, who did not always write respectfully of the state, came to see in it toward the end of his creative life a kind of collective superman, and this precisely because of its emancipation through Machiavellianism and *raison d'état* from the traditional morality. "Multiplicities," he wrote,

> are invented in order to do things for which the individual lacks the courage. It is for just this reason that all communities and societies are a hundred times more upright and instructive about the nature of man than is the individual, who is too weak to have the courage of his own desires. How does it happen that the state will do a host of things that the individual would never countenance? Through division of responsibility, of command and of execution. Through the interposition of the virtues of obedience, duty, patriotism, and loyalty. Through upholding pride, severity, strength, hatred, revenge—in short, all typical characteristics that contradict the herd type. None of you has the courage to kill a man, or even to whip him, but the tremendous machine of the state overpowers the individual, so he repudiates responsibility for what he does (obedience, oath, etc.) [*The Will to Power*].

It does not seem to me at all surprising that the Nazis should have held Nietzsche in such high regard. I cannot see that they required to distort his work or engage in exegetical acrobatics in order to like him. On the contrary it is in order *not* to see him as a proto-Nazi that these acrobatics are required. Not through occasional *obiter dicta*, but through the central thrust of his work, Nietzsche legitimizes ferocity and the politics of ferocity, an authoritarian politics freed from the trammels of Christian, liberal, and democratic tradition—including the trammels of that appearance of piety which was binding on Machiavelli's *Prince*.

Compared with the effects of these "bold strokes in morals and politics" it seems to me that the contradictions which would make Nietzsche unassimilable by the Nazis or make it necessary to distort him are trivial, or the result of misunderstanding. It is true that he speaks contemptuously of the Germany and German nationalism of his contemporaries; indeed it is his way to treat *every* aspect of contemporary life with disdain.

But he does not—and as a good Machiavellian he could not—overlook the value of patriotism; on the contrary it is one of those "salutary interposing virtues" which permit the state to liberate the heroic and frightful powers of man. This surely must have presented very little difficulty to the Nazi ideologists.

What the gentle Nietzscheans always present as their trump card is actually a central weakness in their system. How, they ask, can Nietzsche be a precursor of the Nazis when he is actually on record as being an *anti*-anti-Semite? Now it is quite true that Nietzsche despises contemporary anti-Semites, and most notably his detested brother-in-law Bernhard Forster. It is also true that he sometimes praises the intellectual strength, imagination, and other qualities of Jews. And what he preaches—and he is a preacher—is anti-Christianity, and apparently not anti-Semitism. But—and it is a tremendous but—at the core of his anti-Christianity is anti-Semitism; he uses anti-Semitism as a tool for arousing anti-Christianity, and anyone who becomes anti-Christian by his route will be a hater of Jews.

In *The Antichrist* he writes about the Gospels: "One is among Jews," he writes—the first consideration to keep from losing the thread completely. Paul and Christ were "little superlative Jews." "One would no more associate with the first Christians than one would with Polish Jews—they both do not smell good." "Pontius Pilate is the only figure in the New Testament who commands respect. To take a Jewish affair seriously—he does not persuade himself to do that. One Jew more or less—what does it matter?"

There are many sayings in that vein. One might perhaps find these harmless *boutades*, as the marvelous gentle Nietzscheans do, were it not for their position in the general strategy of his work, helping to establish the picture of the Jews as the arch corrupters of Aryan humanity, inventors of Christianity, the anti-Aryan religion *par excellence* and the revaluation of all Aryan values: Nietzsche's language in *Twilight of the Idols*. The basic image is the old medieval one of the Jew poisoning the well, but the new twist is that the poison is nothing other than Christianity. Freud saw unconscious resentment against Christianity as a cause of Christian anti-Semitism.

Nietzsche's writings encourage that resentment and point to the Jew as the author of the trouble. His real complaint against the vulgar Christian anti-Semites of his day was that they were not anti-Semitic enough; that they did not realize that they were themselves carriers of that Semitic infection, Christianity. The Jews, he wrote in *The Antichrist*, "have made mankind so thoroughly false that even today the Christian can feel anti-Jewish without realizing that he himself is *the ultimate Jewish consequence*." He underlines the last words: they are the ultimate insult, and the ultimate revelation of the real character of

Nietzsche's supposed anti-anti-Semitism. He is in fact the most radically anti-Semitic writer, as well as the most radically anti-Christian writer, known to history.

Nietzsche's writings were widely disseminated in Germany and elsewhere, in popular editions and selections, long before the Nazis came to power, and also after that date. We cannot know what specific effect they had. Certainly it was defeat in the First World War, and not the mad philosopher of whom the Boston ladies heard, which was responsible for the rise of a demogogic, chauvinist, militarist political movement in Germany, and certainly any such movement in Germany would have been anti-Semitic, even if Nietzsche had never lived. But what Nietzsche did was to encourage the substitution of an *anti-Christian* anti-Semitism for the old bumbling self-contradictory Christian anti-Semitism. Nietzschean anti-Semitism was an anti-Semitism without inhibitions—more, an anti-Semitism in the context of a cult of pride, severity, strength, hatred, revenge, and a cult of the state which lets loose these emotions.

Unless one goes so far as to deny all influence to the dissemination of ideas, I think one is forced to see that a mass movement permeated by Nietzsche's ideas—not in their Kaufmannite dilution but straight out of the bottle—is going to be a more dangerous and thoroughgoing affair than one which is still affected by the inhibitions of the traditional ethic. Nazism without Nietzsche would still have been brutally anti-Semitic, but Nietzsche made it easier for Nazism to pursue its inner logic as far as the gas chambers.

Each age, of course, reinvents the authors of the past. The Nazis needed a fierce Nietzsche and found him without any difficulty. In the decades after the defeat of Nazi Germany, *that* Nietzsche became unacceptable, and a gentle Nietzsche was offered to the postwar public. But I suspect that we have not done with Nietzsche, any more than with Machiavelli, and that the fierce Nietzsche may be due for a revival. In part on intellectual grounds: the Nietzsche of the gentle Nietzscheans is a fake, and there are limits to the survival value of fakes. But there are also historical reasons why a Nietzschean ethic may come to recommend itself. The world by the turn of the century is likely to present some terrible aspects. The comfortable countries, if they can keep their hands off one another's throats, will be more comfortable, or at least more affluent than ever. But the poor world is likely to be drowning in the excess of its own population, a human swirl of self-destructive currents, of which the Nigeria-Biafra war may have been a type and forerunner.

The advanced world may well be like, and feel like, a closed and guarded palace, in a city gripped by the plague. There is another metaphor, developed by André Gide, one of the very powerful minds powerfully influenced by Nietzsche: This is the metaphor of the lifeboat, in a sea full of the survivors of a shipwreck. The hands of survivors cling to the sides of the boat. But the boat has already as many passengers as it can carry. No more survivors can be accommodated, and if they gather and cling on, the boat will sink and all be drowned. The captain orders out the hatchets. The hands of the survivors are severed. The lifeboat and its passengers are saved.

Something like this is the logic we apply, when we tighten our immigration laws, and in the general pattern of our relations with the so-called under-developed countries. Something like this, but not exactly the same: it's more as if we were using the hatchets to keep our rations at the existing very high level. As this situation becomes more obvious it is likely to generate its own psychological and moral pressures. The traditional ethic will require larger and larger doses of its traditional built-in antidotes—the force of hypocrisy and cultivated inattention combined with a certain minimum of alms.

But there will be minds, and probably some powerful minds among them, who will go in quest of a morality more appropriate to the needs of the situation and permitting, within the situation, both honesty and a good conscience. Such minds may well turn to Nietzsche, reading him, not in the gentle adaptation, but for his bracing fierceness. There is much there for their comfort, not only in the general ethic, but also in specific applications. Nietzsche approves "Annihilation of decaying races." He also has this to say in *The Will to Power*: "The great majority of men have no right to existence, but are a misfortune to higher men. I do not yet grant the failures (*den Missrathenen*) the right. There are also peoples that are failures (*missrathenen Völker*)."

Professor Kaufmann admits that these words—written but not published by Nietzsche—"sound omnious," but adds that "it is clear from Nietzsche's books"—this is a common gentle Nietzschean use of a blanket reference to smother a particular and precise statement—"that he is not thinking of the Jews, the Poles, the Russians or any other peoples whom the Nazis later decimated."

Who then was Nietzsche thinking of? Professor Kaufmann leaves the question open.

Freud was afraid of Nietzsche, at least I can see no other meaning in his frequent, confused, and obviously agitated references, his tremendous tribute to him and his simultaneous claim not to have really read him. This is understandable. The thought of a man who sees so deep into human nature—or at least into his own nature—and sees there such a need for frightfulness: that is not easy to face. The appeal of Nietzsche simultaneously to the best minds of our century and to the Nazis is another sinister paradox, nor is it consoling to think of what some other future readers of this master may have in store for us. Yet it remains a pity that Freud should have flinched and failed to look Nietzsche in the face—a pity because of the contribution to the understanding of Nietzsche that we have thereby lost but also, more widely, through what "Freud on Nietzsche" might have meant to our understanding of the destuctive forces in our psyche and in our society.

Nietzsche did not invent Fascism: Fascism invented Nietzsche. That was Thomas Mann's idea. It is neat: the society was incubating Fascism, Nietzsche merely expressed the trend of what was happening in the society. Yet it is not enough to say this. The writer is not just a symptom or a clinical indicator. The imagined order which he creates legitimizes in others some image of that order. To legitimize means to free something which would otherwise be at least partly suppressed. In that sense, Nietzsche was one of the great liberators. He freed creative imaginations—Yeats for example might never have developed into a great poet without the Nietzschean permission. He also freed other forces, extended the range of Machiavelli, gave the killers license and a good conscience.

He was sometimes frightened himself, even this most daring of thinkers. Frightened of some travesty of his thought, he said, and the gentle Nietzscheans take comfort from this. Frightened, I think myself, of what he was actually saying, and of what his messages might effect when they reached minds which were as bold in action as he was bold in thought. Let me conclude this by quoting one of the most tragic and moving passages in his works, that passage where the lonely walker of the Engadine looks out to that future which his thought was helping to shape. This is from Book V of *The Gay Science*, first published in 1887:

The background of our cheerfulness. The greatest recent event—that "God is dead," that the belief in the Christian God has ceased to be believable—is even now beginning to cast its first shadows over Europe. For the few, at least, whose eyes, whose *suspicion* in their eyes, is strong and sensitive enough for this spectacle, some sun seems to have set just now.... In the main, however, this may be said: the event itself is much too great, too distant, too far from the comprehension of the many even for the tidings of it to be thought of as having *arrived* yet, not to speak of the notion that many people might know what has really happened here, and what must collapse now that this belief has been undermined—all that was built upon it, leaned on it, grew into it; for example, our whole European morality....

Even we born guessers of riddles who are, as it were, waiting on the mountains, put there between today and tomorrow and stretched in the contradiction between today and tomorrow, we firstings and premature births of the coming century, to whom the shadows that must soon envelop Europe really *should* have appeared by now—why is it that even we look forward to it without any real compassion for this darkening, and above all without any worry and fear for *ourselves*? Is it perhaps that we are still too deeply impressed by the first consequences of this event—and these first consequences, the consequences for us, are perhaps the reverse of what one might expect: not at all sad and dark, but rather like a new, scarcely describable kind of light, happiness, relief, exhilaration, encouragement, dawn?

Indeed, we philosophers and "free spirits" feel as if a new dawn were shining on us when we receive the tidings that "the old god is dead"; our heart overflows with gratitude, amazement, anticipation, expectation. At last the horizon appears free again to us, even granted that it is not bright; at last our ships may venture out again, venture out to face any danger; all the daring of the lover of knowledge is permitted again; the sea, *our* sea, lies open again; perhaps there has never yet been such an "open sea."

31

MR. ALEC FOSTER: AN APPRECIATION

The obituary called Alec Foster "a noted controversialist." He was that, and yet the description may mislead people who didn't know him. A "controversialist" sounds a rather grim type, a man of abstract causes, pedantic, quarrelsome. Alec was the reverse of all that. He did not love abstractions, he loved human beings. Stronger than that—since the word "love" has been bent by so many theologians and patriots—he actually *liked* human beings. I never knew anyone who liked so many different varieties of human beings so much, or who so enjoyed different kinds of company—the young, the old, workers, farmers, teachers, writers, Unionists, Republicans: anyone at all who was willing to talk or to sing or to listen.

He wrote letters to the papers in the same spirit as he wrote—much more often—postcards to his friends: out of the need to communicate with his fellow-creatures. He sang in the same spirit, and loved sport for the same reason. It was his conception of sport, rather than politics, that impelled him to protest publicly against the visit, or visitation, of the Springboks. He saw the white South Africans, not their critics, as being the people who were introducing politics into sport—the politics of racism. Unlike many of those who stood in silence outside the grounds, he

Irish Times, 30 August 1972.
This appreciation of Conor's father-in-law (from his first marriage) followed an *Irish Times* obituary of Alec Foster of 26 August 1972. That obituary was unsigned. It was written by George Hetherington, managing director of the paper, and, by virtue of his having married Conor's former wife, also a son-in-law of Foster.

would dearly have liked to be inside watching the match, but he could not. Indeed, his very first question after the protest march had ended was "Who won?"

The whole idea of *apartheid* in any sense of the word—the whole notion of exclusion and exclusiveness—was not just something he disapproved of: it was the opposite of the generosity that was his nature. He was against it, not just by a gesture of following a fashion but existentially, by being what he was in all the conduct of his daily life and, for exactly the same reason, he was repelled by the notion of personal discourtesy to the South African players. He knew there were versions of anti-apartheid which themselves issued from their own version of apartheid-mindedness.

Similarly he stood against Orange exclusiveness, and wanted to see the unity of Ireland. What he did live to see was an Ireland more bitterly divided than ever, as a result of a murder campaign perpetrated in the name of unity. He did not want to see, and in some strange, splendid way, was never altogether capable of seeing, that human beings can be as implacably self-righteous and as cruel as they were showing themselves to be all round him in Belfast.

He retained right to the end of his long life a noble innocence. Hearing him I was sometimes reminded of lines by the Czech poet, Fred Marnau:

> God was in love and had
> a dream of his own
> And did not notice the scorn in
> people's voices.

That should not be allowed to mislead, either. Alec Foster was a man of exceptionally keen intelligence and deep culture and, unlike most of those so equipped, did not regard these attributes as particularly important. He was at home with the classics as comfortably and casually as he was with a group of small farmers singing in a pub. I know one distinguished classical professor who complained to me about the difficult Latin in the postcards which Alec kept sending him (not difficult to understand, but setting a hard standard for a busy man to keep up in his reply). Alec's total lack of any kind of snobbery in his relation to learning was one of his assets as a teacher. The successes he was proudest of were not those with his brighter pupils—to whom he gave all the credit for their achievement—but the quite small, and to others imperceptible, breakthroughs with the less bright.

In repose, which was seldom, Alec's face seemed set in heavy lines of suffering, and he had in fact suffered much, but when he smiled or laughed the whole great complex of lines and creases took on another meaning altogether: that of joy itself. In reality people's faces don't "light up" as often as they do in the stories, but Alec's change of expression—as when he welcomed a visitor—was like the sun coming out. This was something that even now it is warming, rather than sad, to remember.

He lived long and many people feel the better, and the happier, for having known him.

He died, without pain or long illness, among those who loved him. He is buried on a Kerry hillside, in beautiful country, strikingly resembling his native Swilly shore. His widow, Betty, and his four children know in their sorrow that there are many, of several different generations and kinds, who feel with them some part of their loss, and who know also that things as vital and radiant as Alec Foster's mind and personality are never wholly lost while those who knew him live.

His Christian faith was always central to his life, both in his early and middle years as a Presbyterian, and in his later years as a Catholic. I don't think that that transition ever seemed quite as momentous to him as it would seem—for good or ill—to most people in this island. Like Edmund Burke it was to "Christianity at large," as a religion of love and praise, that he was attached, and not to any form of "polemical theology." One of the sayings most often on his lips was: "I'll sing unto the Lord until I die." And so he did.

32

Now They Talk of
Over-Information

The Evzones stand guard on the terraces of the Royal Palace, while the President's guests go by. The huge guards, in their gawdy clothes, stand as stiffly as any sentry at Buckingham Palace, as far as their bodies are concerned. Their features are taut with apprehension. Their fierce, black eyes dart to and fro. It is as if Groucho Marx has been hired to keep an eye on the spoons, from inside a suit of armour.

These vivid manifestations of distrust on the part of the servants of power are fitting enough. The spoons, in a symbolic sense, are in danger. The guests are journalists.

This was the Twenty-Eighth Assembly of the International Press Institute. Officially we were most welcome, in a Greece which has left the rule of the Colonels behind it.

At the opening of the Assembly, the President of Greece had made a gracious and appropriate speech of welcome, at the Odeon of Herod Atticus. This had been followed by an ungracious and inappropriate "Keynote Address" by Mr. Ferdinand Mayor, a deputy director-general of the United Nations Educational, Scientific and Cultural Organisation (UNESCO).

This discourse necessarily smacked of its place of origin, but it did contain one new word—at least it was new to me. This was the word "over-informed": "*sur-informé.*"

Just as there are people who are overfed so there are, it seems, people who are over-informed, intellectually bloated people. Clearly such people need to be put on some sort of diet—in official Unescan "free and balanced flow of information"—so that they get just the right kind of information, in just the right quantity.

UNESCO is the right body to prescribe and supervise such a diet. After all, most of its member-Governments have been regulating, rationing and filtering the news for years.

I was impressed. In Unescospeak there are many levels, and this was from the Upstairs of that vast Downstairs. To pluck such a flower of speech as "over-informed," a man must needs have climbed to the very highest plateau of Unescience. I gazed upon Mr. Ferdinand Mayor then, with a kind of awe which he would, I am sure, have appreciated —since, concerning the achievements of this gentleman, I am quite adequately under-informed.

Just as Lenin found a wonderful Georgian, so the IPI Executive had found itself a wonderful Unescan. But it is not enough to find a Wonder, you must also know what to do with it when you find it—a problem that Lenin, as his Testament showed, failed to resolve.

The IPI, I thought, had also failed to resolve it. To invite Mr. Mayor to address our assembly—well and good. To have Mr. Mayor engage in dialogue with our members—excellent. But to invite Mr. Mayor to deliver a *keynote address*—how come?

The servants of UNESCO have an Evzonian relationship to journalists. They are there to protect their masters' spoons. Their masters are the member-Governments of UNESCO, most of which are dictatorships of various colours, but have identical views about spoons. The means of communication are the spoons; if not carefully protected, they can be used to cram the minds of the public with excessive and unbalanced information.

Mr. Mayor is a spoon-guarder—nay, the discoverer of the philosophy of spoon-guarding. The Press, on the other hand, are those who want to steal the spoons: that is to make unsupervised use of the means of information in order to gorge the public with an unhealthy diet of unlicensed data: "So how come, please, IPI?"

"Well we wanted the director-general, you know, Amadou-Mahter M'Bow, to come so that our members could put questions to him."

"Fine, but why the Keynote Address?"

"His secretariat told us that, if you invite him to a function, he won't come unless he is to give the Keynote Address. *Pas d'argent, pas de Suisses.* No Keynote, no director-general."

I could think of someone who would have fancied that idea: KEY-NOTE ADDRESS!

By Toad!
Text follows:
Poop! Poop!

In the event the great M'Bow did not even deign to poop in person, and the gentleman who pooped on his behalf did not abide our questions, or stay for the proceedings which his poop was supposed to inspire. It was a hit-and-run Keynote.

So the score: UNESCO 2, IPI Nil.

Speaking of spoons, IPI does not yet have a long enough one to sup with UNESCO. I believe they are having one custom built between this and the next Assembly.

The philosophy of UNESCO probably does not matter very much either in countries where the freedom of the Press from Government control seems securely established, or in countries where Government control over the Press seems securely established. Where it does matter is in those countries where freedom of the Press exists on a kind of sufferance, and under threat. In those countries—India being the most notable example—one of the best defences of the freedom of the Press is the feeling among politicians that to be seen to control the Press impairs one's international image.

MOST TO FEAR

Unescospeak undermines that defence by offering respectable formulae and auspices, under which "responsible" journalists are to be "protected." The people who have most to fear from UNESCO are the journalists of the Third World, whom UNESCO professes to champion.

There is, to be sure, another way of looking at the matter, and this way was advocated most patiently at Athens, by Mr. Sean MacBride, the chairman of the Commission for the Study of International Communications set up by UNESCO. Mr. MacBride's point of view was not a popular one at the Athens Assembly, and he earned some admiration for the courage and pertinacity with which—in contrast with Mr. Mayor—he remained to defend his views. The admiration was more than tinged with exasperation, expressed in such phrases as: "The way you can tell that man isn't Count Dracula is that he likes garlic."

It is true that Mr. MacBride's scowl-like features, old-fashioned aristocratic airs, and cinematic foreign accent appear less ominous and more human to anyone who has enjoyed with him an excellent dinner at (say) Ramponneau's in the Avenue Marceau. However, this subject is one on which I do really suffer from over-information, so I must not pass on that dread contagion.

His argument in any case was to the effect that if you have an international code for the protection of journalists it would in fact give some protection to journalists by having a restraining influence even on dictatorial governments. The counter-argument that the proposed code might actually deprive journalists of protection was swallowed up, like so much else, in Unescience.

Mr. MacBride did not represent UNESCO, he did not even represent his own Commission and (even if he did) that did not speak for UNESCO. His Commission had not reported, drafts were just drafts, and hardly even that.

He sounded very reasonable, without actually being so—a *spécialité de la maison*—and he brought us the kind of reassurance that makes you want to scream.

Pass the garlic.

33

Hands Off

The cause of political violence in Ireland, in particular Northern Ireland, is pressure meeting with resistance. The pressure is toward the unification of Ireland—an effort to move Northern Ireland out of the present United Kingdom and into a separate state of unitary or federal character, embracing the entire island. The resistance is to being incorporated in any form of united Ireland.

The pressure comes almost exclusively from Catholics in the Irish Republic and in the North, and from American descendants of Irish Catholics. The resistance comes mainly from a million Ulster Protestants, who constitute a large majority of the people of Northern Ireland. Both the pressure and the resistance are historical phenomena of long duration, although they have fluctuated in strength from time to time.

In 1886, shortly after mass democracy came to Britain, Prime Minister William Gladstone introduced in Parliament a home rule bill that envisaged a form of self-government for all of Ireland. It became immediately apparent that the Protestants of eastern Ulster—the core population of the present Northern Ireland—resisted incorporation in any self-governing Catholic-majority Irish state. Gladstone at the time dismissed threats of violent resistance by Ulster Protestants as "momentary ebullitions," but there was nothing momentary about them.

Almost a century has passed since then, and over that whole period every electoral consultation has shown that this population supports the

Foreign Policy 37 (Winter 1979–80), pp. 101–10.

union with Britain and resists incorporation in a separate Irish state. That this opposition is deep-rooted is a matter of historical record. That it is also intense—even frighteningly intense— is something that can be witnessed by anyone who visits Northern Ireland and listens to what people say. Those who suggest that, in these conditions, it is in Britain's power to bring about the peaceful unification of Ireland are either deceiving themselves or trying to deceive others. Basically, there are only two options open to Britain—to remain in Northern Ireland or to withdraw.

The great majority of the population of Northern Ireland would pre-fer to remain in the United Kingdom. The core of that majority is Protestant, but the Protestants are by no means alone in their view. A survey carried out by the Economic and Social Research Institute (ESRI) of Dublin last year and published last October puts the proportion of the whole population of Northern Ireland that wishes to remain in the United Kingdom at 72 per cent, made up of 83 per cent of Protestants together with 50 per cent of Catholics. Only 16 per cent of the population—39 per cent of Catholics and 6 per cent of Protestants—wanted unification with the Republic.

The conventional answer to the citation of statistics about the actual preferences of people in Northern Ireland has always been that it is an artificially delimited entity, that the natural unit is the island of Ireland and that in the island there is an overwhelming majority in favor of unity. But no such overwhelming majority exists, and there may not even be any majority at all.

The ESRI survey, like previous surveys, shows a 68 per cent majority in the Republic in favor of unity. But the authors of the survey put the question, "Is there a majority in the whole island of Ireland in favor of unity?" And they returned the answer, "Certainly not a clear majority." They put the figure at between 48 and 52 per cent of the population of the whole island. If the will of a massive majority of the population of Northern Ireland is to be overborne, it is at the behest of a clear major-ity not of the whole island, but of the Republic, which is just as artifi-cially delimited as Northern Ireland.

The real argument that influences people in favor of a united Ireland is not a democratic one. It is that the Irish Republican Army (IRA) seems determined to go on killing as many people as it can until it gets a united Ireland. This argument ignores the fact that if the IRA looks like it is get-ting its way, there are others in the North quite as determined to kill in order not to be incorporated in a united Ireland.

Surveys have shown that direct rule from Britain is acceptable to most Catholics as well as most Protestants and that it is the only political option acceptable to a majority in both communities. Alternative political solutions that have been proposed are simply impracticable. A return to Stormont—the Protestant-dominated Northern Ireland parliament dissolved in 1972—would be unacceptable to Catholics, who have no wish to turn the clock back. Power-sharing would fare no better today than it did in 1974, when a strike by militant Protestants fearing links with the Republic caused the Sunningdale executive (in which Catholics had a guaranteed number of places) to be disbanded only months after its formation. Repartition of Northern Ireland would involve letting Catholic areas, mainly in County Fernmanagh and County Tyrone, join the Republic. Protestants would see this as the first step toward unification.

The second basic option open to Britain is to withdraw its administration and forces from Northern Ireland and to pass legislation ending the existence of the United Kingdom. The effect of this legislation would be to detach from Great Britain an area, the majority of whose population wishes to remain attached. There is no precedent for such an action. But, unprecedented or not, this may happen, for the ESRI survey shows that only 25 per cent of the population of Great Britain wants Northern Ireland to remain in the United Kingdom. Under these conditions, pressure on the British to unify Ireland may eventually induce them simply to pull out.

And if Britain does pull out, what then? There is a viewpoint, often expressed by unity-minded public speakers, that when Britain prepares to withdraw, the representatives of Protestants and Catholics will sit down and work out arrangements for a united Ireland, perhaps on a federal or confederal basis. This is about as pretty a notion as wishful thinking can contrive. And in this case, wishful thinking is exceedingly dangerous. Ordinary people, even in the Republic—where there is much more wishful thinking on this subject than Northern Ireland can afford—refuse to swallow the nonsense about a peaceful settlement following British withdrawal. In the ESRI survey, 57 per cent of the respondents in the Republic believed that British withdrawal would be followed by "great violence," while only a minority of those believed that even the great violence would be followed by a settlement. In Northern Ireland the proportion of those who believed that withdrawal would be followed by great violence was even greater, and they are the people who are in the best position to appreciate the realities of the situation.

Those no doubt well-meaning people in the United States who are exerting pressure on Britain to move Northern Ireland into a united Ireland usually proclaim that they are doing so out of a desire to end the

violence. But if they looked at the situation at all closely, they would realize that the only possible long-term consequence of the pressure they
exert is the much greater violence that most Irish people in the North
and South see as the inevitable consequence of British withdrawal.

This talk of great violence following British withdrawal may sound
vague and alarmist to Americans. No one can predict precisely what
would happen, of course, but the general flow of events is to a great extent predictable. The first thing that would happen would be the setting
up of an executive, representing the Protestant majority in the North,
to conduct the affairs of the province on a go-it-alone basis. Most of the
Protestants do not want an independent Northern Ireland, provided
they are allowed to remain in the United Kingdom. If any Protestant
leaders should sit down with members of a Dublin government to discuss a united Ireland, they would not be merely repudiated but probably, in the volatile conditions following withdrawal, lynched as well.

The first action of such an executive would be to take emergency
measures for the security of the province. For this purpose the executive
could rely on the Ulster Defence Regiment, a domestically recruited
unit of the British army whose allegiance would transfer to the new executive; the Royal Ulster Constabulary (minus those of its officers who
are from mainland Britain); and the Protestant paramilitary organizations, which would be enrolled in some kind of militia.

With these effectives, the executive would proceed to police the
province, the Catholic areas in particular. Neither the executive nor
most Protestants would see this as a punitive measure aimed at
Catholics, although some elements in the militia, and perhaps in the
other units, would see the measure precisely in this light and behave accordingly. The view point of the executive would be that the kid-glove
measures for which Protestants have criticized successive British governments must end, that there must be no more "no-go areas" and no
more safe havens for terrorists. This would require systematic searches
by Protestant forces of Catholic areas.

There is no need to speculate about what would happen then,
because it has been seen before. It was the resistance of Catholics to a
Protestant version of the enforcement of law and order that brought
about the first deployment of British troops in Northern Ireland in
August 1969 to protect the Catholics and stop an incipient civil war.
This time there would be no British troops to deploy and nothing to
stop the process from escalating into full-scale civil war, which would
be detonated by IRA units firing out of Catholic homes at the Protestant
troops. Then the balloon would really go up. What began as a policing
effort would inevitably turn into a massacre. Although there certainly

would be efforts on both sides to bring things under control, there would be at least several hundred dead in a very short time, and a huge exodus of Catholic refugees would pour into the Republic.

In 1975, after Irish Prime Minister Jack Lynch's party, Fianna Fail, decided to call on Britain for a commitment to withdraw, I put a question about the refugee problem that such a withdrawal might generate to two representatives of the Catholic minority in Northern Ireland who were meeting with members of the Dublin government (of which I was a member). The question was a practical one about the number of refugees the Republic might have to expect if things went wrong. The Catholic representatives conferred briefly and came up with an answer: 55,000–65,000 families—that is, about 250,000 people, or half the Catholic population of Northern Ireland. An influx of refugees on that scale would, of course, have ruinous consequences for the economy, social life, and institutions of the Republic.

Disastrous as all this is, it would be only the first stage, confined mainly to the densely populated Protestant-majority core area of Northern Ireland, east of the river Bann. The second stage would develop in the thinly populated Catholic areas west of the Bann and along the border with the Republic. Here the population, obeying instinctive reflexes corresponding to those of the Protestants, would set up Catholic emergency committees for the defense of towns like Derry, Newry, and Strabane against the Protestant forces. Any Catholic area in danger of being taken over would call on the Republic for military aid. No government in the Republic could resist that appeal under such circumstances, especially after the arrival of the Catholic refugees from the Protestant core area, with their tales of horror (partly true and partly exaggerated, like all refugee stories). The forces of the Republic would cross the border—on a humanitarian mission, in the eyes of the Catholics; on a mission to invade Northern Ireland, in the eyes of the Protestants.

Under these conditions, Northern Ireland would turn from grave turbulence to straight intercommunal massacre on a Lebanese scale. Politically, the probable outcome of all this, after thousands of deaths, would be a new border in a different place and two hostile states, one Green and one Orange, preparing for the next round.

It is toward this extremely uninviting scenario that the current pressure to unify Ireland is actually tending. Most people in Ireland, as the surveys show, have at least a strong foreboding about this, although people in the Republic do not yet realize that the great violence they foresee would be likely to damage not only Northern Ireland but the Republic as well. If they did, there would not likely be a majority calling for unity.

A British departure from Northern Ireland is not imminent, mainly because all British political leaders clearly foresee such a chain of consequences following withdrawal and because they fear that these consequences, besides involving the risk of foreign intervention, would spill over in violent forms into mainland Britain. Nonetheless, a worsening economic crisis in Britain, continuing IRA and perhaps other violence, and pressure from America could produce in the British population such weariness and disgust with the whole problem that Britain could decide to withdraw, even with the knowledge that the consequences would be disastrous. Under the circumstances, there are logically only three conceivable ways of ending the violence. One is to increase the pressure to the point where it overcomes the resistance. The second is to increase the resistance to the point where it deters the pressure. The third is to decrease the pressure voluntarily, so that the resistance elicited is also reduced.

The first alternative, increasing the pressure, is currently being attempted, and some of that pressure is coming from Americans (mainly, although not exclusively, Americans of Irish origin). It is applied by two different sets of people, but their efforts are complementary in their effects and are so perceived by those who resist. The two forms the pressure takes are military and political. They are also complementary, because they are directed toward the same end: a united Ireland. Military pressure takes the form of terrorism, conducted mainly by the provisional IRA. This campaign—together with reactions to it by Protestant paramilitaries and British army units— has caused nearly 2,000 deaths, not to mention the injured, the maimed, the bereaved, the robbed, and the terrorized and twisted. There are countless victims, men, women, and children, both Catholic and Protestant. Yet even at this frightening level, the campaign shows no sign at all of reducing Protestant resistance.

Most of those who apply political pressure toward unity disavow and condemn IRA violence. Yet they use the existence of that violence as their main argument for making progress in the same direction as is demanded by the IRA. If that progress is not made, the violence (which they deplore) will continue. From the point of view of those to whom the double pressure is applied, those who apply the political pressure —using the violent pressure as their crucial argument, but also condemning it—seem odiously hypocritical. The two kinds of pressurizers bear an unpleasant resemblance to the proverbial two interrogators: the nasty one who abuses you and hurts you, followed by the nice one who sympathizes with you, offers you a cigarette, and explains what you have to do if you don't want the nasty one to come back.

This kind of pressure, if sustained, may result in British withdrawal. It may, that is to say, bring civil war to all of Ireland. Even such a civil war would not, however, bring unity: the idea that it would is based on unrealistic assumptions about the balance of forces in Ireland. The depth and intensity of the resistance are such that increasing pressure against it cannot end the violence but will of necessity greatly increase it.

The second way, that of increasing the resistance to pressure—that is, Protestant counterviolence againt Catholics—has been tried at various times (most ferociously in the middle of the present decade) and is now on the increase again. It is, in fact, one side of an incipient politico-sectarian civil war.

The third way—that of voluntarily decreasing the pressure—is the only one that points in the direction of peace, rather than war. There are friends of Ireland in the United States who are unwittingly pushing Ireland—all of it—toward the abyss. Men like Governor Hugh Carey (D.-New York), Senator Edward Kennedy (D.-Massachusetts), Senator Daniel Patrick Moynihan (D.-New York), and Speaker Thomas P. O'Neill, Jr. (D.-Massachusetts), would not be applying this pressure if they understood the consequences. Their understanding of Ireland is an inherited one, derived from long-established Irish-Catholic political beliefs, which suffer from one fatal idée fixe: that Ulster Protestants are basically England's puppets and that England (if tightly squeezed) can reverse their political allegiances. This belief is utterly unhistoric and false: and if Britain is induced to pull out of Northern Ireland, its falsity will be amply and horribly demonstrated.

Is there nothing, then, that Americans can do to help in Northern Ireland? Politically, perhaps not very much: although if a leading Irish-American politician were to say that there is no point talking about peaceful unification while the IRA campaign of violence continues, he would be making a substantial positive contribution. To discourage fund raising for the IRA is good, provided the discouragement is not accompanied or followed by insistence that the goal of a united Ireland must be politically attained. For in this case, the political encouragement afforded to the IRA more than cancels out the financial discouragement.

Americans who really want to help and who can see the dangers of political pressure might explore the possibilities of a program of social and economic investment to aid Northern Ireland. The stagnant conditions of certain regions of Northern Ireland (in some regions male unemployment has stood for many years at around 40 per cent) have helped to provide breeding grounds and recruiting grounds for violence. An investment program in those areas could, in the middle and long term, help Northern Ireland toward healthier and more peaceful conditions. But it must be stressed that this would have to be an economic program without political preconditions. Otherwise, it would be just another instrument of pressure, along with the others already applied and tending toward the same disastrous end.

34

Dead Cat Calwell Meets Arctic Dev

The relation between morality and politics was once defined for me by the late Rt Hon. Arthur Calwell, Australian statesman and Labour leader and, at the material time, Minister for Immigration and Information in his country's Government.

Calwell was being entertained to lunch by Eamon De Valera, Irish statesman and at the time, President of Ireland. I was present as an official. The only other guest was the Australian *chargé d'affaires* in Dublin, a Mr. Mulrooney.

The President did not seem at first greatly to take to his guest. For one thing, Calwell was taller than Dev. This was unusual, and faintly discourteous. For another, Calwell was an Australian, and Australians are too much given to coarse language, which Dev was not. However, since utterance of some kind was required of the situation, Dev asked his guest whether, by any chance, he knew a certain Father Dooley, of Melbourne.

It didn't seem a promising opening. I thought I was in for another boring lunch. I could not have been more wrong.

Yes, as it turned out, Calwell did know Father Dooley.

"He's quite a theologian, *he* is. A *profound* theologian. Up he comes to me—this was during the election—and he says:

" 'What's this about nationalising the banks, Artie?'

"I said, 'Well, what about it?'

" 'What about the morality of it,' says he, like that.

Observer, 3 February 1980.

"Says I, 'Bugger the morality of it! It's in the party platform.'"

Artie laughed loud and long, a truly Homeric laugh, shaking that great frame of his, and the room around us.

De Valera did not laugh. The Calwell doctrine may have been close enough to his own political philosophy, but he clearly didn't care for the way it was put. His expression, habitually sombre, darkened frostily. He looked, I thought, a bit as he must have looked on that December day in 1921 when—while presiding over a Dante Commemoration—he heard that his plenipotentiaries had just concluded a Treaty of which he had not personally approved the content. In both cases there was an impropriety involved, and impropriety was something Dev could not abide.

Perhaps by way of reprisal, Dev asked about the health of Robert Menzies, the Liberal leader and former Prime Minister, Artie's great political enemy.

Artie, however, liked this topic too. Menzies was fine, but funny:

"Thing about Bob Menzies is, he's *touchy*. A politician can't really afford to be touchy—not in Australia, anyway. If you know a fellow is touchy you can get at him, if you know what I mean—get him to say something.... "

Saying something was obviously something which a competent politician should avoid at all costs. Dev appreciated that. He nodded slightly, his features showing some signs of Arctic dawn. Artie went on:

"Bob went down to this election meeting in Hobart—Tasmania, you know. We had one of our own men in the audience. He knew what to do. One way you could usually get Menzies sore was to make some reference to the time in the war when he sent Australians to fight in the Middle East, instead of keeping them at home as he ought, to defend Australia against the Japs. But you had to refer to it in just the right way. This man we had there was pretty good at this sort of thing. So when Menzies got into his bit about the defences of the free world, our man gets up, see, and he shouts out—goods lungs he had, too—he shouts out:

"'Where d'yre put yer *knife*, Menzies?'

"Says Menzies, like a fool: '*What* knife?'

"He gets his answer: 'The knife yer stabbled Orstraylia in the back wiv!'"

That was more than poor Bob could take. He calls out: "I came here to talk to gentlemen, not to the sons of convicts."

That answer didn't get Menzies many votes in Tasmania.

Dev liked this anecdote. It was a *politician's* joke, a tale for professionals, and it contained no dirty words, no disrespect for the clergy. Dev smiled that famous smile of his, which a political opponent once compared to moonlight on a tombstone. The party was beginning to swing.

And now, Dev wanted to know, how were the Irish getting on in Australia nowadays?

The Irish, it seemed, were getting on very well indeed. Fine upstanding people, religious, well-behaved, the backbone of the country. Most of them, that is. There were exceptions:

"A few of them—only a few—are little rats like Mulrooney here."

The Minister jerked a colossal thumb in the direction of his country's *chargé d'affaires*.

De Valera, who was at all times the soul of courtesy, showed signs of distress at what sounded to him like personal rudeness. Mr. Mulrooney, for his part, did not look in the least upset.

Artie explained that he meant nothing personal. All he meant was that the *chargé d'affaires*, appointed by a previous government, was unlike most of the Australian Irish, a supporter of the Liberals, and therefore by definition a little rat, in a political sort of way, meaning no harm. With the exception of Bob Menzies, no Australian minded this sort of thing. He himself, Artie Calwell, could take it as well as dish it out.

He explained exactly what it was he could take, and on what scale. It appeared that an Australian, when a political statement fails to meet with his approval, does not do the equivalent of writing a letter to *The Times*. He sends the speaker a dead cat. Artie has received a great many of these furry tributes. After one speech, he had counted as many as 30 in his mail-bag. He believed this well might be an all Australian record. Indeed he was fairly sure it was. He nodded with a certain sober pride.

Dev was impressed. He too had aroused ferocious animosity in his time, and he was inclined to take someone seriously who could establish a national record in that line, even though the unit of measurement in this case might seem repellently exotic. The two great men parted with signs of mutual respect.

It had been, for me, a blissful lunch-time. The comedian in Artie Calwell found the perfect foil in Eamon de Valera—of all the straight men in the world, the King.

The above is not at all what I meant to offer to you today. What I meant for you—and what you have escaped for the time being—was a discourse on the relation of morality to politics, with some consideration on the comparability of the invasions of Afghanistan and the Dominican Republic, and of the fates of Ngo Din Diem and Hafizullah Amin. I was, however, swayed from the point, and from my treatise, by evoking the names, and therefore the spirits, of Artie Calwell and

Eamon de Valera. Those powerful ghosts expanded like a pair of djinns until they filled the column, shouldering abstractions out of it.

Something similar—in a modest way—once happened to the poet Yeats. He had set out to write a poem in praise of Benito Mussolini's system of government. The poem turned into Leda and the Swan, and poor Musso finished nowhere. "Bird and lady," acknowledged the poet, "took possession of the scene." He did not seem to regret the disappearance of the Duce, whom he so much admired, with the part of his mind which did not matter.

35

FWOWING UP WITH DOROTHY PARKER

A dozen or so of Dorothy Parker's wisecracks have entered into the language: some people's language anyway. Almost all of these quips date from Mrs. Parker's heyday, in the late Twenties and early Thirties, when she held the culturally influential position of literary editor of the *New Yorker*, using for that purpose the description "Constant Reader."

Many people remember—and occasionally use—her sassy comment: "Tonstant Weader Fwows Up."

But how many remember the precise word which had this effect on Tonstant Weader, i.e., Dorothy Parker?

What caused her to fwow up was the word "HUMMY."

And I infer, from her claim that the word "hummy" had this emetic effect upon her, that she was neither a good woman nor a good literary critic.

"But my dear Holmes, how on earth....?"

Let us examine the context in which Mrs. Parker chose to express herself in this way.

She was, of course, reviewing a book. The date was 20 October 1928 and the book was A.A. Milne's *The House at Pooh Corner*. Mrs. Parker, queasy from the start, reviewed it under the title "Far from Well." The passage which upset her is that in which Pooh and Piglet set out through the snow to sing Pooh's song to Eeyore. She quotes it from the point where Piglet "begins to weaken a bit":

Observer, 17 February 1980.

"Pooh," he said at last and a little timidly, because he didn't want Pooh to think he was Giving In. "I was just wondering. How would it be if we went home now and practised your song, and then sang it to Eeyore tomorrow —or—the next day, when we happen to see him."

"That's a very good idea, Piglet," said Pooh. "We'll practise it now as we go along. But it's no good going home to practise it, because it's a special Outdoor Song which Has To Be Sung In The Snow."

"Are you sure?" asked Piglet anxiously.

"Well, you'll see, Piglet, when you listen. Because this is how it begins. The more it snows, tiddely-pom—"

"Tiddely what?" said Piglet.

Mrs. Parker here interrupts, for the benefit of the very grown-up readers of the *New Yorker*: ("He took, as you might say, the very words out of your correspondent's mouth.")

Having broken her author's spell, and the stride of his narrative, and thus set him up for destruction—she was a devilish clever lady, you see— she allows him to go on for the last line of her chosen passage, the line which the huntress has isolated as her prey: "'Pom', said Pooh, 'I put that in to make it more 'hummy'.'"

Watch Mrs. Parker now, as she makes her celebrated kill:

"And it is that word 'hummy,' my darlings, that marks the first place in *The House at Pooh Corner* at which Tonstant Weader fwowed up."

The critic can now go home and, like her friend Hemingway, nail that old coonskin to the wall.

I don't think a good woman would be *likely* to single out a children's book for treatment of that kind, before an audience for which it was not intended. But it could be that a good woman, who was also a good critic, could feel obliged to savage a children's book because it was badly written, on the principle that children should not be exposed to bad writing.

That brings me back to that word "hummy," the key to this whole case.

If "hummy" is a bad word, so bad a word that it would make you sick, then Mrs. Parker is a good critic and, if that is so, since she is defending children from the evil of bad prose, she may be allowed also to be a good woman.

But "hummy" is *not* a bad word. It is the perfect word: just such a word as a child might coin, just such a word as a child appreciates for its flavour, in its right place in the story, which is exactly where it is. It is the *mot juste* for Milne's particular audience: children. By writing as well as he did, in stories that delighted children then and delight them now, he was teaching children to love good writing. And Mrs. Parker, *arbitrix elegantiarum* of the place and time, was deterring fashionable parents from encouraging their children in that direction.

So the defence of being a good critic fails. She here shows herself an incompetent critic and therefore, in the circumstances, quite a nasty woman.

But am I making too much of one piece, one crack, one word? No I'm not. The piece is one of Mrs. Parker's most effective, the crack one of her most notable. This is the lady at her best: the word—the fatal "hummy"—and her reaction to it, expose the grand flaw. I have been ploughing through "The Penguin Dorothy Parker"—all 597 pages of it—and most of it is a bore. The poems are talented exercises in the Housman manner, no more. One or two of the stories—notably "The Wonderful Old Gentleman"—make a powerful impact on first reading. But taken as a whole, poems and stories together carry an unbearable cumulative charge of self-pity, gallantly borne.

After immersing myself in this substance for what seemed like a considerable time, I felt I was sinking in what Aimee Temple MacPherson once called "a cloying quicksand." And as the sweet obstruction closed over my head, there wasn't even room to fwow up.

The best of the Penguin "Parker," and the only part you can go on reading for pleasure, is the part that is supposed to contain her literary criticism. These pieces are light, bright, neat and occasionally very funny. The plangent note is sometimes heard indeed, but only faintly. Harold Ross, the editor of the *New Yorker*, was not a man to let the cash-customers be put off by the too-loud rattling of a writer's broken heart. In this respect Mrs. Parker's writing benefited from the Ross discipline.

"Constant Reader" was not a literary critic: "hummy" is not an exception but a give-away. When she writes about something she admired—like André Gide's phoney masterpiece, "Les Faux Monnayeurs" (The Counterfeiters)—the result is embarrassing in its vague excess. (In the course of a six-line review she likens this novel to both the Grand Canyon and the Atlantic Ocean.) What she does best, and most, is to dig up bad books, laugh at them, and get the reader to laugh too. Occasionally she has the misfortune to dig up what, because of her critical inadequacy, she wrongly thinks is a bad book, and give it the same treatment.

Harold Ross, who himself knew nothing of art or literature, had the intuition that, by adopting a certain tone and style, you could sell—and he meant "sell"—to people who do not know about art and literature, the pleasing feeling that they do know about them. The *New Yorker* was founded on that brilliant intuition, and "Constant Reader" fitted perfectly into Ross's strategy. Mrs. Parker's readers were being comfortably assured of their superiority over all these peasants who admire these comical books. "We are the chosen ones: out there are the Philistines."

Actually the lady would have been quite at home in the more fashionable streets of Gath or Askelon.

"Hostess! Some warm water please! This lady has vomited over the gentleman who was telling the children a story."

36

African Self-Righteousness
Is as Tiresome as European

Professor Mazrui has an original mind, with a strong propensity to be intoxicated with its own hypotheses and rhetoric. In his Reith Lectures he has indulged that propensity to the hilt. I did not hear the lectures and it seems they made a good impression on at least some listeners. Professor Mazrui has a pleasing personality and a persuasive manner, and the intellectual excitement which he clearly experiences saves him from being boring. So the lectures no doubt sounded good. In cold print, however, their deficiencies are glaring.

"Let us assume," says Professor Mazrui in the first of these Reith Lectures, "Africa has come to my clinic for varied medical tests on the eve of the 100th anniversary of Europe's rape of her body and her possessions."

No please, let us assume nothing of the sort. Professor Mazrui is not a phenomenon on the scale of a continent, nor is it possible that a continent would consult him. He does not have a clinic, and if he did, Africa would not fit into it. He is too small; Africa too big.

"Let us assume," said the toad, "that I am an ox." The assumption was quickly exploded.

The historical perspective is also badly out, not only in this metaphor, but in the whole discussion which it opens. The apportionment of European political jurisdictions in Africa, which took place in the mid-1880s at Berlin, was a relatively trivial event compared with the

Listener, 103 (1 May 1980), pp. 577–78. Review of *The African Condition: A Political Diagnosis* (The Reith Lectures) by Ali A. Mazrui.

profound and complex social impact of the slave trade, as it developed from the 16th century to the end of the 18th. If we have to use an expression like "Europe's rape of Africa"—and we don't, really—the colossal human exploitation of the centuries of the slave trade would seem to merit such a description much more than does the political and ephemeral late-Victorian scramble for Africa.

But there is a snag there, of which Professor Mazrui (like other African intellectuals who talk in similar vein) is uncomfortably aware. If you want to see history in terms of rape—brutal Europe and suffering Africa—the slave trade is awkward material for your purpose. Professor Mazrui does discuss the slave trade in his second lecture, entitled "The Cross of Humiliation", i.e., humiliation of blacks by whites. Then he runs into the awkwardness, awkwardly. One of the reasons why Africans were enslaved, he says, was their "military weakness": "Their combat culture of spears and bows and arrows was no match for the new firearms. On the contrary, sometimes Europeans traded firearms for slaves, rewarding one set of Africans with guns so that they might continue to produce other sets of Africans for the slave market."

There's the rub. And it wasn't just military weakness. Else why not turn those firearms against the Europeans? It was the same motive as that which drove the Europeans: greed, combined with contempt. Europeans, more successful than Africans, despised the latter comprehensively and bought, sold and exploited those available, usually without mercy. The more successful African peoples and polities likewise despised the less successful ones, attacked them and sold their prisoners, either directly or through African middlemen, to the Europeans.

The notion of one continent "raping" another is a hollow trope. The reality was one of exploitation of weak people by strong people. The strong included many Africans, as well as Europeans. The Europeans, it is true, got most of the loot. Why not? They were the strongest of the strong. Liverpool did better out of the slave trade than Kumasi. But Kumasi, too, did pretty well. And I have never met an Ashanti who was anything but proud of the Ashanti Empire, or who was in the least ashamed of the part played by the slave trade in the growth of that powerful and predatory polity. The Fanti, who did even better out of the trade, are not exactly racked by guilt either. (The only West Africans who have been heard to express compunction for their own share in the slave trade are Dahomeyans, and Dahomey is a special case.) Nor—to turn to Professor Mazrui's own side of the continent—do I know many Arabs, or members of the African peoples associated with the Arab slave-trade, who worry about that long chapter in the history of slavery. Professor Mazrui, in a brief discussion of the Arab role in Africa, in the

Introduction to these lectures, does not allude to the Arab slave trade at all. It is a rather notable omission in the context.

If you want to make Europeans feel guilty about Africa—and that is a main preoccupation of these lectures—the slave trade (that is the acknowledged, or European, one) presents another great inconvenience. The descendants of the *victims* of the African slave trade are not in Africa at all. Most of them are Americans. Some of them remember, as Richard Wright did, that Africans sold their ancestors to the European slavers. And the descendants of the African slave-catchers and slave-sellers are in Africa ... So better to talk about the Berlin Congress of 1884, as Professor Mazrui does, as "the symbol of doom", signifying that "the nightmare of European penetration and colonisation of Africa was now truly under way." The point is that, in the case of Berlin, unlike that of the slave trade—that far more authentic "nightmare"—the participating villains were exclusively European. (In Mogadishu recently a Somali patriot told me that the Emperor of Ethiopia took part in the Congress of Berlin, but nobody else seems to have noticed him.)

African self-righteousness is as tiresome as European or American self-righteousness, and there is far too much of it in these lectures. There is also too much misplaced ingenuity and simply getting things wrong. The lecturer examines "six paradoxes" which are not paradoxes at all —such as the idea that Africa, though "probably the first home of mankind", is poor. He gets excited about Mercator's projection, because it makes Africa too small. He seems to think that imperialists wanted to think of Africa as small. But they didn't. They rejoiced in the thought of the vastness of Africa, as also of the teeming millions of India; all the more credit to us for being able to rule all that, and all *those*. The imperialists had their nonsense, as has Professor Mazrui, but their nonsense was not the sort of nonsense his nonsense thinks it is.

And nonsense, I'm afraid, is mostly what these lectures consist of. Having started from the "rape-diagnosis" trope, which I have tried to dissect, the lecturer ends with a perspective of how the world is to be saved. In this concluding lecture—"In Search of Pax Africana"—the nonsense level rises steeply into obsessive fantasy.

The Third World, it seems, will seek and ensure world peace by "engaging in a nuclear Russian roulette for a short while". Meanwhile, Women's Lib knocks the martial stuffing out of the advanced world. "White adults must be threatened with the danger of big black men wielding nuclear devices." But no sane adult, of any colour (or either sex), gives a damn about the *colour* of anyone who may be threatening him or her with a nuclear device.

It is all a great pity. Professor Mazrui's talents and reputation are such that it was appropriate for him to be invited to deliver the Reith Lectures. But when these particular lectures were handed in in draft, someone at the BBC should have been able to advise the lecturer to think again, and try again. In that way, it should have been possible to avert an intellectual disaster.

37

Kangaroo Tickets and Black Politics

"A Kangaroo ticket makes for a clothes-pin vote"
William Safire

You will find "Kangaroo ticket" in "Safire's Political Dictionary" (Ballantine Books, New York; Third Edition, 1978) defined as follows: "One in which the Vice-Presidential candidate has greater political appeal than the Presidential candidate."

As many people these days seem to find Vice-President Mondale more appealing than President Carter, and Mr. Bush than Mr. Reagan, both current tickets seem to belong to the marsupial order.

You won't find "clothes-pin vote" in Safire's Dictionary, yet. It means a vote which is so repulsive to have to cast that you have to hold your nose, with a clothes-pin. (If you say clothes-*peg*, don't worry —you don't have a vote in an American election.)

"Clothes-pin vote," I predict, will be in the Fourth Edition of Safire: a lexical memorial to the Presidential election of 1980.

It was the great lexicographer of American politics, Safire himself, who presented me—10 days ago in Washington—with the maxim at the head of this column, together with the key to its interpretation, and a copy of his Dictionary. I travelled with the Dictionary across the United States and back again, finding it a marvellous companion, witty, shrewd,

---

Observer, 12 October 1980. The date of the conferral on W.E.B. Dubois was 23 February 1963.

full of history, pertinent anecdote and inside information (Bill Safire was an aide to President Nixon, and is now on the Washington staff of the *New York Times*).

DEPARTURE-POINTS

The current edition of Safire's Dictionary carries on its back cover several richly-deserved tributes, but it lacks the obvious one, so let me now offer that, as my own sincere, if corny tribute: "Safire is a gem."

You can open this book anywhere, and find treasure, and also departure-points for trains of thought and memory. I opened it at "Black, political use of," and found:

> "Cartoonist Jules Feiffer ... pictured a bearded Negro intellectual in 1967 describing the ring-around-the-Rosie of the political use of the word: "As a matter of racial pride we want to be called 'blacks.' Which has replaced the term 'Afro-American'—which replaced 'Negroes'—which replaced 'colored people'—which replaced 'darkies'—which replaced 'blacks'."

There is an awful lot of American history—and not just black history—in that ring-around-the-Rosie. The advent of "black" represents a victory, I think, not only for blacks but for America. "Black" is the right word, not because it is an accurate description—it is no more accurately descriptive of the complexions of most of those concerned than "white" is of whites—but because it is symmetrical, and thus symbolic of equal status.

Already in his Second Edition (1972), Safire noted that "a laudable resistance to euphemism appears to be setting in"; he had observed that "poor" was taking the place of "culturally deprived" and "disadvantaged." "Black" replacing Afro-American is an even more significant rejection of euphemism.

Again, under this same head of "Black, political use of," we have the following:

> "The fear of an unintentional racial slur is real. When New Jersey Governor Richard Hughes held an angry press conference during the 1967 riot in Newark, he said, 'We have determined that the line between a jungle assault on law and order may as well be drawn here as anywhere else in America,' later repeating his condemnation of 'jungle law.' Wrote the *New York Post*: 'While gubernatorial assistants tried to explain that Hughes was referring to 'the law of the jungle' as opposed to 'civil order' and meant no racist connotations, the damage had been done'."

There was an important precedent which Mr. Safire might keep in mind for his next edition. On 15 February 1961, Adlai Stevenson, addressing the Security Council of the United Nations, on behalf of the United States, in the debate on the murder of Patrice Lumumba, asked a rhetorical question: "Are we to abandon the jungles of the Congo (the record here shows *interruption*) to the jungles of internecine warfare and international rivalry?" The interruption that followed "jungles of the Congo" was the prelude to the outbreak, minutes later, of the black riot in the Security Council gallery, which marked the opening of the new phase of black militancy which was to dominate so much of the Sixties. Adlai Stevenson certainly meant no harm by his jungly metaphor, but it was unfortunate all the same; one might wonder what Stevenson's unconscious and that of Governor Hughes were up to.

Still under "Black, etc." Safire quotes a letter written in 1928 by W.E.B. DuBois to a young man who then wanted to stop the use of the word "Negro."

"Historically, of course, your dislike of the word Negro is easily explained. 'Negroes' among your grandfathers meant black folk; 'colored' people were mulattoes. The mulattoes hated and despised the blacks and were insulted if called 'Negroes.' But we are not insulted—not you and I—we are quite proud of our black ancestors, as our white. And perhaps a little prouder."

... "And perhaps a little prouder." As I read those words, I could hear their intonation, for I knew that great man. We were both living in Ghana and I, as Vice-Chancellor of the University of Ghana, had the privilege of conferring an honorary degree on him, in celebration of his life-time of service to the cause of black people. Honorary degrees generally were nothing to him by that time—he had dozens of them, including one from his *Alma Mater*, Harvard—but this was his first from an African University, and that did mean something.

We gave a dinner for him and his wife, Shirley Graham. I remember him sitting after dinner in his wheelchair—he was then over 90 and he had not long to live—on the verandah of the Vice-Chancellor's Lodge on a hill overlooking the Accra plain, not far from the ocean. He looked like a Faulkner Colonel, or a Saudi Prince; a patrician face, high cheekboned, hawk-nosed, olive-skinned, impassive.

The first time he spoke was during a discussion of the case of James Meredith, the black student whose attempt to enter the all-white University of Mississippi was then the focus of all civil rights discussion. In a slow, creaky, Brahmin voice—which most of us were hearing for the first time—DuBois said:

"The only thing ... I can't understand about that young man ... is why *anyone* would want to go ... to the University of Mississippi."

STOOGE OF THE WHITES

When DuBois spoke next, there was no trace of the languid irony which had turned his Meredith remark. This time, a young man had been talking about Moise Tshombe, the nominal leader of Katanga's secession. Treating Tshombe as a stooge of the whites—which was fair enough, by and large—the young man linked Tshombe's name to that of Booker T. Washington, the moderate black leader in the American South in the post-Civil War period, with whom the young and militant DuBois had long engaged in controversy. I think the comparison—implying that Booker T. Washington had been some kind of stooge—was intended to please DuBois. If so, it was a failure. Speaking with great earnestness, in a strong voice, DuBois said:

"When I was young, I once spoke like that about him. My aunt told me: 'Never let me hear you talk like that again. Booker T. Washington was born in slavery and bears the mark of the lash on his back. He lives in the South. You were born free. You live in the North. He does what he can for his people in the South, in his own way. You do what you can here, in your way, but don't insult him.'"

"I have never forgotten that," said DuBois. Nor, I think, will any of us, who heard those words, forget them.

38

PARNELL AND HIS PARTY, RECONSIDERED

Parnell and His Party first appeared in 1957. Since then we have had F.S.L. Lyons's splendid biography and other work shedding light on the period, notably the researches of Emmet Larkin on the Catholic Church and Roy Foster's admirable study of the young Parnell.

These new publications would not in themselves require—at least in my belief—any major recasting of *Parnell and His Party*, and I still feel able to stand over the general line of interpretation in that book with, however, one major exception. That exception derives not so much from the new material—though it is partly prompted by some of Lyons's reflections on Parnell's last period—but results mainly from further consideration of the question of the partition of Ireland. I have now studied this question more attentively than I had when I wrote the book in the 1950s, a time when I was also less skeptical about certain Irish Nationalist assumptions than I am now.

In a footnote to chapter 5 of *Parnell and His Party*, I wrote, with reference to Parnell's insistence that rejection of partition was in the interest of Irish Protestants generally, as follows:

> Parnell's argument is, of course, here directed at English public opinion, which was believed to be anxious about the fate of Irish Protestants in general, rather than about Ulster in particular. Whether he fully understood the strong position of the Ulster unionists in their stronghold of north-east Ulster, and with their power to appeal to deep-rooted English emotions, may

University Publishing (Spring 1981), p. 7.

perhaps be doubted. He acted as if he believed that the status of Ireland could be decided by negotiation between the representatives of Irish and English majorities. This belief may, in the circumstances of the 1880's, have been right; it would be unsafe to say that an English majority led by Gladstone and an Irish majority led by Parnell could not—especially in the favourable climate of opinion created by the exposure, in 1889, of the forgeries published by *The Times* (below, Chap. VII)—have achieved a settlement which preserved Irish unity.

I no longer believe that even Gladstone and Parnell together could have brought about a United Home Rule Ireland. Cautious though the formulation in this footnote was, I believe that when I wrote it I myself was more in the Parnellite tradition than I realized in underestimating the depth and intransigence of Ulster opposition to incorporation in a Home Rule state. Lyons does not think that even Parnell and Gladstone together could have succeeded, and I now agree with him.

The most interesting question—iffish though it is—is what would have happened if Gladstone and Parnell had been able to continue their cooperation to the point of carrying a Home Rule bill through second reading in the Commons, with a majority from the United Kingdom electorate safe enough to make the creation of new peers a credible probability, and if they simultaneously experienced the full storm of Ulster Protestant refusal of Home Rule. What would have happened if in fact the 1912 situation, in its essentials, had come on twenty years earlier, with far more charismatic leadership on the Home Rule side than Asquith and Redmond were later able to supply?

Even that charisma could not have swung the thing. It seems to me now that it was always an inherent impossibility for any British Government to oblige the Ulster Protestant majority areas to come in under a jurisdiction they passionately refused: that of a Dublin parliament. I think therefore that the Home Rule coalition would have had, like Asquith and Redmond, to settle for partition, to which the only real available alternative was no Home Rule at all.

Gladstone would have been likely to see this early; indeed, the careful wording of his second reading speech in 1886 suggests that he wanted to avoid any language that would finally shut the door against a settlement on the basis of partition.

What would Parnell have done on learning from Gladstone that it was either Home Rule with partition or no Home Rule at all?

Politically speaking—that is, if the divorce threat could have been taken out of the equation—I believe Parnell, with his characteristic political realism and force of character, would have gone for Home Rule with partition, concentrating on getting the maximum territory and power for his Home Rule State and for himself as near-absolute ruler of that state. Still leaving the divorce factor out, I believe that he could have imposed that solution on his parliamentary and extra-parliamentary followers (with the loss of a few dissidents) and that he could have defied his American allies. In short, he could have dealt with his radical wing as effectively as he did in less favorable circumstances in 1882.

All this is reckoning, however, without the divorce threat, which cannot really be left out of the political account because Parnell's closest collaborators in England and Ireland had known about the O'Shea situation since before Gladstone's first Home Rule bill. In his biography, Lyons lays considerable stress on the weakness of Parnell's leadership in his last years. In reviews of that biography in *Irish Historical Studies* and elsewhere, I have argued that Lyons somewhat exaggerates this weakness, that nothing short of the earth-quake of the actual divorce proceedings could have ousted Parnell from the leadership or brought any of his rather ill-assorted and—in various ways—unconvincing lieutenants into it. However that may be, Parnell's leadership was by then potentially and implicitly damaged. If he had kept the party firmly on the course—Home Rule for all Ireland—which united that Catholic Ireland whose aspirations he actually represented, then his leadership would have been (in my opinion) absolutely secure. But if he had had to face a new internal conflict—that is, if he did what would now be called a "U-turn" and accepted partition—then the vehement political opposition in Catholic Ireland to such a change of course would certainly have brought the O'Shea situation into public light. Under these conditions, this disclosure would certainly have destroyed his leadership, because both wings of his party, not just one, would have come off.

John O'Leary warned the young W. B. Yeats, in the period we are here discussing, that in Ireland a man must have either the Church or the Fenians on his side. On this particular issue, situated as he was, Parnell would have had both the Church and the Fenians against him, and he would have gone down. With the O'Shea situation in the wings, he would therefore probably have been obliged to break with Gladstone if Gladstone had attempted to go on the partition tack.

Irrespective of Gladstone's options, however, or of Parnell's, or of the divorce limitation on options, the real choice was between Home Rule with partition and no Home Rule at all. That reality has been obscured by an enormous amount of rhetoric—some of the fumes of which I inhaled in my youth—and continues to be so obscured.

39

WHAT ROUGH BEAST?

I must begin by declaring interest. Dr Cullingford says in her introduction that Yeats's "interest in Fascism has laid him open to many 'attacks,' of which the most significant and influential is Conor Cruise O'Brien's article 'Passion and Cunning: An Essay on the Politics of W. B. Yeats'" (published in the Yeats centenary volume: "In Excited Reverie"). Dr Cullingford is determined to repel all such "attacks."

Yeats, Ireland and Fascism is the first book-length treatment of its subject. It is also—and this is a considerable merit—the first study to give serious attention both to Yeats's political philosophy and to his contacts with the practical politics of his own day. (The essay of mine to which she takes exception is concerned, as it says, "not primarily with Yeats's political philosophy but with forms of his actual involvement, at certain critical times, in the political life of his own day.")

The narrowness of my focus in that essay, as I can see in retrospect, is unduly reductive. Dr Cullingford widens the discussion in a salutary way. Her account is also preferable to mine in that she gives an adequate account of Yeats's work as a Senator. I had tended to dwell on the aristocratic, caste and anti-Catholic aspects of Yeats's liberal utterances. Those aspects were there all right, but what I failed to acknowledge was that the liberalism was genuine. Yeats was *both* a liberal *and* a pro-fascist; at different times, in different moods, and under different circumstances. A properly balanced account of Yeats's politics will have to take that contradiction into full consideration.

Observer, 19 July 1981. Review of *Yeats, Ireland and Fascism* by Elizabeth Cullingford.

The book however suffers from two serious defects, which interact, to the book's further detriment.

The first defect is that Dr Cullingford tries too hard to prove too much. She burns to refute, in particular, my "thesis." Her anxiety on that score leads her to over-simplify what she is trying to refute. "O'Brien's thesis is that while Yeats was a self-interested, half-hearted and intermittent nationalist he was an ardent and early Fascist." But my actual argument was that *both* Yeats's nationalism *and* his Fascism were intermittent: sometimes ardent, sometimes not. In challenging, as I was, the then prevailing assumption (which Dr Cullingford now seeks to re-establish) "that Yeat's pro-fascism was either not 'truly Yeats' or not 'truly pro-fascism,'" I wrote that "one must not overlook the intermittent character of his pro-fascism and of all his political activity. If his pro-fascism was real, his irony and caution were real too, and his phases of detachment not less real than his phases of political commitment."

By leaving out the qualifications in an argument one seeks to refute, one can make one's refutation look more effective than it is. Professor Richard Ellmann, who supervised the doctoral thesis on which the book is based, might have done well to warn the author against that temptation.

The over-anxiety to *prove* that Yeats was invariably a thoroughly decent chap shows on every page. The poet is never a snob, never an elitist, but on the contrary one who recoiled from Hegel for humanitarian reasons, inhaled a loving version of Irish nationalism, and so on. She nudges the reader too much. At one point she even nudges Yeats himself. One interpretation of Yeats's "The Second Coming" sees the "rough beast" as prefiguring the rise of Fascism (or something very like it). Dr Cullingford is distressed by Professor Yvor Winters' view that "we may find the beast terrifying but Yeats finds him satisfying...." She cites a passage from "Explorations"—" ... We may be about to accept the most implacable authority the world has known. Do I desire it or dread it, loving as I do the gaming-table of Nature where many are ruined but none is judged, and where all is fortuitous, unforeseen?"— and immediately answers Yeats's question for him: "Very clearly he dreads it, and the poem records that dread." I have a suspicion that Yeats would have found this earnest championship a bit wearing.

The other main defect of this book is that the author does not have enough feel for Yeats's Irish political context. She dispenses instruction with more confidence than understanding. Thus, in defending Yeats's exaltation of poets as against parliamentarians, she says: "But before dismissing this point of view, one must remember that Irish freedom was won not through parliamentary negotiation, but by the unsuccessful poets' rebellion of 1916." That particular piece of cant has been current in official Catholic Ireland for 60 years, but that is no reason for accepting it as a truth that "one must remember."

In fact, the version of "Irish freedom" that "was won"—self-government with partition—was what the "poets" fought and died to *avert*. Yeats, in 1921, when he accepted the Cosgrave Government nomination to a Senate seat, was turning his back (for the moment) on those poets. This decision was a brave one, and I think a sensible one, but if you follow Dr Cullingford's lead about "Irish freedom" being won in 1916, you will entirely misunderstand the nature of that decision.

Along with much else, Dr Cullingford gets the bit about the Blueshirts wrong too. Here she is out to refute a view (mine, again) that the reason why Yeats, after being enthusiastic about the Blueshirts in the summer of 1933, became disillusioned in 1934, was that by 1934 the Blueshirts had begun to look a bit silly. Dr Cullingford predictably espouses the view—entirely tenable if you understand its terms—that the Blueshirts' first six months (completed January 1934) had been "highly successful," and thinks this means that Yeats was abandoning them at the height of their success.

General O'Duffy, the leader of the movement, from having been politically unknown, had emerged, by 1934, as extra-parliamentary leader of the main opposition party in parliament. That *is* success of a kind. But it is not the kind of success of which Yeats had been dreaming in 1933. Yeats had seen in O'Duffy an Irish Mussolini. O'Duffy by 1934 looked as Mussolini would have looked in 1924, if in 1923—in obedience to a government ban—he had cancelled the March on Rome. O'Duffy did the equivalent of that in August 1933. To take disillusionment with O'Duffy, after that date, as proof of disillusionment with Fascism would be imprudent.

Throughout, Dr Cullingford seems to assume that Yeats's Irish nationalism and Fascism are somehow incompatible and that therefore, if it can be shown (as it easily can) that Yeats was a nationalist, he cannot have been a Fascist. It seems an odd idea. In fact at the very end, in 1938, when Yeats's nationalism is most manic—in "The Ghost of Roger Casement" and "On the Boiler"—what comes through is a wish for the defeat of Britain by the Fascist powers. In trying to refute that idea, Dr Cullingford is at her most uncomfortable. She refers to the "unfortunate tone" of a passage from "On the Boiler." Both the tone and the substance are indeed unfortunate, if you are trying to prove what she is trying to prove.

As I said, she set out to refute me, so don't take this review on trust. I hope you will read her book, but if you do I hope you will read my essay also.

40

Blueshirts and Quislings

In July 1933, after a meeting with General O'Duffy, W.B. Yeats wrote to Olivia Shakespear: "Italy, Poland, Germany, then perhaps Ireland. Doubtless I shall hate it (though not so much as I hate Irish democracy) ..."

This was the period in which Yeats wrote his marching songs for the Blueshirts, and used such language as, "our chosen colour is blue ... (the colour of my early book covers)."

The whole situation was full of ironies, some of which still remain with us. To begin with, apologists for the Blueshirts, both then and now, justified the movement in terms of *defence of democratic process* and freedom of speech. This was a period when Republicans were breaking up "Free Staters" meetings with the cry "no free speech for traitors". To the said Free Staters it seemed, with some reason, that the new de Valera government was showing itself remarkably tolerant towards Republican bully-boys. That the Free Staters (Cumann na nGaedheal, Fine Gael) should have responded to that by organising the defence of their own meetings is not surprising. When they went beyond that to ape the symbolism, style and rhetoric of European fascism—in the year in which Hitler came to power—they committed an act of folly for which their party has paid a heavy price over more than forty years.

Some readers will find the word "folly" far too weak; *wickedness*, rather! I stick to folly. The Blueshirts emulated the *style* of the European fascists; they did not emulate their *deeds*. To a Republican who was going on to me about the Blueshirts—as Republicans do even right now, in 1981—I put the question: "How many people did the Blueshirts *kill*?" Answer came there none for none was the answer (in Ireland anyway: I don't know about Spain). The murdered victims of the Republican movement on the other hand, are numbered in their thousands and still rising in the years since the Blueshirts briefly and pathetically lurched across the stage.

Irish democracy both benefitted from this episode and was distorted by it. The existence of the Blueshirts cast Eamonn de Valera in the role of defender of democracy. Although hardly anything in his past career seemed to qualify him for this role, he played it with genius. Paradoxically, the need (real or apparent) to defend democracy against the Blueshirts helped him to move against what was for him and his colleagues (and the country) the far greater danger: their ex-allies in the IRA. In moving against both extremes, de Valera now appeared as a sober father-figure, meting out even-handed justice, defending the citizens against all the wild men, whether in trench coats or coloured shirts.

So the men who had once fought a war against an elected Irish government became identified, and almost identical, with Irish democracy.

And the men who had been that elected government, and who had proved the genuineness of their democratic commitment—by allowing their civil war foes to take over from them in free elections—came to be seen as a democratic security-risk.

Fine Gael had become—I hope John Kelly will forgive me—*contaminated*. Not by any allies, for it had none then, but by its own folly. And by the same blue token, Fianna Fail was *de*contaminated from its anti-democratic past.

There was a certain amount of magic in that blue shirt: for Fine Gael indeed a shirt of Nessus, clinging and corroding. For the blue contamination had the horrid property of getting deeper, instead of fading, with the lapse of time. The victory of the allies in the Second World War, and the revelation of the Holocaust, turned "fascist" and "fascism" into the dirtiest of all political words, universally. So in retrospect, Fine Gael's flirtation with the fascist style looked much worse than it had looked at the time. (*At the time* indeed *The Irish Times*, now very down on fascism, was praising Hermann Goering for telling his Prussian police to shoot communists on sight.) The funny thing is that there were others who had done much more than wear blue shirts but were not thought of as fascists at all. These others had actually tried to bring the Nazis to Ireland. I refer of course to the IRA. If you want to think seriously, instead of fatuously, about Irish fascism, take a trip to Fairview

Park and meditate in front of the statue of Sean Russell. The heirs of Sean Russell today fling around the word "Quisling" as a term of abuse, which it became as a result of the victory of the allies. Yet, *at the time*, Russell's IRA and Quisling were on the same side. Russell's ambition indeed was to become, in relation to Ireland, what Vidkun Quisling was for Norway ...

All that, strangely, is apparently much less memorable, and much less—well, *fascist*—than the Blueshirts. Symbolism is all important. Russell and his friends may have tried to hand our country over to the Nazis but *they didn't wear coloured shirts*. That's the important thing. Similarly the IRA today may be a militarist, authoritarian, ultra-nationalist organisation, which slaughters people—but they don't call themselves fascists. They call other people fascists. So when you hear the word fascist in Irish political usage you don't think of the IRA. You think of Fine Gael. Or have done up to now.

The Blueshirts-under-the-bed bit has been quite strong in the Dublin media, right up to now, especially *The Irish Times*, which no longer has a good word for Goering. The roasting *The Irish Times* gave to the late coalition, over emergency legislation, and especially its foaming inflation of *l'affaire Donegan*, reflected the sincere hostility of certain journalists towards what they see as a fascist tradition in Fine Gael. I think they are looking for fascism in the wrong place.

That may all be ending now. It may prove to be Garret FitzGerald's greatest service to his party—and a great service to his country also—that he has finally laid the ghost of General O'Duffy. It is really not possible, even for the most determined Blueshirt-baiter, to see Garret as a fascist, or Garret's party as a fascist party.

So if that's really over, as I think it may be, perhaps those who want to oppose fascism in Ireland will start opposing it where it is really to be found: at the heart of the Republican Movement.

41

THE FOUR HORSEMEN

TO: Governor Hugh Carey, Senator Edward Kennedy, Senator Daniel Patrick Moynihan, and Speaker Thomas P. O'Neill

I know that you all genuinely want to help Ireland. The trouble is that the Ireland you want to help doesn't exist, and that your efforts have the effect of making things worse, not better, in the Ireland of reality.

The Ireland of your imagination is an island artificially divided by an act of British policy. Since the British divided it, the British can reunite it. As a united Ireland would (you assume) be a peaceful Ireland, the British government, by its refusal to reunite Ireland, has a prime responsibility for the continuing violence. In bringing pressure to bear on Britain to move in the direction of Irish unity, you are therefore working, as you believe, for peace in Ireland.

You know of course—and sometimes even show that you know—that things are more complicated than what is set out in the paragraph above. Nonetheless, that paragraph contains the essentials of what you believe to be true. Your pressure on Britain to unite Ireland only makes sense in terms of an assumption that Britain *can* unite Ireland. It is that assumption, however, that is false. Its falsity makes all your well-meant efforts on behalf of Ireland turn into mischief.

Ireland is divided not by a stroke of British policy but by the conflicting wills of its inhabitants.

Harper's 262 (December 1981), pp. 14, 16, 18–20.

I must ask for your patience at this point because I am going to talk to you about the Ulster Protestants (a majority of the population of Northern Ireland) and I fear that is a topic that you don't find congenial, or particularly worthy of study. In the Irish Catholic tradition in which you were brought up—and in which I was brought up too—the protagonists are Ireland and England, often personified and trailing clouds of positive and negative emotion.

Ulster Protestants have no place in that grand scheme. But since Ulster Protestants are obviously a substantial part of the reality, might it not seem to follow that there is something wrong with the picture? It might, but, as I know to my cost, it doesn't. To minds brought up in that tradition, and still adhering to it in maturity, if Ulster Protestants don't fit into that picture, it doesn't mean there is anything wrong with the picture. It means there is something wrong with the Ulster Protestants. Isn't that right, gentlemen?

I ask you to bear with me for a little, however, while I talk to you about these people, superfluous and incongruous though you may feel them to be.

The Ulster Protestants are descended in the main from settlers who came to Ulster from Scotland and England in the first decade of the seventeenth century. Now, in the eyes of many Africans and Asians, and of left-wing Europeans, the mere word "settlers" in itself decides the question. Settlers, by definition, ought either to go back, in the words of the song, "to from whence they came," or to stay on under political and social institutions devised by the natives.

But you, as Americans, can't quite take that view, can you? After all, these people's ancestors were established in Ulster before—and I imagine quite a long time before—most of your own ancestors left Ireland to settle in America. Clearly the fact of being descended from settlers does not automatically put people in the wrong. There has to be something else.

And of course, there is. These people are descended not from people who left *Ireland* to settle in *America*—obviously a right and proper course of action—but from people who left *Britain* to settle in *Ireland*—obviously a wrong one. I don't know that I could prove precisely why the first is so clearly right, and the second so clearly wrong, but in these matters proof is not what counts: what counts is what you feel in your bones.

But then, you see, these Ulster Protestants also have bones, in which they feel quite as strongly as—probably more strongly than—you do, and their bones tell them quite different things from what your bones tell you. Their bones tell them, most insistently, two things:

First, that they mean to stay in Ulster.

Second, that they will not be included in any political structure in which Irish Catholics are in a majority.

The determination of Ulster Protestants to remain in Ulster is comparable to the determination of Israelis to remain in Israel. And the refusal of Ulster Protestants to be incorporated in a Catholic-majority Irish state is as stubborn as the refusal of Israelis to be incorporated in an Arab-majority Palestine. If you spent any time among Ulster Protestants—even among the very moderate middle-class Protestants of the Alliance Party—you would have to realize that it is so.

In any case, if you follow me so far, you will notice that I am not including loyalty to Britain among the feelings in the bones of this community. Loyalty to Britain is there all right, and important, but it is a qualified, complex, conditional loyalty. It is loyalty to the crown rather than to Parliament. And loyalty to the crown in Ulster is distinguishable from its counterpart in the rest of the United Kingdom. In Ulster, the fact that the crown is a *Protestant* crown, by the laws of the realm, retains an emotional importance that it has lost in the rest of the United Kingdom. Ulster Protestants remember—and many of them annually commemorate, with a grim enthusiasm disturbing to most people—the fact that their ancestors helped to destroy Britain's last Catholic monarch, and that those who were loyal to that particular British monarch, James II, were the Irish Catholics of that time. The marches that commemorate the Battle of the Boyne celebrate the triumph of the Protestant crown.

That itself implies a condition. For if the crown in Parliament—the contemporary constitutional crown—acts in a manner that suggests to Ulster Protestants that they are about to be delivered into the hands of their hereditary Catholic enemies, then the crown, in respect of that transaction, is felt not to be the true crown—the Protestant one, to which Protestants owe and freely accord their loyalty. And, since it is not that true crown, but something masquerading in its place, it not merely *may* but *must* be defied and set at naught.

And so, in the great Home Rule crisis just before the First World War, Ulster Protestants did defy Parliament directly (and the crown in Parliament implicitly), set at naught Asquith's Home Rule Bill, and lay the ground for the partition of Ireland. And again, in 1974, when the Parliament of the United Kingdom almost unanimously approved the Sunningdale arrangements—involving power-sharing between Protestants and Catholics in a joint executive for Northern Ireland and joint participation of that executive and the Dublin government in a Council of Ireland—the resistance of Ulster Protestant workers broke up those arrangements because Protestants saw them as leading in the direction in which they refuse to go: toward a united Ireland.

Irish Catholics are always annoyed, and sometimes infuriated, both by the phenomenon of Ulster Protestant conditional loyalty and by Britain's response to it. The phenomenon itself looks, to Catholics, like an odious compound of hypocrisy and bigotry. Bigotry does come into it but hypocrisy doesn't. British leaders seem, to Catholics, to show criminal weakness in dealing with the rebellions of the nominally loyal (again in Catholic terms). *If only* Asquith in 1912—*if only* Wilson in 1971—had behaved with "firmness" (toward Protestants, that is; toward Catholics "flexibility" is the recommended posture), why, then we should have peace today, and be well on the road to a united Ireland as well.

That is what you four gentlemen expect—or, at any rate, wish—the British to do, is it not?

Well, you may find, though I hope you don't, that part of your wish comes true. In life, as in stories, having part of a wish come true can be a very horrible thing. Some of you, at least, will remember W. W. Jacob's story "The Monkey's Paw," in which a bereaved couple wish for their drowned son to come to them, but fail to stipulate that they want him to be alive and whole when he comes ... I fear your own well-meant wishful activity may tend toward a conclusion no less grisly than that of "The Monkey's Paw."

The part of your wish that you are most likely to get is that a future British government—not this one—may declare its objective to be a united Ireland. You may also, though this is somewhat less likely, get another part of your wish: a serious effort on the part of a British government to move in that direction.

The British Labor Party shows clear signs of beginning to abandon that bipartisan policy with the Conservatives that has prevailed over the last nine years. They are moving toward something much more in line with your wish, with a united Ireland as a declared objective. The Social Democratic leaders, though so far cryptic on the matter, are known to be attracted toward such policies. The Liberals, with their Gladstonian inheritance, are also inclined in that direction, provided public opinion is favorable.

And public opinion is favorable, not so much to a united Ireland in itself as to *anything* that will enable Britain to disengage from Northern Ireland. If a united Ireland will do that, then bully for a united Ireland. This is not surprising. Britain derives no benefit from being in Northern Ireland. That province is a considerable drain on the ailing economy of the entire United Kingdom. British people are tired of having their soldiers and ex-soldiers murdered or maimed, tired of being themselves denounced as oppressors, tired of threats, tired of international pressure. They want to get out if they can.

You have all contributed significantly to this state of affairs. You have made the point that Britain's relations with America are damaged by failure to produce "constructive policies"—meaning green ones—in Northern Ireland. British politicians, and the Foreign Office in particular, are more worried by this than they would be likely to admit. You are all eminent people, key figures in the American political establishment, and what you say has to be taken seriously. You are not creating the pressure, but you are significantly increasing it.

But toward what does that pressure move? Toward a united Ireland? Ostensibly, and initially, yes. But at the point, the predictable part, where it meets determined resistance, the pressure has to swing in another direction.

By now the day may not be far off when the leader of a party committed, in theory at least, to the objective of a united Ireland will become prime minister of the United Kingdom. That in itself might not necessarily mean very much: Sir Harold Wilson, in opposition, favored the idea of a united Ireland—"in fifteen years"—but in office did nothing very effective about it. That might happen again. But it may also happen, as a result of growing British weariness with Northern Ireland, that a prime minister will gain power who is not only nominally committed to unity but is committed to pressing for it, and to attempting to override opposition to it. Such a prime minister, in fact, as all you gentlemen would like to see.

Such a prime minister might be one who genuinely believed in the feasibility of a united Ireland. I could see Dr. David Owen, if he became prime minister in a Social Democrat-Liberal coalition, casting himself with zest in a Gladstonian role. Alternatively, and perhaps more probably, a future prime minister, knowing fully that a united Ireland will not work, might still make a feint in that direction, with the real objective of a simple British disengagement: the dumping of the insoluble Irish question once and for all in the laps of the Irish, and a plague on both their houses.

In any case, if a future prime minister makes such an effort, whether for idealistic or Machiavellian reasons, the immediate consequences are predictable. They would be massive demonstrations of Protestant determination not to move in the desired direction; assertions once more of the conditionality of Protestant loyalty; mass rallies; mass stoppages—with uglier fringe events—all based not on a minority community, like most of the present troubles, but on the majority. Faced with this reaction, the prime minister could either subside spluttering, as Asquith and Wilson did, or he could decide to press on regardless, as he will, I fear, be loudly urged to do by people like yourselves.

But if he does press on, what can he do? The use of force by Britain to induce Ulster Protestants to leave the United Kingdom and enter a united Ireland is out of the question. British public opinion would reject any such policy, which it would rightly see as widening the area of violence and deepening Britain's involvement in it—the very opposite of what British public opinion wants to see. And such a policy would also be repugnant to the army.

The only thing such a prime minister could actually do, having only peaceful means at his disposal to overcome the passionate resistance of a million people, would be to threaten, and perhaps execute, some kind of withdrawal. In Irish Catholic mythology, this would work. It would be "calling the bluff" of the Ulster Protestants. The trouble is that there is no bluff. The mere threat of, for example, withdrawing the subsidies would certainly not induce Ulster Protestants to turn toward a united Ireland. The actual cutting off of subsidies would indeed have effects, but not those intended. In Ulster Protestant eyes, such a policy would represent the penalizing of Protestants for refusing to submit to Catholic power.

If they were faced with such an attempt, Ulster Protestants would not turn toward a united Ireland; they would turn against Britain. Their whole history and traditions and patterns of behavior, including recent patterns (e.g., 1974 and the rise of Paisleyism), imply that. The basic conditions of Protestant loyalty to Britain would have been breached. Protestants would turn en masse toward a policy that a minority among them now advocate: an independent Northern Ireland.

In these conditions, Britain, under varying forms of attack from both communities,[1] and unable to deal with either effectively, would be impelled toward withdrawal, not just of subsidies but of its entire presence in Northern Ireland. The legitimacy of Britain's presence in Northern Ireland depends on acceptance by a majority of the population there. If that acceptance goes, Britain has to go too. The British public would never accept a policy of remaining there, working for a united Ireland, while being attacked from all sides. And the army would advise that its role had become impossible.

So they would go. And what, gentlemen, do you think would happen then? I know, of course, the optimistic rigmarole, long prevalent in Catholic political circles, about what would happen then. The

Protestants, abandoned by the British, would see that their true interests lay in unity with the Republic and would sit down "round a table" with the Dublin government to work out arrangements for some kind of federal Ireland. Like hell they would. A purer example of wishful thinking would be hard to find. The impending and then actual departure of British administration and British troops would create a major crisis: the greatest Ulster has known since the seventeenth century. A crisis of that order does not calm passions, it inflames them. In Northern Ireland, they are already inflamed. A condition of incipient civil war between Catholics and Protestants exists: the materials for full-scale civil war are piled high in Belfast and elsewhere. British withdrawal would ignite them.

You think that is an alarmist point of view? Have you forgotten August 1969, when British troops were first deployed at the request of Catholics, why they were deployed? They were deployed at the request of Catholics, for the protection of the Catholics of Belfast from Protestant reprisals, following a Catholic insurrection in Derry. They were deployed, in short, in order to inhibit the development of politics—sectarian civil war between the two communities in Northern Ireland. And they have been inhibiting it ever since, with only partial success, but still to a greater extent than could be attained without them.

You probably don't find it easy to believe that, either. The fact that the IRA, based in the Catholic areas, is waging "war" against the British Army makes it hard to realize that the British Army, in Protestant-majority areas, is there to protect the Catholics (and in Catholic-majority areas, the Protestants). Nonetheless, that is the reality. If Britain withdraws, each community will look to its own defense: and what each thinks of as defensive activity will look like aggression to the other.

I am not altogether without experience in these matters. I have been, at various times, in the Congo, in Nigeria, on the Bangladesh-Indian border, and in Lebanon, in periods of civil war. I know the smell and the rising dementia of it. And every time I travel in Northern Ireland I get a whiff of that smell, now growing stronger. I have no doubt that British withdrawal would bring on the real thing in full force. You may think that the kind of horrors that happened in those African and Asian countries could not happen in Ireland. If so, you must be forgetting what has already happened in Ireland, inside both communities; the bloodthirsty armed fanatics are already there. If they are let loose on both sides, without any outside restraint, we shall have our Lebanon.

Of course, most people, in both communities, dread civil war and would do anything to avert it, just as in Lebanon. The trouble is that what one community thinks appropriate in order to avert it looks to the other community like an effort to create it. Where radical suspicion and fear exist between two communities, every notable event that occurs serves to feed these emotions, as the recent hunger strikes did, and as they were intended to do by those who organized them.

If Britain decides to withdraw, the reaction of the Protestant majority in the province will be to take over, as of right, the government of what will be, willy-nilly, a new sovereign state. The authority of the Protestant government will be accepted immediately throughout most of the densely populated areas east of the Bann. But it is not likely to be content with that inner area. It will want its writ to run throughout the province. "Security" will be its paramount concern. It will want to "flush-out" the IRA; it will not accept any "no-go" areas; it will reject "kid-glove" methods. These have been well-established shibboleths of Protestant-Unionist discourse for years and they would be the guidelines for the conduct of an independent Protestant government.

So Protestant forces, Protestant-controlled, will enter Catholic areas. These forces will be quite formidable; the RUC, minus the British officers, backed by the Ulster Defence Regiment, no longer under British command; the Ulster Defence Association, as a militia containing some sinister components. To Catholics, unlike Protestants, this will not look like "law and order." It will look like armed invasion by their hereditary enemies.

In short, it will be August 1969 all over again—with the all-important exception that this time there will be no restraint on Protestant force except Catholic force. That is to say, that civil war this time will take its course until it burns itself out.

That course would probably be quite short, but very bloody. It would end in stalemate, following mass migrations of the population: Catholics fleeing from the Protestant heartland, Protestants from the Catholic-majority border areas (which would probably be occupied by troops from the Republic). There would be a new border, approximating to the line of the Bann, separating a smaller, homogeneous Protestant Northern Ireland from the Republic.

This isn't just a private nightmare of my own. Others, including such a persistent unity-pusher as Mr. Jack Lynch, the former Taoiseach, agree that "precipitate" British withdrawal would be likely to have such consequences.

When I was a member of the government in Dublin, and of a Cabinet subcommittee on Northern Ireland, I once asked an SDLP deputation how many refugees we in the Republic would have to prepare for if things "went wrong" following British withdrawal. This was, I believe, in 1975, after Fianna Fail (then, as now, in opposition) had come out in favor of a British "commitment" to withdraw (but not of actual withdrawal). The deputation consisted of two Catholic politicians well known to all of you: one from east of the Bann, and one from west. They said that if things were "very carefully handled," they might not go wrong. Yes, but if, all the same, they did go wrong, how many refugees? They conferred for a few minutes and came back with an agreed answer—between 55,000 and 65,000 families: that is, about 250,000 people, about half the Catholic population of Northern Ireland.

Not my guess—the guess of people who agree with *you*. I didn't have the heart to ask them how many dead there might be; in practical terms our government was directly concerned only with the refugees. But a refugee population move of those dimensions probably implies a death roll of tens of thousands (as compared with slightly over two thousand in all the ten years of violence at present levels). And that is just the Catholic score. There would be Protestant refugees too, though they would not come to the Republic, and there would be Protestant dead.

I know that you have some inkling of the level of danger involved and that you are not looking for immediate (or "precipitate") British withdrawal. What you want the British to do is to find an agreed political solution, involving some kind of united Ireland, and *then* to withdraw. What you refuse to see is that no agreed political solution is available, since the parties are in radical (and increasing) disagreement. The British can't deliver a united Ireland or "an agreed Ireland" (the favored formula of your common guru, Mr. John Hume) and then get out. It would be nice, I agree, but they can't. What they can do is just plain get out. The longer and the more intensely the present combination of physical violence and international political pressure is applied to them, the more likely they are to do just that. And make no mistake; if they do decide to go, they will go quickly: "precipitately," if you prefer. They are not about to say they are going, and then hang around to take the consequences, and the blame for the consequences, as Mr. Lynch and Mr. Haughey would have them do. The gap between the moment they decide to go and their actual departure will be very narrow. As in the case of Palestine.

You will, I know, feel sincerely outraged at being accused of having some share in the responsibility for a buildup toward civil war in Ireland. You have, after all, condemned the Provisional IRA, and opposed its fund-raising efforts in America. You have indeed, and you have run considerable political, and perhaps other, risks in doing so. I respect your courage, and your intentions. Unfortunately, in adding your influential voices to the chorus that insists on the necessity for a united Ireland, you are nonetheless helping those you condemn. By designating their goal as the one that *must* be attained, you, and many others, are helping to validate their cause. That helps them a great deal more than your condemnation of their methods hinders them.

My message to you is that we in Ireland may well be getting quite near the brink of British withdrawal, followed by civil war. American pressure for unity helps to bring us still nearer that brink. You are the most influential of the politicians who have been applying that pressure. I ask you to reflect, and desist. Negative advice, I agree. But there are times when the only helpful advice is "Stop!" and, if that advice is not heeded, no further advice will be of any use.

NOTE

1 You might perhaps expect that when Britain was engaged in confrontation with the Protestants, IRA violence would stop. At the time of the last major British and Protestant confrontation, however—the Sunningdale period, in 1974—IRA violence actually increased.

42

The Artist as Pompous Prig

I first read *A Portrait of the Artist as a Young Man* over 40 years ago. I didn't like it then. I felt uneasy about that at the time because I knew it was supposed to be a great book. I re-read it last week. I still don't like it, found much of it boring and otherwise insufferable and doubt whether anyone today would claim it as a great book if it were not for the fact that it is by the author of *Ulysses*, and tells us a great deal about it.

Most Joyceans—perhaps not quite all—will read me out of the human race at this point. The orthodox position is that Joyce published nothing but masterpieces, so that *A Portrait* is not open to question. The *Times Literary Supplement*, in a judgement quoted on the jacket of the Jonathan Cape edition (1956), says:

"The 'portrait' with its exalted Stephen, its impressionist background, its shadowy cast behind the brilliantly lit central figure and its succession of dramatic monologues, is written in a mood of enraptured fervour."

Quite so. All that is a nice way of saying exactly what I don't like about the book. The author's mood of enraptured fervour about his exalted self is both understandable and even justified: he already knew himself to be a great writer in the making.

But surely I can't be the only reader of *A Portrait* who gets put off by all this relentless rapture about self: fed up by hearing so often how "sensitive" Stephen is, how "sordid" his family and fellow students, and

Sunday Tribune (Dublin), 31 January 1982.

how "coldly", "quietly", or "wearily" he addresses these, and to how impressive an effect.

The only bits of *A Portrait* I love and treasure are those rare moments when members of the "shadowy cast behind the brilliantly lit central figure" are allowed their brief time out in the light, and come to life before our eyes.

The best of these scenes, of course, is the epic Christmas row between Dante, Mr. Casey and Mr. Dedalus over Parnell and the priests. But every time poor Mr. Dedalus is allowed by his son to open his beak, the book wakes up. Can anyone, I wonder, read *A Portrait* without wanting to hear more about Stephen's father, and less about Mr. Dedalus's pompous prig of a son?

It is the members of the "shadowy cast," struggling for their moment on the stage—these and not the self-indulgent self-portraiture—that are the first stirring of the great *Ulysses*.

Of course, *A Portrait* tells us a lot, not only about Joyce, but about what a traditional Irish Catholic upbringing was like. That is a main source of such fascination as it still has, for Catholics and non-Catholics alike. It was, I believe, the first significant portrayal in literature of an Irish Catholic education. For Irish Catholics this had extraordinary interest, because it was about *us*, more intimately than anything before written had been about us.

For some non-Catholics it had an exotic, slightly prurient, appeal; especially as it was, for its day, unusually explicit about sex, as well as about religion.

Joyce brought to art—his art—the kind of fanatic will that other Irishmen had brought to nationalist politics, and to religion. He had been drawn to both those other potent forces, and the final pages of *A Portrait* are about his break with them and his dedication of himself to art. Here Parnell means much to him, as to Yeats. In both cases it is the romantic Parnell, the Parnell of the Split, the great man torn down by little men, that interests the writer. In both cases also, the role of the church in the destruction of the hero is a matter of primary interest.

But there are big differences too. Yeats wanted to stay in Ireland and influence it. He wanted to fill the vacuum left by the fall of Parnell: to fill it with his art indeed, but in a crowded political and social context and not entirely without a political aim. The "Irish Literary Revival" was seen as part of a wider national, and nationalist revival and Yeats encouraged this idea and partly shared in it. He remained an Irish nationalist, and an intermittently political person throughout his life.

Joyce is much more radical. Stephen, in his conversation with Davin, rejects Irish nationalism totally:

"No honourable and sincere man," said Stephen, "has given up to you his life and his youth and his affections from the days of Tone to those of Parnell, but you sold him to the enemy or failed him in need or reviled him and left him for another. And you invite me to be one of you. I'd see you damned first."

For Joyce—by implication—Yeats himself was already among the honourable and sincere men whom the Irish people had let down. Stephen shortly after the conversation with Davin, quotes with lyrical appreciation four lines from Countess Kathleen's dying speech (without identifying either the play or the author). He goes on to recall the "catcalls and hisses and mocking cries" of his fellow students on the night of the opening of the National Theatre, and all the tawdry pathos of that scene.

Joyce seems to have resented the catcalls and so on much more bitterly than Yeats did. It is not hard to imagine why. For Yeats, the people who misbehaved in this way are people he could make allowances for, since they were not exactly his own people, and he was trying to lift them up. For Joyce, not being Anglo-Irish, they *were* his people, exactly, and he despised them for failure to lift themselves up. He washed his hands of them, and left them behind.

Yet he too, in his subtler and even more ambitious way, wanted to lift the poor creatures up, or rather re-invent them: "to forge in the smithy of my soul the uncreated conscience of my race."

A Portrait is, as they say, a chapter in our intellectual and moral history. Perhaps that's among the reasons why I can't like it. Our intellectual and moral history is a lacerating sort of affair.

43

A STEP TO WATCH

"Doubtless I shall hate it," wrote W. B. Yeats, "but not so much as I hate Irish democracy."

What the poet thought he would hate, but not so much as Irish democracy, was Fascism. Yeats was feeling a bit bruised at the time (1933). His deep love of Ireland was a romantic affair and Irish democracy, whatever else it may be, is not a romantic affair. When Cathleen Ni Houlihan—through the magic of the ballot-box—takes visible, tangible form, she often turns out to be no oil-painting.

Through her elected emanations, the lady had recently trodden all over the poet's dreams with those hard, bony feet of hers.

Censorship she wanted then, plenty of that, but no divorce. It didn't matter what the poet thought about that, or anything else. Poets were *in a minority*, you see, especially Protestant poets.

And he could forget that play he wrote about her, back in 1902, and that girl with the English accent who had the impudence to impersonate her, Cathleen—the real one, who was now telling him, Mr. Yeats, where he got off the bus.

No wonder he hated Irish democracy, and no wonder his mind kept going back to Parnell, and his thoroughly democratic destruction, in the three ghastly by-elections of 1891.

Cathleen has mellowed since then of course. She told Charlie he could exempt writers and artists from tax, and she tells Garrett he can

Irish Times, 23 February 1982.

go on as much as he likes about not being beastly to Protestants, because she knows there's no harm in him really.

So that's all right.

But stay! There's something else. Cathleen summons her emanations: Charlie, and Garret and Michael hasten to her side. What can it be? She whispers.

Something about *abortion*? But that's prohibited by law. Surely she can't want the prohibition *repealed* ...?

The lady's eye flashes: The emanations flicker and quail. The unthinkable is unthought. Then the message comes through: She wants the prohibition of abortion *enshrined in the Constitution.*

Enshrined, that's the idea. In the Constitution, get it? They get it.

Garret, writing: Let's see now. We take divorce *out* of the Constitution, and we put abortion *in.* What a super ideal! "Not secular merely, but Catholic as well." Who was it said that? Pearse? Davis? Tone?

Michael: It was Connolly. James Connolly. His last words. It's always been Labour Party policy.

Charlie: Not merely will Fianna Fail put the prohibition of abortion into the Constitution, but we'll put it into the National Anthem as well. *We're* unequivocal about these things. And it wasn't us said anything about divorce, one way or another. That was Garret.

Cathleen: All right, you know the score, the three of you. Get on with it.

As the emanations prepare to leave, Cathleen calls back Garret.

Cathleen (to Garret): I didn't tell you to take divorce out of the Constitution.

Garret (flickering slightly): No?

Cathleen: I told you you could *talk* about *trying* to take divorce out of the Constitution. I don't mind you talking. Shows we're not narrow-minded. If you ever try and do it though, which I doubt, I'll mark your card for you. Oh, and Garret, one other thing. You want to rewrite Articles Two and Three of the Constitution, is that right?

Garret (flickering): Yes, Mother.

Cathleen: Well, I want no messing with my Four Beautiful Green Fields. Remember that.

Garret: You can count on me, Mother.

Cathleen (softening): I know I can, Garret. Sometimes you have me upset with all that modern, liberal stuff. But you're a good boy, at heart. Mind the step as you go out.

As I say, the lady has mellowed quite a bit, but you do still have to watch your step.

A reader objects that, in the above, I am joking about abortion, which is not a joking matter. I agree it is not a joking matter, and I am not joking about it. My joke is about collective hypocrisy: a form of joke for which there are respectable precedents, many of them of Irish origin.

The proposed imposition of a Constitutional prohibition, on top of existing Statutory prohibitions, will change nothing whatever in the realities of abortion. Irish women who want an abortion will continue to go where they can get it: to England, just as much beyond the reach of our Constitution as of our Statutes. If the Oireachtas were determined to deal with these realities, it would have to take measures to prevent pregnant women from leaving the jurisdiction. This would require provision for medical examination of all women of childbearing age at ports, airports and Border posts.

Now, during the recent elections, "Pro Life" lobbyists in some areas did ask candidates to support exactly those measures. These lobbyists were being perfectly logical and consistent, but that, of course, didn't get them any takers.

Measures of the kind proposed would be inconvenient, unpopular, unpleasant and expensive to administer. No political party will lumber itself with stuff like that. Constitutional amendment, on the other hand, costs little, sounds well, requires no follow-through, keeps you sweet with the lobby in question, and so saves you from being outflanked by the other fellow. Also such an amendment arouses no real opposition, since it is altogether devoid of any real effect, here and now.

In short, an ideal reform, which can be favoured by one and all.

You think I'm cynical? No, I accept that hypocrisy is inseparable from democracy, everywhere and always. As democracy is a good, we should be prepared to put up with some hypocrisy. But not too much, I hope.

And we don't have to put up with too much, unless we want to. This is where democracy is different from all other political systems —Fascism, Communism, or whatever.

From them too, hypocrisy is inseparable; but under them hypocrisy is also compulsive. If you don't like the Leader or the Party, you'd better say you do, or lose your job, and perhaps your life.

Under democracy on the other hand, hypocrisy is voluntary. The citizens don't have to practise it, or require it (or even tolerate it) on the part of their representatives. But they often do some or all of these things quite voluntarily. That happens here, perhaps rather more than in other countries.

Yeats was quite wrong. We ought to thank God that we have a lively democracy and a commitment to it. If we let more hypocrisy into it than is probably good for us, it is not for a journalist to complain too much. The mark is there, to shoot at.

44

Death in the Afternoon

Last Wednesday afternoon, in Serpentine Road, North Belfast, a policeman was shot dead. I don't know if you know Serpentine Road. It's a pleasant suburban street that winds itself up from the Shore Road, down by Belfast Lough, up to the Antrim Road in the shadow of the Cave Hill, that romantic eminence on whose summit Wolfe Tone swore his United Irish oath.

The policeman's name was Lindsay McCormack. He was shot while on his way to see children from the local primary school safely across the road. He was in the habit of going there every day at the same time. And this made him an easy target. He was shot in the presence of the children whom he had come to help. The children ran back into the school. Some of them were crying. Two of the murderers ran off towards the Shore Road, the other towards the Antrim Road. The Provisional IRA issued a statement that night to say that they had killed Mr. McCormack.

Nothing unusual about that, is there? Mr. McCormack was the twelfth person, the sixth member of the RUC, to be killed since January, and the fifth person to be killed since the IRA began a new campaign, less than three weeks ago.

Nor was there anything new about the presence of the children. The underground military bureaucracy which sentenced Mr. McCormack to death does not object to the presence of children at the execution of its sentences. Their agents, in recent months, have gunned down a teacher

Irish Times, 8 March 1983.

in front of his class, and the driver of the school bus in the presence of his passengers. These are not freak incidents. They are planned. If you aim to spread terror, terrified children are good carriers. Their vivid voices carry the images of death into homes, streets, schools; other children, and adults as well, pick up the message and re-echo it; the buzz of terror fills the whole neighbourhood. As is intended.

"There's nothing new in any of that. You just said so yourself. And we all condemn violence. So why go on about it?"

I don't know really. Something about children going to school. Our own children, and the ones they know in Howth and Sutton, Clontarf and Artane, live in a suburban area, with a maritime character, rather like the Serpentine Road; some of you certainly live in similar areas, maybe on the South side. You know the pleasant bustle of the morning, with the lollipop persons holding up the traffic to let the children across, and other children boarding the buses, with nothing worse to worry about than Mrs. Hussey. This is Dublin, not Belfast, so these particular Irish children are not going to school in the shadow of the gunmen and the godfathers. It is not likely that they will come back at the end of the day to tell us how their teacher, or their bus driver, or the nice garda who used to help them across the road, was murdered before their eyes, and how much blood there was, and which way it went.

It is not likely that these things will happen to our children, here, soon. It may, however, be on the cards for the future, if we are not careful. We ought not to forget—though we rather easily do—that it is only for tactical reasons that the Provisional IRA generally (though not invariably) confine their operations to Northern Ireland and Britain. The democratic system of this Republic—which is not *their* Republic—is as illegitimate, in their eyes, as Northern Ireland is. Therefore, it will be legitimate to use, against this State and its servants, the same methods that have done service in Northern Ireland, whenever the godfathers deem that course opportune.

That moment may possibly be nearer than most of us assume. Mr. Owen Carron, Provisional Sinn Fein MP for Fermanagh-South Tyrone, had something ominous to say in that connection recently. Mr. Carron was speaking, on Sunday, February 27th, at a Labour Party conference in Manchester on the use of plastic bullets.

Mr. Carron is against plastic bullets. He has nothing against lead bullets, such as those deliberately used to take the life of Lindsay McCormack. Mr. Carron cannot have anything against that, because the shooting in Serpentine Road was an acknowledged incident in the Provisional IRA's armed struggle, an armed struggle for which Mr. Carron and his colleagues were pledged to provide "unambiguous support."

In any case, Mr. Carron, addressing this humanitarian gathering, told his listeners that the goal of his movement was "a 32-County United Socialist Republic." And he added: "We need to intervene to destabilise the South."

Now, there is a strange thing about this. You would expect, would you not, that a threat to "destabilise the South" would arouse more interest in the South than in the North? But the reverse was the case. *The Irish News*, Belfast, ran the story on its front page, under an eight-column headline as follows: "DESTABILIZE SOUTH" CALL FROM CARRON.

For *The Irish News*, that Monday, Mr. Carron's threat was the big story. In Dublin, however—the capital city which is proposed as the centre of the destabilising attentions of Mr. Carron and his friends—the big story that day, and almost the only story, was that ard-fheis. Mr. Carron and his proposed intervention simply got lost.

It's a pity really, because there is a connection between the two stories. How many of those who cheered for "Troops Out" and Mr. Blaney would have cheered as hard if they had realised that the destabilisation of the South is part of the Republican movement's plans for a United Ireland?

"Sinn Fein strategy," said Mr. Carron, according to *The Irish News*, "was a combination of fighting electoral campaigns in the North and South, political agitation and armed resistance."

Mr. Carron is not reported as having indicated that "armed resistance" would be inappropriate as an element in the proposed destabilisation of the South. We know how these people have destabilised the North, and it would be prudent for us to prepare against similar efforts here. I hope our Government, and the security forces, have taken Mr. Carron's statement seriously. Otherwise our children—yours, reader, and mine—may before very long have interesting things to tell us as they come home from school.

45

Islam's Example

Judge Noel Ryan and the Bishop of Limerick, Dr Jeremiah Newman, have something peculiar in common. Both seem to be fascinated by the Muslim way of life, and to feel that there is something in it for our instruction.

Dr Newman not long ago opined that the Muslim world was "way ahead of us"; apparently in the public deference paid to religion, and accredited teachers of religion. The judge, in giving judgment last week against Eileen Flynn, the schoolteacher who lost her job after she became pregnant by a married man with whom she was living, said: "In other places women are being condemned to death for this sort of offence." The "other places" are countries like Saudi Arabi or Sudan, where the Islamic penalty is to stone to death the convicted woman.

The judge, a more cautious Islamophile than the bishop, added that he did not agree with the death sentence in such cases. Why he brought the subject up was not altogether clear. The point seemed to be that, since Muslims actually kill female adulterers, it is pretty moderate and reasonable conduct, on the part of Christians, just to sack them. *Some* kind of penalty is clearly called for. And the Muslims—though they push the thing too far, of course—have, on the whole, got hold of the right end of the stick, or stone.

Personally, though, I should advise caution, in the matter of our taking a leaf out of the Koran. The Muslim attitude to sexual misconduct, especially on the part of women, may indeed have been exemplary

Irish Times, 10 July 1984.

— though severe to excess—but there are other aspects to be considered. Before introducing the Shari'a—Muslim religious law—we should take a careful look at it. It will be found to be distressing and inconvenient to many respectable persons, even males of absolute chastity. But the fact is that strict Islam, however admirable in other respects, is hell on booze, and boozers.

Only a few weeks ago, a Catholic religious was publicly flogged in the Sudan. His offence was that he had in his possession, for his own personal use, certain quantities of beer and whiskey.

I don't know about Dr Newman himself, but I feel reasonably sure that a fair number both of his flock and his clergy would contemplate without enthusiasm the introduction of the Islamic penal code into the diocese of Limerick.

The Muslims may be way ahead of us, but many of us won't mind if they get right out of sight.

This interest in Islam is telling us something, though, about an intellectual current in our society.

The thing about Islam, in those societies which accept it unreservedly, is that it is theocratic and totalitarian. Those tiresome distinctions which evolved in Western societies from the 18th century on are rejected by the fully Islamic society.

Not for them the blasphemous notions of a secular sphere, and secular laws, not subject to divine authority. The authority of Allah is absolute over all aspects of life, both private and public. And Allah's laws are interpreted by the accredited teachers of the law ... That is the way in which the Muslims are way ahead of us. Way behind us as well, though. The modern Muslim view of the relation of religion to society is very similar to the medieval Catholic view. And there are those amongst us who hold that the medieval Catholic view was very much sounder than the secular and liberal values to which the Church, in modern Western societies, has been forced to give so much ground. The magnetism of modern Islam, for such minds, lies in the force of its example. In certain countries—most spectacularly in Iran—devout Muslims have shown that it is possible to stop the secular rot. To put the clock back, to put God (as it were) back into the Sabbath.

Way ahead, oh way ahead altogether.

And there are likenesses between our historical situation, in this island, in relation to secular and liberal values, and the situation of the Muslims in relation to the same. Neither we nor the Muslims dreamt up those values for ourselves. We took them in, along with a lot of other things, from the advanced countries of the West. The Muslims who reject them—as is increasingly happening throughout the Islamic

World—feel themselves thereby to become more thoroughly themselves. It is a nativist revolution as well as a traditionalist one. By rein-
stating stoning for adultery, and flogging for drink, Muslims have
reasserted their collective identity, rejecting the whole heritage of the
alien and infidel West.

Might not something of the same kind be attempted here—minus
the flogging-for-drink bit of course? The idea is around, as a twinkle in
some people's eyes, a flicker in some people's minds: a bishop here and
judge there. The fact that it is present at all even as a rather wistful as-
piration, makes our society significantly different from many other
Western societies. But we are hardly likely to catch up with Islam.

The mass of the Islamic people have been protected against (or deprived of) the advance of secular ideas by their use of languages
—Arabic, Farsi, etc.—which have not been permeated by the ideas in
question.

We, on the other hand, have been speaking English for more than
five generations. We are part of the North Atlantic English-speaking
world, and deeply penetrated by its assumptions, conventions and habits
of mind. These include the notion that a person ought not to be
penalised just for acting in a manner contrary to someone else's religious beliefs.

We have that notion, but it doesn't really agree with some of us.
Hence the prestige of Islam.

If you hear a Christian clergyman praise the Muslims, you might
think he was being broadminded, but you would be mistaken. What he
envies about the Muslims is how narrow-minded they can get away with
being.

46

UN Theater

Twenty million people are estimated to have died in wars since 1945, the year the United Nations was born. Why did the UN not *do* something to prevent those wars?

The question is misconceived. The United Nations cannot do anything, and never could. It is not an animate entity or agent. It is a place, a stage, a forum, and a shrine. It can be manipulated, just as the ancient shrine at Delphi used to be. It is also—and this has been its most useful function—a place to which powerful people can repair when they are fearful about the course on which their own rhetoric seems to be propelling them. People go there in certain kinds of crises to save their people's—and their own—skins.

But the main thing that endears the United Nations to member governments, and so enables it to survive, is its proven capacity to fail, and to be seen to fail. If there is something you are expected to do, but don't want to do, or even have done for you, you can safely appeal to the UN, in the comfortable certainty that it will let you down. This capacity is useful for the selfish purposes of the governments concerned, but it also helps, in its own rather sordid way, to make the world slightly less dangerous.

The UN has developed a set of rituals that make it possible for powerful people who have made fools of themselves to climb down and not look quite as foolish as they deserve to look. The classic examples of this

New Republic 193 (4 November 1985), pp. 17–19.

use of the United Nations stage are provided by the Suez crisis of 1956, and the Cuban missile crisis of 1962.

Britain and France had intervened in the Canal Zone on the pretext of "separating the combatants," Egypt and Israel. In fact, of course, the intervening powers were acting in collusion with Israel. Once the combatants were separated, Britain and France wanted to get out. They had initially prevented the UN from intervening in the crisis; now they called upon the UN to shoulder the burden of their acts. A token force made up of contingents from friendly countries—the United Nations Expeditionary Force—was sent to Egypt to pretend to execute the mission for which Britain and France had pretended to go in. The combatants were no longer combating, but never mind. The British government professed itself well satisfied with this outcome. By its principled intervention, in the interests of international peace and security, Britain had finally induced the United Nations "to act."

That piece of stagecraft saved perhaps a few thousand lives. Britain and France, under superpower pressure, would soon have been obliged to go, with or without the UN's help. But six years later, millions of lives were at stake. In the famous eyeball-to-eyeball confrontation over Cuban missiles, Khrushchev too needed a decorous retreat. Again, the UN proved useful, Secretary General U. Thant appealed to *both* parties: to the United States to "avoid direct confrontation with Soviet ships," and to the Soviet Union to keep its ships away from Cuban waters. Khrushchev immediately agreed. He went on about the Soviet Union's respect for international legality and the principles of the Charter. The Soviet Union was setting an example; now let the United States follow suit. It was not hard for Kennedy to comply with his part of the secretary general's appeal.

It was obviously important to Khrushchev to be seen to "bow" to the secretary general rather than to the power of the United States. If no plausible face-saving machinery had been available, would Khrushchev have let the ships go ahead, in the hope that it was Kennedy who was bluffing? We can never know, but it does seem possible. Khrushchev was a vain, choleric gambler who at times seemed intoxicated by the thought of the enormous power at his disposal. The small factor of the availability of a plausible face-saving device may well have tilted the balance.

Thomas M. Franck, the author of a recent book on the UN, *Nation Against Nation*, calls the acceptance by both superpowers of the secretary general's appeal "a modest success" for the United Nations. The verdict seems a bit patronizing under the circumstances. More than any other episode in the UN's history, the Cuban missile crisis suggests that the world might be even more unsafe if it weren't for the UN's unimpressive repertoire of tricks.

The Suez and Cuban crises were cases in which political leaders had gotten into trouble and wanted to wriggle out of it. But there are also cases where political leaders have used the United Nations in order to stay out of trouble that their friends and supporters expected them to get into. The United States used it in this way in 1956 over Hungary; and the Soviet Union in 1982 over Lebanon.

The Eisenhower administration had given many Hungarians the impression that if they set out "to roll back the Iron Curtain," they could count on help from the US. When a Hungarian government decided to defy the Soviets, however, the United States decided that backing Hungary was too risky. Understandably, this prudent course was likely to be regarded as reprehensible by those who had believed in Eisenhower-Dulles rhethoric. Eisenhower and Dulles successfully deflected the rising tide of resentment away from the White House and onto the United Nations.

To understand how this worked, one has to consider the peculiar symbiotic relationship that existed between the United States and the United Nations in the UN's first decade. The advent of the United Nations was initially hailed in the United States with enormous ballyhoo. It was expected to be the theater and instrument of a millennial expansion of US power and influence in the world, in "the American Century." And these hopes were not altogether disappointed. From 1945 to 1958, the United States could count on the support of a two-thirds majority in the General Assembly for any proposition for which the US cared enough to lobby and, if necessary, to "twist arms."

Now, in terms of power in the world and the defense of US interests, a two-thirds majority in the UN General Assembly isn't very important. But in terms of American *domestic* politics, that majority was very useful indeed. It meant that administration policies would automatically be validated by "world opinion." In these conditions, it was natural for the State Department to glorify the General Assembly, customarily hailed in that epoch as "the moral conscience of mankind." With the Security Council paralyzed by the "Soviet veto," the General Assembly became the focus of all the hopes and idealisms that Americans, far more than any other people, had been encouraged to place in the UN.

The United States fought the Korean War under a United Nations flag. The flag was obtained by a bit of luck (and perhaps illegally) through a Security Council vote during the temporary absence of the Soviet representative. When the Soviet representative hurriedly returned, the Americans threw the matter into the General Assembly, which duly upheld the American position by the customary two-thirds. For us purposes, all that was needed was legitimation, a blessing on American arms.

So when the Eisenhower-Dulles government threw the Hungarian case into the United Nations in 1956, it was not immediately apparent that this was designed to sacrifice the Hungarians. But there was a difference between the two cases. In the first, what the us had wanted was an explicit legitimation of us intervention. In the second, what it wanted was an implicit legitimation of us *non*-intervention. The Hungarian rising was crushed, but the United States was not blamed. The us supposedly had its hands tied by the Charter. It looked to the United Nations for action. The United Nations was inherently incapable of action, but could be blamed for failure to act.

The Soviet Union made similar use of the United Nations in 1982. It masked its decision to refrain from intervention in Lebanon—even after the defeat there of its ally Syria, armed with Soviet weapons—by a dramatic performance at the un in the role of champion of the Arabs. The Arabs had to appear to take this seriously because they were making the same sort of use of the un themselves at the time, and because they did not want the Soviets to intervene or to intervene themselves, other than verbally.

Steam was let off; parties were championed in words only; someone was sold down the river; direct confrontation between the superpowers was averted; the "failure of the United Nations" was deplored. Business as usual. Shoddy, but probably preferable to the honest, brave courses whose rejection the United Nations theater facilitated by obscuring. Preferable, that is, to American intervention in support of the Hungarians, and Soviet intervention in support of the Syrians (and/or PLO).

These procedures work only if one of the parties wants to get off the hook—as over Suez and Cuban missiles—or avoid getting onto the hook—as over Hungary and Lebanon. In cases where both parties are prepared to go to the bitter end—as, for example, over the Falklands— there is no real role for the un. If Margaret Thatcher's government had decided to let General Galtieri get away with his invasion while saving face, it would have left the matter to the United Nations, and the islands to Argentina. But that was not the course chosen.

At the emergency session of the General Assembly, in August 1958, in the wake of the Anglo-American landings at Suez, the United States failed for the first time to muster a two-thirds majority for a draft resolution that it felt it seriously needed. On that day the General Assembly ceased to be the moral conscience of mankind. The general aura of holiness that the United States public had originally been encouraged to imagine as surrounding the UN began to dim.

Still, the thing has survived. Almost all countries belong to it, and no country shows any serious sign of starting to get out, US warnings notwithstanding. In certain situations, and in the hole-and-corner ways I have described, it has probably helped others—perhaps millions of others—to survive.

47

An Exalted Nationalism

Twenty-four years ago, in connection with the centenary of Yeats's birth, I wrote an essay on Yeats's politics under the title *Passion and Cunning* (recently reprinted, in a collection with the same title).

Today, on the fiftieth anniversary of Yeats's death, I should like to return to the same subject, but looking at it this time from a significantly different angle.

In 1965, what interested me most about Yeats's politics was his intermittent, but potent and recurring, attraction towards fascism. Today what interests me most is his propensity—also intermittent, but potent and recurring—to exalted (or manic) Irish nationalism, and his capacity to evoke the same in some of his Irish readers, both in his own day and later.

Yeats was, throughout his life, as he has told us, an Irish nationalist. Mostly his nationalism remained a rather quiet and abstract sort of thing, with not much bearing on his writing and activities. But on the rare occasions when nationalism found expression in his work, it did so to some purpose.

By far the most important of Yeats's nationalist writings is the play *Cathleen Ni Houlihan*, which was first performed in 1903 with Maud Gonne in the title role. It electrified its Dublin audiences with its summons to fight and die for Ireland, and will be remembered for ever. The Old Woman who is Cathleen, the symbolic figure representing Ireland, says, in her last lines on stage:

Times (London), 28 January 1989.

"They that have red cheeks will have pale cheeks for my sake." *She goes out: her voice is heard outside singing.*

> "They shall be remembered for ever,
> They shall be alive for ever,
> They shall be speaking for ever,
> The people shall hear them for ever."

The play ends with the lines:

> *Peter (to Patrick laying a hand on his arm): "Did you see an old woman going down the path?"*
> *Patrick: "I did not, but I saw a young girl, and she had the walk of a queen."*

Thirteen years later, Constance Markievicz, in jail in England under sentence of death for her part in Dublin's Easter Rising of 1916, was comforted by the thought that the promise of Yeats's Cathleen would now apply to her: "They shall be remembered for ever ...", she quoted in a letter to her sister, adding "and even poor me shall not be forgotten".

More than 20 years after that, the dying Yeats asked himself the question:

> Did that play of mine send out
> Certain men the English shot?

I believe, not only that it clearly did, but that it is still sending them out. *Cathleen Ni Houlihan* is unique among Yeats's political writings in that it is entirely free from ambivalence, ambiguity and the cryptic. It is a straightforward, red-hot piece of physical-force-nationalist propaganda. If someone today were to put on *Cathleen Ni Houlihan* as a benefit performance in support of the Provisional IRA, they would not have to alter a single line. There is nothing there that would not serve their purpose.

But they do not have to put the play on, for it has become internalized. It has entered the Irish nationalist bloodstream. In particular, it is part of the sub-culture that has given us the Provisional IRA.

Some might dispute that. English people often think of the Provisionals as mindless thugs—the sort of people who would not know about a poet like Yeats. In reality, the Provisionals, like other similar movements, have their share of intellectuals, some of whom are quite at home with Yeats, in their way.

One such was Dáithi O'Conaill, one of the IRA leaders in the 1970s. One day, O'Conaill was asked why IRA operations in mainland Britain were so seldom successful. O'Conaill explained that there were certain difficulties in communication. And then he quoted, from Yeats's *The Second Coming*, the line:

> The falcon cannot hear the falconer.

O'Conaill was the falconer; the falcon represented the people O'Conaill sent out to blow other people up.

Not perhaps quite what the poet had in mind when he wrote that particular line but not remote, either, from the general subject matter of that poem. In any case it is clear that this IRA leader knew his Yeats.

The year after the final curtain went down on *Cathleen Ni Houlihan*, Maud Gonne went off and married Major John MacBride (later executed for his part in the Easter Rising). From then on, and for a long time, Yeats abandoned the wilder shores of Irish nationalism. He refused to allow his Abbey Theatre to become a centre for nationalist propaganda and was denounced by the nationalists.

Yeats did not return to a nationalist theme until after the Easter Rising and the execution of its leaders. Yeats's four "1916" poems, as a whole, are quite unlike *Cathleen Ni Houlihan*. They are reflective and, in large part, sceptical and apprehensive. But they do contain lines that can be read in the spirit of *Cathleen Ni Houlihan*, and these were the lines that entered into the bloodstream of Irish republicanism. Most especially the line:

> A terrible beauty is born.

One day in 1971 I was speaking in the Dáil, the Irish parliament, and I happened to quote some lines of Yeats. This was just after the opening of the Provisional IRA's "offensive" in Northern Ireland, and shortly after the Arms Trials, in which C. J. Haughey—now Taoiseach—had been acquitted on charges of importing arms illegally into the Republic.

As it happened, Haughey was in the chamber when I spoke and he called out loudly: "Complete the quotation!" Completing the quotation would have entailed quoting the line about a terrible beauty. In the context, I took—and I still take—Haughey's demand to imply that, with the renewal of the arms struggle, this time in Northern Ireland, a terrible beauty had been born again.

In the Irish Civil War of 1922–23, Yeats took the government side, the side of the Anglo-Irish treaty. Those who were true to the tradition of *Cathleen Ni Houlihan*, the republicans, including the political ancestors of today's Provisional IRA, were on the other side. For that reason Yeats, personally, has never been any kind of hero to the republicans. All the same, parts of his work are part of their culture and part of what keeps them going.

Fifty years after his death, Yeats is still very much alive, in many senses. Unfortunately the part that is most alive in Ireland, out of all the rich complexity of his work, is the *Cathleen Ni Houlihan* part. Through that play, the poet doomed himself to a share in the Valhalla of his blood-thirsty Irish Valkyrie.

> "They shall be remembered for ever,
> They shall be alive for ever,
> They shall be speaking for ever,
> The people shall hear them for ever."

48

A Vindication of Edmund Burke

I. TRUTH AND CONSEQUENCES

On November 1, 1790, Edmund Burke's most famous book, *Reflections on the Revolution in France*, was published. It is important to get the title right. The book is often referred to as *Reflections on the French Revolution*. The book's real title adequately reveals Burke's intentions. Burke's point, in wording the title as he did, was that this was not just a "French Revolution" but a general revolution begun in France but likely to spread to other countries, as indeed it began to do, through military expansion, less than two years after the publication of the *Reflections*.

But already well before the period of military expansion, and before Burke began to write his *Reflections*, the revolution that began in France was beginning to expand in another way. This was an expansion through the movement of ideas, and through the strong sympathy, admiration, and spirit of emulation which various revolutionary transactions and declarations in France had aroused in certain circles in other countries, including Britain, by the end of 1789. Burke's *Reflections* was written with the deliberate aim of sounding the alarm against this form of revolutionary expansion. The *Reflections* resembles George Orwell's *Nineteen Eighty-Four* in two important ways. Both books were written about a revolution in another country and its consequences, and both were directed against British sympathizers with that revolution, and intended to isolate them.

National Review, 42 (17 December 1990), pp. 28–35.

Philosophically, the origins of Burke's opposition to French Revolutionary ideas go back a long way: to his first book, *A Vindication of Natural Society*, published in 1756—34 years before the publication of the *Reflections*.

A Vindication was a prophetic work. In it, Burke set out to show—in an ironic mode—that an attempt to substitute "natural religion" for revealed religion would have revolutionary consequences for civil society. Burke's immediate target was Henry Bolingbroke, an English Voltairean of the early eighteenth century and a spiritual ancestor of the English sympathizers with the French Revolution, who are Burke's targets in the *Reflections*. There is an impressive continuity of thought and perception between these two books, separated as they are by more than thirty eventful years. It is a continuity that refutes the superficial contention of so many of Burke's detractors that he "changed his principles" over the French Revolution. He didn't change his principles. He held to them with fierce tenacity in the *Reflections*, and in the rest of his writings and speeches against the French Revolution.

A Vindication of Natural Society, that remote predecessor, or ancestor, of the *Reflections*, is not a treatise against the Enlightenment as a whole. Burke was himself a child of the Enlightenment: a child, that is, of the early, English or English-inspired, phase of the Enlightenment. This was the Enlightenment of Locke and Montesquieu, an Enlightenment that was compatible with a tolerant version of Christianity. This was Burke's Enlightenment. But from the second quarter of the eighteenth century on, a different strain of Enlightenment emerged, and became dominant in France by the mid 1760s. This was the Voltairean Enlightenment, radically hostile to all forms of revealed religion, and contemptuously rejecting the entire Judaeo-Christian heritage. Burke, who was a deeply religious man—although there is some doubt about what his religion actually was—attacked the anti-religious strain of the Enlightenment with *A Vindication*, just as with the *Reflections* he would attack what he saw as the results of that strain in the French Revolution.

As Burke had foreseen (in general terms) in *A Vindication*, the discrediting of religion had the effect of condemning the established social and political system in that country where the discredit of religion was pushed to the greatest lengths. That country was France. The discredit of religion automatically discredited the monarchy, since reverence for the monarch—His Most Christian Majesty—rested essentially on the theory that the monarch was God's anointed. If there was no God—at least no God Who personally intervened in human politics—then the monarchy was a fraud. The monarch was delegitimized by being desacralized, and the way was laid open for his deposition and execution. Edmund Burke opposed that whole process, or project, from near its beginning, with *A Vindication*, to near its end, with the *Reflections*.

Philosophically, then, the *Reflections* has deep roots in Burke's thought. Politically it is also in strict accordance with a principle that he had laid down as early as December 1783, explaining his initial—and protracted—unwillingness to attack the system of government of the East India Company. Burke, in that context, explained his "insuperable reluctance to destroy any established system of government, upon a theory." That reluctance is at the root of the *Reflections*, politically speaking. And Burke had given expression to that reluctance nearly six years before the Revolution in France began. Those who seek to cast doubt on Burke's sincerity and consistency over the French Revolution have a very poor case.

Burke had had serious qualms about the Revolution from the very beginning. His earliest known thoughts about it are contained in a letter to Lord Charlemont, dated August 9, 1789:

> Our thoughts of everything at home are suspended by our astonishment at the wonderful Spectacle which is exhibited in a Neighbouring and rival Country—what Spectators and what actors. England gazing with astonishment at a French struggle for Liberty and not knowing whether to blame or to applaud! The thing indeed, though I thought I saw something like it in progress for several years, has still something in it paradoxical and Mysterious. The spirit it is impossible not to admire; but the old Parisian ferocity has broken out in a shocking manner. It is true this may be no more than a sudden explosion ... But if it should be character rather than accident, then that people are not fit for Liberty, and must have a Strong hand like that of their former masters to coerce them.

Burke did not, at any time, approve of the French Revolution, but he did not, during 1789, experience any need to combat it. Burke's decision that he must sound the alarm against the English sympathizers with the Revolution in France was reached in the third week of January 1790, when he read a pamphlet containing the proceedings of the Revolution Society on November 4 of the previous year. The Revolution Society was an old established body, consisting mainly of Dissenters, which existed to commemorate the English Revolution of 1688. The Society met annually on November 4, that being the birthday of William III. The 1789 meeting was the first since the fall of the Bastille, and the participants used the occasion to celebrate and extol the French Revolution. The proceedings consisted of a sermon by a well-known

Dissenting minister, the Reverend Richard Price; a resolution carried by the Society; a dinner at the London Tavern; and an address to the National Assembly. In the *Reflections*, the part of the proceedings which Burke concentrates on is the Price sermon. But it was the pamphlet as a whole that inflamed Burke and set him to composing the *Reflections*. The pamphlet firmly placed the British welcome for the French Revolution in a context of anti-Popery. The resolution carried by the Revolution Society at the London Tavern on the evening following Price's sermon ran as follows:

> This Society, sensible of the important advantages arising to this Country by its deliverance from Popery and Arbitrary Power, and conscious that, under God, we owe that signal blessing to the Revolution, which seated our Deliverer, King William the Third, on the Throne; do hereby declare our firm attachment to the civil and religious principles which were recognised and established by that glorious event and which have preserved the succession in the Protestant line; and our determined resolution to maintain and, to the utmost of our power, to perpetuate those blessings to the latest posterity.

On the same occasion, Price moved the Congratulatory Address to the National Assembly in Paris, which was duly carried, conveyed to the Assembly, and warmly welcomed there.

Thus, a society set up to celebrate the Revolution of 1688 was emphasizing the anti-Catholic character of that Revolution, while welcoming the French Revolution, which had already assumed an anti-Catholic character, notably through the annexation of Church property (November 1789).

This combination hurt Burke deeply, for it hit him along a fault line in his political personality. Politically, Burke was a Whig, and thus *ex officio* committed to the principles of the Glorious Revolution of 1688. But he was disqualified from sharing the feelings of normal English Whigs toward that Revolution. Burke needed to play down its anti-Catholic elements, and when the Revolution Society played them up, Burke suffered, and needed to strike back.

Burke's mother was, and remained all her life, a practicing Catholic, as were her people, the Nagles, a family of Catholic gentry in the Blackwater Valley, County Cork. Burke spent six years of his childhood among the Nagles, and he shared their feelings about the anti-Catholic Penal Code, which unfavorably governed so many aspects of their lives.

Edmund Burke's father, Richard Burke, was, at least outwardly, a member of the Established Church of Ireland, of which Edmund was brought up as a member. But Richard Burke, too, may have been a victim of the Penal Laws, though in a more insidious way. I have reason to believe that Richard had been a Catholic, but conformed to the Established Church in order to safeguard his career as an attorney.

Burke's problem with the Glorious Revolution was that he was committed to its general principles, which had brought great benefits to Britain, but that he detested that Revolution's most conspicuous and oppressive monument in Ireland, the Penal Code.

In his political career, Burke dealt with this problem by seeking to extend the benefits of the Glorious Revolution—the civil and religious liberty that it promised—to Roman Catholics, in Britain and in Ireland. In this effort, Burke had been assisted by the more liberal Zeitgeist of the late eighteenth century—the progress of the Enlightenment. Aided by this tendency, Burke had succeeded in masterminding the first measure of Catholic Emancipation—the Catholic Relief Act of 1778. He had paid for that, by losing his parliamentary seat for Bristol in the general election of 1780, as a result of the anti-Catholic reaction which followed that Act and found its most dramatic expression in the Gordon Riots of the summer of that year, in which Lord George Gordon publicly blamed Burke for the measure of relief against which the rioters were protesting.

We can see, therefore, why the proceedings of the English Revolution Society of November 4, 1789, were so repugnant to Edmund Burke. But let me not be misunderstood here. The anti-Catholic elements in the English welcome for the French Revolution do *not* constitute "the reason why" Burke was against that Revolution. Burke was against it, on rational grounds, from the beginning, because of his objection to radical social innovations made on grounds of theory. What the proceedings of the Revolution Society accomplished was to enlist Burke's emotions, in addition to his reasoning power, against the French Revolution. The *Reflections* is the fruit of that alliance.

Burke, while already at work on what would become the *Reflections*, was headed toward a break with his old friend, now the leader of his party, Charles James Fox. This became apparent in a debate in the House of Commons, on the Army Estimates Bill, on February 9, 1790. Fox had spoken with enthusiasm of various revolutionary developments in France. Burke fired a warning shot:

> The House must perceive from my coming forward to mark an expression or two of my best friend, how anxious I am to keep the distemper of France from the least countenance in England ... I am so strongly opposed to even the least tendency towards the means of introducing a democracy like theirs ... that much as it would afflict me, if such a thing could be attempted, and

that any friend of mine could concur in such measures (I am far, very far, from believing they could) I would abandon my best friends and join with my worst enemies to oppose either the means or the end, and to resist all violent exertions of the spirit of innovation, so distinct from all principles of true and safe reformation: a spirit well calculated to overturn States, but perfectly unfit to amend them.

Fox rose to reply, according to the *Parliamentary History*, "with a concern of mind which it was impossible to describe." He acknowledged his deep intellectual indebtedness to Burke, and explicitly disavowed any attempt "to introduce any dangerous element into our excellent Constitution." Burke immediately and gracefully accepted the *amende honorable*, but the parliamentary episode did not end there. Richard Brinsley Sheridan, then the most prominent member of the Whigs after Burke and Fox, marred the reconciliation scene by declaring that he "differed decidedly from Burke" in "almost every word that he had uttered respecting the French Revolution." Burke curtly replied that "henceforward" Sheridan and he "are separated in politics."

The rift between the leading Whigs did not force itself on the attention of Parliament again until April-May of 1791. In the meantime (November), the *Reflections* had been published, widening the rift. This was a quiet period in the history of the Revolution in France, and to most Whigs, Burke and his book appeared extravagantly alarmist. Fox, under Sheridan's influence, was becoming extravagant on the other side.

On April 15, Fox declared, in the course of a parliamentary debate, that the new French Constitution was "the most stupendous and glorious edifice of liberty which had been erected on the foundation of human liberty in any place or country." According to the *Parliamentary History*, "as soon as Mr. Fox sat down, Mr. Burke rose, mid visible emotion," but was shouted down by the Whigs. He did not get a chance of taking the matter up until April 21, which saw a sort of preliminary round between Fox and Burke, each man indicating that he was not prepared to back away.

On May 6, the storm broke. Burke began with a long speech in the spirit of the *Reflections*. He ended with a direct attack upon the French Constitution which Fox so venerated: "I regard the French Constitution, not with approbation but with horror, as involving every principle to be detested, and pregnant with every consequence to be dreaded and abominated."

Fox replied with heavy sarcasm, certain to raise the temperature. When Burke rose again, his speech was interrupted by frequent calls for order coming from his own benches. Burke took these calls to be organized by Fox. He was probably mistaken in that—though Fox could have discouraged these demonstrations had he wished to do so. However that may be, it was Burke's belief that Fox was encouraging the chorus of his former friends against him that led to the final break: "An attempt is being made by one who was formerly my friend to bring down upon me the censure of the House. In the course of our long acquaintance, no one difference of opinion has ever before for a single moment interrupted our friendship." Fox is here recorded as whispering: "There was no loss of friends."

Burke: "Yes, there is a loss of friends. I know the price of my conduct. I have done my duty at the price of my friend. Our friendship is at an end." At this point, the *Parliamentary History* goes on:

> Mr. Fox rose to reply: but his mind was so much agitated, and his heart so much affected by what had fallen from Mr. Burke, that it was some minutes before he could proceed. Tears trickled down his cheeks, and he strove in vain to give utterance to feelings that dignified and exalted his nature. The sensibility of every member of the House appeared uncommonly exalted upon that occasion.

The opening part of Fox's speech to which this was the prelude was kind and respectful to Burke, and it seemed for a moment as if the reconciliation of February 1790 might be repeated. But then Fox bethought himself of the *Reflections*, and opened his mind on that subject: "As soon as that book was published, I condemned it, both in public and in private, and every one of the doctrines which it contained."

That tore it.

Edmund Burke could not possibly remain a member of a party whose leader, in Burke's presence and on the floor of the House of Commons, had totally condemned all the doctrines contained in *Reflections on the Revolution in France*.

Burke replied coldly—referring to "pretenses of friendship"—and the quarrel between Burke and Fox became irreparable.

As it happened, the break with Burke came at a bad time for the Whigs. In the month following the quarrel between Burke and Fox, Louis XVI and Marie-Antoinette attempted their flight to Varennes and were brought back to Paris as prisoners. The French Revolution accelerated until it vindicated—fully by 1792–93—what had been regarded as the alarmist picture which Burke had painted in the *Reflections*. The Whigs, who had rejected the author of the *Reflections*, had cut themselves off from British public opinion because of their enthusiasm for the Revolution in France.

II. INSIGHT AMOUNTING TO PROPHECY

I have considered, so far, the genesis of the *Reflections* and its immediate consequences in British politics. I shall now consider the content of the work itself.

The book began as a letter, addressed to "a very young gentleman" in Paris, who had asked Burke for reassurance regarding the future course of the French Revolution. Burke's original reply, forwarded by him to Paris toward the end of 1789, explains, calmly and courteously, why he cannot provide the desired reassurance. Burke tells his French correspondent: "You may have subverted Monarchy, but not recover'd freedom ... You are now to live in a new order of things; under a plan of Government of which no Man can speak from experience ... The French may be yet to go through more transmigrations."

Those three sentences are developed at length in the *Reflections*, which is also still, in form, a letter to the same correspondent. But the *Reflections* is in other respects very different, in character and tone, from the original letter. In the interim, from mid January 1790 on, Burke had learned of those "proceedings of certain societies" in London, in which unrestricted admiration for the French Revolution was expressed and a desire to emulate it in England was implied.

Burke felt great alarm and anger at those proceedings, and having denounced them, from his place in the House of Commons, in February 1790 he set out to write a tract to warn the British public against the dangers of any such tendencies. That tract, in the form of a letter, is the *Reflections*.

Burke's passionate indignation against the French Revolution—and above all against any attempt to imitate it in the British Isles—is evident in the *Reflections*, sustains it, and is the source of a part of its power. But a part only. The text of the *Reflections* takes up nearly three hundred pages. I reckon that 90 per cent of that consists of argument and analysis. There is an emotional undercurrent throughout, but it breaks through to the surface only rarely. When it does the resultant rhetoric is spectacular. The most spectacular—that about the Queen of France, as Burke saw her in 1773—has been quoted far more often than anything else in the book. Repetition of this quotation has created the misleading impression that the *Reflections* is mostly gorgeous rhetoric. In reality, most of the book is made up of plain and cogent argument. Passion is present, but Burke keeps it well under control, except on the rare occasions when he decides not to do so.

The grand distinguishing feature of the *Reflections* is the power of Burke's insight into the character of the French Revolution, then at an early stage. This insight is so acute as to endow him with prophetic power. He sees what way the Revolution is heading. No one else seems to have done so at the time. The spring and summer of 1790—the period in which Burke wrote the *Reflections*—was the most tranquil stage, in appearance, in the history of the Revolution. It was a period of constitution-making, of benevolent rhetoric, and of peaceful jubilation, as in the *Déclaration de Paix au Monde* on May 21, 1790, or the *Fête de la Fédération* on July 14, 1790, celebrating the first anniversary of the fall of the Bastille.

Contemplating that attractive scene, in the spring and summer of 1790, most people seem to have assumed that the French Revolution *had already taken place*, and that all that remained was to reap its benign consequences. Burke sensed that the Revolution was only beginning. In the penultimate paragraph of the *Reflections*, Burke warned that the French "commonwealth" could hardly remain in the form it had taken in 1790: "But before its final settlement it may be obliged to pass, as one of our poets says, 'though great varieties of untried being,' and in all its transmigrations to be purified by fire and blood."

Reading the *Reflections* with an undergraduate class in New York in the 1960s, I found that my students assumed that the direst events of the Revolution—the September Massacres, the Terror, the executions of the King and Queen—had already taken place when the *Reflections* was written. In reality, those events all lay in the future. And yet there is a sense in which those events are already present in the *Reflections*. They are present in the sense that the ferocious dynamic which Burke ascribes to the Revolution, even in 1790, became viable to the world through those events of 1792–94.

Burke foresaw not merely "transmigrations, fire, and blood." In a remarkable passage—on page 342 of the Penguin Classics edition—Burke foresaw how those transmigrations would end up, in military despotism:

It is known that armies have hitherto yielded a very precarious and uncertain obedience to any senate, or popular authority; and they will least of all yield it to an assembly which is to have only a continuance of two years. The officers must totally lose the characteristic disposition of military men, if they see with perfect submission and due admiration, the dominion of pleaders; especially when they find that they have a new court to pay to an endless succession of those pleaders, whose military policy, and the genius of whose command (if they should have any) must be as uncertain as their duration is transient. In the weakness of one kind of authority, and in the fluctuation of all, the officers of an army will remain for some time mutinous and full of faction, until some popular general, who understands the art of conciliating the soldiery, and who possesses the true spirit of command, shall draw the eyes of all men upon himself. Armies will obey him on his personal account. There is no other way of securing military obedience in this state of things. But the moment in which that event shall happen, the person who really commands the army is your master; the master (that is little) of your king, the master of your assembly, the master of your whole republic.

The seizure of power by Napoleon Bonaparte—the event predicted in this remarkable passage—occurred on 18 *brumaire* 1799, nine years after the publication of the *Reflections*, and more than two years after the death of the author.

Burke's astonishing capacity to see into the ways in which events were moving derived, not from any mystical intuition, but from penetrating powers of observation, judicious inference from what was observed, and thorough analysis of what was discerned by observation and inference. Burke had immense respect for *circumstances*, and observed them with proportionate attentiveness. There is a passage about circumstances in relation to liberty which occurs very near the beginning of the *Reflections* (pages 89–91 in the Penguin Classics edition), and is fundamental to Burke's political thinking, not alone in the *Reflections*, but generally. In this passage Burke is referring to the congratulations conveyed by the English Revolution Society to the French National Assembly, in November 1789, on France's achievement of liberty. The passage runs:

> I flatter myself that I love a manly, moral, regulated liberty as well as any gentleman of the Revolution Society; be he who he will; and perhaps I have given as good proofs of my attachment to that cause, in the whole course of my public conduct. I think I envy liberty as little as they do, to any other nation. But I cannot stand forward, and give praise or blame to any thing which relates to human actions, and human concerns, on a simple view of the object, as it stands, stripped of every relation, in all the nakedness and solitude of metaphysical abstraction. Circumstances (which with some gentlemen pass for nothing) give in reality to every political principle its distinguishing colour, and discriminating effect. The circumstances are what render every civil and political scheme beneficial or noxious to mankind. Abstractedly speaking, government, as well as liberty, is good; yet could I, in common sense, ten years ago, have felicitated France on her enjoyment of a government (for she then had a government) without enquiry what the nature of that government was, or how it was administered? Can I now congratulate the same nation upon its freedom? Is it because liberty, in the abstract, may be classed amongst the blessings of mankind, that I am seriously to felicitate

a madman, who has escaped from the protecting restraint and wholesome darkness of his cell, on his restoration to the enjoyment of light and liberty? Am I to congratulate an highwayman and murderer, who has broke prison, upon the recovery of his natural rights? This would be to act over again the scene of the criminals condemned to the gallies, and their heroic deliverer, the metaphysic Knight of the Sorrowful Countenance.

When I see the spirit of liberty in action, I see a strong principle at work; and this, for a while, is all I can possibly know of it. The wild gas, the fixed air is plainly broke loose: but we ought to suspend our judgment until the first effervescence is a little subsided, till the liquor is cleared, and until we see something deeper than the agitation of a troubled and frothy surface. I must be tolerably sure, before I venture publicly to congratulate men upon a blessing, that they have really received one. Flattery corrupts both the receiver and the giver; and adulation is not of more service to the people than to kings. I should therefore suspend my congratulations on the new liberty of France, until I was informed how it had been combined with government; with public force; with the discipline and obedience of armies; with the collection of an effective and well-distributed revenue; with morality and religion; with the solidity of property; with peace and order; with civil and social manners. All these (in their way) are good things too; and, without them, liberty is not a benefit whilst it lasts, and is not likely to continue long. The effect of liberty to individuals is, that they may do what they please: We ought to see what it will please them to do, before we risque congratulations, which may be soon turned into complaints. Prudence would dictate this in the case of separate insulated private men; but liberty, when men act in bodies, is power. Considerate people, before they declare themselves, will observe the use which is made of power; and particularly of so trying a thing as new power in new persons, of whose principles, tempers, and dispositions, they have little or no experience, and in situations where those who appear the most stirring in the scene may possibly not be the real movers.

III. THE END OF ANOTHER REVOLUTION

I now consider the relation of the *Reflections* to our own time. 1990 was like 1790 in an important way. Both years were aftermaths of epochal changes. 1790 saw the first anniversary of the fall of the Bastille. 1990 saw the first anniversary of the destruction of the Berlin Wall. The 1990 anniversary was celebrated, as the 1790 anniversary was (but not by Burke), as a feast of liberation. But the two versions of liberation are diametrically opposed. In July 1790, what was being celebrated was the beginning of the Revolution in France. In November 1990, what was celebrated was the undoing of the Communist Revolution.

In July 1790, while France was celebrating the Feast of the Federation, and British friends of the French Revolution were celebrating in sympathy, Edmund Burke was at work on the great counter-revolutionary tract which was the *Reflections on the Revolution in France*. From the principles laid down in the *Reflections*, we know that Burke would have rejoiced at the destruction of the Berlin Wall and the comprehensive discredit of the Communist Revolution.

There is a real continuity between the Revolution in France and the Revolution in Russia. That continuity is often denied—especially by French anti-Communists. Last year's bicentenary celebrations in Paris were organized around the theme of universal liberation, supposedly inspired by the 1789 Declaration of the Rights of Man and of the Citizen. As pageantry, the celebration was brilliantly successful. As history, it was nonsense. The edifying sentiments expressed in the Declaration had no influence over the conduct of the French Revolutionaries themselves, or of anybody else, anywhere. What that document influenced was *other documents*: principally, the constitutions of a number of Latin American countries, whose governments were, in practice, no more influenced by the edifying sentiments in question than the original French Revolutionaries had allowed themselves to be.

The true heirs to the French Revolution—and specifically to the Jacobin tradition—were the Communists. We can see this particularly clearly when we apply Burkean categories. What Burke most detested, and dreaded, about the French Revolutionaries was their commitment to radical social and political innovation: the transformation of an established order in accordance with theoretical prescriptions. In all that, Marx and Lenin are clearly heirs to the Jacobins. The only difference is that the commitment of the Marxists, in these respects, outdid that of the Jacobins. In every phase of the French Revolution, the Revolutionaries left private property intact, with just one great exception, bitterly denounced by Burke. That exception was the nationalization of the property of the Church, in November 1789. What the Jacobins did to Church property, the Marxists did to almost all property. The result was the command economy, whose abject failure is now acknowledged in all the European lands which were unlucky enough to have been subjected to it.

What we have been witnessing in 1989–90, in the Soviet Union and in Eastern Europe, is the bankruptcy of the greatest experiment in social and political innovation ever made. What stronger vindication could there be of the principles laid down, and the warning contained, in *Reflections on the Revolution in France*?

Modern British society is widely different from the British society that Burke knew, but there is a clear continuity between the two. The

society changed, politically and socially, not through any burst of innovation, but through a series of partial reforms, as Burke hoped it would
do. The heritage of the great French innovative effort was not so happy.
The Revolution and its consequences left the French a deeply divided
people throughout the nineteenth century and the first half of the
twentieth. After 1917, those of the French who felt themselves to be
in the tradition of their own great Revolution flocked to the French
Communist Party. In the Second World War, the fact that the party of
the working-class (as the French Communist Party then still was) was
opposed to the war-effort—because of the Stalin-Hitler pact—was
among the reasons for the fall of France.

From 1970 on, however, the Revolutionary heritage, which had be-
deviled the French for so long, went into decline, as did the French
Communist Party. The 1989 celebration of the bicentenary was essentially a gorgeous farewell party—a sort of wake—for a Revolution which
is at last over, though it took nearly two centuries for it to die.

One of the consequences of the decline of the cult of the French
Revolution in France itself has been the emergence of a new respect for
Edmund Burke, and for the *Reflections* in particular, among French historians. For many years the dominant school of French historians were
really the priests of a cult of the great Revolution. As long as that was
the case, the author of *Reflections on the Revolution in France—ce livre in-
fâme*, as Michelet called it—was necessarily anathema. French historians of today take quite a different view. The monumental *Critical
Dictionary of the French Revolution*, edited by François Furet and Mona
Ozouf and published in 1988, contains an entry on Burke by Gérard
Gengembre which concludes with a tribute to his "penetrating clair-
voyance, revealing the depths of what was at stake in the Revolution."
There are many other references to Burke, and his name is cross-listed
in at least 16 of the *Dictionary*'s entries. Last year saw the publication of
a new French translation of the *Reflections*—together with a selection of
Burke's other writings on the Revolution—with a weighty and profoundly respectful preface by Philippe Raynaud (who was also a contrib-
utor to the *Critical Dictionary*). Raynaud describes the author of the
Reflections as "liberal and counter-revolutionary," which is exactly right.

British scholarship is less respectful toward the author of the
Reflections than French scholarship now is. At least that is the conclusion
toward which one would be impelled by comparing Raynaud's edition
with the corresponding English publication of the same year: Volume
VIII (*The French Revolution, 1790–1794*) of *The Writings and Speeches of
Edmund Burke* (Clarendon Press, Oxford); Volume VIII is edited by
L.G. Mitchell. Raynaud's preface provides 105 pages of respectful
interpretation and comment, ending with a tribute to Burke's "in-

comparable art." Mitchell gives us 51 pages of disparagement and depreciation, interspersed with a veritable anthology of sneers directed at Burke by his numerous enemies. If Mitchell is aware that Burke's writings on the Revolution have any merit, he nowhere reveals this. He thinks of Burke as a failure. His preface ends with the words: "For him there was only the bitterness of the dishonored prophet."

A quirky introduction might be excused if the edition were otherwise satisfactory. It is in fact lamentably defective. It is hard to believe, but this volume of *The Writings and Speeches of Edmund Burke* contains no speeches at all; Yet some of Burke's most important speeches were made on the subject—the French Revolution—with which Volume VIII is supposed to be concerned, and fall within its chronological limits: 1790–1794. The relevant speeches omitted include the series which culminated in the breach between Edmund Burke and Charles James Fox (referred to above). It seems almost inconceivable that these speeches could be omitted from the relevant volume of a scholarly series entitled *The Writings and Speeches of Edmund Burke*. The two volumes previously published in this series gave their readers what those readers were entitled to expect: the writings *and the speeches*; including—quite rightly—a number of speeches which are of little importance compared with a number of those omitted from Volume VIII. This miserable edition also omits one of Burke's major writings on the French Revolution, the great *Appeal from the New to the Old Whigs*, which is the sequel and justification of the *Reflections*.

If this series is to retain its previously high reputation, Volume VIII should be withdrawn from circulation, and a new Volume VIII prepared, to the same standards as were followed in Volumes II and V.

Turning away, with relief, from Volume VIII, let me conclude with one of the most remarkable passages in the *Reflections*. It is a passage which is highly relevant to the present scene in the former empire of Communism, and to some of the forces which are trying to fill the vacuum left by the collapse of Communism. It is, in effect, a treatise on the versatility of evil:

> We do not draw the moral lesson we might from history. On the contrary, without care it may be used to vitiate our minds and to destroy our happiness. In history a great volume is unrolled for our instruction, drawing the materials of future wisdom from the past errors and infirmities of mankind. It may, in the perversion, serve for a magazine, furnishing offensive and defensive weapons for parties in church and state, and supplying the means of keeping alive, or reviving dissensions and animosities, and adding fuel to civil

fury. History consists, for the greater part, of the miseries brought upon the world by pride, ambition, avarice, revenge, lust, sedition, hypocrisy, ungoverned zeal, and all the train of disorderly appetites, which shake the public with the same

> troubled storms that toss
> The private state, and render life unsweet.

These vices are the causes of those storms. Religion, morals, laws, prerogatives, privileges, liberties, rights of men, are the pretexts. The pretexts are always found in some specious appearance of a real good. You would not secure men from tyranny and sedition, by rooting out of the mind the principles to which these fraudulent pretexts apply? If you did, you would root out every thing that is valuable in the human breast. As these are the pretexts, so the ordinary actors and instruments in great public evils are kings, priests, magistrates, senates, parliaments, national assemblies, judges, and captains. You would not cure the evil by resolving, that there should be no more monarchs, nor ministers of state, nor of the gospel; no interpreters of law; no general officers; no public councils. You might change the names. The things in some shape must remain. A certain quantum of power must always exist in the community, in some hands, and under some appellation. Wise men will apply their remedies to vices, not to names; to the causes of evil which are permanent, not to the occasional organs by which they act, and the transitory modes in which they appear. Otherwise you will be wise historically, a fool in practice. Seldom have two ages the same fashion in their pretexts and the same modes of mischief. Wickedness is a little more inventive. Whilst you are discussing fashion, the fashion is gone by. The very same vice assumes a new body. The spirit transmigrates; and far from losing its principle of life by the change of its appearance, it is renovated in its new organs with the fresh vigour of a juvenile activity. It walks abroad; it continues its ravages; whilst you are gibbeting the carcass, or demolishing the tomb. You are terrifying yourself with ghosts and apparitions, whilst your house is the haunt of robbers. It is thus with all those, who attending only to the shell and husk of history, think they are waging war with intolerance, pride, and cruelty, whilst, under colour of abhorring the ill principles of antiquated parties, they are authorizing and feeling the same odious vices in different factions, and perhaps in worse.

Those last four words should be borne in mind as we contemplate some of the patterns emerging in the disintegrating empire of ruined Communism: the aftermath of the most ambitious and sustained innovative effort in human history.

49

PRIDE IN THE LANGUAGE

The Cultural Capital of Europe did not distinguish itself last week. On Saturday last, a day of brilliant sunshine, the Memorial Service for Sean O'Faolain was held at St. Joseph's Church, Glasthule.

Sean O'Faolain, who died at the age of 91, could aptly (though not elegantly) be described as the Grand Old Man of Irish Letters. If a writer of comparable distinction, belonging to any other nation, were being commemorated in the national capital, the Memorial Service would have been crowded with representatives of the nation's entire Establishment.

That applies to every other nation in the European Community (with the possible exception of Belgium) and to other European nations, such as Poland, Czechoslovakia, Sweden and Norway. Not so with us.

Let it be recorded here, for the information of posterity that, at the Memorial Service for Sean O'Faolain, on May 4, 1991, there was present not one single member of the Oireachtas, the Parliament of Ireland.

There was, indeed, a degree of official representation: the bare bleak minimum. The President was represented by an aide-de-camp; so was the Taoiseach. I am not reproaching either the President or the Taoiseach with their absence; both may well have had prior commitments.

But the absence of all members of an entire Parliament cannot be similarly explained. What that symbolises is a gaping hole in the heart

Irish Independent, 11 May 1991.

of our national culture. Dublin, in the 1990s, isn't fit to be the Cultural Capital of anything.

I reflected sadly, during the week, on the meaning of that act of cultural absenteeism, on the part of the elected representatives of the Irish people. That act has to mean something: what does it mean?

I believe that it reflects a skewed relationship, on our collective part, to language and consequently to literature.

We speak, read and write one language: English. That was the language in which Sean O'Faolain habitually wrote and through which he became famous. But we feel obscurely that we ought to be speaking, reading and writing a language other than that which we actually do speak, read and write.

We have two official languages: the second is the one we use: the first is the one we think we ought to be using. We don't read—and most of us can't read—the writers who use the first official language, but we have some respect for them, in a vague and perfunctory sort of way.

We do read the writers who write in the language we habitually use, but we don't feel much collective pride in them. Their collective product is denominated "Anglo-Irish Literature." We are unlikely to feel warm towards anything labelled "Anglo-Irish."

The Gaelic Revival movement will be a hundred years old in two years time. It did not succeed. It failed to preserve even what was then left. There were over 600,000 Irish speakers at the turn of the century, and most of these would have been native speakers.

A report published this week shows the number of native speakers is down to 10,000.

The Revival Movement failed to revive, and its only movement was backwards. But it did generate a huge amount of political hypocrisy and—what was worse, because more insidious—a habit of listening to official nonsense, in an approving sort of way, as you might listen to the prattle of an innocent child.

The Gaelic Revival failed to persuade the Irish people to speak Irish. But it did succeed in something. It succeeded in securing the lip-service of the great majority of the elected representatives of the Irish people (in this Republic).

And it succeeded in making the Irish people a little ashamed of the fact that they continue to speak English, and not Irish. The shame is not sufficient to bring about a resolve to learn Irish properly, and use it habitually.

If it were sufficient to do that, that might be a very good thing. But it *is* sufficient to make us feel permanently ill at ease with the language we actually do speak.

We use it pragmatically, and as a matter of expediency. But we don't love it. We don't take pride in it. We even tend to resent it as something imposed on us by the ancient oppressor.

We forget that our people chose to become English-speakers, of their own free will, at a time when they could have gone on speaking Irish had they chosen to do so.

I don't know whether there is any other people which habitually speaks one language, while feeling that it ought to be speaking another. (Some of the Welsh, perhaps, or some of the Scots). In any case, it is a curious condition and cannot be a healthy one, psychologically speaking.

And it is that condition, I believe, that accounts for the complete absence of our parliamentarians from the Memorial Service for Sean O'Faolain.

Since we have collectively—and silently—decided to go on speaking English, we must, for the sake of our psychological health, come to terms with that decision. We must learn both to respect and to love the language we actually speak.

We must learn to honour the men and women of our stock who have enriched the literature of that language. As long as we have not learned these things, we shall be lacking in self respect.

People who have no respect for the language they speak can have no respect for their own selves.

50

YOUR LORDSHIPS: AN OPEN LETTER TO THE IRISH CATHOLIC HIERARCHY

Your lordships have never before been subjected to an Open Letter. The publication of this one, here, is a sign of the times, which you will do well to ponder.

An Open Letter is a statement in which a writer, believing himself (or herself) to speak for a number of citizens, addresses the representatives of a powerful institution, deemed to have abused its power. The archetype of the Open Letter is Emile Zola's letter to the President of the French Republic on 13 January, 1898, published under a title which became famous: *J'accuse!*

Zola was protesting against the persecution of an innocent man: Captain Dreyfus. You are primarily responsible for the passage of a constitutional amendment under which an unknown number of innocent women can be, have been, and are being, persecuted in the name of a supposed absolute: "the right to life of the unborn." The most conspicuous victim is the girl nominated X in this week's Supreme Court decision. That girl now is free to travel thanks to that decision. The loophole of "going to England" is now restored.

But the "equal" "right to life of the unborn" apparently remains intact within our jurisdiction and governs, for example, the treatment in our hospitals of pregnant cancer victims (I say, apparently, because we won't know the current status of our laws in this matter until the Supreme Court has made known the grounds on which it struck down the injunction).

Irish Independent, 29 February 1992.

Much indignation was expressed, and rightly so, following Mr. Justice Costello's injunction. The lobbyists who led the public campaign for the Eighth Amendment—notably SPUC and PLAC—have been severely embarrassed. Your Lordships, however, the prime movers in that campaign, as we all know, have been largely immune from criticism.

Old habits of deference die hard. SPUC and PLAC would be of little significance, without the backing of your Lordships. I address you, therefore, rather than them. If one has complaints about the behaviour of the monkeys, it is more sensible to address oneself to the organ grinder, rather than to the little creatures who pass the cap around for him. It was to your music that our people gave ourselves the Eighth Amendment which has disgraced us in the eyes of the world, and to a great extent in our own eyes also.

I accuse you of abusing your power by causing to be inserted into the fundamental law of the State, binding on all the citizens, a simplified version of the teaching of your Church, and yours only. This is manifestly unjust to those of us who conscientiously reject your teaching in that matter.

I accuse you also of deceiving the public, in the sense that you knowingly permitted your agents to present a crudely simplified version of Catholic teaching on this matter. We were given to understand that it has always been the teaching of the Church that the foetus, from the moment of conception, is fully a human being, whose right to be born is (at least) equal to its mother's right to live. As you know, this is untrue. For most of your Church's long lifetime, its teaching was quite different, and much more similar to what people outside your Church generally believe today.

Until the 19th century your Church's official teaching was that: "the abortion of a male foetus up until 40 days after conception and of a female foetus (*sic*) up to 80 days after conception carried no penalty with it. In practice this meant—since there was no way of determining the sex of the foetus—that abortion was exempt from punishment for the first 80 days of pregnancy." (See Uta Ranke-Heinemann, *Eunuchs for the Kingdom of Heaven: Women, Sexuality and the Catholic Church*, Penguin Books 1991, a work which I warmly commend to my lay readers, and commend also to any of your Lordships who may not already be familiar with it).

In the late 19th century, for reasons unknown to me, the Catholic Church infallibly decided that what it had been infallibly teaching up to then was now infallibly wrong. From this late period in the history of your ancient institution dates the doctrine of the right of life of the foetus from the moment of conception.

That doctrine is absolute and peremptory, verbally speaking. In practice, it does not work like that. Your Church has permitted abortion, specifically in the case of victims of rape. It is well known that in the summer of 1960 some of those nuns who were victims of rape in the Congo (now Zaire) underwent operations to ensure that they would not give birth.

The right to life of those particular foetuses was not respected. I don't know what sophistries were invoked to pretend that abortion was not abortion in those cases. You and your somewhat less obnoxious Catholic counterparts in other lands have always an abundant supply of sophistries and sophists at your disposal, to mitigate, in practice, the absolute principles you are so addicted to affirming, at the level of theory.

In any case you made no specific exception for the benefit of rape victims in the law you foisted on us in 1983. I wonder did any of you regret that omission during the crisis of your authority—for it is no less—that followed the Attorney-General's interim injunction on February 6 last?

You now apparently feel that the crisis is over: that the Supreme Court decision has let you off the hook. In a statement issued immediately after the Supreme Court decision striking down the High Court's injunction you expressed satisfaction "that the legal issues in this case have been resolved with a minimum of delay."

To this expression of satisfaction with the Supreme Court decision, you add the following moral rider: "It remains the concern of the Catholic Church that, as always, whatever the circumstances, innocent new life should not be made to pay the penalty of death for the crime of another."

Your Lordships, who do you think you are fooling? The legal outcome at which you express satisfaction is one which permits a girl to go to England to get an abortion. You then go on, as if nothing had happened, to reiterate, in all its purity, the very doctrine on which was based the High Court injunction, whose striking down by the Supreme Court you receive with satisfaction!

I have never read a statement which so happily combines absurdity, complacency, impudence, incoherence and incongruity as does that 14-line fatwa issued on your behalf by the Catholic Press and Information Office on Wednesday. I am afraid your Lordships are so accustomed to having your utterances treated with respect that you have forgotten that nonsense is not entitled to respect, however exalted the personages who may choose to offer it to the public.

Your Lordships have just had a bad couple of weeks, as a result of your own gratuitous Constitution-making venture of nine years ago. I suggest that you now take a rest.

Specifically, I suggest you refrain, for the future, from efforts to shape the laws of this State, which are for all the citizens, and not just for what you call your flock. Your flock is increasingly less flock-like. It is traditionally credulous but you have taxed its credulity. It no longer follows your teaching on contraception. It was largely due to your pastoral failure in that domain that you moved to change the laws of the State to embody your teaching on abortion. The result of that misguided attempt has been a further diminution of that authority.

You may preach your peculiar doctrines to those who are willing to listen to you, even restlessly, but please don't try, any more, to impose those doctrines on the rest of us by manipulating the laws of the State. Hierarchy and democracy go ill together, both in theory and in practice. If you didn't learn that lesson this month, you never will.

I am, your Lordships, with all the respect that is due from one citizen to any group of fellow-citizens,

yours sincerely
Conor Cruise O'Brien.

BIBLIOGRAPHY

The following bibliography of the writings of Conor Cruise O'Brien is comprehensive, but not complete. It includes all of Conor's major pieces through the year 1992; however, I have been selective in the matter of short newspaper articles and ephemera.

If there are significant items that I have either overlooked or excluded, I would appreciate hearing from other scholars, so that corrections may be made in any future edition.

I wish to indicate my debt to the pioneering checklist compiled by Joanne L. Henderson for *Conor Cruise O'Brien: An Appraisal* by Elisabeth Young-Bruehl and Robert Hogan (Newark, Del.: Proscenium Press, 1974). There are also some bibliographic items in D.R. O'Connor Lysaght, *End of a Liberal: The Literary Politics of Conor Cruise O'Brien* (Dublin: Plough Books, 1978), and Risteard O'Glaisne, *Conor Cruise O'Brien agus an Liobralachas* (Dublin: Clódhanna Teo, 1974).

SYNOPSIS OF BIBLIOGRAPHY

   I. Books, pamphlets, and chapters in books (in chronological order, listed by primary edition)
  II. Articles in periodicals (in chronological order)
 III. Newspaper essays (each section in chronological order)
    Observer
    Irish Times
    Times (London)
    Irish Independent

I. Books, Pamphlets, and Chapters in Books

1952
["Donat O'Donnell"], *Maria Cross: Imaginative Patterns in a Group of Modern Catholic Writers* (New York: Oxford University Press, 1952; London: Chatto and Windus, 1953). Second ed. under Conor Cruise O'Brien (London: Burns and Oates, 1963).

1957
Parnell and His Party, 1880–90 (Oxford: Clarendon Press, 1957; corrected impression, 1964).

1960
(Editor), *The Shaping of Modern Ireland* (London: Routledge and Kegan Paul, 1960). By O'Brien: "Foreword," pp. 1–11; "1891–1916," pp. 13–23.

1962
To Katanga and Back: A UN Case History (London: Hutchinson, 1962).

1964
Conflicting Concepts of the United Nations (Leeds: Leeds University Press, 1964). The Montague Burton Lecture. Reprinted in *Writers and Politics* (1965), pp. 195–214.

1965
"Passion and Cunning: An Essay on the Politics of W.B. Yeats." In A. Norman Jeffares and K.G.W. Cross, eds., *Excited Reverie: A Centenary Tribute to William Butler Yeats, 1865–1939* (London: Macmillan, 1965), pp. 207–78. Reprinted in George Abbot White and Charles Newman, eds., *Literature in Revolution* (New York: Holt Rinehart and Winston, 1972), pp. 142–203; *Passion and Cunning: Essays on Nationalism, Terrorism and Revolution* (London: Weidenfeld and Nicolson; New York: Simon and Shuster, 1988), pp. 8–61; and abridged in Irving Howe, ed., *The Idea of the Modern in Literature and the Arts* (New York: Horizon Press, 1972), pp. 303–17.
Writers and Politics (London: Chatto and Windus, 1965).

1967
Ireland, the United Nations, and Southern Africa (Dublin: Irish Anti-Apartheid Movement, 1967).

"Politics and the Morality of Scholarship." In Max Black, ed., *The Morality of Scholarship* (Ithaca: Cornell University Press, 1967), pp. 59–74. Reprinted in *Power and Consciousness* (1969), pp. 33–42.

1968
"The Calculus of Pain, of Peace and of Prestige," Foreword in John Gerassi, *North Vietnam: A Documentary* (London: George Allen and Unwin, 1968), pp. 21–29. Reprinted in *Herod* (1978), pp. 82–91.

"The Embers of Easter 1916–66," in O. Dudley Edwards and Fergus S. Pyle, eds., *1916: The Easter Rising* (London: MacGibbon and Kee, 1968), pp. 225–40.

Murderous Angels: A Political Tragedy and Comedy in Black and White (Boston: Little Brown, 1968; London: Hutchinson, 1969).

The United Nations: Sacred Drama (London: Hutchinson, 1968). Drawings by Feliks Topolski.

1969
Conor Cruise O'Brien Introduces Ireland, ed. Owen Dudley Edwards. (London: Andre Deutsch, Ltd., 1969). By O'Brien: "Introducing Ireland," pp. 13–20; "Ireland in International Affairs," pp. 104–34.

"Imagination and Politics," in J.C. Laidlaw, ed., *The Future of the Modern Humanities* (New York: Modern Humanities Research Association, 1969), pp. 73–85.

"Introduction," and "Edmund Burke: A Biographical Note," in Edmund Burke, *Reflections on the Revolution in France and on the Proceedings in Certain Societies in London Relative to that Event* (Harmondsworth: Penguin Books, 1968), pp. 7–81.

(Edited with William Dean Vanich), *Power and Consciousness* (New York: New York University Press, 1969). By O'Brien: "Introduction," pp. 1–13; "Politics and the Morality of Scholarship," pp. 33–42; "Imagination and Politics," pp. 205–14; and "Politics as Drama as Politics," pp. 215–28.

1970
Camus (London: William Collins, 1970). US ed. entitled *Albert Camus of Europe over Africa* (New York: Viking, 1970).

1972
(Maire and Conor Cruise O'Brien), *A Concise History of Ireland* (London: Thames and Hudson, 1972; 2d rev. ed., 1973).

States of Ireland (London: Hutchinson, 1972).

The Suspecting Glance (London: Faber and Faber, 1972).

1978
Herod: Reflections on Political Violence (London: Hutchinson, 1978).

1980
Neighbours: The Ewart-Biggs Memorial Lectures, 1978–1979 (London: Faber and Faber, 1980).

The Press and the World (London: Birkbeck College, 1980). The Haldane Memorial Lecture.

1981
"Introductory Remarks," in *Patricia Slattery, ed., The Irish Question: An Inquiry into the Cultural, Historical and Political Issues at the Root of the Conflict in Northern Ireland* (Winooski, Vt., 1981), pp. 3–19. Proceedings of a conference held at St. Michael's College, Vermont, 1981.

"Patriotism and *The Need for Roots*: The Antipolitics of Simone Weil," in George Abbot White, ed., *Simone Weil: Interpretations of a Life* (Amherst: University of Massachusetts Press, 1981), pp. 95–110. Orig. pub. in limited edition, George Abbot White, ed., *Simone Weil: Live Like Her?* (Cambridge: Technology and Cultural Seminar, Massachusetts Institute of Technology, 1976).

1986
The Siege: The Saga of Israel and Zionism (London: Weidenfeld and Nicolson, 1986 and New York: Simon and Shuster, 1986).

1988
God Land: Reflections on Religion and Nationalism (Cambridge: Harvard University Press, 1988). The William E. Massey Sr. Lectures in the History of American Civilization.

"Introduction to the Cresset Library Edition," in Matthew Arnold, ed., *Irish Affairs: Edmund Burke* (orig. pub. as *Letters, Speeches and Tracts on Irish Affairs*, 1881; new ed., London: Cresset Library, 1988), pp. vii-xxxvi.

"Nationalism and the French Revolution," in Geoffrey Best, ed., *The Permanent Revolution: The French Revolution and Its Legacy, 1789–1989* (London: Fontana Press, 1988), pp. 17–48.

Passion and Cunning: Essays on Nationalism, Terrorism and Revolution (London: Weidenfeld and Nicolson; New York: Simon and Shuster, 1988).

1989
"Warren Hastings in Burke's Great Melody," in Geoffrey Carnall and Colin Nicolson, eds., *The Impeachment of Warren Hastings: Papers from a Bicentenary Commemoration* (Edinburgh: Edinburgh University Press, 1989), pp. 58–75.

1991
"Foreword," in Andrée Sheehy-Skeffington, *Skeff: The Life of Owen Sheehy Skeffington, 1909–1970* (Dublin: Lilliput Press, 1991), pp. vii-xii.

1992
The Great Melody: A Thematic Biography and Commented Anthology of Edmund Burke (London: Sinclair-Stevenson, Ltd.; Chicago: University of Chicago Press, 1992).

"Introduction," in André Malraux, *The Walnut Trees of Altenburg* (Chicago: University of Chicago Press, 1992).

Second Ian Gow Memorial Lecture (London: Friends of the Union, 1992).

II. Articles in Periodicals

1938
[Donat], "Poisson d'Avril/Poison d'Autrui" (poem), *T.C.D.: A College Miscellany* (26 May 1938), p. 173.

[Donat], "Said to Me Francis Winterbotham" (poem), *T.C.D.: A College Miscellany* (3 Nov. 1938), p. 234.

[Shrdlu], "Sir Horace: A Ballad" (poem), *T.C.D.: A College Miscellany* (3 Nov. 1938), p. 229.

1939
Unsigned editorial on European situation, *T.C.D.: A College Miscellany* (26 Oct. 1939), pp. 1–2.

Unsigned editorial (ascription not totally certain), on women in college, *T.C.D.: A College Miscellany* (9 Nov. 1939), pp. 25–26.

1940
[Donat], "Materialist May Song" (poem), *T.C.D.: A College Miscellany* (23 May 1940), pp. 160–61.

[Donat], "In County Wicklow, Now" (poem), *T.C.D.: A College Miscellany* (12 June 1940), pp. 200–201.

[Donat], "The Swan to Iona" (poem), *T.C.D.: A College Miscellany* (12 June 1940), p. 200.

1945

[Donat O'Donnell], "The Fourth Estate: The Irish Independent: A Business Idea," *The Bell* (Feb. 1945), pp. 386–94.

[Donat O'Donnell], "The Catholic Press: A Study in Theopolitics," *The Bell* (April 1945), pp. 30–40.

[Donat O'Donnell], "A Rider to the Verdict," addendum to Vivian Mercier, "Verdict on *The Bell*," *The Bell* (May 1945), pp. 164–67.

[Donat O'Donnell], "Parnell's Monument," *The Bell* (Oct. 1945), pp. 566–73.

1946

[Donat O'Donnell], "Horizon," *The Bell* (March 1946), pp. 1030–38.

[Donat O'Donnell], "Raffles, Stalin and George Orwell," *The Bell* (May 1946), pp. 167–71. Review of *Critical Essays* and *Animal Farm* by George Orwell.

[Donat O'Donnell], "The Pieties of Evelyn Waugh," *The Bell*; (Dec. 1946), pp. 38–49. Reprinted in *Kenyon Review* 9 (Summer 1947), pp. 400–11; and with minor changes in *Maria Cross* (1952), pp. 119–34.

1947

[Donat O'Donnell], "Donat O'Donnell Replies to T.J. Barrington," *The Bell* (March 1947), pp. 57–62. Reply to a letter by T.J. Barrington, "Mr. Waugh's Pieties," *The Bell* (Feb. 1947), pp. 58–63.

[Donat O'Donnell], "Beauty and Belfast: A Note on 'Odd Man Out,'" *The Bell* (May 1947), pp. 55–62.

[Donat O'Donnell], "The Universe of François Mauriac: I. The Sun and the Rain," *The Bell* (Aug. 1947), pp. 9–19.

[Donat O'Donnell], "The Universe of François Mauriac: II. Women and Boys," *The Bell* (Sept. 1947), pp. 45–55.

[Donat O'Donnell], "The Universe of François Mauriac: III. The Catholic and the Novelist," *The Bell* (Nov. 1947), pp. 47–59. Part III is reprinted, with small changes and with a new coda in *Kenyon Review* 10 (Summer 1948), pp. 454–71; and with minor changes, in *Maria Cross* (1952), pp. 3–37.

1948

[Donat O'Donnell], "The Parnellism of Sean O'Faolain," *Irish Writing* 5 (July 1948), pp. 59–76. Reprinted in *Maria Cross* (1952), pp. 95–118.

1949

[Donat O'Donnell], "The Faust of Georges Bernanos," *Kenyon Review* 11 (Summer 1949), pp. 405–23. Reprinted in *Maria Cross* (1952), pp. 41–62.

[Donat O'Donnell], "The Unfallen," *Envoy* 1 (Dec. 1949), pp. 44–50. Review of *The Irish* by Sean O'Faolain and of *The Face of Ireland* by Arland Usher.

1950

[Donat O'Donnell], *Envoy* 1 (Feb. 1950), pp. 89–90. Reply to a letter by S. O'Faolain, *Envoy* 1 (Jan. 1950), pp. 87–90.

[Donat O'Donnell], "L'Unité de l'Irlande et les Irlandais d'Amérique," *Revue Générale Belge* 57 (July 1950), pp. 1–9.

1951
[Donat O'Donnell], "The Temple of Memory: Péguy," *Hudson Review* 3 (Winter 1951), pp. 548–74. Reprinted in *Maria Cross*, (1952) pp. 137–68.

1952
[Anonymous], "Profile: Mr. Sean MacBride, T.D.," *The Leader* (2 Aug. 1952), pp. 19–20.

1953
[Donat O'Donnell], "The Abbey: Phoenix Infrequent," *Commonweal* 57 (30 Jan. 1953), pp. 423–24.

[Donat O'Donnell], "The Magic of Mauriac," *Commonweal* 58 (15 May 1953), pp. 144–46, 148–50. Excerpt reprinted in *Commonweal* 71 (30 Oct. 1959), pp. 161–62.

[Donat O'Donnell], "The Ambiguities of Purity," *The Bell* (Nov. 1953), pp. 632–35. Review of *Purity of Diction in English Verse* by Donald Davie.

[Donat O'Donnell], "Mauriac after Gide," *The Bell* (Dec. 1953), pp. 49–59.

1954
[Donat O'Donnell], "Baudelaire," *Spectator* (1 Jan. 1954), p. 21. Review of *Baudelaire: A Study of His Poetry* by Martin Turnell.

[Donat O'Donnell], "The Conjurer's Apprentice," *Spectator* (2 April 1954), pp. 406–7. Review of *The Art of Paul Valéry* by F. Scarfe.

[Donat O'Donnell], "Belloc Uprooted," *Spectator* (11 June 1954), pp. 719–20. Review of *Hilaire Belloc* by Frederick Wilhelmsen.

[Donat O'Donnell], "Liberty in Ireland," *Spectator* (30 July 1954), pp. 152–53. Review of *The Freedom of the Press in Ireland, 1784–1841* by Brian Inglis.

[Donat O'Donnell], "A Sunday in East Berlin," *Commonweal* 61 (29 Oct. 1954), pp. 90–91.

[Donat O'Donnell], "Discipline and Self-Discipline," *Spectator* (3 Dec. 1954), p. 728. Review of *Language as Gesture* by R.P. Blackmur.

1955
[Donat O'Donnell], "No Bishop, no Bonfire," *New Statesman* (5 March 1955), p. 320. Review of "The Bishop's Bonfire" at the Gaiety Theatre, Dublin.

[Donat O'Donnell], "The Novels and Stories of Sommerville and Ross," *Irish Writing* 30 (March 1955), pp. 7–15. Reprinted in *Writers and Politics* (1965), pp. 106–15.

[Donat O'Donnell], "A Pillar in the Cloud," *New Statesman* (30 April 1955), pp. 617–18. Review of *The Theme of Beatrice in the Plays of Claudel* by Ernest Beaumont.

[Donat O'Donnell], "Poetry, Inspiration and Criticism," *Spectator* (8 July 1955), pp. 53, 55–56. Review of *Inspiration and Poetry* by C.M. Bowra. Reprinted in *Writers and Politics* (1965), pp. 154–59.

[Donat O'Donnell], "Sartre as Critic," *New Statesman* (27 Aug. 1955), pp. 247–48. Review of *Literary and Philosophical Essays* by Jean-Paul Sartre. Reprinted in *Writers and Politics* (1965), pp. 72–75.

[Donat O'Donnell], "Paris Theatre," *Spectator* (28 Oct. 1955), pp. 554–55. Review of the "Oresteia" at the Marigny Theatre, Paris.

[Donat O'Donnell], "Two Cheers for the New Byzantium," *New Statesman* (19 Nov. 1955), pp. 654–56.

[Donat O'Donnell], "Paris Theatre," *Spectator* (25 Nov. 1955), p. 716. General discussion of the Paris theater season.

[Donat O'Donnell], "Conversation with Mauriac," *Commonweal* 63 (2 Dec. 1955), pp. 220–22.

[Donat O'Donnell], "Mr. Greene's Battlefield," *Spectator* (10 Dec. 1955), p. 804. Review of *The Quiet American* by Graham Greene.

1956

[Donat O'Donnell], "A Question of Confidence," *Commonweal* 63 (6 Jan. 1956), pp. 347–49.

[Donat O'Donnell], "Proust at the Ball," *Spectator* (10 Feb. 1956), p. 190. Review of *Marcel Proust at the Ball* by Marthe Bibesco.

[Donat O'Donnell], "Class-conscious Comedy," *Spectator* (24 Feb. 1956), p. 256. Review of *The Town Traveller* by George Gissing.

[Donat O'Donnell], "Sancta Simplicitas," *New Statesman* (17 March 1956), pp. 251–52. Review of *The Archbishop and the Lady* by Michael de la Bedoyere.

[Donat O'Donnell], "The People's Victor," *Spectator* (20 April 1956), p. 550. Review of *Victor Hugo* by André Maurois. Reprinted in *Writers and Politics* (1965), pp. 61–64.

[Donat O'Donnell], "New Novels," *New Statesman* (19 May 1956), pp. 575–76. Review of novels by Robert Penn Warren, Peter Vansittart, David Unwin, and W. John Morgan.

[Donat O'Donnell], untitled, *Spectator* (1 July 1956), p. 24. Short review of *Hillaire Belloc: A Memoir* by J.B. Morton.

[Donat O'Donnell], "The Colonist," *Spectator* (21 Sept. 1956), pp. 391–92. Review of *An Introduction to the French Poets: Villon to the Present Day* by Geoffrey Brereton.

1957

[Donat O'Donnell], "Sensitive Register," *Spectator* (14 June 1957), p. 784. Review of *Emergence from Chaos* by Stuart Holroyd.

[Donat O'Donnell], "Some Letters of James Joyce," *Spectator* (28 June 1957), p. 850. Review of *Letters of James Joyce*, ed. Stuart Gilbert.

[Donat O'Donnell], "Thou Art Pierpoint," *Spectator* (12 July 1957), pp. 56–57. Review of *Wyndham Lewis* by Geoffrey Wagner.

[Donat O'Donnell], "The Loved One," *Spectator* (19 July 1957), p. 112. Review of *The Ordeal of Gilbert Pinfold* by Evelyn Waugh.

[Donat O'Donnell], "Island Intellectual," *Spectator* (16 Aug. 1957), pp. 223–24. Review of *Preliminary Essays* by John Wain.

[Donat O'Donnell], "The Tang of Vichy," *Spectator* (6 Sept. 1957), pp. 312–13. Review of *Pétain* by Glorney Bolton.

1958

[Donat O'Donnell], "Revised Reporting," *Spectator* (25 April 1958), pp. 536–38. Review of *The American Earthquake* by Edmund Wilson.

[Donat O'Donnell], "Mr. Dooley in Paris," *Spectator* (23 May 1958), p. 648.

[Donat O'Donnell], "Head of Protocol," *Spectator* (1 Aug. 1958), p. 172. Review of *Quai d'Orsay* by Jacques Dumaine.

[Donat O'Donnell], "Mr Dooley on Indirect Aggression," *Spectator* (15 Aug. 1958), p. 217.

[Donat O'Donnell], "Southern Writers," *Spectator* (29 Aug. 1958), p. 284. Review of *The Fugitives* by John M. Bradbury.

[Donat O'Donnell], "Carey Bloom," *Atlantic* 202 (Nov. 1958), pp. 142–46, 148.

[Donat O'Donnell], "Queer World," *Spectator* (7 Nov. 1958), p. 620. Review of *Borstal Boy* by Brendan Behan. Reprinted in *Writers and Politics* (1965), pp. 126–27.

[Donat O'Donnell], "Joyce at School," *Nation* 187 (6 Dec. 1958), pp. 432–33. Review of *Joyce among the Jesuits* by Kevin Sullivan.

1959
[Donat O'Donnell], "Irishness," *New Statesman* (17 Jan. 1959), p. 78. Review of *The Oxford Book of Irish Verse*, ed. Donagh MacDonagh and Lennox Robinson. Reprinted in *Writers and Politics* (1965), pp. 97–99.

[Donat O'Donnell], "The Great Conger," *Spectator* (22 May 1959), p. 736. Review of *Mythologies* by W.B. Yeats and *Yeats as I Knew Him* by Monk Gibbon. Reprinted in *Writers and Politics* (1965), pp. 119–20.

[Donat O'Donnell], "The New Yorker," *Spectator* (3 July 1959), pp. 11–12. Reprinted in *Writers and Politics* (1965), pp. 3–7.

[Donat O'Donnell], "Mother's Tongue," *Spectator* (14 Aug. 1959), p. 201. Review of *J.M. Synge* by David H. Greene and Edward M. Stephens). Reprinted in *Writers and Politics* (1965), pp. 121–22.

[Donat O'Donnell], "Re-enter the Hero," *Spectator* (4 Sept. 1959), pp. 637–38. Review of *The Age of Defeat* by Colin Wilson. Reprinted in *Writers and Politics* (1965), pp. 149–53.

[Donat O'Donnell], "Life with Freud," *Spectator* (6 Nov. 1959), p. 638. Review of *Free Associations* by Ernest Jones.

1960
[Donat O'Donnell], "Generation of Saints," *Spectator* (15 Jan. 1960), p. 80. Review of *The Picaresque Saint* by R.W.B. Lewis. Reprinted in *Writers and Politics* (1965), pp. 139–43.

[Donat O'Donnell], "A Rejoinder," *Spectator* (26 Jan. 1960), pp. 293–94. Reply to comments of Angus Wilson on the works of Albert Camus.

[Donat O'Donnell], "Free Spenders," *Spectator* (4 March 1960), pp. 325–26. Review of books by Vance Packard, Thomas Griffith, and Emmet Hughes. Reprinted in *Writers and Politics* (1965), pp. 23–27.

[Donat O'Donnell], "Bears," *Spectator* (22 April 1960), pp. 577–78. Review of *Tolstoy or Dostoevsky* by George Steiner. Reprinted in *Writers and Politics* (1965), pp. 144–48.

[Donat O'Donnell], "Over the Precipice," *Spectator* (29 April 1960), pp. 634–35. Review of *The Fall of Parnell* by F.S.L. Lyons. Reprinted in *Writers and Politics* (1965), pp. 116–18.

[Donat O'Donnell], "Serpents," *Spectator* (27 May 1960), p. 773. Review of *Apologies to the Iroquois* by Edmund Wilson.

[Donat O'Donnell], "Men of Letters," *Spectator* (26 Aug. 1960), p. 317. Review of *The Goncourt Brothers* by André Billy.

1961
[Donat O'Donnell], "Our Men in Africa," *Spectator* (20 Jan. 1961), p. 80. Review of *A Burnt-Out Case* by Graham Greene.

[Donat O'Donnell], "Orwell Looks at the World," *New Statesman* (26 May 1961), pp. 837–38. Review of *George Orwell* by Richard Rees and *Collected Essays* by George Orwell. Reprinted in *Writers and Politics* (1965), pp. 31–35.

1963
"Our Wits About Us," *New Statesman* (15 Feb. 1963), p. 237. Review of *The Irish Comic Tradition* by Vivian Mercier. Reprinted in *Writers and Politics* (1965), pp. 101–5.

"Chorus or Cassandra," *New Statesman* (19 April 1963), pp. 591–92. Review of *The New Statesman* by Edward Hyams.

"A New Yorker Critic," *New Statesman* (28 June 1963), pp. 972–73. Review of *Against the American Grain* by Dwight Macdonald. Reprinted in *Writers and Politics* (1965), pp. 8–12.

"Varieties of Anti-Communism," *New Statesman* (13 Sept. 1963), pp. 319–21. Review of books by Constantine Fitz Gibbon, Peter Howard, and John Mander. Reprinted in *Writers and Politics* (1965), pp. 174–92.

"Journal de Combat," *New Statesman* (20 Dec. 1963), pp. 911–12. Review of *Encounters*, ed. Stephen Spender, Irving Kristol, and Melvin Lasky. Reprinted in *Writers and Politics* (1965), pp. 169–73.

1964
"Glimpses of Gaitskell," *New Statesman* (31 Jan. 1964), p. 172. Review of *Hugh Gaitskell*, ed. W.T. Rodgers.

"White Gods and Black Americans," *New Statesman* (1 May 1964), pp. 681–82. Review of *Notes of a Native Son* and *Nobody Knows My Name* by James Baldwin. Reprinted in *Writers and Politics* (1965), pp. 17–22.

"Critic into Prophet," *New Statesman* (15 May 1964), pp. 765–66. Review of *The Cold War and the Income Tax* by Edmund Wilson. Reprinted in *Writers and Politics* (1965), pp. 163–68.

"The Schweitzer Legend," *New York Review of Books* (20 Aug. 1964), pp. 7–8. Review of *Verdict on Schweitzer* by Gerald McKnight. Reprinted in *Writers and Politics* (1965), pp. 234–38.

"A Vocation," *New Statesman* (9 Oct. 1964), pp. 538–39. Review of *Words* by Jean-Paul Sartre.

"The Perjured Saint," *New York Review of Books* (19 Nov. 1964), pp. 2–4. Review of *Cold Friday* by Whittaker Chambers. Reprinted in *Writers and Politics* (1965), pp. 183–91.

1965
"Yeats and Irish Politics," *Tri-Quarterly* 4 (1965), pp. 91–98.

"Neo-Colonialism," *New Statesman* (29 Jan. 1965), pp. 154–56. Review of *Neo-Colonialism* by Brian Crozier.

"Yeats and Fascism," *New Statesman* (26 Feb. 1965), pp. 319–21. Closing sequence of Yeats article in *Excited Reverie* (1965).

"A Curious Queen," *New York Review of Books* (11 March 1965), pp. 3–4. Review of *Queen Victoria* by Elizabeth Longford.

"The Congo, the United Nations and Chatham House," *New Left Review* 31 (May-June 1965), pp. 3–27.

"Big Jim," *New Statesman* (7 May 1965), pp. 722–23. Review of *James Larkin* by Emmet Larkin.

"A Long Engagement," *New York Review of Books* (20 May 1965), pp. 4–5. Review of *Force of Circumstance* by Simone de Beauvoir.

"Pseudo-History," *New Statesman* (18 June 1965), pp. 962–63. Review of *Struggle for the World* by Desmond Donnelly.

"The Neurosis of Colonialism," *Nation* 200 (21 June 1965), pp. 674–76. Review of *The Wretched of the Earth* by Frantz Fanon.

"Contemporary Forms of Imperialism," *Studies on the Left* 5 (Fall 1965), pp. 13–40. Reprinted in Arthur I. Blaustein and Roger R. Woock, eds., *Man Against Poverty: World War II* (New York: Random House, 1968), pp. 296–309.

"The Last of the Highest?" *New Statesman* (26 Nov. 1965), pp. 831–32. Review of *Neo-Colonialism* by Kwame Nkrumah.

"The Dylan Cult," *New York Review of Books* (9 Dec. 1965), pp. 12–13. Review of *The Life of Dylan Thomas* by Constantine Fitzgibbon and *Dylan Thomas and Poetic Dissociation* by David Holbrook.

"The Dean's Identity," *New Statesman* (24 Dec. 1965), p. 1002. Review of *Jonathan Swift* by Nigel Dennis.

1966
"The Life and Death of Kennedy," *New Statesman* (14 Jan. 1966), pp. 50–51. Review of *A Thousand Days* by Arthur Schlesinger, Jr., and *Kennedy* by Theodore Sorensen.

"Africa's Answer to Schweitzer," *Atlantic* 217 (March 1966), pp. 68–71.

"The Counterrevolutionary Reflex," Columbia University *Forum* (Spring 1966), pp. 21–24. Reprinted in *Commonweal* 85 (3 March 1967), pp. 619–21; and P. Spackman and L. Ambrose, eds., *The Columbia University Forum Anthology* (New York: Atheneum, 1968).

"An Irishman at Large in the U.S.A.," *Saturday Review* 49 (12 March 1966), pp. 59–60, 108–15.

"Non-Alignment," *New Statesman* (8 April 1966), p. 507–8.

"Conor Cruise O'Brien on Ghana," *Toward Freedom* 15 (May 1966), pp. 2 and 4. Reprinted from *Observer* (24 April 1966).

"The Embers of Easter 1916–1966," *New Left Review* 37 (May-June 1966), pp. 3–14. Orig. publ. in *Irish Times* (7 April 1966). Reprinted in *1916: The Easter Rising* (1968), pp. 225–40; and *Massachussets Review* 7 (Autumn 1966), pp. 621–37.

"Politics and the Writer," *Book Week* (12 June 1966), pp. 1 and 12.

"Digging," *New Statesman* (17 June 1966), p. 885. Review of *Five Years* by Deirdre Levinson.

"Changing the Guard," *New York Review of Books* (23 June 1966), pp. 11–12. Review of *African Tightrope* by H.T. Alexander.

"Autonomy and Academic Freedom in Britain and Africa," *Minerva* 4 (Aug. 1966), pp. 89–92.

"Churchill and Macmillan," *New York Review of Books* (15 Dec. 1966), pp. 5–6. Review of *Winston S. Churchill*, vol. 1, by Randolph S. Churchill and *Winds of Change* by Harold Macmillan.

1967

"Insecure Democracy," *Socialist Register* (1967), pp. 229–37.

"'Losing Our Cool'—in Ghana," *Nation* 204 (6 March 1967), pp. 309–11. Review of *The Rise and Fall of Kwame Nkrumah* by Henry L. Bretton.

"Comments on 'What's Happening to America,'" *Partisan Review* 34 (Spring 1967), pp. 251–54.

"Two-Faced Cathleen," *New York Review of Books* (29 June 1967), pp. 19–21. Review of *The Imagination of an Insurrection* by William Irwin Thompson.

"Some Encounters with the Culturally Free," *New Left Review* 44 (July–Aug. 1967), pp. 60–63. Reprinted in *Rights* (Spring 1967), pp. 11–13.

"In Quest of Uncle Tom," *New York Review of Books* (14 Sept. 1967), pp. 10–11. Review of *Dublin: A Portrait* by V.S. Pritchett and *Irish Journal* by Heinrich Boll.

"The Shadow of Octavian," *Listener* 78 (21 Sept. 1967), pp. 374–75. Review of *To Move a Nation* by Roger Hilsman.

"McCarthyism," *Listener* 78 (7 Dec. 1967), pp. 757–58. Review of *McCarthy and the Intellectuals* by Michael Rogin.

"A Condemned People," *New York Review of Books* (21 Dec. 1967), pp. 14–19.

1968

"Bright Small Boy," *New York Review of Books* (15 Feb. 1968), pp. 11–14. Review of *The Blast of War, 1939–45* by Harold Macmillan and *Macmillan* by Anthony Sampson.

"Shadows on the Acropolis," *Saturday Review*, 51 (17 Feb. 1968), pp. 31–32. Review of *The Death of a Democracy: Greece and the American Conscience* by Stephen Rousseau.

"Irish Republican," *Listener* 79 (7 March 1968), pp. 308–9. Review of *The Fenian Chief: A Biography of James Stephens* by Desmond Ryan.

"How the UN Could End the War," *New York Review of Books* (28 March 1968), pp. 22–25.

"Satirical Pastoral," *New York Review of Books* (25 April 1968), pp. 19–20, 22. Review of *The Triumph* by John Kenneth Galbraith.

"Jokes and Peace—Conor Cruise O'Brien in Conversation with Michael Barratt," *Listener* 79 (30 May 1968), pp. 698–99.

"Confessions of the Last American," *New York Review of Books* (21 June 1968), pp. 16–18. Review of *The Armies of the Night* by Norman Mailer.

"Views," *Listener* 80 (24 Oct. 1968), p. 526.

"Beware of Melancholy," *New York Review of Books* (7 Nov. 1968), pp. 18–19, 22–23. Review of books by Douglas Brown, Edward Feit, E.J. Kahn, Jr., John Laurence, Alan Paton, and Theodore Bull.

"Mission Impossible," *New York Review of Books* (21 Nov. 1968), pp. 8, 10. Review of *The "Other" State Department* by Arnold Beichman.

"Honest Men," *Listener* 80 (12 Dec. 1968), pp. 797–98.

1969
"Genocide and Discretion," *Listener* 81 (30 Jan. 1969), pp. 129–30.

"Biafra Revisited," *New York Review of Books* (22 May 1969), pp. 15–23, 26–27. Abridged as "What More Must Biafrans Do?" in *Observer* (11 May 1969).

"Camus, Algeria, and 'The Fall,'" *New York Review of Books* (9 Oct. 1969), pp. 6, 8, 10–12.

"Holy War," *New York Review of Books* (6 Nov. 1969), pp. 9–16.

"Imagination and Order: Machiavelli," *Times Literary Supplement* (13 Nov. 1969), pp. 1309–11.

1970
"What Exhortation?" *Irish University Review* 1 (1970), pp. 48–61.

"America First," *New York Review of Books* (29 Jan. 1970), pp. 8, 10, 12–14.

"Vulnerable Ireland," *Listener* 84 (27 Aug. 1970), pp. 281–82. Review of *The Correspondence of Edmund Burke*, vol. 8, ed. R.B. McDowell.

"The Gentle Nietzscheans," *New York Review of Books* (5 Nov. 1970), pp. 12–16. Reprinted in modified form in *The Suspecting Glance* (1972), pp. 51–65.

1971
"Irish Troubles: The Boys in the Back Room," *New York Review of Books* (8 April 1971), pp. 35–39.

"The Scholar and the Man of Affairs," *New Statesman* (22 Sept. 1971), pp. 396–97. Review of *The Study of International Affairs: Essays in Honour of Kenneth Younger*, ed. Roger Morgan.

"Violence in Ireland: Another Algeria?" *New York Review of Books* (23 Sept. 1971), pp. 17–19.

"On Reading Crossman's Irish Diary," *New Statesman* (24 Sept. 1971), pp. 384–85.

"Thoughts on Commitment," *Listener* 86 (16 Dec. 1971), pp. 834, 836.

1972
"Not Europe Only," *Massachusetts Review* 13, no. 4 (1972), pp. 529–38.

[Anonymous], "Ulster's Differences," *Times Literary Supplement* (17 March 1972), pp. 297–98. Review of books by Richard Rose, R.S.P. Elliot and John Hickie, and Constantine FitzGibbon. Reprinted in *Herod* (1978), pp. 92–98.

"Northern Ireland: Its Past and Its Future," *Race* 14 (July 1972), pp. 11–20.

1973
"Ireland: Dying for Bones," *New York Review of Books* (25 Jan. 1973), pp. 36–39. Review of *The Green Flag* by Robert Kee and *Towards a New Ireland* by Garret Fitzgerald.

"On the Rights of Minorities," *Commentary* 55 (June 1973), pp. 46–50. Reprinted in *Current* 153 (July 1973), pp. 38–46.

"A Reply from Conor Cruise O'Brien," *Hibernia* (8 June 1973), pp. 8–9.

"In Search of Morality—Conor Cruise O'Brien Talks to Brian Inglis," *The Listener* 90 (23 Aug. 1973), pp. 233–36.

"A Funny Sort of God," *New York Review of Books* (18 Oct. 1973), pp. 56–58. Review of *The Honorary Consul* and *Collected Stories* by Graham Greene.

1974
"An Ulster Fable," *New York Review of Books* (21 Feb. 1974), pp. 13–14. Review of *World Without End, Amen* by Jimmy Breslin.

"An Interview with Conor Cruise O'Brien," *James Joyce Quarterly* 11 (Spring 1974), pp. 201–9.

1975
"An Unhealthy Intersection," *New Review* 2 (July 1975), pp. 3–9. Reprinted in *Irish Times* (21 and 22 Aug. 1975).

"A Slow North-east Wind," *Listener* 94 (25 Sept. 1975), pp. 404–5. Review of *North* by Seamus Heaney.

1976
"Reflections on Terrorism," *New York Review of Books* (16 Sept. 1976), pp. 44–48. Review of books by J. Bowyer Bell, Edward Hyams, Sam C. Sarkesian, and H. Jon Rosenbaum and Peter C. Sederberg. Reprinted in *Herod* (1970), pp. 57–70.

"Ireland Will not Have Peace," *Harper's* 253 (Dec. 1976), p. 42.

1977
"Nationalism and the Reconquest of Ireland," *Crane Bag* 1, no. 2 (1977), pp. 8–13.

"For Political Ends," *New York Times Book Review* (23 Jan. 1977), pp. 4–5. Reprinted in *Herod* (1978), pp. 71–77.

"The Anti-Politics of Simone Weil," *New York Review of Books* (12 May 1977), pp. 23–28.

"Liberty and Terrorism," *International Security* 2 (Fall 1977), pp. 56–67. Slightly altered as "Liberty and Terror" in *Encounter* 49 (Oct. 1977), pp. 34–41.

"On Violence and Terror," *Dissent* 24 (Fall 1977), pp. 433–36.

"Anti-Barbarian," *New York Review of Books* (15 Sept. 1977), pp. 37–38. Review of *The Gentle Barbarian* by V.S. Pritchett.

"Two Edmund Burkes?" *New York Review of Books* (29 Sept. 1977), pp. 3–4, 6. Review of *The Rage of Edmund Burke* by Isaac Kramnick.

"Dead Hippo," *Listener* 98 (2 Nov. 1977), pp. 590–91. Review of *The Colonial Encounter: A Reading of Six Novels* by M.M. Mahood.

1978
"The End of White Rule?" *New York Review of Books* (9 March 1978), pp. 21, 24–28.

"The Theatre of Southern Africa," *New York Review of Books* (23 March 1978), pp. 33–38.

"Greene's Castle," *New York Review of Books* (1 June 1978), pp. 3–5. Review of *The Human Factor* by Graham Greene.

1979
"Martyr," *New York Review of Books* (15 June 1979), p. 8. Review of *Biko* by Donald Woods.

"South Africa and the UN," *The Tablet* (4 Aug. 1979), pp. 743–45.

"Violence: A Summary," *Journal of Medical Ethics* 5 (Sept. 1979), p. 132.

"Americans and Ireland," *International Herald Tribune* (8 Sept. 1979).

"Hands Off," *Foreign Policy* 37 (Winter 1979–80), pp. 101–10.

1980
"Purely American," *Harper's* 260 (April 1980), pp. 32–34. Reprinted from *Observer* (27 Jan. 1980).

"African Self-Righteousness Is as Tiresome as European," *Listener* 103 (1 May 1980), pp. 577–78.

1981
"The Protestant Minority: Within and Without," *The Crane Bag* 5 (1981), pp. 46–49.

"A Journalist Doesn't Stop Being a Citizen," *Listener* 105 (22 Jan. 1981), p. 108.

"Parnell and His Party, Reconsidered," *University Publishing* (Spring 1981), p. 7.

"Babies, Wild Dogs, and Coalition," *Magill* 4 (June 1981), pp. 15–16.

"Blueshirts and Quislings," *Magill* 4 (June 1981), p. 25.

"Thank God," *Listener* 105 (18 June 1981), p. 772.

"Saints, Sinners and Sincerity," *Magill* 4 (July 1981), pp. 15–16.

"Picture of Dorian Gray," *New York Review of Books* (16 July 1981), pp. 3–4. Review of *The Backbench Diaries of Richard Crossman*, ed. Janet Morgan.

"The Roots of Terrorism," *New Republic* 185 (25 July 1981), pp. 29–32. Review of *The Terror Network* by Claire Sterling.

"Miss De Valera's Grandfather Speaks," *Magill* 4 (August 1981), pp. 16–17.

"An Open Letter to John Kelly," *Magill* 4 (Sept. 1981), pp. 17–19.

"With the Irish Troops in the Lebanon," *Magill* 4 (Oct. 1981), pp. 27–29.

"How Long Can They Last?" *New York Review of Books* (5 Nov. 1981), pp. 26–31. Review of books on South Africa by L.H. Gann and Peter Duignan, John S. Saul and Stephen Gelb, and the Study Commission on US Policy toward Southern Africa.

"The Four Horsemen," *Harper's* 262 (Dec. 1981), pp. 14, 16, 18–20.

1982
"The Artist as Pompous Prig." *Sunday Tribune* (Dublin), 31 Jan. 1982.

"'Are You Sure You Are so Sure, Paul?'" *Listener* 107 (25 Feb. 1982), pp. 20–21. Review of *Pope John Paul II and the Catholic Restoration* by Paul Johnson.

"'A Great Man Whose Greatness Has Actually Benefitted His People,'" *Listener* 107

(15 April 1982), p. 19. Review of *Davitt and Irish Revolution, 1846–82* by T.W. Moody.

"Ireland: The Shirt of Nessus," *New York Review of Books* (29 April 1982), pp. 30–33. Review of *Irish Nationalism: A History of Its Roots and Ideology* by Sean Cronin. Reprinted with postscript in *Passion and Cunning*, (1988) pp. 213–25.

"The Angel of the Absurd," *Times Literary Supplement* (7 May 1982), p. 505. Review of *Camus* by Patrick McCarthy.

"'Holy Men Are not Averse to Passing on a Bit of Gossip,'" *Listener* 107, (27 May 1982), pp. 20–21. Review of books on the Vatican by Lord Longford, Norman St. John-Stevas, George Bull, and Malachi Martin.

"'Israel Will Be on the Lookout for any Rifts that May Be Going,'" *Listener* 107, (24 June 1982). Review of *The Arab-Israeli Wars* by Chaim Herzog and *Inside the Middle East* by Dilip Hiro.

"Peres v. Begin," *Listener* 108 (30 Sept. 1982), pp. 18–19.

1983
"Timmerman's War: Some Critical Notes," *Encounter* 60 (Jan. 1983), pp. 49–55, "Reply" to comment by Patrick Seale, pp. 85–86.

"Unreliable Witness," *New Republic* 188 (24 Jan. 1983), pp. 37–40. Review of *The Longest War* by Jacobo Timmerman.

"'The House of War Is not so Black as It's Painted,'" *Listener* 109 (17 March 1983), pp. 20–21. Review of *Faith and Power: The Politics of Islam* by Edward Mortimer.

"International Episodes," *New York Review of Books* (29 Sept. 1983), p. 14. Review of *Present History* by Theodore Draper.

1984
"Israel in Embryo," *New York Review of Books* (15 March 1984), pp. 34–38. Review of *The High Walls of Jerusalem* by Ronald Sanders.

"'The PLO Is on Israel's Borders No Longer,'" *Listener* 111 (26 April 1984), p. 29. Review of *The PLO* by Jillian Becker and *Between Battles and Ballots* by Yoram Peri.

"Prophets of the Holy Land," *Harper's* 269 (Dec. 1984), pp. 42–43. Part of a written symposium on the Middle East.

1985
"Some Reflections on Religion and Nationalism," *Studies in Zionism* 6, no. 2 (1985), pp. 161–69.

"The Charms of Certitude," *New York Review of Books* (17 Jan. 1985), pp. 21–23. Review of *How Democracies Perish* by Jean-François Revel.

"Wishful Thinking," *New York Review of Books* (28 Feb. 1985), pp. 9–12. Review of *The British Empire in the Middle East* by William Roger Louis.

"Conor Cruise O'Brien Talks to Michael Charlton about the UN in the Congo," *Listener* 113 (14 March 1985), pp. 6–8.

"The Fall of Africa," *New Republic* 192 (18 March 1985), pp. 31–35. Review of *The First Dance of Freedom* by Martin Meredith. Reprinted in *Passion and Cunning* (1988), pp. 268–76.

"Odd Man Out," *New York Review of Books* (11 April 1985), pp. 3–7. Review of *Breaking with Moscow* by Arkady N. Shevchenko.

"The Afrikaner Mentality," *Atlantic* 255 (May 1985), pp. 101–3. Review of *Waiting: The Whites of South Africa* by Vincent Crapanzano.

"Three Who Made a Revolution," *New Republic* 192 (17 June 1985), pp. 25–31. Review of biographies of Chaim Weizman, David Ben-Gurion, and Berl Katznelson. Reprinted in *Passion and Cunning* (1988), pp. 256–67.

"'Jimmy Carter Was a Sir Galahad, but He Desperately Wanted to Be Re-elected,'" *Listener* 114 (1 Aug. 1985), pp. 26–27. Review of *The Blood of Abraham: Inside the Middle East* by Jimmy Carter.

"'What Mr. McGuinness Actually Says ...,'" *Listener* 114 (8 Aug. 1985), pp. 4–5.

"'Those Rulers Who Fail to Cut, Stone or Flog Are Seen by Khomeini as Bad Muslims,'" *Listener* 114 (26 Sept. 1985), pp. 24–25. Review of *Islam and Revolution: Writings and Declarations* by Imam Khomeini.

"Virtue and Terror," *New York Review of Books* (26 Sept. 1985), pp. 28–31.

"Why Israel Can't Take 'Bold Steps' for Peace," *Atlantic* 256 (Oct. 1985), pp. 45–55.

"The Liberal Pope," *New York Review of Books* (10 Oct. 1985), pp. 13–15.

"The Nationalist Trend," *Times Literary Supplement* (1 Nov. 1985), pp. 1230–31. Review of *The Irish Mind*, ed. Richard Kearney. Reprinted in *Passion and Cunning* (1988), pp. 192–98.

"U.N. Theater," *New Republic* 193 (4 Nov. 1985), pp. 17–19.

"Bloody Business," *New Republic* 193 (2 Dec. 1985), pp. 34–38. Review of *Political Murder* by Franklin L. Ford.

1986

"The Intellectual in Power" (discussion between O'Brien and John Lukacs), *Salmagundi* 69 (Winter 1986), pp. 257–66.

"The Very Model of a Secretary-General," *Times Literary Supplement* (17 Jan. 1986), pp. 63–64. Review of *In the Eye of the Storm* by Kurt Waldheim.

"Press Freedom and the Need to Please," *Times Literary Supplement* (21 Feb. 1986), pp. 179–80. Reprinted in *Passion and Cunning* (1988), pp. 238–46.

"What Can Become of South Africa?" *Atlantic* 257 (March 1986), pp. 41–68. Portions in *Irish Times* (8, 10, and 11 March 1986). Reprinted in *Passion and Cunning* (1988), pp. 122–68.

"Rattling the Bag," *Times Literary Supplement* (14 March 1986), pp. 179–80. Review of *Move Your Shadow* by Joseph Lelyveld.

"'Was Irish National Feeling not Noble and Enlightened by Definition, Then?'" *Listener* 115 (20 March 1986), pp. 24–25. Review of *Collected Letters of W.B. Yeats*, vol. 1, ed. John Kelly.

"Ireland: The Mirage of Peace," *New York Review of Books* (24 April 1986), pp. 40–46. Review of *Bobby Sands and the Tragedy of Northern Ireland* by John Feehan. Reprinted, with alterations, in *Passion and Cunning* (1988), pp. 199–212.

"Intellectuals in the Post-Colonial World" (discussion by O'Brien, Edward Said, and John Lukacs), *Salmagundi* 70–71 (Spring-Summer 1986), pp. 65–81.

"The Responsibility of Intellectuals" (discussion by O'Brien, George Steiner, Leszek Kolakowski, Robert Boyers), *Salmagundi* 70–71 (Spring-Summer 1986), pp. 164–95.

"Blood on the Border," *New York Review of Books* (8 May 1986), pp. 42–43. Review of *Nothing Happens in Carmincross* by Benedict Kiely.

"Thinking about Terrorism," *Atlantic* 257 (June 1986), pp. 62–66. Reprinted in *Passion and Cunning* (1988), pp. 226–33.

"God and Man in Nicaragua," *Atlantic* 258 (Aug. 1986), pp. 50–72. Reprinted in *Passion and Cunning* (1988), pp. 80–122.

"Trop de Zèle," *New York Review of Books* (9 Oct. 1986), pp. 11–12, 14. Review of *The Bloody Crossroads* by Norman Podhoretz. Reprinted in *Passion and Cunning* (1988), pp. 247–55.

(With Patrick Cruise O'Brien), "Camouflage Apartheid," *New Republic* 195 (13 Oct. 1986), pp. 14–15. Substantially the same as O'Brien column in *Irish Independent* (20 Sept. 1986). Reprinted in *Passion and Cunning* (1988), pp. 173–76.

(With Patrick Cruise O'Brien), "Tutu's Enthronment," *New Republic* 195 (27 Oct. 1986), pp. 9–11. Substantially the same as O'Brien column in *Irish Independent* (4 Oct. 1986). Reprinted in *Passion and Cunning* (1988), pp. 181–84.

(With Patrick Cruise O'Brien), "Boycott Buster," *New Republic* 195 (3 Nov. 1986), pp. 12–13. Reprinted in *Passion and Cunning* (1988), pp. 185–87.

"The Cant of Pity," *Atlantic* 258 (Dec. 1986), pp. 101–2. Review of *The Tears of the White Man* by Pascal Bruckner.

(With Patrick Cruise O'Brien), "Timing Is Everything," *New Republic* 195 (1 Dec. 1986), pp. 9–10.

1987

" 'His Firm Belief that God Is on the Side of the Ulster Protestants Is Mr. Paisley's Greatest Asset,' " *Listener* 117 (22 Jan. 1987), pp. 23–24. Review of *Paisley* by Ed Maloney and Andy Pollak and *God Save Ulster: Religion and the Politics of Paisleyism* by Steve Bruce.

"Coping with Terrorism," *Center Magazine* 20 (March-April 1987), pp. 45–49.

"The Green Haze," *Atlantic* 259 (April 1987), pp. 89–91. Review of *The Green Haze: US Guns, Money and Influence in Northern Ireland* by Jack Holland.

"Sandinismo: The Nationalist Faith of Nicaragua," *Center Magazine* 20 (July-Aug. 1987), pp. 31–34.

"Foxed by a Bible-Banging Maori," *New York Times Book Review* (2 Aug. 1987), p. 9. Review of *Season of the Jew* by Maurice Shadbolt.

"At the Shrine of Honourable Failure," *Times Literary Supplement* (6–12 Nov. 1987), pp. 1211–12. Review of *The UN: In or Out?* by Ernest Van den Haag and John P. Conrad.

"The Treason of the Clerks," *Nature* (19 Nov. 1987), pp. 275–76. Review of *Academic Freedom and Apartheid: The Story of the World Archaeological Congress* by Peter Ucko.

1988

"Nobs and Snobs," *New York Review of Books* (4 Feb. 1988), pp. 3–4, 6. Review of *Evelyn Waugh: The Early Years* by Martin Stannard.

"West Bank: The Way Out," *Quadrant* 32 (July 1988), pp. 23–24.

"The Pragmatist," *New York Review of Books* (22 Dec. 1988), p. 22. Part of symposium, "The Election and the Future."

1989

"Burke's Great Melody: Warren Hastings' 'Opera of Fraud,'" *Encounter* 72 (Feb. 1989), pp. 30–37.

"A Last Chance to Save the Jews?" *New York Review of Books* (27 April 1989), pp. 27–28, 35.

"Danger in Indignation," *Times Literary Supplement* (28 April-4 May 1989), p. 447. Review of *Prepared for the Worst* by Christopher Hitchens.

"Bad News for Spies," *New York Times Book Review* (21 May 1989), p. 3. Review of *The Russia House* by John le Carré.

1990

"The Decline and Fall of the French Revolution," *New York Review of Books* (15 Feb. 1990), pp. 46–51. Review of *A Critical Dictionary of the French Revolution*, ed. François Furet and Mona Ozour.

"A Linchpin of Democracy," *Times Literary Supplement* (23 Feb.-1 March 1990), pp. 189–90. Review of *Higher Than Hope: A Biography of Nelson Mandela* by Fatima Meer.

"His Year of Living Dangerously," *New York Times Book Review* (15 April 1990), p. 7. Review of *Tribes with Flags* by Charles Glass.

"German Horse, French Rider," *National Review* 42 (28 May 1990), p. 19.

"A Tale of Two Nations," *New York Review of Books* (19 July 1990), pp. 33–36. Review of *Ulster: Conflict and Consent* by Tom Wilson.

"A Vindication of Edmund Burke," *National Review* 42 (17 Dec. 1990), pp. 28–35.

1991

"From Titusville to Baghdad: The Oil Factor in Peace and War," *Times Literary Supplement* (8 Feb. 1991), pp. 9–10. Review of *The Prize* by Daniel Yergin.

"Paradise Lost," *New York Review of Books* (25 April 1991), pp. 52–60. Review of *The Crooked Timber of Humanity* by Isaiah Berlin.

"Coming Together," *World Monitor* (4 May 1991), pp. 65–66.

"Exorcizing the English Demon," *Times Literary Supplement* (21 June 1991), pp. 9–10. Review of *Douglas Hyde* by Janet Dunleavy and Gareth Dunleavy.

"Nationalists and Democrats," *New York Review of Books* (15 Aug. 1991), p. 31.

"Track II," *New Republic* 205 (30 Sept. 1991), pp. 10–11.

1992

"Pursuing a Chimera: Nationalism at Odds with the Idea of a Federal Europe," *Times Literary Supplement* (13 March 1992), pp. 3–4. Reprinted as "Toward European Disunion" in *Harper's* 285 (14 July 1992), pp. 18, 20, 22.

"Nationalism and Democracy," *Queen's Quarterly* 99 (Spring 1992), pp. 72–83.

(With Patrick Cruise O'Brien), "Better but not all Better," *Atlantic* 270 (July 1992), pp. 72–82.

"Bosnia: Hands Off," *Atlantic* 270 (Nov. 1992), pp. 34, 36.

"Out of the Hedge-school," *Times Literary Supplement* (4 Dec. 1992), p. 5.

"Jean Jacques Rousseau," *Independent Magazine* (12 Dec. 1992), p. 62.

"The Future of the West," *The National Interest* 30 (Winter 1992–93), pp. 33–40.

III. Newspaper Essays

Observer

1961
"My case" (Part 1), 10 December 1961.
"My case" (Part 2), 17 December 1961.
"Dr. O'Brien replies" (letter), 24 December 1961.

1964
"Integrity and the party line," 28 June 1964. Reprinted in *Writers and Politics* (1965), pp. 81–83.
"Mercy and Mercenaries," 6 December 1964. Reprinted and expanded in *Writers and Politics* (1965), pp. 223–29.

1966
"Nkrumah—the man I knew," 27 February 1966.
"Return to Ghana," 24 April 1966. Reprinted in *Toward Freedom* 15 (May 1966), pp. 2 and 4.

1967
"Inside Biafra," 8 October 1967.

1969
"What more must Biafrans do?" 11 May 1969.

1971
"Ireland: The smell of civil war," 12 September 1971.
"Little hope now of help from Dublin," 28 November 1971.
"The green card and Mr. Wilson," 28 November 1971.
"Celebrating patriotic violence," 12 December 1971.

1972
"Different roads to the cemetery," 6 February 1972.

1974
"Extremists: A delusion," 14 April 1974.
"A solution of despair," 9 June 1974.

1976
"White man's burden," 25 July 1976. Review of *Albert Schweitzer* by James Brabazon.

1977
"What the Irish voters didn't want to know," 26 June 1977.

"The Queen's message to King Billy," 14 August 1977.

"Incendiary passions," 28 August 1977. Review of *Maud Gonne* by Samuel Levenson.

"The politics of flattery," 4 September 1977.

"Dublin, Downing Street and Rome—a troubled triangle with Ulster at every apex," 25 September 1977.

1978

"Linking the separate tables," 22 January 1978.

"A song of disembafflement," 29 January 1978. Review of "Kingdom Come" by Stewart Parker at the King's Head Theatre Club, London.

"The long shadow of the terrorist," 5 February 1978.

"The agonizing dilemma of two just men," 19 February 1978.

"After the Comber massacre," 26 February 1978.

"Voice of Dublin," 12 March 1978.

"Fearsome prospects in Scots dreams," 19 March 1978.

"Waldheim: Mandate on terror?" 26 March 1978.

"Why they made Biko a martyr," 30 April 1978.

"The four freedoms," 28 May 1978.

"When lords of the word get it wrong," 2 July 1978.

"Rhodesia poll shock: Smith not finally committed," 6 August 1978.

Interview with Ian Smith, 6 August 1978.

"Ian Smith and the unmaking of UDI," 13 August 1978.

"The case for censoring television violence," 10 September 1978.

"Breach of faith," 24 September 1978.

"Peace people get on with their job—peace," 15 October 1978.

"UNESCO's original sin," 22 October 1978.

1979

"Lands where the coup is king," 21 January 1979.

"No to a nauseous Marxist-Methodist cocktail," 28 January 1979.

"Long day's journey into prayer," 4 February 1979.

"Sir Harold, Mr. Toad, and history," 18 February 1979.

"Spirit of one Germany stirs again," 4 March 1979.

"On being kicked by a New York cop," 4 March 1979.

"Which of you can make a horse?" 18 March 1979.

"The great beast versus yooklid," 1 April 1979.

"Mr. Callaghan and other crusaders," 15 April 1979.

"Where Mr. Powell is a moderate," 22 April 1979.

"The siren song of Mrs. Thatcher," 29 April 1979.

"On being a Jewish wild goose," 3 June 1979.

"Dropping the pilot" (unsigned editorial), 3 June 1979.

"An open letter to Senator Moynihan," 10 June 1979.

"The Marat-Sade of David Frost," 17 June 1979.

"Freeing the news flow," 24 June 1979.

"Now they talk of over-information," 1 July 1979.

"Confessions of a near hangman," 15 July 1979.

"Metamorphoses of apartheid," 22 July 1979.

"The guilt of Afrikanerdom," 29 July 1979.

"The Pope meets Frankenstein," 29 July 1979.

"Ulster appeasement" (unsigned editorial), 12 August 1979.

"Decade of violence," 19 August 1979.

"The spiral into civil war," 26 August 1979.

"Why the elephant is terrified of the mouse," 26 August 1979.

"Killing of initiatives" (unsigned editorial), 2 September 1979.

"In the shadow of US ethnicity," 30 September 1979.

"The Pope and the unwanted child," 14 October 1979.

"Refined and vulgar Marxism," 28 October 1979.

"Blind alley in Ulster" (unsigned editorial), 28 October 1979.

"Testing the power of magic blood," 11 November 1979.

"Changing styles in punishing traitors," 25 November 1979.

"Sulphurous charms of Charles Haughey," 9 December 1979.

1980

"Softening women, sobering bombs," 6 January 1980.

"America: The long search for innocence," 27 January 1980. Reprinted in *Harper's* 260 (April 1980), pp. 32–34.

"Dead Cat Calwell meets Arctic Dev," 3 February 1980.

"Fwowing Up with Dorothy Parker," 17 February 1980.

"Plight of the Ogaden refugees," 2 March 1980.

"Africa's powder horn," 9 March 1980.

"With Oxfam and a Land-Rover through Ethiopia," 16 March 1980.

"Where have all the nomads gone?" 23 March 1980.

"How to succeed without teaching," 13 April 1980.

"Lenin and the Olympic Games," 13 April 1980.

"A success of Soviet Empire," 20 April 1980.

"Freedom, equality, and Aini's choice," 27 April 1980.

"How fairs the world from Sarajevo?" 27 April 1980.

"In praise of Belfast," 18 May 1980.

"The non brigade walk tall," 18 May 1980.

"The creaky voice of Nero's mother," 8 June 1980.

"Why Germans are not afraid any more," 15 June 1980.

"Survival, defence and freedom," 6 July 1980.

"The British deterrent" (unsigned editorial), 20 July 1980.

"Modest proposal of Chairman Zee," 20 July 1980.

"In all directions like sour dough," 3 August 1980.

"Incorporation of Western Europe," 10 August 1980.

"Terminal ideology or prudent reason?" 31 August 1980.

"Pot shots from a Serbian bazooka," 28 September 1980.
"All quiet on the campus: But what do the think-tanks think?" 12 October 1980.
"Kangaroo tickets and black politics," 12 October 1980.
"The bitter end of entertainment," 26 October 1980.
"Appeasing the IRA," (unsigned editorial), 26 October 1980.
"Reagan: The promise and the peril" (unsigned editorial), 9 November 1980.
"The prayer-book and the knife," 16 November 1980.
"Coppers' narks and journalists' ethics," 30 November 1980.
"A curious ethical border zone," 14 December 1980.
"Don't bet on catastrophe," 28 December 1980.

1981
"Doctor consults ethical oracle," 4 January 1981.
"A place without Christmas trees," 11 January 1981.
"We shall be the masters of medicine," 25 January 1981.
"The sun setting over *The Times*," 1 February 1981.
"Our song: Yes, we are no bananas," 8 March 1981.
"Happy hour at the Madison Inn," 5 April 1981.
"Blessings of the sun—and gun," 12 April 1981.
"A political kiss and the hate vote," 19 April 1981.
"The crime of Captain Colthurst," 3 May 1981.
"A kind of mourning in Dublin," 10 May 1981.
"Ah the harpings, salvoes and shouting," 17 May 1981.
"Ireland: Can the border be redrawn?" 31 May 1981.
"Burke for our time?" 31 May 1981. Review of *Burke* by C.P. Macpherson and *Edmund Burke and the Critique of Political Radicalism* by Michael Freeman.
"A choice of risks in Ulster," 7 June 1981.
"Saint Patrick and the yellow snake," 21 June 1981.
"Fitzgerald peddles no faery myths," 5 July 1981.
"Violence, television and original sin," 19 July 1981.
"What rough beast?" 19 July 1981. Review of *Yeats, Ireland and Fascism* by Elizabeth Cullingford.
"Ghost lecturer, flying Dutchman," 2 August 1981.
"What can he lick off the ground?" 13 September 1981.
"Search for a 'final solution,'" 27 September 1981.
"Why Christians in Lebanon commit 'ultimate treason,'" 18 October 1981.
"Survival—and other UN dodges," 25 October 1981.
"You could be red first—then dead," 8 November 1981.
"Where Ian Paisley loses Carson's trail," 6 December 1981.
"Peace and Polish connection," 20 December 1981.

1982
"Colour itself is not the problem," 3 January 1982.
"The boggling of Al Haig's brain," 17 January 1982.

"Haigspeak: A new guide to power," 24 January 1982.
"Kissinger's way of helping the Poles," 31 January 1982.
"Peace, freedom and hypocrisy," 7 February 1982.
"Mr. Haughey and the Ed Flynn effect," 14 February 1982.
"Mr. Haughey's pyrrhic victory," 21 February 1982.
"In defence of my 'facile parallel,'" 28 February 1982.
"Never stand between a hippo and the water," 1 March 1982.
"Uncharted waters with a conger eel," 14 March 1982.
"Peace need not pass understanding," 21 March 1982.
"Maybe the world will find a way," 28 March 1982.
"I like the Pope—but not this visit," 4 April 1982.
"An offer from Prior they can't refuse," 11 April 1982.
"The donkey, the UN and the minaret," 18 April 1982.

Irish Times

1966
"The embers of Easter," 7 April 1966.

1968
"King Herod explains: A Christmas charade," 2 December 1968.

1969
"The Irish question—1969," 21 January 1969.
"The Villagers," 24 February 1969.
"Black anti-semitism," 3 March 1969.
"Student unrest," 10 March 1969.
"Aspects of American education," 17 March 1969.
"Nixon's choice," 24 March 1969.

1970
"Future of the United Nations," 24 and 26 October 1970. Address to the Royal Institute
   of International Affairs, Chatham House, London.

1972
"Mr. Alex Foster: An appreciation," 30 August 1972.

1973
"European parliament gets breath of fresh air," 27 February 1973.

1975
"Shades of republicanism," 27 March 1975.
"An unhealthy intersection," 21 and 22 August 1975. Reprinted from *New Review* 2 (July
   1975), pp. 3–9.

1982
"In the winter it snows," 12 January 1982.
"Bishops and another cult," 19 January 1982.
"Second Coming comes unstuck," 26 January 1982.

"Episcopal epiphanies," 2 February 1982.
"The Gath syndrome," 9 February 1982.
"The man who will be Thursday," 16 February 1982.
"A step to watch," 23 February 1982.
"Last week in the Holy City," 2 March 1982.
"Jews, Arabs, Prods and Micks," 9 March 1982.
"Davitt, the failed angel," 16 March 1982.
"Saint Patrick was British," 23 March 1982.
"In the dog house," 30 March 1982.
"Year of the dog," 6 April 1982.
"Give Prior a chance," 13 April 1982.
"Ulster: Is it Scottish?" 20 April 1982.
"Haughey and Collins get it right," 27 April 1982.
"Reading between the lines," 4 May 1982.
"The end of the affair," 11 May 1982.
"Jingoes of blue and green," 18 May 1982.
"Jaws, ears and feet," 25 May 1982.
"A Dear John letter," 1 June 1982.
"So we like the British?" 8 June 1982.
"Give me George and boredom," 15 June 1982.
"Israel is an Irish issue," 22 June 1982.
"A view from the piazza," 29 June 1982.
"Hunting for a moral issue," 6 July 1982.
"Crusades, Moranism and two nations," 13 July 1982.
"Collins mucks things up," 20 July 1982.
"Listening to the sound of silence," 27 July 1982.
"Fine Gael misses the bus," 3 August 1982.
"When Bloom turns to bluster," 10 August 1982.
"Circuses but no bread," 17 August 1982.
"Unsafe at any speed," 24 August 1982.
"A quest for identity," 31 August 1982.
"Wet turf and shy secrets," 7 September 1982.
"We have ways of making you talk," 14 September 1982.
"An Oscar for Gerry Collins," 21 September 1982.
"The plot thickens at RTE," 28 September 1982.
"One step forward, two steps back," 5 October 1982.
"Blessed are the timid," 12 October 1982.
"Three De Valera memories," 18 October 1982.
"Obituary for the 'Benign Scenario,'" 25 and 26 October 1982.
"Dropping the pilot," 2 November 1982.
"Thinking up some innuendoes," 9 November 1982.
"Shut up about the north," 14 December 1982.

"Doing what you're told," 21 December 1982.
"Theocracy's winning ways," 25, 27, and 28 December 1982.

1983
"Tin-pot Salazars of RTE," 4 January 1983.
"The land of the GUBU," 18 January 1983.
"The only move is checkmate," 25 January 1983.
"Let the hare sit," 1 February 1983.
"The divine dimension," 8 February 1983.
"A bug never flew on one wing," 15 February 1983.
"A word of advice for Garret," 22 February 1983.
"Genuine fully paid-up Irish," 1 March 1983.
"Death in the afternoon," 8 March 1983.
"An idea for Mr. Hume," 15 March 1983.
"A Marxist sense of Ireland," 22 March 1983.
"Casting the IRA figleaf aside," 29 March 1983.
"With charity for all," 5 April 1983.
"What UN chief wants for Middle East," 12 April 1983.
"How far the rot has gone," 19 April 1983.
"Decent people and vigilantes," 26 April 1983.
"A good dean's work," 3 May 1983.
"The best Taoiseach we have," 10 May 1983.
"The IRA and 'other political parties,'" 17 May 1983.
"Vulgar rubbish for the reader," 24 May 1983.
"Standing against violence," 31 May 1983.
"'Please do go on, Mr. Hume,'" 14 June 1983.
"The let's pretend forum," 21 June 1983.
"Keeping out of the sun," 28 June 1983.
"What kind of state?" 5 July 1983.
"Cod can be bad for your health," 12 July 1983.
"Our poor boggled minds," 19 July 1983.
"To the health of Lord Fitt," 26 July 1983.
"Truth and fantasy on the British presence," 2 August 1983.
"No guts for thinking," 9 August 1983.
"Dealing with the lesser breeds," 16 August 1983.
"What is put in can be taken out," 23 August 1983.
"Dazzled by the bishops," 30 August 1983.
"Bossing us to be perfect," 6 September 1983.
"The ones who stayed away," 13 September 1983.
"Crown and half-crown reveal all," 20 September 1983.
"Sancho Panza's New Ireland," 27 September 1983.
"The Mullah of Limerick," 4 October 1983.
"United Ireland without 'Prots,'" 11 October 1983.

"If Dev had not been there," 18 October 1983.
"Foreign armies and regrettable rhetoric," 25 October 1983.
"Questions from history," 31 October 1983.
"Letter to a noble lord," 8 November 1983.
"War and peace," 29 November, 1983.
"Cryptic words from Mr. Haughey," 6 December 1983.
"Frank's holy show," 13 December 1983.
"Leaders worth respect," 20 December 1983.

1984
"The boss," 2 and 3 January 1984.
"A risk of GUBU," 10 January 1984.
"God help us all," 24 January 1984.
"CIE's black hole on wheels," 31 January 1984.
"Logic is good for you," 7 February 1984.
"Victims of silent panic," 14 February 1984.
"UN force of a different colour," 21 February 1984.
"Drums, whistles, hot air," 28 February 1984.
"Get Brian on the line," 6 March 1984.
"Treated with contempt," 13 March 1984.
"Senile, how are you!" 20 March 1984.
"A whole new tap-dance," 27 March 1984.
"One tough guy," 3 April 1984.
"Cynical for an ideal?" 10 April 1984.
"Do not let him use us," 17 April 1984.
"Cult of blood sacrifice," 24 April 1984.
"Forum wager," 1 May 1984.
"Fantasy at the forum," 8 May 1984.
"A worse bugbear than CJ," 15 May 1984.
"You have been warned," 22 May 1984.
"Loaded words," 29 May 1984.
"Vote for new blood," 5 June 1984.
"Corpo's manners," 12 June 1984.
"On the other foot," 19 June 1984.
"Play for today," 26 June 1984.
"Ireland needs a Sadat," 3 July 1984.
"Islam's example," 10 July 1984.
"Bleating to Britain," 17 July 1984.
"On the road to Tel Aviv," 24 July 1984.
"A spell that needs breaking," 7 August 1984.
"Still a free country," 14 August 1984.
"That name again, please," 11 September 1984.
"Votes or prayers," 18 September 1984.

"God helps Reagan," 25 September 1984.
"'Right to life' violence," 2 October 1984.
"Catholics are 'in,'" 9 October 1984.
"IRA realism," 16 October 1984.
"When forum thinking fails," 23 October 1984.
"Jackson boosts Reagan," 29 and 30 October 1984.
"Reagan camp is happy," 6 November 1984.
"The next time," 13 November 1984.
"Land of blessed hedonism," 20 November 1984.
"Ethnic badge," 27 November 1984.
"Crime, justice and Mr. Dooley's wisdom," 4 December 1984.
"Helping Haughey back," 11 December 1984.
"Tough times at the trough," 18 December 1984.

1985
"Hurrah for God," 8 January 1985.
"A folk hero of the subway," 15 January 1985.
"No obituary needed yet for democrats," 22 January 1985.
"Civil reception from charitable Irish," 29 January 1985.
"Hitting the keynote with a loud bang," 5 February 1985.
"Faith is good for the Rev. O. Roberts," 12 February 1985.
"Shedding the blacks to keep the Jews," 19 February 1985.
"How God helped Oral Roberts get a brand new car," 26 February 1985.
"The seduction of Arkady Shevchenko," 5 March 1985.
"Real Zionism and its Irish counterfeit," 19 March 1985.
"The lesson of guns that guard schools," 26 March 1985.
"Patter of Teddy's feet heard in the land," 2 April 1985.
"Reagan's offer 'apple with the razorblade,'" 9 April 1985.
"Turning Al Capone into a man to admire," 16 April 1985.
"The soothing sound of rock music," 23 April 1985.
"Ronnie's always smiling in the last reel," 30 April 1985.
"President Reagan and the Republicans," 7 May 1985.
"Different troops of ghosts on parade," 14 May 1985.
"So the nuclear cloud has a silver lining," 21 May 1985.
"The UNIFIL question that awaits an answer," 28 May 1985.
"A nip of Neo-McCarthyism in the air," 4 June 1985.
"UNIFIL mission in Lebanon useless," 11 June 1985.
"Herzog—a welcome kind of presidency," 18 June 1985.
"Reagan staggers under Carter's cross," 25 June 1985.
"Terror wins on the road to Damascus," 2 July 1985.
"Back to a problem that won't go away," 9 July 1985.
"Yes to sanctions, no to sanctimonious talk," 16 July 1985.
"The cardinal and the hate percentage," 23 July 1985.

"What Garret should do with Britain's offer," 30 July 1985.
"Putting money where one's faith is," 3 September 1985.
"Nationalist doctrine does not fit the facts," 10 September 1985.
"An electoral danger to Irish democracy," 17 September 1985.
"Waiting for the church leaders to move," 24 September 1985.
"A sleepwalker heads for a fog-bound summit," 12 November 1985.
"In the steps not of Lemass, but of Haughey," 19 November 1985.
"Britain's unspoken fallback position," 26 November 1985.
"Isolated by the isolated men of violence," 3 December 1985.
"Does intelligent life exist on Tom King?" 10 December 1985.
"The naked emperor of Hillsborough," 17 December 1985.
"Happy Christmas to all, whatever it means," 24 December 1985.
"Selling a pup to Margaret Thatcher," 31 December 1985.

1986
"Wishful thinking about the Iron Lady," 7 January 1986.
"The Iron Lady suffers metal fatigue," 14 January 1986.
"In England lying is a mortal sin, if caught," 21 January 1986.
"Poor acoustics keep unionist 'NO' inaudible," 28 January 1986.
"Garret stumbles in the soft-shoe shuffle," 18 February 1986.
"The yuppies may be our last line of defence," 25 February 1986.
"Bringing 'peace and stability' to the North," 4 March 1986.
"Cracks beginning to show in the 'bulwark,'" 11 March 1986.
"What can become of South Africa?" 8 March 1986.
"Apartheid—mind boggling self deception," 10 March 1986.
"A black bourgeois government?" 11 March 1986. This, and the preceding two columns
    reprinted and expanded in *Atlantic* 257 (March 1986), pp. 41–68; and *Passion
    and Cunning* (1988), pp. 122–68.

Times (London)

1971
"Ballot box or the bullet in Northern Ireland," 14 August 1971.

1986
"States of the union," 28 July 1986. Reprinted in *Passion and Cunning* (1988), pp. 277–81.

1988
"Lumbering to the right," 18 August 1988.
"Ignorance makes easy prey," 31 August 1988.
"Swatting the wasps," 14 September 1988.
"Can Bush kill by kindness?" 16 September 1988.
"Raking over the pledge," 21 September 1988.
"TV round to the Duke," 27 September 1988.
"Groomed out of existence," 7 October 1988.
"Jackson's boon to Bush," 15 October 1988.

"Blacking out the IRA," 19 October 1988.
"Codename for a landslide," 29 October 1988.
"Bush's touch of the blues," 2 November 1988.
"Black mark for Bush," 11 November 1988.
"Denounced—for the truth," 16 November 1988.
"Arafat's declining power," 23 November 1988.
"Discord that pays dividends," 7 December 1988.
"If terror stalked America," 14 December 1988.
"Last chance for Hillsborough," 21 December 1988.

1989
"Sweeping all before him," 10 January 1989.
"A kinder, gentler, Bush?" 20 January 1989.
"Bush shuffle on abortion," 28 January 1989.
"An exalted nationalism," 28 January 1989.
"Blowing in the wind," 2 February 1989.
"Could Pius XI have averted the Holocaust?" 10 February 1989.
"Tower's just treatment," 17 February 1989.
"Tower's regrettable leanings," 1 March 1989.
"Bush's phony drugs war," 10 March 1989.
"Martyrdom of the leprechaun," 17 March 1989.
"Hollow critics of the IRA," 24 March 1989.
"Votes to end the violence," 5 April 1989.
"Mirage of a settlement," 19 April 1989.
"Abortion battle re-opened," 1 May 1989.
"Irangate: Bush on trial," 8 May 1989.
"Sick man of the world," 8 May 1989. Review of *The Closed Circle: An Interpretation of the Arabs* by David Pryce-Jones.
"Reagan's own monster," 15 May 1989.
"The explosive electioneer," 23 May 1989.
"Power that must be denied," 30 May 1989.
"The shadow on Congress," 2 June 1989.
"Shadow boxing the Taoiseach," 9 June 1989.
"How Haughey could fall," 19 June 1989.
"Where Deng scores over democracy," 27 June 1989.
"Haughey's hands tied," 4 July 1989.
"Why Israel will pay for its kidnap coup," 1 August 1989.
"Hostages: Faith misplaced," 8 August 1989.
"Can the army ever leave?" 10 August 1989. Reprinted in *World Press Review* 36 (October 1989), p. 38.
"Who follows de Klerk?" 25 August 1989.
"A triumph of racist theory over family love," 29 August 1989.
"Damning with faint and half-felt sentiments," 26 September 1989.

"No more pussy-footing: Hit the IRA," 9 February 1991.
"Devaluing the university," 5 March 1991.
"Mrs. Thatcher's Passachendaele," 11 March 1991.
"Saddam's dangerous freedom," 22 March 1991.
"Does pax Americana start here?" 28 March 1991.
"Blood on our hands," 5 April 1991.
"Sacrificed to cynicism," 11 April 1991.
"We can only grieve and hope," 18 April 1991.
"Moscow bares its teeth as army star rises," 24 April 1991.
"Up Ireland's blind alley," 30 April 1991.
"Gulf morality the archbishop overlooks," 11 May 1991.
"No yield for the brokers," 15 May 1991.
"No tears for a bad loser," 21 May 1991.
"If it's good to be godless, why do they kill?" 30 May 1991.
"Untying the Gordian knot," 7 June 1991.
"The bear on a slippery slope," 12 June 1991.
"Why do some nations still see themselves as the chosen people?" 25 June 1991.
"Is patience running out?" 6 July 1991.
"Will Gorbachev be the spectre at the rich man's feast?" 12 July 1991.
"Islam's immunity from law," 19 July 1991.
"Not all blacks are liberals," 26 July 1991.
"Government-funded murder has failed to shock most white South Africans," 31 July 1991.
"Sinking differences is the way ahead," 8 August 1991.
"Will Yeltsin choose force or chaos?" 14 August 1991.
"Quit the West's dependable friends first," 15 August 1991.
"The dawning of a new ice age," 21 August 1991.
"Breaking up is not hard to do," 4 September 1991.
"Who inherits this UN seat?" 11 September 1991.
"America is not abandoning Israel, its best ally in the Middle East, but the Republicans would like a concession," 18 September 1991.
"Haughey: Not quite dead yet," 25 September 1991.
"Jekyll the patriot, Hyde the nationalist," 3 October 1991.
"Charles Haughey will not be able to cling to office for long, once scandalized Ireland goes to the polls," 10 October 1991.
"Irish Americans have prospered from their anti-British attitude," 16 October 1991.
"The Judge Thomas row draws a wedge into the alliance of feminists and blacks," 23 October 1991.
"What hope for Middle East peace?" 30 October 1991.
"Settlement in the way of peace," 6 November 1991.
"Ireland's Machiavelli," 13 November 1991.
"Victim of voodoo economics," 20 November 1991.
"Democracy is not enough," 28 November 1991.

"After Terry Anderson's release the way to stop future hostage taking is to prove it never pays," 5 December 1991.

"Federalism's mask begins to slip," 11 December 1991.

"Time to rout the godfathers," 18 December 1991.

1992

"German domination of Europe will make political union a much less attractive idea in the year ahead," 1 January 1992.

"Syria's threat to peace," 8 January 1992.

"Auschwitz's true origin," 22 January 1992.

"An Irish cat with nine lives," 29 January 1992.

"The rogue who ruled Ireland," 4 February 1992.

"All roads lead to internment," 12 February 1992.

"Ireland's cruel hypocrisy" (on abortion), 19 February 1992.

"History's power to haunt us," 26 February 1992.

"J'accuse: The Irish church," 4 March 1992.

"We may mock conspiracy theorists, but watch out for the real conspirators," 12 March 1992.

"Clinton for the White House," 18 March 1992.

"Slaves to race and sex," 25 March 1992.

"A constitutional change could get Ireland out of a tight spot on abortion," 1 April 1992.

"Time to get tough in Ulster," 15 April 1992.

"The doctrine of hellfire has more to do with hatred of others than with fear," 22 April 1992.

"A scandal that won't go away," 20 May 1992.

"Why Bush will vote for war," 27 May 1992.

"Playing black man's bluff," 16 June 1992.

"Winning votes in foreign fields," 30 June 1992.

"Dublin's provocation," 8 July 1992.

"Only fools step in," 6 August 1992.

"Winning votes in Sarajevo," 11 August 1992.

"Servant of too many masters," 18 August 1992.

"Why women will desert Bush," 28 August 1992.

"Unfit to rule Ireland," 6 November 1992.

"Ireland's Albert factor," 19 November 1992.

"Slow collapse of the Irish colossus," 28 November 1992.

"Avoid Bosnia's blood trap," 4 December 1992.

"Will India fall to the zealots?" 8 December 1992.

"Blundering into Bosnia," 15 December 1992.

"Why security comes first," 29 December 1992.

Irish Independent

1986

"America's Irish reach the age of reason at long last," 22 March 1986.

"Reagan works abroad for votes at home," 28 and 29 March 1986.

"Mexico's revolution loses some," 5 April 1986.

"The church at war," 12 April 1986.

"Bonded by bombs," 19 April 1986.

"Trouble in paradise," 26 April 1986.

"Romero: A ghost that will not die," 3 May 1986.

"us 'spooks' in action," 10 May 1986.

"The stigma we share with Jews," 17 May 1986.

"Divorce: The need for consciousness," 24 May 1986.

"Is there intelligent life on Tom King?" 31 May 1986.

"Playing safe with our neutrality," 7 June 1986.

"Blood bath unless the un moves in," 14 June 1986.

"Hierarchy and unholy alliance," 21 June 1986.

"Victory for a grand alliance," 28 June 1986.

"Unreality of our claim on the north," 5 July 1986.

"Why we must not invite Waldheim," 12 July 1986.

"Needed: A painful cure for the pts," 19 July 1986.

"Terror in Tuscany," 26 July 1986.

"South Africa could put uk in crisis," 2 August 1986.

"Educating Laurie—the problem of us cable tv," 9 August 1986.

"Paving the way to a disaster," 16 August 1986.

"Sectarian politics are flourishing," 23 August 1986.

"Time to get out of the Lebanon," 30 August 1986.

"One-man rule O.K.?" 6 September 1986.

"The racial chill in Sunshine City," 20 September 1986. Reprinted in *Passion and Cunning* (1988), pp. 173–76.

"Fire in the eyes of blacks on campus," 27 September 1986. Reprinted in *Passion and Cunning* (1988), pp. 177–80.

"Archbishop Tutu on being a leader," 4 October 1986. Reprinted in *Passion and Cunning* (1988), pp. 181–84.

"The real betrayal of anti-apartheid," 13 October 1986. Reprinted in *Passion and Cunning* (1988), pp. 169–72.

"Will apartheid end in anarchy?" 18 October 1986. Reprinted in *Passion and Cunning* (1988), pp. 188–91.

"Student apathy, Reagan guile," 25 October 1986.

"Prostitution of the professors," 1 November 1986.

"Reagan—the spell is broken," 8 November 1986.

"Ronnie trots out the dirty tricks brigade," 15 November 1986.

"Ronnie and his men do it yet again," 29 November 1986.

"You would have had a ball at the inquisition," 6 December 1986.

"The thoughts of Chairman Charlie," 20 December 1986.

"Some collisions in the pursuit of happiness," 25, 26, and 27 December 1986.

1987
"Why I stand by Section 31," 3 January 1987.
"The Donlong affair and the quest for power," 10 January 1987.
"Lebanon—the price is now far too high," 17 January 1987.
"The problem with one-party states," 24 January 1987.
"Cosgrave was right about kidnappers," 31 January 1987.
"Why I won't vote for Labour this time out," 7 February 1987.
"Don't fear to dwell on flawed pedigrees," 14 February 1987.
"The fantasy man," 21 February 1987.
"Damned if he knew ... and double damned if he did not," 28 February 1987.
"Nancy gets her man," 7 March 1987.
"A new cabinet—but is it built to last?" 14 March 1987.
"Uncle Sam finds he can love Paddy," 21 March 1987.
"Prime time religion beats out the devil," 4 April 1987.
"A bridge too far for Reagan," 11 April 1987.
"Campus peace still pretty fragile," 17 and 18 April 1987.
"The black and white of race relations," 25 April 1987.
"The men already after Reagan's shoes," 2 May 1987.
"Affairs of the Hart ...," 10 May 1987.
"Politics of AIDS," 16 May 1987.
"The real America is no gay haven," 23 May 1987.
"Canada's Irish keep the fragile peace," 30 May 1987.
"Uncle Sam was never really an Irishman," 6 June 1987.
"Nuked on the road to No. 10," 13 June 1987.
"Hillsborough: How far have we really come?" 20 June 1987.
"A wobbly hand on the Fine Gael tiller," 27 June 1987.
"At last: The truth about Dev's constitution," 4 July 1987.
"Thatcher: Is she facing a doorstep rebellion?" 11 July 1987.
"Gaybo's too good for American T.V.," 18 July 1987.
"So whose bloody war is this anyway?" 25 July 1987.
"Neutrality—politics, not morality," 1 August 1987.
"Censor is not a 4-letter word ...," 8 August 1987.
"Hoover: Just the man to suck up the dirt," 15 August 1987.
"Whatever you do, *don't* take Hart," 12 September 1987.
"A welcome confession from the Cardinal," 19 September 1987.
"Is the gulf bridgeable?" 26 September 1987.
"Kinnock could yet be the end of Maggie," 3 October 1987.
"Must we always be the bloody Irish?" 10 October 1987.
"No wonder they're baulking at Bork," 17 October 1987.
"The bottom's falling out of our world," 24 October 1987.
"The beginning of the end," 31 October 1987.
"The truth kept me out of the graveyard," 7 November 1987.

"Time for internment—northland south," 14 November 1987.
"As Enniskillen fades ... the old tunes again," 21 November 1987.
"The Provos aren't good television," 28 November 1987.
"The wrong green noises at a red-letter time," 5 December 1987.
"Summit dream won't change reality," 12 December 1987.
"An open letter to Alan Dukes," 19 December 1987.

1988
"Not so much a city ... more a state of mind," 1–2 January 1988.
"Religion isn't oil on troubled waters," 9 January 1988.
"Hume-ouring the Provos," 16 January 1988.
"Noel Browne is not a saint," 23 January 1988.
"If the boot were on the other foot," 30 January 1988.
"Shooting to kill the Hillsboro Accord," 6 February 1988.
"Why Waldheim must go," 13 February 1988.
"India behind the poor mouth," 20 February 1988.
"The dark forces of the Golden Temple," 27 February 1988.
"So-phoney encounter of the fatal kind," 5 March 1988.
"Trial and terror," 12 March 1988.
"Hotting up the Holy War," 19 March 1988.
"The long shadow of the lynchers," 26 March 1988.
"Is America ready to crown a black king?" 1 and 2 April 1988.
"Let's just hope it doesn't all end in tears," 9 April 1988.
"A touch of the old hot gospel," 16 April 1988.
"Bush may be on a hiding to nothing," 23 April 1988.
"Sir Geoffrey doesn't speak for Maggie," 30 April 1988.
"Pain, learning ... and the Accord," 7 May 1988.
"Things are looking up," 14 May 1988.
"I wouldn't expect too much if I were you," 21 May 1988.
"The summit with a little too much pique," 28 May 1988.
"It's a good job peace isn't left to the women," 4 June 1988.
"The Brothers," 11 June 1988.
"You can't have it both ways," 18 June 1988.
"To the end of the earth," 25 June 1988.
"Don't turn the page so fast on Lisnaskea," 2 July 1988.
"The siege reality," 9 July 1988.
"Time to stop talking to the Provos," 16 July 1988.
"The loser takes all ...," 23 July 1988.
"A spring in the right direction," 30 July 1988.
"Peace at last for Palestine?" 6 August 1988.
"The last straw," 13 August 1988.
"The odd couple," 20 August 1988.
"Internment could work," 27 August 1988.

"On the home straight," 10 September 1988.
"Softening up the Unionists," 17 September 1988.
"America—still a land of the fastest gun," 24 September 1988.
"Dukakis wins battle of the box," 1 October 1988.
"Oh Danny Boy you blew it," 8 October 1988.
"Losing to the long black shadow," 15 October 1988.
"And about time too," 22 October 1988.
"Danny Boy's hood-lums," 29 October 1988.
"Mr. President," 5 November 1988.
"It's not Bush who worries me ...," 12 November 1988.
"Hillsborough is sounding hollow," 19 November 1988.
"Waiting for a Michael Collins," 26 November 1988.
"Why I refused to go to tea with Waldheim," 3 December 1988.
"Send this priest to England," 10 December 1988.
"The cracks that will not heal," 17 December 1988.
"The deerest American tale," 24 December 1988.
"Give peace a chance," 31 December 1988.

1989
"A way with tragic women," 7 January 1989.
"Reagan's last reel," 14 Jan 1989.
"A kinder and gentler America?" 21 January 1989.
"Bush baby dilemma," 28 January 1989.
"Did Hitler order the poisoning of Pope Pious XI?" 4 February 1989.
"Tip O'Neill—a shallow love affair with Ireland," 11 February 1989.
"Lie still ... and think of Ireland," 18 February 1989.
"Faint praise for Charlie," 25 February 1989.
"Tower comes tumblin' down," 4 March 1989.
"Leprechauns, Provos and fairy tales," 11 March 1989.
"Poison on parade," 18 March 1989.
"Facing up to the terrorists," 24 and 25 March 1989.
"A peace for Palestine," 1 April 1989.
"The machine takes Chicago," 8 April 1989.
"Where's the beef, Garret?" 15 April 1989.
"The wrongs of Wright," 22 April 1989.
"Thinking again on abortion," 29 April 1989.
"You're just a little bit right, Garret," 6 May 1989.
"The blind leading the blind," 13 May 1989.
"Oh, don't be so dull, George," 20 May 1989.
"He'll be worse if they win big," 27 May 1989.
"That other coalition ...," 3 June 1989.
"Who said I had a vengeful disposition?" 24 June 1989.
"Dessie should back Haughey," 1 July 1989.

"Good week for democracy," 8 July 1989.
"Imagine if Wolfe Tone had won ...," 22 July 1989.
"Tom King and the winds of change," 29 July 1989.
"The thin line," 5 August 1989.
"Burntollet and the Bogside," 12 August 1989.
"I welcome this action," 19 August 1989.
"Alan Dukes and the bishops," 26 August 1989.
"Eagle had landed," 2 September 1989.
"Haughey spell is broken," 9 September 1989.
"The informers," 16 September 1989.
"Phone trial is all Greek to us," 23 September 1989.
"RTE seems sadly lacking in self-respect," 30 September 1989.
"Sex and the 'singular' man," 7 October 1989.
"An amendment that should worry us all," 14 October 1989.
"Who's to blame?" 21 October 1989.
"Listen, for a change," 28 October 1989.
"The ghost of GUBU," 4 November 1989.
"Brooke boos for IRA," 11 November 1989.
"Germany will be united," 18 November 1989.
"Czechs—what now after Jakes?" 25 November 1989.
"Come on, Levin—chuck it," 2 December 1989.
"Kohl in hot seat at Summit table," 9 December 1989.
"The killing goes on," 16 December 1989.
"Happy Christmas—but war's not over," 23 December 1989.
"The new Europe," 30 December 1989.

1990
"Don't cry for Noriega," 6 January 1990.
"Why won't we listen?" 13 January 1990.
"Athy noon," 20 January 1990.
"Blind alleys," 27 January 1990.
"Black power's new statesman," 3 February 1990.
"Silence is golden," 10 February 1990.
"Meet de Klerk half way," 17 February 1990.
"Who's playing games?" 24 February 1990.
"Nothing but most abject nonsense," 3 March 1990.
"Turning to the east," 10 March 1990.
"Whistling in the graveyard," 17 March 1990.
"Inside Austria, looking out," 24 March 1990.
"Doherty adds to GUBU image," 24 March 1990.
"A star's lost luster," 7 April 1990.
"Real link that exists," 13 and 14 April 1990.
"Does Ireland really need a president?" 21 April 1990.

"The theatre of illusion," 28 April 1990.
"Never likely to meet the real captors," 5 May 1990.
"Still chasing a will-o-the-wisp," 12 May 1990.
"Flowers of the North may wither," 19 May 1990.
"Give it a lash, Jack," 26 May 1990.
"Democracy itself at risk," 2 June 1990.
"Watch out, Mr. Barry," 9 June 1990.
"Classical GUBU," 16 June 1990.
"Scots may lead way on North," 23 June 1990.
"The hidden enemies," 30 June 1990.
"Neither liked nor respected," 7 July 1990.
"Roasting Ridley," 14 July 1990.
"Haughey to the rescue?" 21 July 1990.
"Prevention is better," 28 July 1990.
"US status is at stake," 4 August 1990.
"The writing on the wall," 11 August 1990.
"It's time to flee Saudi," 18 August 1990.
"Our role as rats," 25 August 1990.
"No reply to hatred," 1 September 1990.
"Neutrality biz," 8 September 1990.
"Green light for the war," 15 September 1990.
"Lenihan: *Really* no problem?" 22 September 1990.
"Collins: Shadow of a gunman," 29 September 1990.
"It's German lessons time," 6 October 1990.
"Trembling balance," 13 October 1990.
"Stopping the rot," 20 October 1990.
"F.F. won't forgive or forget," 3 November 1990.
"C.J. in terminal trouble," 10 November 1990.
"Over the rainbow," 17 November 1990.
"Margaret Thatcher and me," 24 November 1990.
"Mixing the colours of the 'rainbow,'" 24 November 1990.
"Heave on Haughey," 1 December 1990.
"Big heave begins," 8 December 1990.
"It was sheer Blarney," 15 December 1990.
"Threat of war," 29 December 1990.

1991
"IRA truce an old sham," 5 January 1991.
"Mission impossible?" 12 January 1991.
"Saddam survivor," 19 January 1991.
"Post-war peace lies with Israel," 26 January 1991.
"Neutrality blinding us to our role," 2 February 1991.
"A sinister combination," 9 February 1991.

"White flag propaganda," 16 February 1991.
"Nobody believes in Saddam anymore," 23 February 1991.
"Israel is not yet at peace," 2 March 1991.
"The use of language," 9 March 1991.
"Medieval values," 16 March 1991.
"Novel looks at roots of FF," 23 March 1991.
"A blind alley breakthrough," 29 and 30 March 1991.
"Standing by at the slaughter," 6 April 1991.
"Satan-like art of the possible," 13 April 1991.
"Accepting some bitter realities," 20 April 1991.
"Sinister child of glasnost," 27 April 1991.
"Reading between the lines," 4 May 1991.
"Pride in the language," 11 May 1991.
"Round One to Unionists as Brooke falters," 18 May 1991.
"Claimed by conflicting stances," 25 May 1991.
"O'Malley holds the key on North," 1 June 1991.
"Does boot fit on the other foot?" 8 June 1991.
"Playing Russian roulette," 15 June 1991.
"Storming all the way to a 2nd term," 22 June 1991.
"Aiming for a failure," 29 June 1991.
"A path that could only lead to war," 6 July 1991.
"Mandate for the dead is long gone," 13 July 1991.
"Dublin happy to sit on the green fringed fence," 20 July 1991.
"Brazening through Inkatha-gate," 27 July 1991.
"After Inkatha-gate, what now for the shanty town?" 3 August 1991.
"S. Africa: The way ahead," 10 August 1991.
"They're free, but I still felt sick," 17 August 1991.
"We must not let it happen again," 24 August 1991.
"The Baltics—a missed chance," 31 August 1991.
"Double standards that let the IRA raise the stakes," 7 September 1991.
"The Fitzgerald that I know," 14 September 1991.
"Neutrality: The end is nigh," 21 September 1991.
"Good to see you back, GUBU," 28 September 1991.
"The vindication game ...," 5 October 1991.
"Doubting Thomas," 12 October 1991.
"Smashing the black-feminist alliance," 19 October 1991.
"Vote with no confidence whatever," 26 October 1991.
"It could only happen here," 2 November 1991.
"Either way, it's quite OK," 16 November 1991.
"Haughey is unsafe at any speed," 16 November 1991.
"Bush takes a beating," 23 November 1991.
"Fear and loathing in Washington," 30 November 1991.

"Who wants to be a Euro governor?" 7 December 1991.
"When things go wrong: A simple rule," 14 December 1991.
"Season's Greetings from Iran," 21 December 1991.
"My best wishes for the new year," 28 December 1991.

1992
"Giving off the wrong message," 4 January 1992.
"So complacent," 11 January 1992.
"Maudling and 'that bloody awful place,'" 18 January 1992.
"Don't write him off just yet," 25 January 1992.
"He's gone—but is it the end of GUBU?" 1 February 1992.
"The chink in despair," 8 February 1992.
"Well done, taoiseach! But ...," 15 February 1992.
"Hypocrisy need not be cruel," 22 February 1992.
"Your Lordships," 29 February 1992.
"Maastricht doesn't matter any more," 7 March 1992.
"Making a law for everyone," 14 March 1992.
"Blarney time," 21 March 1992.
"A recipe for inaction," 28 March 1992.
"My plea for the North," 4 April 1992.
"Power, not right to life, is the issue," 11 April 1992.
"Stealing a march on the civil war spectre," 17/18 April 1992.
"Steering clear of the fires of hell," 25 April 1992.
"Feminism: New force at the polls," 2 May 1992.
"The craziest kind of GUBU," 9 May 1992.
"Time for a little humility," 16 May 1992.
"The holy show is still on the road," 23 May 1992.
"Bishops bide their time—for now," 30 May 1992.
"Learning to live with the Viking veto," 6 June 1992.
"£68? What £68?" 13 June 1992.
"'Yes' no guarantee of Euro unity," 20 June 1992.
"Making the peace—piece by piece," 27 June 1992.
"Breakthrough into a blind alley," 4 July 1992.
"Decoding the talk on talks," 11 July 1992.
"My money is on Bill Clinton," 18 July 1992.
"More nonsense about sex," 25 July 1992.
"All smiles ... but still not an inch," 1 August 1992.
"War games amid a new Holocaust," 8 August 1992.
"Gamble on Sarajevo," 15 August 1992.
"Family values—Bush's big mistake," 22 August 1992.
"Flawed logic of secrecy," 27 August 1992ep
"The wind of change," 5 September 1992.
"'Mass action' must end," 12 September 1992.

"Another spoilt chance," 19 September 1992.

"Labour have their fun—but Major is off the hook," 26 September 1992.

"A return to old decency," 3 October 1992.

"This time round, a starker choice," 10 October 1992.

"Rebounding on Bush," 17 October 1992.

"Goodbye George and hello President Clinton," 31 October 1992.

"The knives are out," 7 November 1992.

"Albert's heavy hand on the North," 14 November 1992.

"Why Labour should opt out of coalition," 21 November 1992.

"Rainbow arithmetic will determine Albert's fate," 28 November 1992.

"Bringing Albert back from the dead," 5 December 1992.

"Albert now ready to pay price," 12 December 1992.

"Hang on—bacon's not home yet," 19 December 1992.

INDEX

This book was typeset by Typo Litho Composition Inc., Québec, in 10/12 Janson, and printed and bound by Friesen Printers, Altona, Manitoba. Design is by Miriam Bloom, Expression Communications Inc.